COMMIRE, ANNE.
SOMETHING ABOUT THE
AUTHOR.
V.170
37565004963988 CENT

SOMETHING ABOUT THE AUTHOR®

Something about the Author *was named an "Outstanding Reference Source,"* the highest honor given by the American Library Association Reference and Adult Services Division.

ISSN 0276-816X

something about the author®

Facts and Pictures about Authors
and Illustrators of Books for Young People

volume 170

THOMSON
GALE

Detroit • New York • San Francisco • New Haven, Conn. • Waterville, Maine • London • Munich

Something About the Author, Volume 170

Project Editor
Lisa Kumar

Editorial
Amy Elisabeth Fuller, Michelle Kazensky, Joshua Kondek, Julie Mellors, Mary Ruby, Stephanie Taylor

Permissions
Margaret Chamberlain-Gaston, Jacqueline Key, Lisa Kincade

Imaging and Multimedia
Leitha Etheridge-Sims, Lezlie Light

Composition and Electronic Capture
Tracey L. Matthews

Manufacturing
Drew Kalasky

Product Manager
Leigh Ann Deremer

© 2007 Thomson Gale, a part of the Thomson Corporation.

Thomson and Star Logo are trademarks and Gale is a registered trademark used herein under license.

For more information, contact
Thomson Gale, Inc.
27500 Drake Rd.
Farmington Hills, MI 48331-3535
Or you can visit our internet site at
http://www.gale.com

ALL RIGHTS RESERVED
No part of this work covered by the copyright herein may be reproduced or used in any form or by any means —graphic, electronic, or mechanical, including photocopying, recording, taping, Web distribution, or information storage retrieval systems — without the written permission of the publisher.

This publication is a creative work fully protected by all applicable copyright laws, as well as by misappropriation, trade secret, unfair competition, and other applicable laws. The authors and editors of this work have added value to the underlying factual material herein through one or more of the following: unique and original selection, coordination, expression, arrangement, and classification of the information.

For permission to use material from this product, submit your request via the Web at http://www.gale-edit.com/permissions, or you may download our Permissions Request form and submit your request by fax or mail to:

Permissions Department
Thomson Gale
27500 Drake Rd.
Farmington Hills, MI 48331-3535
Permissions Hotline:
248-699-8006 or 800-877-4253, ext. 8006
Fax 248-699-8074 or 800-762-4058

Since this page cannot legibly accommodate all copyright notices, the acknowledgments constitute an extension of the copyright notice.

While every effort has been made to secure permission to reprint material and to ensure the reliability of the information presented in this publication, Thomson Gale neither guarantees the accuracy of the data contained herein nor assumes any responsibility for errors, omissions or discrepancies. Thomson Gale accepts no payment for listing; and inclusion in the publication of any organization, agency, institution, publication, service, or individual does not imply endorsement of the editors or publisher. Errors brought to the attention of the publisher and verified to the satisfaction of the publisher will be corrected in future editions.

LIBRARY OF CONGRESS CATALOG CARD NUMBER 62-52046

ISBN 0-7876-8794-4
ISSN 0276-816X

This title is also available as an e-book.
ISBN 1-4144-1071-9
Contact your Thomson Gale sales representative for ordering information.

Printed in the United States of America
10 9 8 7 6 5 4 3 2 1

Contents

Authors in Forthcoming Volumes ix
Introduction xi
SATA Product Advisory Board xiii

A

Ashby, Ruth 1
Atwater-Rhodes, Amelia 1984- 3
Atwood, Margaret 1939- 7
Atwood, Margaret Eleanor
   See Atwood, Margaret 7

B

Barbour, Karen 1956- 15
Bates, Martine
   See Leavitt, Martine 127
Birdsall, Jeanne 1951- 17
Boerst, William J. 1939- 19
Bottner, Barbara 1943- 20
Bowen, Anne 1952- 23
Brimner, Larry Dane 1949- 24
Brown, Jo 1964- 29
Brown, Ruth 1941- 30
Butler, M. Christina 1934- 33

C

Camper, Cathy 1956- 36
Carey, Charles W., Jr. 1951- 37
Carheden, Görel Kristina
   See Näslund, Görel Kristina 142
Carney, Mary Lou 1949- 38
Carter, David A. 1957- 40
Coney, Michael G. 1932-2005
   Obituary Notice 43
Coney, Michael Greatrex
   See Coney, Michael G. 43

Coney, Mike
   See Coney, Michael G. 43
Cummings, Priscilla 1951- 44

D

Dale, Anna 1971- 48
Daley, Michael J. 1959- 50
D'Amico, Carmela 51
D'Amico, Steve 52

E

Edwards, Wallace 1957(?)- 54
Ericsson, Jennifer A. 1957- 56
Ermatinger, James W. 1959- 57

F

Feiffer, Kate 1964- 59
Flutsztejn-Gruda, Ilona 1930- 60
Forde, Catherine 1961- 61
Fox, Aileen 1907-2005
   Obituary Notice 62

G

Gaffney, Timothy R. 1951- 64
George, Jean
   See George, Jean Craighead 65
George, Jean Craighead 1919- 65
Gerber, Merrill Joan 1938- 74
   Autobiography Feature 76
Goode, Diane 1949- 97
Goode, Diane Capuozzo
   See Goode, Diane 97
Gorrell, Gena K. 1946- 102
Gorrell, Gena Kinton
   See Gorrell, Gena K. 102

Graber, Janet 1942- 104
Green, John 1978(?)- 105
Griessman, Annette 1962- 106

H

Hannigan, Katherine 108
Henderson, Aileen Mary
   See Fox, Aileen 62
Henriquez, Emile F. 1937- 110
Hill, Laban Carrick 110
hooks, bell 1952- 112

J

Jacobson, Jennifer
   See Jacobson, Jennifer Richard 116
Jacobson, Jennifer Richard 1958- 116
Jacobson, Rick 118

K

Keep, Richard 1949- 121
Keep, Richard Cleminson
   See Keep, Richard 121
Kimmel, Elizabeth Cody 122
Kulikov, Boris 1966- 125

L

Leavitt, Martine 1953- 127
Lehman, Barbara 1963- 129
Lehmann, Debra Lynn
   See Vanasse, Deb 186

M

Mansir, A. Richard 1932- 131
Marchetta, Melina 1965- 132
Mason, Cherie 134
McKendry, Joe 1972- 135
Milligan, Bryce 1953- 136
Munger, Nancy 140

N

Näslund, Görel Kristina 1940- 142
Neubecker, Robert 142

O

Ostow, Micol 1976- 143

P

Paver, Michelle 148
Perez, Lana
   See Perez, Marlene 147
Perez, Marlene 147
Plume, Ilse 148

R

Reeve, Philip 151
Richards, Chuck 1957- 153
Roche, Luane 1937- 154
Romano, Ray 1957- 155
Romano, Raymond
   See Romano, Ray 155
Ross, Michael Elsohn 1952- 157

S

Sabuda, Robert 1965- 165
Sabuda, Robert James
   See Sabuda, Robert 165
Skye, Obert 170
Smith, Z.Z.
   See Westheimer, David 193
Stille, Darlene R. 1942- 170
Stille, Darlene Ruth
   See Stille, Darlene R. 170

T

Taback, Simms 1932- 174
Teague, Mark 1963- 177
Teague, Mark Christopher
   See Teague, Mark 177
Toft, Kim Michelle 1960- 182

V

Vanasse, Deb 1957- 186
VanOosting, James 1951- 187

W

Walsh, Lawrence 1942- 188
Walsh, Suella 189
Watkins, Gloria Jean
   See hooks, bell 112
Watts, Jeri Hanel 1957- 189
Webber, Desiree Morrison 1956- 190
Weigel, Jeff 1958- 192

Westheimer, David 1917-2005
   Obituary Notice 193

Westheimer, David Kaplan
   See Westheimer, David 193

Wilson-Max, Ken 1965- 194

Y

Yang, Belle 1960- 197

Z

Zalben, Jane Breskin 1950- 198

Zhang, Song Nan 1942- 204

Authors in Forthcoming Volumes

Below are some of the authors and illustrators that will be featured in upcoming volumes of *SATA*. These include new entries on the swiftly rising stars of the field, as well as completely revised and updated entries (indicated with *) on some of the most notable and best-loved creators of books for children.

K.P. Bath ∎ A medieval European city that time forgot is the setting for Bath's fantasy novels *The Secret of Castle Cant: Being an Account of the Remarkable Adventures of Lucy Wickwright, Maidservant and Spy* and *Escape from Castle Cant*. In this tiny, technologically backward kingdom, Bath's humorous, fantastical fables center on a young servant girl embroiled in a series of dastardly court intrigues; meanwhile, readers can delight in Bath's sea of puns, similes, alliteration, and other wordplay.

Maurine F. Dahlberg ∎ Dahlberg won critical acclaim with her debut children's book *Play to the Angel*. Centering on a twelve-year-old Viennese girl who aspires to become a concert pianist, the story, with its World War II setting, focuses on how the tragedy of war changes people's lives. Other novels by Dahlberg, such as *Escape to West Berlin*, continue the author's focus on brave teens forced by circumstance to deal with extraordinary times.

Adam Gopnik ∎ Gopnik's byline has become well known to readers of the *New Yorker* through his work as a cultural and art critic. While living in France with his young son during a stint as the magazine's Paris correspondent, the literate journalist was inspired to dabble in fiction, with the YA fantasy *The King in the Window* the result. A sophisticated mix of fantasy, wordplay, and whimsy, Gopnik's novel can be read on several levels, entertaining both teens and adult readers.

Murray Kimber ∎ Raised on the Canadian prairie, Kimber was inspired to begin his career as a painter after discovering the superhero comics of the 1930s and 1940s. Now an award-winning artist and illustrator, Kimber's work appears in mainstream magazines as well as in picture books such as an illustrated version of Alfred Noyes' classic poem *The Highwayman* and Jim McGugan's *Josepha: A Prairie Boy's Story*, the last earning Kimber the 1994 Canadian Governor General's Award for illustration.

***Margaret Mahy** ∎ Considered a national treasure in her native New Zealand, Mahy shows respect for her young readers through her sophisticated use of language, imagery, and metaphor. Winner of the 2006 Hans Christian Andersen Author Award—one of many other honors she has received in her long career—the prolific Mahy is known for combining fantasy and the supernatural in young-adult novels such as *The Haunting*. Her many beginning readers seduce budding wordsmiths by weaving whimsy into an easy-to-read text, while her picture books are consistently cited for their engaging rhyming texts.

Frances Park ∎ Together with sister Ginger Park, Park is known for creating picture books that reflect her family's Korean heritage. In books such as *My Freedom Trip: A Child's Escape from North Korea* and *Good-bye, 382 Shin Dang Dong* she focuses on young children forced to leave familiar surroundings due to changes in the adult world that they cannot understand. In the more lighthearted *Where on Earth Is My Bagel?* Park helps young children learn to embrace such changes by introducing a Korean boy who longs to sample a different way of life.

***Philip Ridley** ∎ Ridley's knack for storytelling, which developed as he created tales as a way to calm his nervous younger brother, has resulted in a successful career as a dramatist and screenwriter. In addition to screenplays such as *The Krays*, Ridley's energetic wit and engaging, off-kilter characters have also found a perfect home in children's literature, as evidenced by books such as *Dakota of the White Flats*, *Meteorite Spoon*, and the comic fantasy *Krindlekrax; or, How Rushkin Splinter Battled a Horrible Monster and Saved His Entire Neighborhood*.

***Elizabeth Ann Scarborough** ∎ A popular author of fantasy fiction, Scarborough blends humor and fantasy to create stories featuring strong female protagonists who befriend charming animal characters and embark on exciting quests. In addition to fantasy series and standalone novels such as *The Lady in the Loch* and the Nebula Award-winning *The Healer's War*, Scarborough collaborates with fantasist Anne McCaffrey on the popular "Acorna" series for young adults. Her "Acorna" books, as well as her other novels, are acknowledged for their originality, fast pace, and unconventionality as well as for their author's wit and light-hearted approach.

Victor E. Villaseñor ∎ Award-winning author, journalist, and motivational Villaseñor is known for penning compelling memoirs such as *Rain of Gold* and *Burro Genius* that focus on young Latinos making a life for themselves in a new country, where both opportunity and discrimination exist. The author of novels, short fiction, and nonfiction, Villaseñor has also inspired younger Latinos with pride in their Hispanic heritage and culture through his bilingual picture books, which include *Little Crow to the Rescue/Cuervito al rescate* and *Mother Fox and Mr. Coyote/Mama Zorra y Don Coyote*.

Adrienne Yorinks ∎ The versatile Yorinks has worked as a dog groomer and breeder as well as a writer, illustrator, quilt artist, and textile designer. With *Quilt of States: Piecing Together America* she combines several of her talents, using colored and patterned fabrics to create a hand-stitched history of the fifty states that is enhanced by short narrative histories contributed by librarians from around the country. Other projects that have benefitted from Yorinks' textile collage art include the picture book *Quack!*, by Arthur Yorinks, and Marian Wright Edelman's nonfiction title *Stand for Children*.

Introduction

Something about the Author (*SATA*) is an ongoing reference series that examines the lives and works of authors and illustrators of books for children. *SATA* includes not only well-known writers and artists but also less prominent individuals whose works are just coming to be recognized. This series is often the only readily available information source on emerging authors and illustrators. You'll find *SATA* informative and entertaining, whether you are a student, a librarian, an English teacher, a parent, or simply an adult who enjoys children's literature.

What's Inside SATA

SATA provides detailed information about authors and illustrators who span the full time range of children's literature, from early figures like John Newbery and L. Frank Baum to contemporary figures like Judy Blume and Richard Peck. Authors in the series represent primarily English-speaking countries, particularly the United States, Canada, and the United Kingdom. Also included, however, are authors from around the world whose works are available in English translation. The writings represented in *SATA* include those created intentionally for children and young adults as well as those written for a general audience and known to interest younger readers. These writings cover the entire spectrum of children's literature, including picture books, humor, folk and fairy tales, animal stories, mystery and adventure, science fiction and fantasy, historical fiction, poetry and nonsense verse, drama, biography, and nonfiction. Obituaries are also included in *SATA* and are intended not only as death notices but also as concise overviews of people's lives and work. Additionally, each edition features newly revised and updated entries for a selection of *SATA* listees who remain of interest to today's readers and who have been active enough to require extensive revisions of their earlier biographies.

Autobiography Feature

Beginning with Volume 103, many volumes of *SATA* feature one or more specially commissioned autobiographical essays. These unique essays, averaging about ten thousand words in length and illustrated with an abundance of personal photos, present an entertaining and informative first-person perspective on the lives and careers of prominent authors and illustrators profiled in *SATA*.

Two Convenient Indexes

In response to suggestions from librarians, *SATA* indexes no longer appear in every volume but are included in alternate (odd-numbered) volumes of the series, beginning with Volume 57.

SATA continues to include two indexes that cumulate with each alternate volume: the Illustrations Index, arranged by the name of the illustrator, gives the number of the volume and page where the illustrator's work appears in the current volume as well as all preceding volumes in the series; the Author Index gives the number of the volume in which a person's biographical sketch, autobiographical essay, or obituary appears in the current volume as well as all preceding volumes in the series.

These indexes also include references to authors and illustrators who appear in *Gale's Yesterday's Authors of Books for Children, Children's Literature Review,* and *Something about the Author Autobiography Series*.

Easy-to-Use Entry Format

Whether you're already familiar with the *SATA* series or just getting acquainted, you will want to be aware of the kind of information that an entry provides. In every *SATA* entry the editors attempt to give as complete a picture of the person's life and work as possible. A typical entry in *SATA* includes the following clearly labeled information sections:

PERSONAL: date and place of birth and death, parents' names and occupations, name of spouse, date of marriage, names of children, educational institutions attended, degrees received, religious and political affiliations, hobbies and other interests.

ADDRESSES: complete home, office, electronic mail, and agent addresses, whenever available.

CAREER: name of employer, position, and dates for each career post; art exhibitions; military service; memberships and offices held in professional and civic organizations.

MEMBER: professional, civic, and other association memberships and any official posts held.

AWARDS, HONORS: literary and professional awards received.

WRITINGS: title-by-title chronological bibliography of books written and/or illustrated, listed by genre when known; lists of other notable publications, such as plays, screenplays, and periodical contributions.

ADAPTATIONS: a list of films, television programs, plays, CD-ROMs, recordings, and other media presentations that have been adapted from the author's work.

WORK IN PROGRESS: description of projects in progress.

SIDELIGHTS: a biographical portrait of the author or illustrator's development, either directly from the biographee—and often written specifically for the *SATA* entry—or gathered from diaries, letters, interviews, or other published sources.

BIOGRAPHICAL AND CRITICAL SOURCES: cites sources quoted in "Sidelights" along with references for further reading.

EXTENSIVE ILLUSTRATIONS: photographs, movie stills, book illustrations, and other interesting visual materials supplement the text.

How a *SATA* Entry Is Compiled

SATA editors examine a wide variety of published sources to gather information for an entry. Biographical and bibliographic sources are consulted, as are book reviews, feature articles, published interviews, and material sometimes obtained from the biographee's family, publishers, agent, or other associates. Whenever possible, the author or illustrator is sent a copy of the entry to check for accuracy and completeness.

Entries that have not been verified by the biographees or their representatives are marked with an asterisk (*).

Contact the Editor

We encourage our readers to examine the entire *SATA* series. Please write and tell us if we can make *SATA* even more helpful to you. Give your comments and suggestions to the editor:

Editor
Something about the Author
Thomson Gale
27500 Drake Rd.
Farmington Hills MI 48331-3535

Toll-free: 800-877-GALE
Fax: 248-699-8070

Something about the Author Product Advisory Board

The editors of *Something about the Author* are dedicated to maintaining a high standard of excellence by publishing comprehensive, accurate, and highly readable entries on a wide array of writers for children and young adults. In addition to the quality of the content, the editors take pride in the graphic design of the series, which is intended to be orderly yet inviting, allowing readers to utilize the pages of *SATA* easily and with efficiency. Despite the longevity of the *SATA* print series, and the success of its format, we are mindful that the vitality of a literary reference product is dependent on its ability to serve its users over time. As literature, and attitudes about literature, constantly evolve, so do the reference needs of students, teachers, scholars, journalists, researchers, and book club members. To be certain that we continue to keep pace with the expectations of our customers, the editors of *SATA* listen carefully to their comments regarding the value, utility, and quality of the series. Librarians, who have firsthand knowledge of the needs of library users, are a valuable resource for us. The *Something about the Author* Product Advisory Board, made up of school, public, and academic librarians, is a forum to promote focused feedback about *SATA* on a regular basis. The nine-member advisory board includes the following individuals, whom the editors wish to thank for sharing their expertise:

Eva M. Davis
Youth Department Manager,
Ann Arbor District Library,
Ann Arbor, Michigan

Joan B. Eisenberg
Lower School Librarian,
Milton Academy,
Milton, Massachusetts

Francisca Goldsmith
Teen Services Librarian,
Berkeley Public Library,
Berkeley, California

Susan Dove Lempke
Children's Services Supervisor,
Niles Public Library District,
Niles, Illinois

Robyn Lupa
Head of Children's Services,
Jefferson County Public Library,
Lakewood, Colorado

Victor L. Schill
Assistant Branch Librarian/Children's Librarian,
Harris County Public Library/Fairbanks Branch,
Houston, Texas

Caryn Sipos
Community Librarian,
Three Creeks Community Library,
Vancouver, Washington

Steven Weiner
Director,
Maynard Public Library,
Maynard, Massachusetts

SOMETHING ABOUT THE AUTHOR

ASHBY, Ruth

Personal

Female.

Addresses

Home—Huntington, NY. *Agent*—c/o Author Mail, William B. Eerdmans, Publishing, 255 Jefferson Ave. SE, Grand Rapids, MI 49503.

Career

Writer of children's books.

Awards, Honors

Outstanding Science Trade Book selection, National Science Teachers Association/Children's Book Council, 2004, for *Rocket Man*.

Writings

Quest for King Arthur, illustrated by Scott Caple, Bantam (New York, NY), 1988.
Sea Otters, Atheneum (New York, NY), 1990.
Tigers, Atheneum (New York, NY), 1990.
The Orangutan, Dillon Press (New York, NY), 1994.
(Editor, with Deborah Gore Ohrn) *Herstory: Women Who Changed the World*, Viking (New York, NY), 1995.
Elizabethan England, Benchmark Books (New York, NY), 1999.
T-Rex: Back to the Cretaceous, Scholastic (New York, NY), 2000.
Boss Tweed and Tammany Hall, Blackbirch Press (San Diego, CA), 2002.
Steve Case: America Online Pioneer, Twenty-first Century Books (Brookfield, CT), 2002.
Lincoln, Smart Apple Media (North Mankato, MN), 2003.
Lee vs. Grant: Great Battles of the Civil War, Smart Apple Media (North Mankato, MN), 2003.
The Outer Planets, Smart Apple Media (North Mankato, MN), 2003.
1800, Benchmark Books (New York, NY), 2003.
How the Solar System Was Formed, Smart Apple Media (North Mankato, MN), 2003.
Gettysburg, Smart Apple Media (North Mankato, MN), 2003.
Victorian England, Benchmark Books (New York, NY), 2003.
Fury on Horseback, Smart Apple Media (North Mankato, MN), 2003.
The Underground Railroad, Smart Apple Media (North Mankato, MN), 2003.
Extraordinary People, Smart Apple Media (North Mankato, MN), 2003.
The Earth and Its Moon, Smart Apple Media (North Mankato, MN), 2003.
(Editor) *The Letters of Elinore Pruitt Stewart, Woman Homesteader*, illustrated by Laszlo Kubinyi, Benchmark Books (New York, NY), 2004.

Rocket Man: The Mercury Adventure of John Glenn, Peachtree (Atlanta, GA), 2004.

The Diary of Sam Watkins, a Confederate Soldier, illustrated by Laszlo Kubinyi, Benchmark Books (New York, NY), 2004.

The Amazing Mr. Franklin; or, The Boy Who Read Everything, Peachtree (Atlanta, GA), 2004.

Pteranodon: The Life Story of a Pterosaur, illustrated by Phil Wilson, Abrams (New York, NY), 2005.

John and Abigail Adams, World Almanac Library (Milwaukee, WI), 2005.

James and Dolly Madison, World Almanac Library (Milwaukee, WI), 2005.

Ronald and Nancy Reagan, World Almanac Library (Milwaukee, WI), 2005.

George W. and Laura Bush, World Almanac Library (Milwaukee, WI), 2005.

George and Martha Washington, World Almanac Library (Milwaukee, WI), 2005.

Franklin and Eleanor Roosevelt, World Almanac Library (Milwaukee, WI), 2005.

John and Jacqueline Kennedy, World Almanac Library (Milwaukee, WI), 2005.

Bill and Hillary Rodham Clinton, World Almanac Library (Milwaukee, WI), 2005.

Woodrow and Edith Wilson, World Almanac Library (Milwaukee, WI), 2005.

Abraham and Mary Todd Lincoln, World Almanac Library (Milwaukee, WI), 2005.

Anne Frank: Young Diarist, Aladdin (New York, NY), 2005.

My Favorite Dinosaurs, illustrated by John Sibbick, Milk & Cookies, 2005.

Caedmon's Song, illustrated by Bill Slavin, W.B. Eerdmans (Grand Rapids, MI), 2006.

Sidelights

Ruth Ashby is a children's writer who focuses on nonfiction topics ranging from biology and paleontology to history and biography. She has also edited such volumes as *Herstory: Women Who Changed the World* and *The Letters of Elinore Pruitt Stewart, Woman Homesteader. Herstory* features short biographies of 120 of history's prominent women rulers, scientists, and athletes. According to a reviewer for *Publishers Weekly,* the "highly readable thumbnail sketches cover areas from literature to politics, fashion to aviation, music to science." A *Booklist* contributor noted that "women of all times, places, and professions are treated," and felt that the coeditors "admirably do justice to the topic and audience." Kristen Oravec, reviewing *The Letters of Elinore Pruitt Stewart* along with another title for *School Library Journal,* commented that "the past comes strikingly to light in these first-person accounts."

Several of Ashby's original titles for young readers discuss dinosaurs. *T-Rex: Back to the Cretaceous,* a tie-in for the IMAX film of the same name, follows the characters from the film while also providing trivia on Tyrannosaurus rex. "The author has constructed a book to appeal to dinophiles," wrote Patricia Manning in her *School Library Journal* review. *My Favorite Dinosaurs,* which covers various dinosaurs from different prehistoric eras, was considered "a browsing delight for dinosaur fans" by Todd Morning in *Booklist. Pteranodon: The Life Story of a Pterosaur* is an imagined day in the life of a pterosaur that is based on scientific field studies of the albatross; scientists theorize that the furry, flying dinosaur had similar habits to the modern-day bird. "Dinosaur lovers will enjoy this handsomely illustrated picture book full of drama and speculation," wrote a contributor to *Kirkus Reviews.* Patricia Manning, writing for *School Library Journal,* noted that "the simple text includes . . . dramatic moments," and that the work is "an attractive and rewarding look at the possibilities in a long-lost life history."

Ashby has written a number of biographies on notable figures in U.S. history, including astronaut John Glenn, inventor and politician Benjamin Franklin, and several U.S. presidents and their wives. In *The Amazing Mr. Franklin; or, The Boy Who Read Everything,* she offers a "lively narrative account," in the words of Carolyn Phelan in *Booklist,* describing Ashby's take on Franklin's varied career as a scientist, writer, politician, and inventor. Rebecca Sheridan, writing in *School Library Journal,* noted that "Ashby's clearly written narrative . . . flows smoothly and will hold the interest of children." *Rocket Man: The Mercury Adventure of John Glenn* recounts Glenn's childhood and the career that led to his becoming an astronaut and returning to space at age seventy-seven. "This book describes Glenn's life in a highly readable style," wrote Lana Miles in *School Library Journal.*

Ashby's series of titles about U.S. presidents and their first ladies includes short biographies that "are well designed and neatly tie together the lives of presidential couples," wrote Ilene Cooper in her *Booklist* review of *Bill and Hillary Rodham Clinton. School Library Journal* reviewer Janet Gillen, considering other titles in the series, deemed the books "readable, interesting, and accurate."

Along with biographies of famous Americans, Ashby has also penned fictionalized biographies of Anne Frank, whose diary has helped many young people to learn about the Holocaust, and Caedmon, the seventh-century monk who is considered by many to be the first English poet. *Caedmon's Song* fills in imagined details of how a tongue-tied, disgruntled cowherd who hated poetry dreamed a hymn, leading him to become a monk so he could continue to create songs of praise. Ashby "creates a sympathetic protagonist, a man who is not ambitious but who, when the time is right, answers his calling," wrote Kara Schaff Dean in *School Library Journal.* "The episode is a significant one in our cultural history, and it's been many a year since any other version of it has been offered for young readers," noted a contributor to *Kirkus Reviews.* A *Publishers Weekly* critic considered the book an "accessible tale," and commented that

Cover of Ruth Ashby's Rocket Man, *illustrated by Robert Hunt.* (Text copyright © 2004 by Ruth Ashby. Illustrations copyright © 2004 by Robert Hunt. Published by Peachtree. Reproduced by permission.)

"young readers will likely find the brief profile of a little-known figure intriguing."

Biographical and Critical Sources

PERIODICALS

Booklist, October 1, 1995, review of *Herstory: Women Who Changed the World,* p. 349; July, 2004, Carolyn Phelan, review of *The Amazing Mr. Franklin; or, The Boy Who Read Everything,* p. 1838; March 1, 2005, Ilene Cooper, review of *Bill and Hillary Rodham Clinton,* p. 1188; April 1, 2005, Todd Morning, review of *My Favorite Dinosaurs,* p. 1361.
Kirkus Reviews, March 15, 2005, review of *My Favorite Dinosaurs,* p. 347; June 1, 2005, review of *Pteranodon: The Life Story of a Pterosaur,* p. 632; December 15, 2005, review of *Caedmon's Song,* p. 1317.
Publishers Weekly, June 19, 1995, review of *Herstory,* p. 62; January 30, 2006, review of *Caedmon's Song,* p. 72.
School Library Journal, July, 1990, Ruth S. Vose, review of *Tigers,* p. 80; August, 1994, Helen Rosenberg, review of *The Orangutan,* p. 160; November, 1995, Maureen Connelly, review of *Herstory,* p. 133; January, 2001, Patricia Manning, review of *T-Rex: Back to the Cretaceous,* p. 113; February, 2003, Deborah Rothaug, review of *Extraordinary People,* p. 151; March, 2004, review of *The Letters of Elinore Pruitt Stewart, Woman Homesteader,* p. 224; November, 2004, Rebecca Sheridan, review of *The Amazing Mr. Franklin,* p. 121; December, 2004, Lana Miles, review of *Rocket Man: The Mercury Adventure of John Glenn,* p. 156; April, 2005, Patricia Manning, review of *My Favorite Dinosaurs,* and Rita Soltan, review of *Anne Frank: Young Diarist,* p. 118; July, 2005, Patricia Manning, review of *Pteranodon,* p. 86; August, 2005, Janet Gillen, review of *Bill and Hillary Rodham Clinton* and others, p. 140; October, 2005, review of *My Favorite Dinosaurs,* p. S31; March, 2006, Kara Schaff Dean, review of *Caedmon's Song,* p. 206.
Voice of Youth Advocates, August, 1996, review of *Herstory,* p. 148; April, 2003, review of *Fury on Horseback,* p. 75.*

* * *

ATWATER-RHODES, Amelia 1984-

Personal
Born April 16, 1984, in Silver Spring, MD; daughter of William (a public-policy consultant in econometrics) and Susan (a school vice principal). *Education:* Attended University of Massachusetts, beginning c. 2002. *Hobbies and other interests:* Cross-stitch, playing piano, gardening, cooking, carpentry, debate, learning new things.

Addresses
Home—Concord, MA. *Agent*—c/o Author Mail, Delacorte Press, Bantam Dell, 1745 Broadway, New York, NY 10019.

Career
Novelist.

Awards, Honors
Quick Picks for Reluctant Young Readers citation, American Library Association, 2001, for *Demon in My View* and *Shattered Mirror; School Library Journal* Best Books of the Year designation, 2003, for *Hawksong.*

Writings

NOVELS

In the Forests of the Night, Delacorte (New York, NY), 1999.
Demon in My View, Delacorte (New York, NY), 2000.

Shattered Mirror, Delacorte (New York, NY), 2001.
Midnight Predator, Delacorte (New York, NY), 2002.

"KIESHA'RA" NOVEL SERIES

Hawksong, Delacorte (New York, NY), 2003.
Snakecharm, Delacorte (New York, NY), 2004.
Falcondance, Delacorte (New York, NY), 2005.
Wolfcry, Delacorte (New York, NY), 2006.

Adaptations

The "Kiesha'ra" series has been adapted for audiobook by Recorded Books.

Work in Progress

Further novels.

Sidelights

Amelia Atwater-Rhodes had an early dose of fame when, in 1999 at age fifteen, *In the Forests of the Night,* her first published book, drew positive reviews from mainstream critics. *In the Forests of the Night* is a vampire novel that the author wrote at age thirteen; finishing the book and submitting the manuscript, she signed the publishing contract on her fourteenth birthday. In the years since, the young writer has continued to produce imaginative fiction on a regular basis, including the "Kiesha'ra" fantasy series. Not surprisingly considering the author's celebrity, Atwater-Rhodes's books are popular with teen readers; whereas young-adult books normally sell in four-digit editions, *In the Forests of the Night* required repeat printings, and sales had reached over 50,000 copies only months after publication.

A prolific writer, Atwater-Rhodes has continued to attract critical praise, her second novel, *Demon in My View,* cementing critics' faith in her abilities. Despite the demands of fulfilling the contracts of her publishers for more novels featuring a mix of witchcraft and vampirism, however, the young novelist still had to navigate her teen years, which included high-school graduation and enrollment at the University of Massachusetts. "Her mother still makes her do the dishes," commented Susan Carpenter in the *Los Angeles Times,* describing the life of the then-sixteen-year-old writer following publication of *Demon in My View.*

Atwater-Rhodes was born in Silver Spring, Maryland, in 1984, but subsequently moved to Concord, Massachusetts, where she attended high school. While both parents—her mother is a high-school vice principal and her father is a public-policy consultant—acknowledged being fans of the books of horror fiction-writer Anne Rice, Atwater-Rhodes particularly credits her mother with whetting her appetite for the genre. As she told *USA Today* writer Katy Kelly, "She pretty much raised me on Stephen King and Dracula and aliens. She'd say, 'Just keep in mind: it's fiction. You're not supposed to take an ax to your neighbor. You're not to bite your friend.'"

Cover of Amelia Atwater-Rhodes's In the Forests of the Night, *featuring artwork by Eric Dinyer.* (Text copyright © 1999 by Amelia Atwater-Rhodes. Jacket illustration © 2000 by Eric Dinyer. Published by Dell Laurel Leaf. Reproduced by permission of Eric Dinyer.)

The urge to create seized Atwater-Rhodes early, and she was at work on a science-fiction novel by the second grade. By age nine, she had discovered Christopher Pike's *The Last Vampire,* a book that, as she once explained, "served as an inspiration by pointing out that vampires do not have to fit into stereotypes." She began writing in earnest following the fifth grade, working after school, in the middle of the night, or whenever inspiration struck. Sometimes she would write sixty pages at a sitting, and while composing *In the Forests of the Night* she balanced a tiger Beanie Baby on her head and took inspiration from singer Alanis Morisette's *Jagged Little Pill* album. After reading the novel, a former teacher signed on as her agent and sent the novel to Delacorte Press. While celebrating her fourteenth birthday, Atwater-Rhodes received a phone call telling her that the publisher had accepted *In the Forests of the Night* for publication.

Taking place in the present day and set in its author's New England hometown, *In the Forests of the Night* is the story of a 300-year-old vampire named Risika, who was "turned" while a teenager and living in colonial Concord. Risika's human persona, Rachel Weatere, was born in 1684; now, after centuries as an Undead, Risika has adjusted to her status, and as Holly Koelling noted in *Booklist,* "has grown distant from the mortal world. Humans are prey, needed solely for nourishment." Risika sleeps by day and goes hunting in New York City by night, seeking fresh blood. One night, returning home, she discovers a black rose on her pillow just as she had centuries before, on the eve of her own changeover from human to vampire. The rose is a sign, a challenge from her archenemy, a powerful vampire named Aubrey, who long ago helped Risika arrange her transformation and who she believes murdered her human brother. Risika goes into action, deciding to confront her old enemy.

Reviews of *In the Forests of the Night* were generally favorable, albeit with some reservations. A reviewer for *Publishers Weekly* cited Atwater-Rhodes as "skillful at building atmosphere, insightful in creating characters and imaginative in varying and expanding upon vampire lore," while also noting a strain of "easy, adolescent cynicism." In *Booklist,* Koelling dubbed the novel's storyline "derivative" and "meandering," but went on to comment that Atwater-Rhodes's "use of language is surprisingly mature and polished for a thirteen-year-old writer." As Koelling correctly predicted, "Both the book's subject and the age of the author will ensure its popularity, especially with middle-schoolers, and it may encourage other young writers to pursue the craft." Kendra Nan Skellen, reviewing the novel for *School Library Journal,* wrote that *In the Forests of the Night* "is well written and very descriptive, and has in-depth character development. . . . This first novel by an author with great ability and promise is sure to be popular." *New Yorker* contributor Melanie Thernstrom summed up critical response by writing: "Amelia has an uncanny understanding of the kind of narrative that makes for a successful potboiler: she's skilled at creating characters the reader easily and instantly bonds with, and she's resourceful when it comes to putting them in jeopardy. . . . No one in the world of young-adult publishing has managed to come up with an analogy to Amelia: other early-teenage writers simply don't write coherent multiple-character, time-weaving, metafictional novels."

Atwater-Rhodes served up another slice of her favorite genre—horror—in her second novel, *Demon in My View.* Like *In the Forests of the Night, Demon in My View* chronicles a portion of the elaborate genealogy of vampires and related supernatural beings created by the author. By 2001, Atwater-Rhodes calculated, she had written the equivalent of over twenty-five novels, and had dozens of story ideas saved on her computer. As Thernstrom noted, "It will require a dizzying number of books to straighten . . . out" the histories of the young novelist's elaborate character genealogy, some 260 and growing. "Unless Amelia manages to achieve the immortality of her characters, her imagination has already extended beyond her own life span," the critic added.

Demon in My View focuses on Jessica Ashley Allodola, a high school student who briefly appeared in *In the Forests of the Night.* Writing under the pen name of Ash Night, Jessica has just published her first novel, a vampire tale titled *Tiger, Tiger.* At school she is an outsider, something of a misfit, but writing takes her into a dreamlike state in which she can describe the world of vampires and witches in vivid detail. Jessica marvels at the way her fertile imagination works; what she does not realize is that these visions are, in fact, real. As a reviewer for *Publishers Weekly* noted of the novel's plot, the vampires "aren't too happy that she's spilled their secrets and wittingly alerted vampire-hunting witches to the location of their undead village, New Mayhem." To gain vengeance, Aubrey—the nemesis of *In the Forests of the Night*—appears at Jessica's high school disguised as a new student named Alex. Attracted to Jessica's aura, Aubrey is then torn between a desire for revenge and the wish to turn the young writer into a vampire like himself. Jessica, too, finds herself attracted to Aubrey. Meanwhile, the plot thickens with the arrival of another student, actually a witch of the Smoke Line, Caryn, who has arrived to protect Jessica from the vampires. "The clash between the witches and the vampires and the truth of Jessica's birth take the plot down many twisting and suspenseful paths," according to Jane Halsall, writing in *School Library Journal.*

A reviewer for *Publishers Weekly* commented that in *Demon in My View* "fantastic fights will keep readers turning pages quickly," and concluded that "Atwater-Rhodes exercises impressive control over the complex lineages she has imagined, and she comes up with creative solutions to advance her story. Readers will drain this book in one big gulp." Not all reviewers were quite so enthusiastic about the young writer's second outing, however. Ellen Creager wrote in the *Detroit Free Press* that the book "is nowhere near as polished as the first," lacking its "compelling plot" and "immediacy." Creager further noted that *Demon in My View* "is a bit too close to [the television series] 'Buffy the Vampire Slayer' for comfort," and Halsall wrote in *School Library Journal* that the second novel "is not as tightly plotted or generally as well written as . . . [the] first."

Atwater-Rhodes's vampire and witch saga continues in the novels *Shattered Mirror* and *Midnight Predator. Shattered Mirror* tells the story of Sara Vida, a high school student and witch who must grapple with her upbringing and values when she befriends brother and sister vampires Christopher and Nissa. When Sara learns that Christopher's twin brother is Nikolas, a notoriously evil vampire who murdered one of Sara's own ancestors, the tension and suspense build. *Midnight Predator* finds relentless vampire hunter Turquoise Draka joining

Cover of Atwater-Rhodes's Shattered Mirror, *featuring artwork by Cliff Nielsen.* (Text copyright © 2001 by Amelia Atwater-Rhodes. Illustration by Cliff Nielson. Used by permission of Random House Children's Books, a division of Random House, Inc.)

fellow tracker Ravyn on the trail of notorious undead Jeshickah, even though the creature's trail leads into the vampire realm known as the Midnight Empire.

While a *Publishers Weekly* contributor found that "some of [Atwater-Rhodes's] writing . . . is over the top," in *Shattered Mirror* the young author "chooses an interesting theme . . . and she builds some creative elements around it." Similarly, *School Library Journal* contributor Elaine Baran Black commented that with *Shattered Mirror,* "Atwater-Rhodes does another fine job of building a suspenseful mood and sustaining it throughout." Black further remarked that, "though the ending isn't necessarily a big surprise, readers will be racing to reach it as they devour this compelling tale." Praising *Midnight Predator* for its "thoughtful" conclusion, Molley S. Kinney noted in *School Library Journal* that Atwater-Rhodes's "plot and characters are . . . skillfully intertwined," and "the harshness and violence" of her story are balanced by "the soulful searching" of the tale's central protagonists.

In 2003 Atwater-Rhodes introduced her "Kiesha'ra" series with *Hawksong*. A shapeshifter who can move from human to hawk form, Danica Shardae is heir to the throne of her kingdom. Hoping to end the war between her kind and the serpiente, she agrees to wed Zane Cobriana. Professing an equal commitment to a peace between their two shapeshifter races, Zane nonetheless presents a real threat to his bride while in his alternate cobra form, forcing Danica to keep removed from him in private. As some attempt to end their alliance, Danica and Zane try to forge a bond of trust in a novel that *School Library Journal* contributor Saleena L. Davidson dubbed an "engaging fantasy" that is both "a love story and . . . an intriguing look at a world that is teeming with tension and danger and beauty." While a *Kirkus Reviews* writer bemoaned Atwater-Rhodes's use of a "stock romance plot," the critic added that *Hawksong* is "enjoyable for that genre," and in *Publishers Weekly* a critic praised the author for "creat[ing] . . . impressively complex cultures for both the avian and serpiente people."

Atwater-Rhodes continues her "Kiesha'ra" saga with *Snakecharm, Falcondance,* and *Wolfcry,* which continue to detail the fragile alliance between avian and serpiente shapeshifters. In *Snakecharm* Danica and Zane hope that their heir will strengthen the bond between their peoples, until Syfka, a member of the falcon clan, arrives and begins to stir up discontent in the Wyvern court. *Falcondance* finds falcon Nicias Silvermead isolated from his kind and living amid the avians and serpientes as a guard to Danica and Zane's daughter, Oliza Shardae Cobriana, in the Wyvern court. Haunted by visions of his home in Anhmik, Nicias finally returns to his homeland, hoping to find the powerful falcon who can help him harness his growing magic powers. Back in the Wyvern court, Princess Oliza comes of age and hopes for a peaceful future, until her kidnapping by a wolf band forces her to realize that peace in her kingdom is a fragile thing. According to Lisa Prolman in *School Library Journal, Snakecharm* contains a "compelling" story in which "there is enough suspense to keep readers interested," while the tale unfolding in *Falcondance* is "detailed and intertwined with [falcon] myth and legend," according to Janis Flint-Ferguson in her *Kliatt* review.

In an interview with Kellie Vaughan for *Teen People,* a then-fourteen-year-old Atwater-Rhodes offered an assessment of her creative strengths as a younger writer: "As a teen, I bring a different perspective to writing. I can offer immediate emotions, experiences and insight that adult writers often have to reach back and find in order to write about them." Her advice to other would-be writers is shared by older, more experienced authors: "Write when you feel like writing. . . . Write because you love to write. Write for yourself and no one else."

Biographical and Critical Sources

PERIODICALS

Booklist, June 1, 1999, Holly Koelling, review of *In the Forests of the Night,* p. 1812; September 1, 2001, John Peters, review of *Shattered Mirror,* p. 96; August, 2002, Debbie Carton, review of *Midnight Predator,* p. 1948.

Book Report, November-December, 1999, p. 65.

Detroit Free Press, July 16, 2000, Ellen Creager, "Fifteen Year Old Is on a Roll with Her Second Novel," p. E5.

Entertainment Weekly, March 26, 1999, p. 80.

Kirkus Reviews, June 15, 2003, review of *Hawksong,* p. 855; September 1, 2004, review of *Snakecharm,* p. 859.

Kliatt, September, 2005, Janis Flint-Ferguson, review of *Falcondance,* p. 5.

Los Angeles Times, July 30, 2000, Susan Carpenter, "Teen Author's Novel Approach," p. E2.

New Yorker, October 18-25, 1999, Melanie Thernstrom, "The Craft," pp. 136, 138, 140-142.

People, August 9, 1999, William Plummer and Tom Duffy, "Author Rising," pp. 103-104.

Publishers Weekly, May 24, 1999, review of *In the Forests of the Night,* p. 80; April 24, 2000, review of *Demon in My View,* p. 92; September 24, 2001, review of *Shattered Mirror,* p. 94; June 30, 2003, review of *Hawksong,* p. 80.

School Library Journal, July, 1999, Kendra Nan Skellen, review of *In the Forests of the Night,* p. 92; May 1, 2000, Jane Halsall, review of *Demon in My View,* p. 166; September, 2001, Elaine Baran Black, review of *Shattered Mirror,* p. 223; May, 2002, Molley S. Kinney, review of *Midnight Predator,* p. 146; August, 2003, Saleena L. Davidson, review of *Hawksong,* p. 154; October, 2004, Lisa Prolman, review of *Snakecharm,* p. 154; September, 2005, Sharon Rawlins, review of *Falcondance,* p. 198.

Seventeen, June, 1999, Curtis Sittenfeld, "Freshman Debut."

Teen People, February, 1999, Kellie Vaughan, interview with Amelia Atwater-Rhodes.

USA Today, May 6, 1999, Katy Kelly, "A Writer Grave beyond Her Years," p. D1.

ONLINE

Random House Web site, http://www.randomhouse.com/ (April 26, 2006), "Amelia Atwater-Rhodes."*

* * *

ATWOOD, Margaret 1939-
(Margaret Eleanor Atwood)

Personal

Born November 18, 1939, in Ottawa, Ontario, Canada; daughter of Carl Edmund (an entomologist) and Margaret Dorothy (Killam) Atwood; married Jim Polk, 1967 (divorced 1977); married Graeme Gibson (a writer); children: (second marriage) Jess (daughter). *Education:* University of Toronto, B.A., 1961; Radcliffe College, A.M., 1962; Harvard University, graduate study, 1962-63, 1965-67. *Politics:* "William Morrisite." *Religion:* "Immanent Transcendentalist."

Margaret Atwood (Photograph copyright © Christopher Felver/Corbis.)

Addresses

Home—Toronto, Ontario, Canada. *Agent*—c/o Author Mail, House of Anansi Press, 110 Spadina Ave., Ste. 801, Toronto, Ontario M5V 2K4, Canada.

Career

Novelist, poet, and educator. University of British Columbia, Vancouver, British Columbia, Canada, lecturer in English literature, 1964-65; Sir George Williams University, Montreal, Quebec, Canada, lecturer in English literature, 1967-68; York University, Toronto, Ontario, Canada, assistant professor of English literature, 1971-72; House of Anansi Press, Toronto, editor and member of board of directors, 1971-73; University of Toronto, writer-in-residence, 1972-73; University of Alabama—Tuscaloosa, writer-in-residence, 1985; New York University, New York, NY, Berg Visiting Professor of English, 1986; Macquarie University, North Ryde, Australia, writer-in-residence, 1987. Formerly worked as a camp counselor and waitress.

Awards, Honors

E.J. Pratt Medal, 1961, for *Double Persephone;* President's Medal, University of Western Ontario, 1965;

YWCA Women of Distinction Award, 1966, 1988; Governor General's Award, 1966, for *The Circle Game,* and 1986, for *The Handmaid's Tale;* first prize in Canadian Centennial Commission Poetry Competition, 1967; Union Prize for poetry, 1969; Bess Hoskins Prize for poetry, 1969, 1974; City of Toronto Book Award, Canadian Booksellers' Association Award, and Periodical Distributors of Canada Short Fiction Award, all 1977, all for *Dancing Girls, and Other Stories;* St. Lawrence Award for fiction, 1978; Radcliffe Medal, 1980; *Life before Man* selected a notable book of 1980, American Library Association; Molson Award, 1981; Guggenheim fellowship, 1981; named companion, Order of Canada, 1981; International Writer's Prize, Welsh Arts Council, 1982; Book of the Year Award, Periodical Distributors of Canada/Foundation for the Advancement of Canadian Letters, 1983, for *Bluebeard's Egg, and Other Stories;* named Woman of the Year, *Ms.* magazine, 1986; Ida Nudel Humanitarian Award, Toronto Arts Award for writing and editing, and *Los Angeles Times* Book Award, all 1986, and Arthur C. Clarke Award for Best Science Fiction, and Commonwealth Literature Prize, both 1987, all for *The Handmaid's Tale;* Council for the Advancement and Support of Education silver medal, 1987; Humanist of the Year award, 1987; Booker Prize shortlist, City of Toronto Book Award, Coles Book of the Year Award, Canadian Booksellers' Association Author of the Year Award, Foundation for Advancement of Canadian Letters citation, Periodical Marketers of Canada Award, and Torgi Talking Book Award, all 1989, all for *Cat's Eye;* Harvard University Centennial Medal, 1990; named to Order of Ontario, 1990; Trillium Award for Excellence in Ontario Writing, and Book of the Year Award, Periodical Marketers of Canada, both 1992, both for *Wilderness Tips, and Other Stories;* Commemorative Medal, 125th Anniversary of Canadian Confederation; Booker Prize shortlist, Trillium Award, Canadian Authors' Association Novel of the Year Award, Commonwealth Writers' Prize for Canadian and Caribbean Region, and *Sunday Times* Award for Literary Excellence, all 1994, and Swedish Humour Association's International Humourous Writer Award, 1995, all for *The Robber Bride;* named chevalier, French Ordre des Arts et des Lettres, 1994; Trillium Award, 1995, for *Morning in the Burned House;* Norwegian Order of Literary Merit, 1996; Booker Prize shortlist, and Giller Prize, both 1996, both for *Alias Grace;* International IMPAC Dublin Literary Award shortlist, Dublin City Library, 1998; Booker Prize, 2000, and Dashiell Hammett Award, International Association of Crime Writers, 2001, both for *The Blind Assassin;* Booker Prize shortlist, 2003, for *Oryx and Crake;* Enlightenment Award, Edinburgh International Festival, 2005. Recipient of honorary degrees from Trent University, 1973, Concordia University, 1980, Smith College, 1982, University of Toronto, 1983, Mount Holyoke College, 1985, University of Waterloo, 1985, University of Guelph, 1985, Victoria College, 1987, University of Montreal, 1991, University of Leeds, 1994, Queen's University, 1994, Oxford University, 1998, Cambridge University, 2001, and others.

Writings

FOR CHILDREN

(And illustrator) *Up in the Tree* (juvenile), McClelland & Stewart (Toronto, Ontario, Canada), 1978, reprinted, Groundwood Books (Toronto, Ontario, Canada), 2006.
(With Joyce Barkhouse) *Anna's Pet* (juvenile), James Lorimer, 1980.
For the Birds, illustrated by John Bianchi, Firefly Books (Richmond Hill, Ontario, Canada), 1991.
Princess Prunella and the Purple Peanut (juvenile), illustrated by Maryann Kovalski, Workman (New York, NY), 1995.
Rude Ramsay and the Roaring Radishes (juvenile), illustrated by Dušan Petričić, Key Porter Books (Toronto, Ontario, Canada), 2003, Bloomsbury (New York, NY), 2004.
Bashful Bob and Doleful Dorinda, illustrated by Dušan Petričić, Key Porter Books (Toronto, Ontario, Canada), 2004.

POETRY

Double Persephone, Hawkshead Press (Ontario, Canada), 1961.
The Circle Game, Cranbrook Academy of Art (Bloomfield Hills, MI), 1964, revised edition, House of Anansi Press (Toronto, Ontario, Canada), 1978.
Kaleidoscopes Baroque: A Poem, Cranbrook Academy of Art (Bloomfield Hills, MI), 1965.
Talismans for Children, Cranbrook Academy of Art (Bloomfield Hills, MI), 1965.
Speeches for Doctor Frankenstein, Cranbrook Academy of Art (Bloomfield Hills, MI), 1966.
The Animals in That Country, Little, Brown (Boston, MA), 1968.
The Journals of Susanna Moodie, Oxford University Press (Toronto, Ontario, Canada), 1970.
Procedures for Underground, Little, Brown (Boston, MA), 1970.
Power Politics, House of Anansi Press (Toronto, Ontario, Canada), 1971, Harper (New York, NY), 1973.
You Are Happy, Harper & Row (New York, NY), 1974.
Selected Poems, 1965-1975, Oxford University Press (Toronto, Ontario, Canada), 1976, Simon & Schuster (New York, NY), 1978.
Marsh Hawk, Dreadnaught Press (Toronto, Ontario, Canada), 1977.
Two-headed Poems, Oxford University Press, 1978, Simon & Schuster (New York, NY), 1981.
Notes toward a Poem That Can Never Be Written, Salamander Press (Toronto, Ontario, Canada), 1981.
True Stories, Oxford University Press (Toronto, Ontario, Canada), 1981, Simon & Schuster (New York, NY), 1982.
Snake Poems, Salamander Press (Toronto, Ontario, Canada), 1983.
Interlunar, Oxford University Press (Toronto, Ontario, Canada), 1984.

Selected Poems II: Poems Selected and New, 1976-1986, Oxford University Press (Toronto, Ontario, Canada), 1986.
Morning in the Burned House, Houghton Mifflin (Boston, MA), 1995.
Eating Fire: Selected Poetry, 1965-1995, Virago Press (London, England), 1998.

Also author of *Expeditions,* 1966, and *What Was in the Garden,* 1969.

NOVELS; FOR ADULTS

The Edible Woman, McClelland & Stewart (Toronto, Ontario, Canada), 1969, Little, Brown (Boston, MA), 1970, reprinted, Anchor Press (New York, NY), 1998.
Surfacing, McClelland & Stewart (Toronto, Ontario, Canada), 1972, Simon & Schuster (New York, NY), 1973, reprinted, Anchor Press (New York, NY), 1998.
Lady Oracle, Simon & Schuster (New York, NY), 1976, reprinted, Anchor Press (New York, NY), 1998.
Life before Man, Simon & Schuster (New York, NY), 1979, reprinted, Anchor Press (New York, NY), 1998.
Bodily Harm, McClelland & Stewart (Toronto, Ontario, Canada), 1981, Simon & Schuster (New York, NY), 1982, reprinted, Anchor Press (New York, NY), 1998.
Encounters with the Element Man, William B. Ewert (Concord, NH), 1982.
Unearthing Suite, Grand Union Press (Toronto, Ontario, Canada), 1983.
The Handmaid's Tale, McClelland & Stewart (Toronto, Ontario, Canada), 1985, Houghton Mifflin (Boston, MA), 1986.
Cat's Eye, McClelland & Stewart (Toronto, Ontario, Canada), 1988, Doubleday (Garden City, NY), 1989.
The Robber Bride, Doubleday (New York, NY), 1993.
Alias Grace, Doubleday (New York, NY), 1996.
The Blind Assassin, Nan A. Talese (New York, NY), 2000.
Oryx and Crake, Nan A. Talese (New York, NY), 2003.
The Tent, Nan A. Talese, (New York, NY), 2006.

SHORT FICTION

Dancing Girls, and Other Stories, McClelland & Stewart (Toronto, Ontario, Canada), 1977, Simon & Schuster (New York, NY), 1982, reprinted, Anchor Press (New York, NY), 1998.
Bluebeard's Egg, and Other Stories, McClelland & Stewart (Toronto, Ontario, Canada), 1983, Anchor Doubleday (New York, NY), 1998.
Murder in the Dark: Short Fictions and Prose Poems, Coach House Press (Toronto, Ontario, Canada), 1983.
Wilderness Tips, and Other Stories, Doubleday (New York, NY), 1991.
Good Bones, Coach House Press (Toronto, Ontario, Canada), 1992, published as *Good Bones and Simple Murders,* Doubleday (New York, NY), 1994.
A Quiet Game: And Other Early Works, edited and annotated by Kathy Chung and Sherrill Grace, Juvenilia Press (Edmonton, Alberta, Canada), 1997.

OTHER

The Trumpets of Summer (radio play), Canadian Broadcasting Corporation (CBC-Radio), 1964.
Survival: A Thematic Guide to Canadian Literature, House of Anansi Press (Toronto, Ontario, Canada), 1972.
The Servant Girl (teleplay), CBC-TV, 1974.
Days of the Rebels, 1815-1840, Natural Science Library, 1976.
The Poetry and Voice of Margaret Atwood (recording), Caedmon (New York, NY), 1977.
(Author of introduction) Catherine M. Young, *To See Our World,* GLC Publishers, 1979, Morrow (New York, NY), 1980.
Snowbird (teleplay), CBC-TV, 1981.
Second Words: Selected Critical Prose, House of Anansi Press (Toronto, Ontario, Canada), 1982.
(Editor) *The New Oxford Book of Canadian Verse in English,* Oxford University Press (Toronto, Ontario, Canada), 1982.
(Editor with Robert Weaver) *The Oxford Book of Canadian Short Stories in English,* Oxford University Press (Toronto, Ontario, Canada), 1986.
(With Peter Pearson) *Heaven on Earth* (teleplay), CBC-TV, 1986.
(Editor) *The Canlit Foodbook,* Totem Books (New York, NY), 1987.
(Editor with Shannon Ravenal) *The Best American Short Stories, 1989,* Houghton Mifflin (Boston, MA), 1989.
(Editor with Barry Callaghan and author of introduction) *The Poetry of Gwendolyn MacEwen,* Exile Editions (Toronto, Ontario, Canada), Volume 1: *The Early Years,* 1993, Volume 2: *The Later Years,* 1994.
Strange Things: The Malevolent North in Canadian Literature (lectures), Oxford University Press (Toronto, Ontario, Canada), 1996.
Some Things about Flying, Women's Press (London, England), 1997.
(With Victor-Levy Beaulieu) *Two Solicitudes: Conversations* (interviews), translated by Phyllis Aronoff and Howard Scott, McClelland & Stewart (Toronto, Ontario, Canada), 1998.
(Author of introduction) *Women Writers at Work: The "Paris Review" Interviews,* edited by George Plimpton, Random House (New York, NY), 1998.
Negotiating with the Dead: A Writer on Writing (nonfiction), Cambridge University Press (New York, NY), 2002.
(Author of introduction) *Ground Works: Avant-garde for Thee,* edited by Christian Bök, House of Anansi (Toronto, Ontario, Canada), 2002.
Moving Targets: Writing with Intent, 1982-2004, House of Anansi (Toronto, Ontario, Canada), 2004, published as *Writing with Intent: Essays, Reviews, Personal Prose, 1983-2005,* Carroll & Graf (New York, NY), 2005.
The Penelopiad: The Myth of Penelope and Odysseus (play), Knopf (Toronto, Ontario, Canada) 2005.

Contributor to anthologies, including *Five Modern Canadian Poets,* 1970; *The Canadian Imagination: Dimensions of a Literary Culture,* Harvard University

Press, 1977; *Women on Women,* 1978; and *Story of a Nation: Defining Moments in Our History,* Doubleday Canada, 2001. Contributor to periodicals, including *Atlantic Monthly, Poetry, New Yorker, Harper's, New York Times Book Review, Saturday Night, Tamarack Review,* and *Canadian Forum.*

Atwood's works have been translated into French.

Adaptations

Reflections: Progressive Insanities of a Pioneer, a six-minute visual interpretation of Atwood's poem by the same name, was produced by Cinematics Canada, 1972, and by Universal as *Poem as Imagery: Progressive Insanities of a Pioneer,* 1974. *The Journals of Susanna Moodie* was adapted as a screenplay, Tranby, 1972; *Surfacing* was adapted for film, Pan-Canadian, 1979; *The Handmaid's Tale* was filmed by Cinecom Entertainment Group, 1989, and was adapted as an opera by Danish composer Poul Ruders, for the Royal Danish Opera Company, 2002. *The Atwood Stories,* adaptations of Atwood's fiction, appeared as six half-hour episodes on W Network. Many of Atwood's books have been adapted as audiobooks.

Sidelights

Margaret Atwood is considered one of Canada's major novelists and has attained a measure of celebrity; according to Ann Marie Lipinski, writing in the *Chicago Tribune,* the writer is "one of the leading literary luminaries, a national heroine of the arts, the rara avis of Canadian letters." Atwood's books, which have been highly lauded in the United States and Europe as well in as her native Canada, have won numerous literary awards, among them Great Britain's prestigious Booker Prize in 2000. In her works, she often examines the relationship between humanity and nature, and she also looks at power as it pertains to gender and politics, although she rejects the label of feminist that many have attached to her. Employing symbolism, irony, and self-conscious narrators, Atwood takes literary chances in her writing, borrowing techniques from science fiction and detective-genre fiction.

While Atwood's fame rests on such novels as *The Handmaid's Tale, Alias Grace, Cat's Eye,* and *The Blind Assassin,* the author is also a published poet, playwright, essayist, and author of short fiction. She has also published books for younger readers throughout her decades-long career. Praised as a "silly romp" by a *Publishers Weekly* contributor, Atwood's 1996 picture book, *Princess Prunella and the Purple Peanut,* features a rhythmic text that rejoices in the sound of the letter "P" while telling the story of a pretty princess who is prompted to do three good deeds after a wise old woman weaves a convincing magic.

Born in 1939, in Ottawa, Ontario, Canada, Atwood was raised in a tight-knit family that also included a brother and a sister. Until her late teens, she spent at least half the year in the remote regions of northern Ontario and Quebec, where her etymologist father researched forest insects for the Canadian government while the family lived in a cabin without running water or electricity. Educated by her mother, she delved into books of all sorts during these long sojourns away from civilization, particularly Greek and Celtic mythology and the often brutal fairy tales collected by the Brothers Grimm. Her family's itinerant lifestyle combined with her exposure to etymological and mythic metamorphosis to build a fascination with the concepts of destruction and rebirth as inevitabilities. As a six year old, Atwood had already started dabbling with poetry, writing a series she called "Rhyming Cats." The following year, in 1946, she and her family moved to Toronto, where her father took a university post. While attending Toronto's city schools, Atwood still spent half the year living close to nature in Canada's north woods.

By the time she reached high school, Atwood had decided to become a professional writer. As she told Kim Hubbard in *People,* she was somewhat frightened by her decision, for she had few female role models in her chosen profession. "Emily Dickinson lived in a cupboard, Charlotte Brontë died in childbirth. They were weird like Christina Rossetti, or they drank or committed suicide like Sylvia Plath. Writing seemed like a call to doom. I thought I would probably get [tuberculosis] and live in a garret and have a terrible life."

Graduating from Toronto's Leaside High School in 1957, Atwood attended the University of Toronto's Victoria College and entered the English honors program. Studying under well-known critic Northrop Frye, she became versed in the use of mythical and biblical imagery. As an undergraduate she wrote for the college literary magazine and had her first poem published at age nineteen. Four years later, in 1961, the soon-to-graduate Atwood published her first volume of poetry, the award-winning *Double Persephone.* She then earned an M.A. at Radcliffe College, studying Victorian literature, and also attended Harvard University. When her second poetry collection, *The Circle Game,* won Canada's Governor General's award in 1964, its author was teaching at the college level. Five years later, Atwood published her first novel, *The Edible Woman*, marking the start of her meteoric fiction-writing career.

Atwood's novels are known for their strong female characters. Early novels such as *Surfacing, Bodily Harm,* and the well-known *The Handmaid's Tale* feature female protagonists who are characteristic of Atwood: they are, as Judy Klemesrud reported in the *New York Times,* "intelligent, self-absorbed modern women searching for identity" who "hunt, split logs, make campfires and become successful in their careers, while men often cook and take care of their households." In Atwood's plots, the lives of these women are shattered by overwhelming threats: "cancer, divorce, violence—and those that persist quietly, naggingly—solitude, loneliness, desperation," according to Lipinski.

In *The Handmaid's Tale* Atwood draws readers into Gilead, a future America in which Fundamentalist Christians have killed the president and members of Congress and imposed their own patriarchal dictatorial rule. In this future world, polluted by toxic chemicals and nuclear radiation, few women can bear children and the birthrate has dropped alarmingly. Those women able to bear children are forced to become "Handmaids," Gilead's official breeders, while those not deemed suitable are reduced to slaves under the repressive religious government. As Elaine Kendall explained in the *Los Angeles Times Book Review,* Atwood's novel is strongly grounded in current laws and regulations, and depicts "a future firmly based upon actuality, beginning with events that have already taken place and extending them a bit beyond the inevitable conclusions. *The Handmaid's Tale* does not depend upon hypothetical scenarios, omens, or straws in the wind, but upon documented occurrences and public pronouncements; all matters of record." Atwood's *Oryx and Crake* also draws readers into a provocative future world, this time focusing on a man who, his psyche shattered by violent memories, attempts to make sense of the post-apocalyptic wasteland he now inhabits.

In *Cat's Eye* Atwood narrows her focus and explores the dynamic of a family that resembles, on its surface, the one she was raised in, with its etymologist father, unconventional mother, and home-schooled children. However, the novel's pivotal tragedy hinges on the cruelty of children. The story focuses on Elaine, a successful painter who returns to her family's home in Toronto for an exhibition of her work. In a flashback to her childhood, Elaine relives her time with her childhood nemesis, a girl named Cordelia whom Elaine thought was her best friend but who actually made Elaine the object of a series of potentially deadly pranks. The young Elaine feels helpless to defend herself and is unable to confide in her parents. As Cordelia enters her teen years, however, she becomes overweight and unhappy, and she eventually goes insane. By the book's conclusion, the adult Elaine discovers how these events have influenced her art and her life. As Hermione Lee noted of *Cat's Eye* in the *New Republic,* "Under Atwood's sharp satire on girls' codes is a nightmare of persecution, which is the ugly heart of the novel. . . . Atwood's account of this torture is horrifyingly brilliant, and will strike home to anyone who was ever involved in childhood gang warfare, whether as bullier or bullied."

Alias Grace and the Booker Prize-winning *The Blind Assassin* venture into the genre of historical fiction. *The Blind Assassin* draws readers back to the early twentieth century to explore a family tragedy and its aftershocks. Based on an actual incident, *Alias Grace* centers on Grace Marks, a servant found guilty of murdering her employer and his mistress in northern Canada in 1843. Some doubt Grace's guilt, however, and as she serves out her sentence of life in prison with no memory of the murders, reformers agitate for clemency. In a quest for evidence to support their position, they assign a young doctor, Simon Jordan, who is versed in the new science of psychiatry, to evaluate her soundness of mind. Over many meetings, Grace tells the doctor the harrowing story of her life, which has been marked by extreme hardship. Much about Grace, though, remains puzzling: she is haunted by flashbacks of the supposedly forgotten murders and by a woman who died from a mishandled abortion. Praised by many reviewers for its evocation of day-to-day life during the mid-1800s, *Alias Grace* was dubbed "pure enchantment" by *Los Angeles Times Book Review* critic Richard Eder. Reviewing the novel in *Maclean's,* Diane Turbide wrote of Atwood's complex protagonist that Grace is more than an intriguing character: she is also "the lens through which Victorian hypocrisies are mercilessly exposed."

Like her adult novels, Atwood's books for children also depict a world slightly off-kilter, but instead of looming secrets, murderous servants, and the threat of cultural annihilation young readers are introduced to petulant princesses, likeable misfits, and challenges that resolve in happy-ending fashion. In fact, books like *Bashful Bob and Doleful Dorinda, Rude Ramsay and the Roaring Radishes,* and *Princess Prunella and the Purple Peanut* provide Atwood with an excuse to engage in all manner of wordplay. While her first book for children, 1976's self-illustrated and hand-lettered *Up the Tree,* relates a simple story that *Booklist* contributor Gillian Engberg deemed "whimsical" and a "refreshing return to basics," the generous helping of humorous alliterations, slapstick plot-lines, and complex vocabulary to be found in Atwood's more recent books make them almost interactive: readers need to keep a dictionary at the ready in order to get the writer's most sophisticated jokes. Still, these books appeal on several levels, and as *Resource Links* reviewer Adriane Pettit noted of *Bashful Bob and Doleful Dorinda,* "the wittiness and creativity in this wonderful tongue-twisting book make it an enjoyable read" for both adults and children. While a *Publishers Weekly* contributor cautioned that readers of *Rude Ramsay and the Roaring Radishes* might "feel overstuffed with rococo remarks" as they tackle Atwood's tale about a clueless man who, with his pet rat Ralph, leaves his "ramshackle rectangular residence" and eventually finds a new home with red-haired Rillah (who lives, not surprisingly, in a rectory), other critics disagreed. In *Kirkus Reviews* a contributor praised Atwood's text as "both amusing and enlightening in its use of rich vocabulary," while *School Library Journal* writer Caroline Ward maintained that the author's "command of wordplay is impressive, and unfamiliar words . . . may afford youngsters an opportunity for vocabulary enrichment."

Although her writing has been grist to many critics and scholars, and has been labeled everything from Cana-

In Rude Ramsay and the Roaring Radishes, *illustrated by Dušan Petričić, the life story of Atwood's well-meaning hero is peppered with the letter "R."* (Text copyright © 2003 by Margaret Atwood. Illustrations copyright © 2003 by Dušan Petričić. Reproduced by permission of Bloomsbury Children's Books.)

dian nationalist and feminist to gothic, the versatile Atwood continues to defy easy categorization and her books are enjoyed as much for their compelling plots and characters as for their intellectual depth. Writing in *Saturday Night,* Linda Sandler described the writer as "all things to all people . . . a nationalist . . . a feminist or a psychologist or a comedian. . . a maker and breaker of myths . . . a gothic writer. She's all these things, but finally she's unaccountably . . . elusive, complex, passionate." In *World and I* Linda Simon quoted Atwood's comments regarding the central quandary of choosing a writer's life: "There's always this tug of war. If you're writing, you're not living, and if you're living you're not writing. So which are you going to do?"

Biographical and Critical Sources

BOOKS

Bloom, Harold, editor, *Margaret Atwood,* Chelsea House (Philadelphia, PA), 2000.

Contemporary Literary Criticism, Thomson Gale (Detroit, MI), Volume 2, 1974, Volume 3, 1975, Volume 4, 1975, Volume 8, 1978, Volume 13, 1980, Volume 15, 1980, Volume 25, 1983, Volume 44, 1987.

Cooke, Nathalie, *Margaret Atwood: A Biography,* ECW Press (Toronto, Ontario, Canada), 1998.

Dictionary of Literary Biography, Volume 53: *Canadian Writers since 1960,* Thomson Gale (Detroit, MI), 1986.

Howells, Coral Ann, *Margaret Atwood,* St. Martin's Press (New York, NY), 1996.

Ingersoll, Earl G., editor, *Waltzing Again: New and Selected Conversations with Margaret Atwood,* Ontario Review Press (Princeton, NJ), 2006.

McCombs, Judith, and Carole L. Palmer, *Margaret Atwood: A Reference Guide,* G.K. Hall (Boston, MA), 1991.

St. James Guide to Young Adult Writers, 2nd edition, St. James Press (Detroit, MI), 1999.

Sullivan, Rosemary, *The Red Shoes: Margaret Atwood Starting Out,* HarperFlamingo Canada (Toronto, Ontario, Canada), 1998.

Twigg, Alan, *For Openers: Conversations with Twenty-four Canadian Writers,* Harbour, 1981.

Woodcock, George, *The Canadian Novel in the Twentieth Century,* McClelland & Stewart (Toronto, Ontario, Canada), 1975.

PERIODICALS

Booklist, December 15, 1995, Hazel Rochman, review of *Princess Prunella and the Purple Peanut,* p. 702; June 1, 2000, Donna Seaman, review of *The Blind Assassin,* p. 1796; April 1, 2006, Gillian Engberg, review of *Up in the Tree,* p. 47.

Books in Canada, January, 1979; December, 1980, review of *Anna's Pet,* p. 18; June-July, 1980: March, 1981; December, 1995, review of *Princess Prunella and the Purple Peanut,* p. 18.

Canadian Book Review Annual, 2003, review of *Rude Ramsay and the Roaring Radishes,* p. 445.

Canadian Forum, February, 1970, John Stedmond, review of *The Edible Woman,* p. 267; January, 1973; November-December, 1974; December-January, 1977-78; June-July, 1981, Chaviva Hosek and Scott Lauder, review of *True Stories;* December-January, 1981-82, Frank Davey, review of *Life after Man,* pp. 29-30.

Canadian Review of Materials, March, 1991, review of *For the Birds,* p. 93.

Globe & Mail (Toronto, Ontario, Canada), July 7, 1984; October 5, 1985; October 19, 1985; February 15, 1986; November 15, 1986; November 29, 1986; November 14, 1987.

Kirkus Reviews, August 15, 2004, review of *Rude Ramsay and the Roaring Radishes,* p. 802.

Library Journal, August 9, 2000, Beth E. Andersen, review of *The Blind Assassin;* December, 2003, Laurie Selwyn, review of *Oryx and Crake,* p. 184

Los Angeles Times, March 2, 1982; April 22, 1982; May 9, 1986; January 12, 1987; September 26, 2000, p. E1.

Los Angeles Times Book Review, October 17, 1982; February 9, 1986, Elaine Kendall, review of *The Handmaid's Tale;* December 23, 1987; November 14, 1993, pp. 3, 11; December 15, 1996, Richard Eder, review of *Alias Grace,* p. 2.

Maclean's, January 15, 1979; October 15, 1979, Roy MacGregor, review of *Life before Man;* December 15, 1980, Ann Johnston, review of *Anna's Pet,* p. 52; March 30, 1981; October 5, 1992, John Bemrose, review of *Good Bones;* October 3, 1993, Judith Timson, "Atwood's Triumph," pp. 56-61; February 6, 1995, John Bemrose, review of *Morning in the Burned House;* September 23, 1996, Diane Turbide, "Amazing Atwood," pp. 42-45; October 14, 1996, p. 11; July 1, 1999, Margaret Atwood, "Survival, Then and Now," p. 54; September 11, 2000, John Bemrose, review of *Margaret's Museum,* p. 54.

New York Review of Books, December 16, 1993, Gabrielle Annan, review of *The Robber Bride,* pp. 14-15; December 19, 1996, Hilary Mantel, review of *Alias Grace,* pp. 4-6.

New York Times, December 23, 1976; January 10, 1980; February 8, 1980; March 6, 1982, Anatole Broyard, review of *Bodily Harm,* p. 13; March 28, 1982, Judy Klemesrud, "Canada's High Priestess of Angst," p. 21; September 15, 1982; January 27, 1986, Christopher Lehmann-Haupt, review of *The Handmaid's Tale,* p. C24; February 17, 1986, Mervyn Rothstein, "Atwood Finds No Balm in Gilead," p. C11; November 5, 1986; October 26, 1993, Michiko Kakutani, review of *The Robber Bride,* p. C20; November 23, 1993, Sarah Lyall, "An Author Who Lets Women Be Bad Guys," pp. C13, C16; September 8, 2000, Michiko Kakutani, review of *The Blind Assassin,* p. E43.

New York Times Book Review, October 18, 1970, Millicent Bell, review of *The Edible Woman;* March 4, 1973; April 6, 1975; September 26, 1976; May 21, 1978; February 3, 1980, Marilyn French, review of *Life before Man,* pp. 1, 26; October 11, 1981; February 9, 1986, Mary McCarthy, "Breeders, Wives, and Unwomen," pp. 1, 35; February 5, 1989, Alice McDermott, "What Little Girls Are Really Made Of," pp. 1, 35; October 31, 1993, Lorrie Moore, review of *The Robber Bride,* pp. 1, 22; December 11, 1994, Jennifer Howard, review of *Good Bones and Simple Murders;* April 28, 1996, p. 22; December 29, 1996, Francine Prose, review of *Alias Grace,* p. 6; September 3, 2000, p. 7.

People, May 19, 1980; February 27, 1989, Susan Toepfer, review of *Cat's Eye,* pp. 22-23; March 6, 1989, Kim Hubbard, "Reflected in Margaret Atwood's *Cat's Eye,* Girlhood Looms as a Time of Cruelty and Terror," pp. 205-206; December 18, 1995, review of *Princess Prunella and the Purple Peanut,* p. 29.

Publishers Weekly, August 23, 1976; October 3, 1994, review of *Good Bones and Simple Murders;* August 28, 1995, pp. 107-108; January 1, 1996, review of *Princess Prunella and the Purple Peanut,* p. 70; October 7, 1996, p. 58; April 13, 1998, p. 65; July 24, 2000, review of *The Blind Assassin,* p. 67, and interview with Atwood, p. 68; August 23, 2004, review of *Rude Ramsay and the Roaring Radishes,* p. 54.

Quill & Quire, April, 1981, Robert Sward, review of *True Stories;* September, 1984; September, 1995, review of *Princess Prunella and the Purple Peanut,* p. 73.

Resource Links, December, 2003, Denise Parrott, review of *Rude Ramsay and the Roaring Radishes,* p. 1; April, 2005, Adriane Pettit, review of *Bashful Bob and Doleful Dorinda,* p. 1.

School Library Journal, November, 2004, Caroline Ward, review of *Rude Ramsay and the Roaring Radishes,* p. 90.

Times (London, England), March 13, 1986; June 4, 1987; June 10, 1987; January 26, 1989, Philip Howard, review of *Cat's Eye;* November 8, 2000, p. 3.

Times Literary Supplement, March 21, 1986; June 12, 1987; September 29, 2000, p. 24.

Tribune Books (Chicago, IL), November 21, 1993, p. 1.

Washington Post Book World, September 26, 1976; December 3, 1978; January 27, 1980; March 14, 1982; February 2, 1986; November 7, 1993, Francine Prose, review of *The Robber Bride,* p. 1; September 3, 2000, Michael Dirda, review of *The Blind Assassin,* pp. 15-16; November 7, 2004, Elizabeth Ward, review of *Rude Ramsay and the Roaring Radishes,* p. 12.

Writer's Digest, October, 2000, p. 34.

World and I, January, 2003, Linda Simon, "Words and Their Glories: Margaret Atwood's Journey," p. 236.

ONLINE

Atwood Society Web site, http://www.mscd.edu/~atwoodso/ (May 10, 2006).

Margaret Atwood Information Site, http://www.owtoad.com/ (May 10, 2006).

Random House Web site, http://www.randomhouse.com/ (May 10, 2006), "Margaret Atwood."*

* * *

ATWOOD, Margaret Eleanor
See ATWOOD, Margaret

B

BARBOUR, Karen 1956-

Personal
Born October 29, 1956, in San Francisco, CA; daughter of Donald C. (a physician) and Nancy B. Barbour; married Hermann Lederle (an artist), 1981. *Education:* University of California, Davis, B.A., 1976; San Francisco Art Institute, M.F.A., 1980.

Addresses
Home—Point Reyes Station, CA. *Agent*—c/o Author Mail, HarperCollins Children's, 1350 Avenue of the Americas, New York, NY 10019.

Career
Freelance illustrator, author, animator, and painter.

Awards, Honors
Certificate of Excellence, American Institute of Graphic Arts Book Show, and Parents' Choice Award, Parents' Choice Foundation, both 1987, both for *Little Nino's Pizzeria;* Parents' Choice Gold Award, 1997, for *Marvelous Math: Poems,* selected by Lee Bennett Hopkins.

Writings

FOR CHILDREN; SELF-ILLUSTRATED

Little Nino's Pizzeria, Harcourt (San Diego, CA), 1987.
Nancy, Harcourt (San Diego, CA), 1989.
Mr. Bow Tie, Harcourt (San Diego, CA), 1991.
Mr. Williams Henry Holt (New York, NY), 2005.

ILLUSTRATOR

Helen Barolini, *Festa: Recipes and Recollections of Italy,* Harcourt (San Diego, CA), 1988.
Arnold Adoff, *Flamboyan,* Harcourt (San Diego, CA), 1988.
James Berry, *When I Dance: Poems,* Harcourt (San Diego, CA), 1991.
Anna Kate Winsey, *Toby Is My Best Friend,* Silver Burdett (Morristown, NJ), 1992.
Arnold Adoff, *Street Music: City Poems,* HarperCollins (New York, NY), 1995.
Jane Yolen, *A Sip of Aesop,* Blue Sky Press (New York, NY), 1995.
Eric Metaxas, *Princess Scargo and the Birthday Pumpkin: The Native American Legend,* Rabbit Ears (New York, NY), 1996.
Lee Bennett Hopkins, editor, *Marvelous Math: A Book of Poems,* Simon & Schuster (New York, NY), 1997.
Juan Felipe Herrere, *Laughing out Loud, I Fly: Poems in English and Spanish,* HarperCollins (New York, NY), 1998.
Eve Bunting, *I Have an Olive Tree,* HarperCollins (New York, NY), 1999.
Tony Johnston, *The Ancestors Are Singing,* Farrar Straus & Giroux (New York, NY), 2003.
Andrea Griffing Zimmerman and David Clemesha, *Fire! Fire! Hurry! Hurry!,* Greenwillow Books (New York, NY), 2003.
Lee Bennett Hopkins, selector, *Wonderful Words: Poems about Reading, Writing, Speaking, and Listening,* Simon & Schuster (New York, NY), 2004.
Julius Lester, *Let's Talk about Race,* HarperCollins (New York, NY), 2005.

Adaptations
Princess Scargo and the Birthday Pumpkin: The Native American Legend was adapted for videocassette, 1993.

Sidelights
The work of artist Karen Barbour has graced the pages of a number of well-received children's books, including *I Have an Olive Tree* by Eve Bunting and *A Sip of Aesop* by Jane Yolen. In addition to working with other picture-book authors, Barbour has created several original works, including *Nancy* and *Little Nino's Pizzeria.*

Karen Barbour's illustrations for I Have an Olive Tree *reflect the folktale elements of Eve Bunting's story about a girl's exploration of her Greek culture.* (Illustrations copyright © 1999 by Karen Barbour. Text copyright © 1999 by Eve Bunting. Used by permission of HarperCollins Publishers.)

In *Nancy* a newcomer extends a hand of friendship as a way to break into an established clique of four best friends in her new neighborhood and finds that creativity is the key to acceptance. "Barbour has a real fix on what it is to be young," observed *New York Times Book Review* contributor Christina Olson in praise of *Nancy.* "While the story . . . has its appeal, it is the raucous artwork that grabs readers' attention and holds it," added Ilene Cooper in her *Booklist* appraisal. Cooper also noted Barbour's uninhibited use of wavy lines, polka dots, and fun, vibrant colors.

Born in San Francisco in 1956, Barbour attended both the University of California and the San Francisco Art Institute, earning her master of fine arts degree in 1980. Her first picture-book effort, *Little Nino's Pizzeria,* proved to be a success, winning her both a commendation from the American Institute of Graphic Arts and a Parents' Choice Foundation award. Published in 1987, *Little Nino's Pizzeria* sparked the interest of book publishers looking for talented artists to enhance the work of established authors. Barbour's move to New York City put her in proximity to a number of these publishers, and she was quick to gain illustration assignments. Her first illustration job—a cookbook titled *Festa: Recipes and Recollections of Italy*—was published in 1988; moving from there to picture books was a short step to a successful career.

When I Dance: Poems, a collection by James Berry, meshes the sounds of English with those of Berry's native Caribbean, and critics remarked that Barbour's artwork adds to the overall effect with its use of folk-style motifs. Also praised by reviewers are Barbour's bright and fanciful paintings for Lee Bennett Hopkins' *Marvelous Math: A Book of Poems. School Library Journal* contributor Lee Bock called them "lively illustrations [that] dance and play around the poems." In yet another poetry collection, Arnold Adoff's *Street Music: City Poems,* Barbour's whimsical artwork brings to life the hustle and bustle of crowded city streets. "Graceful, stylized forms fill the pages with pattern and texture against vibrant background colors," noted *Horn Book* reviewer Nancy Vasilakis. Similarly, a *Publishers Weekly* critic said that Barbour's pictures "vibrate a jazzy fluidity and rhythm."

Written and illustrated by Barbour, *Mr. Bow Tie* deals with the grave issue of homelessness. The main character of the title is a homeless man who is constantly seen wearing a bow tie and wandering the streets of New York. The homeless man is later befriended by a shopkeeper and his family. As the story progresses it is revealed to young readers that "Mr. Bow Tie" is actually an aristocrat who strayed from his elderly parents and he is eventually reunited with them. Some reviewers commented on Barbour's unrealistic approach, Dinitia Smith writing in the *New York Times* that the story presents "little information and provide[s] no understanding" of the human plight of the homeless. However, *School Library Journal* contributor Kate McClelland described the book's storyline as "a gentle, humane introduction to homelessness."

Barbour's artwork for *I Have an Olive Tree,* a picture book by Eve Bunting, has been praised for both its historical accuracy and its overall technique. Noting that the illustrations "have the flavor of Greek folk art," a *Horn Book* reviewer commended in particular Barbour's use of a "multi-hued palette and curving lines." A *Publishers Weekly* contributor called the book "visually arresting," while *Booklist* reviewer Hazel Rochman explained that the artist's flat, bright paintings, with their heavy, black lines, "combine folk art and magic realism to show the circles of connection that sweep across time and place."

Barbour has also contributed illustrations to *Fire! Fire! Hurry! Hurry!,* written by Andrea Griffing Zimmerman and David Clemesha. Created for pre-schoolers, *Fire! Fire! Hurry! Hurry!* spotlights the daily commotion going on in a firehouse station and stars a firefighting crew that includes a blue bear, a lime-green elephant, a yellow lion, and a pink mouse. The story is enlivened by Barbour's colorful folkloric illustrations, which a *Kirkus Reviews* critic commended for its "eye-popping color." Leslie Barban, in *School Library Journal,* also commented on Barbour's use of bold color, noting that the artist's gouache illustrations are "awash with color that can be seen from a distance."

With *The Ancestors Are Singing* Barbour illustrates in black-and-white drawings, giving life to Tony Johnston's collection of children's poems celebrating the history of Mexico. The poems in *The Ancestors Are Singing* present a variety of perspectives on Mexico's traditions and mythologies. Sharon Korbeck, writing in *School Library Journal,* noted that Barbour's "bold, swirling black-and-white illustrations convey a vivid sense of place," through their depiction of the Mexican people. A *Kirkus Reviews* critic also applauded the book's folkloric drawings for their "childlike energy" and for their ability to meld the past with the present.

Mr. Williams presents the oral history of J.W. Williams, a family friend of the author's mother. *Mr. Williams* offers a personal depiction of growing up on a Louisiana farmstead during the 1930s and 1940s as an African American. The story tells of the man's many hardships in the face of the racism present in the rural South during the early twentieth century; with personally elicited details, "readers gain a wealth of information about the era" remarked a *Publishers Weekly* reviewer. In addition, a *Kirkus Reviews* critic noted that Barbour's ink-and-gouache illustrations add depth to the narrative and are full of "lovely colors] that [perfectly match the simplicity of the text."

Biographical and Critical Sources

PERIODICALS

Booklist, October 1, 1989, Ilene Cooper, review of *Nancy,* p. 343; February 1, 1995, Carolyn Phelan, review of *Street Music: City Poems,* p. 1005; May 15, 1999, Hazel Rochman, review of *I Have an Olive Tree,* p. 1702; March 15, 2000, review of *Laughing out Loud, I Fly,* p. 1342.

Horn Book, July-August, 1991, Mary M. Burns, review of *When I Dance,* p. 469; May-June, 1995, Nancy Vasilakis, review of *Street Music,* p. 337; July, 1999, review of *I Have an Olive Tree,* p. 452.

Kirkus Reviews, August 15, 1991, review of *Mr. Bow Tie,* p. 1086; March 15, 2003, review of *The Ancestors Are Singing,* p. 468; March 15, 2003, review of *Fire! Fire! Hurry! Hurry!,* p. 482; August 1, 2005, review of *Mr. Williams,* p. 844.

New York Times Book Review, November 26, 1989, Christina Olson, review of *Nancy,* p. 23; November 10, 1991, Dinitia Smith, review of *Mr. Bow Tie,* p. 52.

Publishers Weekly, September 6, 1991, review of *Mr. Bow Tie,* p. 103; December 19, 1994, review of *Street Music,* p. 54; August 7, 1995, review of *A Sip of Aesop,* p. 460; May 24, 1999, review of *I Have an Olive Tree,* p. 78; October 10, 2005, review of *Mr. Williams,* p. 61.

School Library Journal, November, 1989, Karen Litton, review of *Nancy,* p. 74; December, 1991, Kate McClelland, review of *Mr. Bow Tie,* p. 78; September, 1995, JoAnn Rees, review of *A Sip of Aesop,* p. 198; October, 1997, Lee Bock, review of *Marvelous Math: A Book of Poems,* p. 118; April, 2003, Leslie Barban, review of *Fire! Fire! Hurry! Hurry!,* p. 144; April, 2003, review of *The Ancestors Are Singing,* p. 183.*

* * *

BATES, Martine
See LEAVITT, Martine

* * *

BIRDSALL, Jeanne 1951-

Personal
Born 1951; married William Diehl, 1994; children: two stepchildren. *Education:* Attended Boston University, 1969; attended California College of Arts and Crafts, 1972.

Addresses
Home—Northampton, MA. *Agent*—Barbara S. Kouts Literary Agency, P.O. Box 560, Bellport, NY 11713.

Career
Children's book author.

Awards, Honors
Booklist Top Ten First Novels for Youth inclusion, *School Library Journal* Best Books designation, and National Book Award for Young People's Literature, all 2005, all for *The Penderwicks.*

Writings

The Penderwicks: A Summer Tale of Four Sisters, Two Rabbits, and a Very Interesting Boy, Knopf (New York, NY), 2005.

Adaptations

The Penderwicks was adapted as an audiobook, Listening Library, 2006.

Work in Progress

A sequel to *The Penderwicks.*

Sidelights

Inspired by the novels of Edward Eager and E. Nesbit, Jeanne Birdsall's 2005 book *The Penderwicks: A Summer Tale of Four Sisters, Two Rabbits, and a Very Interesting Boy* was described as "so retro, it's almost radical" by *School Library Journal* interviewer Rick Margolis. The story of four sisters who encounter adventure during a summer vacation spent on a cottage in the Berkshire mountains, the novel surprised many—including its author—when it earned first-time writer Birdsall the National Book Award for Young People's Literature in 2005.

Growing up in Strafford, Pennsylvania, Birdsall had a childhood that was scarred by alcoholism, and reading became a way for her to escape into another world. Her love of childrens' literature has stayed with her throughout her life. Although in her primary career she has excelled at the visual arts and has become well known for her art photography, at age forty-two she decided to fulfill a childhood goal, and channel some creative energy into writing a book that carried on the legacy of Nesbit and Eager. *The Penderwicks* was the result.

In *The Penderwicks* readers meet the Penderwick sisters: twelve-year-old Rosalind, eleven-year-old Skye, ten-year-old Jane, and four-year-old Batty. Together with their widowed father, a loving but rather absent-minded botany professor, the sisters and the family dog vacation in a cozy cottage on a country estate called Arundel hall. With few children living nearby, the girls soon befriend Jeffrey, the lonely son of the hall's upper-crusty owner, Mrs. Tifton. As the summer passes, the children encounter a series of adventures in which the magic comes from their imaginative view of their novel surroundings. Jeffrey's doomed fate—to be sent to a dreaded military school—is something to be liberated from, while the usually dependable Rosalind suddenly finds herself doe-eyed over the hall's handsome young gardener. Feisty Skye battles the restrictions placed on the children by the snooty Mrs. Tifton, while Jane narrates the children's activities with a wry yet humorously melodramatic eye.

Praise for *The Penderwicks* was wide-ranging, many critics acknowledging Birdsall's nod to a pantheon of writers that range from Louisa May Alcott and Frances Hodgson Burnett to Elizabeth Enright and Lemony Snicket. "Nostalgic but never stale, this fresh, satisfying novel is like a cool breeze on a summer's day," concluded *Horn Book* contributor Carolyn Shute, describing *The Penderwicks* as "suffused with affectionate humor." In her "timeless tale," Birdsall captures "spirited family dynamics and repartee," wrote a contributor to *Publishers Weekly,* the critic adding that the Penderwick sisters exhibit "delightfully diverse personalities" that "propel the plot." Praising the author's "superb writing style," B. Allison Gray wrote in *School Library Journal* that Birdsall's "wonderful, humorous book . . . features characters whom readers will immediately love," characters who engage in what a *Kirkus Reviews* writer described as "the sorts of lively plots and pastoral pastimes we don't read much about these days."

In her writing Birdsall openly pays homage to the books she loved as a child: escapist fiction featuring a band of curious children, a daunting challenge, and an everyday world that is transformed by the imagination into a place rife with the possibility of adventure. When she first approached publishers, she was advised to add a strong dose of adolescent strife, and make her story reflect what publishers maintained is demanded by modern readers weaned on so-called "problem novels." Fortunately, her manuscript fell into the hands of a more open-minded editor at Knopf, and *The Penderwicks* was ultimately published with relatively minor changes. As Birdsall explained to Rick Margolis in *School Library Journal,* "People are saying children who lead traumatic lives need books that validate the trauma, and I'm not saying they're wrong. But I also think because it worked so well for me, that there are children who lead difficult lives who need to understand that it doesn't have to be so bad. I also think that there are a lot of children out there who are still leading wonderful lives, and . . . they need to have something to read too."

Working on a sequel to her award-winning novel, Birdsall makes her home in Western Massachusetts, together with her husband and assorted cats, rabbits, a dog, and even a snail. As she remarked of writing in an interview on her home page: "Most authors do work very hard. I know that I do, partly because I write slowly, so I have to write almost every day to make any progress at all. But mostly I work hard because I'm happiest when I'm writing."

Biographical and Critical Sources

PERIODICALS

Bulletin of the Center for Children's Books, September, 2005, Timnah Card, review of *The Penderwicks: A Summer Tale of Four Sisters, Two Rabbits, and a Very Interesting Boy,* p. 9.

Horn Book, July-August, 2005, Carolyn Shute, review of *The Penderwicks,* p. 465.

Kirkus Reviews, June 1, 2005, review of *The Penderwicks,* p. 633.
Publishers Weekly, July 25, 2005, review of *The Penderwicks,* p. 77.
School Library Journal, July, 2005, B. Allison Gray, review of *The Penderwicks,* p. 95; January, 2006, Rick Margolis, "Seems like Old Times" (interview), p. 60.

ONLINE

Boston Globe Online, http://www.boston.com/ (December 12, 2005), David Mehegan, "A Storybook Beginning."
Jeanne Birdsall Home Page, http://www.jeannebirdsall.com (April 26, 2006).
R. Michelson Galleries Web site, http://www.rmichelson.com/ (April 26, 2006), "Jeanne Birdsall."

* * *

BOERST, William J. 1939-

Personal

Born February 17, 1939; married July 5, 1968; wife's name, Rachel M. (a guidance secretary); children: Robin K., Julie M. *Education:* State University of New York College at Fredonia, B.S. (education); also attended State University of New York College at Potsdam, Syracuse University, and College of Saint Rose. *Politics:* Democrat. *Religion:* "Atheist." *Hobbies and other interests:* Kayaking, reading, gardening.

Addresses

Home—40 Meadow La., Jamestown, NY 14701. *Office*—Fenton 250, SUNY Fredonia, Fredonia, NY 14063. *E-mail*—bill2@alltel.net.

Career

English teacher at a public school in northern New York, 1962-63; U.S. Peace Corps, Washington, DC, elementary schoolteacher in Liberia, 1963-65; teacher of English and speech at a high school in Watertown, NY, 1965-67; Board of Education, Jamestown, NY, junior high school teacher, then high-school English teacher, 1967-2000; writer, 2000—. State University of New York, Fredonia, lecturer in English. Founding member, Chautauqua Area Writers and Chautauqua County Writing/Reading Process Teachers.

Awards, Honors

New York Public Library Book for the Teen Age designation, 2004, for *Johannes Kepler: Discovering the Laws of Celestial Motion.*

Writings

Isaac Asimov: Writer of the Future, Morgan Reynolds (Greensboro, NC), 1999.
Time Machine: The Story of H.G. Wells, Morgan Reynolds (Greensboro, NC), 2000.
Edgar Rice Burroughs: Creator of Tarzan, Morgan Reynolds (Greensboro, NC), 2000.
Generous Anger: The Story of George Orwell, Morgan Reynolds (Greensboro, NC), 2001.
Tycho Brahe: Mapping the Heavens, Morgan Reynolds (Greensboro, NC), 2003.
Johannes Kepler: Discovering the Laws of Celestial Motion, Morgan Reynolds (Greensboro, NC), 2003.
Isaac Newton: Organizing the Universe, Morgan Reynolds (Greensboro, NC), 2004.
Galileo Galilei and the Science of Motion, Morgan Reynolds (Greensboro, NC), 2004.

Contributor of articles, poems, and short fiction to periodicals, including *English Journal, Language Arts, Iowa English Bulletin, Not Your Average Zine, Poet,* and *Artifacts.* Newsletter editor, Vegetarian Society of Chautauqua/Allegheny.

Sidelights

Before turning to writing full time in 2000, William J. Boerst worked for many years as an English teacher. Among his books for young readers, many focus on noted inventors and theorists, among them *Isaac Newton: Organizing the Universe, Galileo Galilei and the Science of Motion,* and *Tycho Brahe: Mapping the Heavens.* Part of the "Renaissance Scientists" series, *Galileo Galilei* was praised for its balance between the personal and the scientific; in *Booklist* Carolyn Phelan wrote: "Unusually detailed and free from the taint of legend," Boerst's biography of the noted astronomer and physicist "is more complex, more understandable, and probably more accurate" than similar works for younger readers.

In *Isaac Newton* Boerst delves into the life of the seventeenth-century British mathematician credited with devising the three laws of motion and reveals Newton's introverted nature. From birth through his death at age eighty-four, the reclusive Newton made a number of notable discoveries, and devoted much of his adult life to study and research. Boerst's "well-written book makes an excellent choice for teens exploring scientists or just looking for a good biography," according to Jenna Miller in *School Library Journal,* while Phelan commented that in *Isaac Newton* the biographer "offers a vivid portrayal of Newton's difficult childhood and adolescence."

Boerst provides readers with a detailed background of another of the world's most notable scientists, this time an astronomer, in *Tycho Brahe.* In addition to discussing the Danish Brahe's astronomical observations—made in the 1500s, prior to the invention of the telescope—Boerst also provides readers with a detailed account of the man's upringing, education, career, and personality. One fascinating personal revelation is that Brahe wore a silver and gold nose for much of his life, having lost his own in a sword fight. Phelan, writing in *Booklist,* stated that "Boerst provides a clearly written account" of the legendary astronomer.

Biographical and Critical Sources

PERIODICALS

Booklist, December 1, 1998, Roger Leslie, review of *Isaac Asimov: Writer of the Future,* p. 657; January 1, 2000, Carolyn Phelan, review of *Time Machine: The Story of H.G. Wells,* p. 908; July, 2000, Carolyn Phelan, review of *Edgar Rice Burroughs: Creator of Tarzan,* p. 2019; March 15, 2003, Carolyn Phelan, review of *Tycho Brahe: Mapping the Heavens,* p. 1316; June 1, 2003, Carolyn Phelan, review of *Johannes Kepler: Discovering the Laws of Celestial Motion,* p. 1789; November 1, 2003, Carolyn Phelan, review of *Galileo Galilei and the Science of Motion,* p. 488; February 1, 2004, Carolyn Phelan, review of *Isaac Newton: Organizing the Universe,* p. 967; June 1, 2001, Hazel Rochman, review of *Generous Anger: The Story of George Orwell,* p. 1858.

School Library Journal, January, 2001, Marilyn Fairbanks, review of *Edgar Rice Burroughs,* p. 138; August, 2003, review of *Johannes Kepler,* p. 170; December, 2003, Todd Morning, review of *Galileo Galilei and the Science of Motion,* p. 164; April, 2004, Jenna Miller, review of *Isaac Newton,* p. 166.

Voice of Youth Advocates, October, 2000, review of *Time Machine,* p. 284; June, 2001, review of *Edgar Rice Burroughs,* p. 137; February, 2004, Morgan Reynolds, review of *Tycho Brahe,* p. 517.

ONLINE

Morgan Reynolds Web site, http://www.morganreynolds.com/ (April 11, 2006).*

* * *

BOTTNER, Barbara 1943-

Personal

Born May 25, 1943, in New York, NY; daughter of Irving (a business executive) and Elaine (Schiff) Bottner; married Gerald Kruglik, 1988. *Education:* Attended Boston University, 1961-62, and École des Beaux Arts, 1963-64; University of Wisconsin—Madison, B.S., 1965; University of California, Santa Barbara, M.A., 1966; studied animation at School of Visual Arts. *Hobbies and other interests:* Dancing, travel, politics, Buddhism.

Addresses

Home—2297 W. 21st St., Los Angeles, CA 90018. *E-mail*—bhb1@sbcglobal.net.

Barbara Bottner (Photograph reproduced by permission of Barbara Bottner.)

Career

Writer, illustrator, producer, actor, and educator. Formerly taught kindergarten; set designer for off-Broadway theater; Café La Mama, New York, NY, actor in touring productions in United States and Europe; producer of short animated films; Parsons School of Design, New York, NY, instructor, beginning 1973; instructor at Oris Art Institute of Los Angeles County and New School for Social Research, c. 1990; staff writer for television series *Nickelodeon,* 1992. Director of short animated films, including *Goat in a Boat* and *Later That Night.* Mentor for WriteGirl (nonprofit), Los Angeles. *Exhibitions:* Work has been represented in film festivals in London, England; Melbourne, Australia; Ottawa, Ontario, Canada; and New York, NY.

Member

Writers Guild of America, Author's Guild.

Awards, Honors

Best Film for Television award, International Animation Festival (Annecy, France), 1973, for *Goat in a Boat;* Children's Choice citation, International Reading Association/Children's Book Council, 1980, for *Mean Maxine;* Distinguished Teaching Award, New School for Social Research, 1990; Cine Golden Eagle, Council for International Nontheatrical Events, for animated film *Later That Night;* Bank Street College honor citation, and *School Library Journal* best books designation, both 2005, both for *Wallace's Lists;* books included on several notable book and children's choice lists.

Writings

What Would You Do with a Giant?, Putnam (New York, NY), 1972.

Fun House, Prentice-Hall (Englewood Cliffs, NJ), 1975.
Eek, a Monster, Macmillan (New York, NY), 1975.
The Box, Macmillan (New York, NY), 1975.
What Grandma Did on Her Birthday, Macmillan (New York, NY), 1975.
Doing the Toledeo, Four Winds Press (New York, NY), 1977.
Big Boss! Little Boss!, Pantheon (New York, NY), 1978.
Jungle Day! Delacorte (New York, NY), 1978.
There Was Nobody There, Macmillan (New York, NY), 1978.
Messy, Delacorte (New York, NY), 1979.
Dumb Old Casey Is a Fat Tree, Harper (New York, NY), 1979.
Myra, Macmillan (New York, NY), 1979.
Horrible Hannah, illustrated by Joan Drescher, Crown (New York, NY), 1980.
Mean Maxine, Pantheon (New York, NY), 1980.
The World's Greatest Expert on Absolutely Everything . . . Is Crying, Harper (New York, NY), 1985.
Nothing in Common (young-adult novel), Harper (New York, NY), 1986.
Zoo Song, illustrated by Lynn Munsinger, Scholastic (New York, NY), 1987.
Let Me Tell You Everything: Memoirs of a Lovesick Intellectual (young-adult novel), Harper (New York, NY), 1989.
Bootsie Barker Bites, illustrated by Peggy Rathmann, Putnam (New York, NY), 1992.
Hurricane Music, illustrated by Paul Yalowitz, Putnam (New York, NY), 1995.
Nana Hannah's Piano, illustrated by Diana Cain Bluthenthal, Putnam (New York, NY), 1996.
Bootsie Barker, Ballerina, illustrated by G. Brian Karas, HarperCollins (New York, NY), 1997.
Two Messy Friends, Scholastic (New York, NY), 1998.
Marsha Makes Me Sick, illustrated by Denise Brunkus, Golden Books (New York, NY), 1998.
Marsha Is Only a Flower, illustrated by Denise Brunkus, Golden Books (New York, NY), 2000.
(With husband, Gerald Kruglik) *It's Not Marsha's Birthday,* illustrated by Denise Brunkus, Golden Books (New York, NY), 2001.
Be Brown!, illustrated by Barry Gott, Grosset & Dunlap (New York, NY), 2002.
Charlene Loves to Make Noise, illustrated by Alex Stadler, Running Press (Philadelphia, PA), 2002.
The Scaredy Cats, illustrated by Victoria Chess, Simon & Schuster (New York, NY), 2003.
Wallace's Lists, illustrated by Olof Landström, Katherine Tegen Books (New York, NY), 2004.
Rosa's Room, illustrated by Beth Spiegel, Peachtree (Atlanta, GA), 2004.
(With Gerald Kruglik; and illustrator) *Pish and Posh,* HarperCollins (New York, NY), 2005.
(With Gerald Kruglik; and illustrator) *Pish and Posh Wish for Fairy Wings,* HarperCollins (New York, NY), 2005.
Raymond and Nelda, illustrated by Nancy Hyashi, Peachtree (Atlanta, GA), 2006.
You Have to Be Nice to Someone on Their Birthday, illustrated by Tatjana Mai-Wyss, Putnam's Sons (New York, NY), 2007.
(And illustrator) *Miss Mabel Is Able,* Knopf (New York, NY), 2007.

Writer for television series *Shelley Duvall's Bedtime Stories* and *Winnie the Pooh,* for Disney Channel; author of *Mrs. Piggle Wiggle* (television program), Showtime. Contributor to periodicals, including *Los Angeles Times Book Review;* contributor of short fiction to *Cosmopolitan* and *Playgirl.* Contributing editor, *LA Weekly, Lion and the Unicorn,* and *Miami Herald;* contributor of illustrations to periodicals, including *New York Times, Viva,* and *Ms.;* contributor of cartoons to *Viva, Penthouse,* and the *New York Times* op-ed page.

Bottner's work has been translated into French and Swedish.

Adaptations

Myra was adapted into an animated film by Churchill Films, 1980.

Work in Progress

A novel for adults titled *Don't Look Me Like That;* work for other media.

Sidelights

As a child, Barbara Bottner grew up dreaming of becoming an artist, a dancer, and a story teller. After studying painting in Paris, she was asked to create sets for an off-Broadway theatrical company, Café La MaMa, where she worked alongside company founder and director Ellen Stewart. Bottner's set-design career with Café La MaMa ended prematurely, however, when she was told that her set designs were too large and eclipsed the actors. She then studied acting and toured for two years both in the United States and Europe. Bottner became a substitute teacher to supplement her acting wages, and after a year of teaching, she decided to establish a career in children's book illustration. Since then, she has become known for writing children's books, young-adult novels, and "I Can Read"s. She has also written a novel for adults, works with at-risk teenage girls through the Los Angeles-based mentoring nonprofit WriteGirl, and teaches and consults privately in Los Angeles.

In her young-adult novel *Nothing in Common,* Bottner chronicles the lives of Melissa Warren, a wealthy teenager, and Sara Gregori, the daughter of Melissa's maid. Mrs. Grigori had a motherly relationship with both girls, and following her death Melissa and Sara each attempt to circumvent their grief, in different ways.

Let Me Tell You Everything: Memoirs of a Lovesick Intellectual introduces Brogan Arthur, a high-school senior who is passionate about books, politics, and the

A collaboration between Bottner, husband Gerald Kruglik, and illustrator Olof Landström, **Wallace's Lists** *finds a young mouse recording lists about every part of his life.* (Text copyright © 2004 by Barbara Bottner and Gerald Kruglik. Illustrations copyright © 2004 by Olof Landström. Used by permission of Katherine Tegen Books /HarperCollins Publishers.)

world of ideas. Brogan's feminist ideals are confused, however, by her infatuation with her handsome social studies teacher. Hazel Rochman commented in *Booklist* that Bottner's "witty voice is nicely controlled as she mocks feminist rhetoric, yet at the same time affirms her commitment."

Written for younger readers, *Zoo Song* dramatizes the simple theme of working together despite differences of opinion. "Although a replay of an old song, Bottner's moral tale is light, and readers will harken to it," maintained a *Publishers Weekly* reviewer.

In one of several books Bottner has created featuring an unusual heroine, *Bootsie Barker Bites* illustrates a theme in keeping with that of *Zoo Song,* but with a somewhat darker tone. The dreadful Bootsie Barker appears to be sweet, but when the adults disappear she becomes thoroughly cruel. Bootsie terrorizes the story's narrator, a younger girl forced to play with Bootsie while the girls' mothers visit with one another. A *Kirkus Reviews* contributor called *Bootsie Barker Bites* "an entertaining, insightful glimpse into a child's real world," while Ann A. Flowers concluded in *Horn Book:* "The satisfaction of seeing a bully get her comeuppance is guaranteed to make a young reader's heart sing." Bootsie returns in *Bootsie Barker, Ballerina.*

The comical *Hurricane Music* represents another example of Bottner's effective use of humor. As a *Kirkus Reviews* critic remarked, in *Hurricane Music* "Bottner makes her playful, syncopated text tongue-in-cheek from start to finish." After discovering a clarinet in her basement, Aunt Margaret finds herself unable to afford music lessons and opts to "study the sounds of life" instead. *Booklist* reviewer Mary Harris Veeder noted that "any child who's ever tried to master an instrument will identify with [Aunt Margaret's] vigorous glee."

Another Bottner story with musical undertones is *Nana Hannah's Piano,* which puts a spin on the time-tested story about a boy who would rather play baseball than practice the piano. However, a week spent with Nana Hannah while recovering from a sprained ankle changes the boy's attitude. A *Kirkus Reviews* critic praised *Nana Hannah's Piano*, commenting: "Sharing, caring and a patch of common ground—Bottner knows the ingredients, and fashions them into a minor ode to encouragement."

In the picture book *Be Brown!*, illustrated by Barry Gott, Bottner tells a story about a boy who attempts to train his disobedient brown pup. Each time his young master orders the young dog to do a task, the animal disobeys and does the complete opposite. *Be Brown!* is sparse in words, including only one command per page, but is not sparse in content; as a *Kirkus Reviews* critic noted, "Bottner is nicely communicative about the absence of communication" and her story "commands attention."

Bottner touches on the subject of fear in *The Scaredy Cats*, which introduces a feline family whose members are too afraid to do anything. Mother and Father cat are afraid to drive because they fear the car will go too fast; they do not open their mail because they are afraid of being disappointed; and they are afraid to let Baby Scaredy wear her new dress because they fear she will stain it. *The Scaredy Cats* presents "a funny and revealing look at our fears," according to a *Kirkus Reviews* critic. Kathleen Kelly MacMillan, in *School Library Journal*, noted of Bottner's stylistic approach that the author's "serious tone is a perfect counterpoint to the increasing ridiculousness of the Scaredy Cats' fears." In 2003, *The Scaredy Cats* was chosen as a "One Picture Book, One Community" title for Miami-Dade first graders.

Wallace's Lists is one of several comic collaborations between Bottner and her husband, Dr. Gerald Kruglik. Focusing on the disadvantages of planning too much, the book introduces Wallace, a mouse who starts each day of his orderly life by checking his to-do lists. Wallace's life is thrown asunder when he meets a new neighbor, Albert the mouse, who approaches life in a more impetuous way. Under Albert's influence, Wallace gradually gives up his systematic approach to life, and learns to appreciate the value of spontaneity. Critics applauded Bottner's story, remarking on the author's humor and ability to engage readers. Lauralyn Persson, writing in *School Library Journal*, reviewed the title and noted: "The writing is memorable . . . and the authors provide just the right amount of details," making "this picture book . . . a winner." Similarly a *Publishers Weekly* reviewer stated of the book that *Wallace's Lists* "goes on the recommended list."

Biographical and Critical Sources

BOOKS

Bottner, Barbara, *Be Brown!*, Grosset & Dunlap (New York, NY), 2002.

Bottner, Barbara, and Gerald Kruglik, *The Scaredy Cats*, Simon & Schuster (New York, NY), 2003.

PERIODICALS

Booklist, July, 1989, p. 1891; June 1-15, 1995, p. 1782.
Bulletin of the Center for Children's Books, December, 1984, p. 62; January, 1987, p. 83; September, 1992, pp. 6-7; April, 1997, p. 277.
Horn Book, March-April, 1993, pp. 193-194.
Kirkus Reviews, May 15, 1989, p. 760; September, 1, 1992, p. 1126; September 10, 1996, p. 1147; April 1, 1997, p. 549; December 15, 2001, review of *Be Brown!*, p. 1754; March 15, 2003, review of *The Scaredy Cats*, p. 76.
Publishers Weekly, December 21, 1984, p. 87; August 28, 1987, p. 78; June 7, 2004, review of *Wallace's Lists*, p. 49.
School Library Journal, November, 1986, p. 97; February, 1993, p. 69; May, 1995, pp. 81-82; April, 2003, Kathleen Kelly MacMillan, review of *The Scaredy Cats*, p. 116; June, 2004, Lauralyn Persson, review of *Wallace's Lists*, p. 96.
Voice of Youth Advocates, June, 1989, p. 98.

ONLINE

Barbara Bottner Home Page, http://www.barbarabottnerbooks.com (April 10, 2006).

* * *

BOWEN, Anne 1952-

Personal
Born 1952; married; children: two sons.

Addresses
Agent—c/o Author Mail, Carolrhoda Books, Inc., 241 1st Ave. N., Minneapolis, MN 55401.

Career
School teacher for approximately twenty-five years, including work with hearing-impaired children.

Awards, Honors
Utah Language Arts Teacher of the Year, 1996-97.

Writings

I Loved You Before You Were Born, illustrated by Greg Shed, HarperCollins Publishers (New York, NY), 2001.
How Did You Grow So Big, So Soon?, illustrated by Marni Backer, Carolrhoda Books (Minneapolis, MN), 2003.

When You Visit Grandma & Grandpa, illustrated by Tomek Bogacki, Lerner Publishing Group (Minneapolis, MN), 2004.

Tooth Fairy's First Night, illustrated by Jon Berkeley, Carolrhoda Books (Minneapolis, MN), 2005.

Sidelights

A teacher with over two decades of experience, Anne Bowen turned to writing children's books later in life after she became a grandparent. Her stories often offer pictures of the simple joys of living and enjoying young members of the family. For example, her first picture book, *I Loved You Before You Were Born,* is about a grandmother's eager anticipation of the arrival of a newborn grandchild in a story in which "poetic descriptions . . . brim with sentimental tenderness," according to a *Publishers Weekly* reviewer. *When You Visit Grandma & Grandpa* is a similar story, only this time it is about a child's anticipated visit to her grandparents' home, not about the birth itself. A *Publishers Weekly* reviewer described the story as a "touching testimony to the deliciousness of anticipation and intergenerational love." Bowen's *How Did You Grow So Big, So Soon?* is also about an adult's love for a child as she watches the baby grow, but here the tale is told from the mother's viewpoint. More recently, Bowen explored a more fanciful tale with *Tooth Fairy's First Night,* a "charmer" of a story, according to one *Kirkus Reviews* contributor, about a tooth fairy who is new to her profession and must overcome some unexpected obstacles.

Biographical and Critical Sources

PERIODICALS

Kirkus Reviews, March 1, 2005, review of *Tooth Fairy's First Night,* p. 284.

Publishers Weekly, April 2, 2001, review of *I Loved You Before You Were Born,* p. 62; November 8, 2004, review of *When You Visit Grandma & Grandpa,* p. 54.

School Library Journal, March, 2004, Leanna Manna, review of *How Did You Grow So Big, So Soon?,* p. 154.

ONLINE

HarperTeacher.com, http://www.harperchildrens.com/teacher/ (June 14, 2005), brief biography of Anne Bowen.*

* * *

BRIMNER, Larry Dane 1949-

Personal

Born November 5, 1949, in St. Petersburg, FL; son of George Frederick (a military officer) and Evelyn A. Brimner (a homemaker). *Education:* San Diego State University, B.A. (literature), 1971, M.A. (writing), 1981. *Hobbies and other interests:* Reading, snow skiing, animals, pine furniture, travel, American folk art.

Addresses

Office—P.O. Box 87257, Tucson, AZ 85754. *Agent*—c/o Author Mail, 21 Hillside Cir., Bayfield, CO 81122. *E-mail*—ldb@brimner.com.

Career

Central Union High School, El Centro, CA, writing teacher, 1974-84; San Diego State University, San Diego, CA, lecturer, 1984-91; freelance writer, 1985—.

Member

International Reading Association, Authors' Guild, Society of Children's Book Writers and Illustrators, National Council of Teachers of English, California Association of Teachers of English, Southern California Council on Literature for Children and Young People, Sierra Club, AmFar.

Awards, Honors

Children's Choice Award, International Reading Association, 1988, for *BMX Freestyle* and *Snowboarding,* 2000, for *The Official M & M's Brand Book of the Millennium;* Pick of the List designation, American Booksellers Association, 1988, for *Country Bear's Good Neighbor;* Best Children's Science Book listee, *Science Books and Films,* 1991, for *Animals That Hibernate;* Notable Trade Book in the Field of Social Studies designation, National Council of Social Studies/Children's Book Council, 1992, for *A Migrant Family;* Junior Library selection, 2004, for *Subway: The Story of Tunnels;* Oppenheim Gold Medal for Best Book, 2002, San Diego Books Award, 2002, Great Lakes' Great Books Honor Book, 2004, and Arkansas Diamond Award, 2005, all for *The Littlest Wolf.*

Writings

Country Bear's Good Neighbor, Orchard Books (London, England),1988.

Cory Coleman, Grade 2, Henry Holt (New York, NY), 1990.

Country Bear's Surprise, Orchard Books (London, England), 1991.

A Migrant Family, Lerner Publishing (Minneapolis, MN), 1992.

Max and Felix, Boyds Mills Press (Honesdale, PA), 1993.

Elliot Fry's Goodbye, illustrated by Eugenie Fernandes, Boyds Mills Press (Honesdale, PA), 1994.

Voices from the Camps: Internment of Japanese Americans during World War II, F. Watts (New York, NY), 1994.

Merry Christmas, Old Armadillo, illustrated by Dominic Catalano, Boyds Mills Press (Honesdale, PA), 1995.

Being Different: Lambda Youths Speak Out, F. Watts (New York, NY), 1995.
If Dogs Had Wings, illustrated by Chris L. Demarest, Boyds Mills Press (Honesdale, PA), 1996.
Skiing, Children's Press (New York, NY), 1997.
Mountain Biking, F. Watts (New York, NY), 1997.
How Many Ants?, illustrated by Joan Cottle, Children's Press (New York, NY), 1997.
The Harvest Fair, illustrated by Steve Henry, Children's Press (New York, NY), 1997.
Figure Skating, Children's Press (New York, NY), 1997.
The Cool Hot Day, illustrated by Steve Henry, Children's Press (New York, NY), 1997.
Letters to Our Children: Lesbian and Gay Adults Speak to the New Generation, F. Watts (New York, NY), 1997.
Snowboarding, F. Watts (New York, NY), 1997.
Praying Mantises, Children's Press (New York, NY), 1999.
The Official M & M's Brand Book of the Millennium, illustrated by Karen Pellaton, Charlesbridge (Watertown, MA), 1999.
Flies, Children's Press (New York, NY), 1999.
The World Wide Web, Children's Press (New York, NY), 1997, revised edition, 2000.
E-mail, Children's Press (New York, NY), 1997, revised edition, 2000.
Cat on Wheels, illustrated by Mary Peterson, Boyds Mills Press (Honesdale, PA), 2000.
Caving: Exploring Limestone Caves, F. Watts (New York, NY), 2001.
The Littlest Wolf, illustrated by José Aruego and Ariane Dewey, HarperCollins (New York, NY), 2002.
Everybody's Best Friend, illustrated by Christine Tripp, Children's Press (New York, NY), 2002.
Trash Trouble, illustrated by Christine Tripp, Children's Press (New York, NY), 2003.
The New Kid, illustrated by Christine Tripp, Children's Press (New York, NY), 2003.
Subway: The Story of Tunnels, Tubes, and Tracks, illustrated by Neil Waldman, Boyds Mills Press (Honesdale, PA), 2004.

"FIRST BOOKS" SERIES

BMX Freestyle, F. Watts (New York, NY), 1987.
Karate, F. Watts (New York, NY), 1988.
Footbagging, F. Watts (New York, NY), 1988.
Snowboarding, F. Watts (New York, NY), 1989.
Animals That Hibernate, F. Watts (New York, NY), 1991.
Unusual Friendships . . ., F. Watts (New York, NY), 1993.
Rolling . . . In-line!, F. Watts (New York, NY), 1994.
Rock Climbing, F. Watts (New York, NY), 1997.
Surfing, F. Watts (New York, NY), 1997.
Mountains, Children's Press (New York, NY), 2000.

"TRUE BOOKS" SERIES

Polar Mammals, Children's Press (New York, NY), 1996.
Bobsledding and the Luge, Children's Press (New York, NY), 1997.
Speed Skating, Children's Press (New York, NY), 1997.
The Winter Olympics, Children's Press (New York, NY), 1997.
Earth, Children's Press (New York, NY), 1998.
Mars, Children's Press (New York, NY), 1998.
Mercury, Children's Press (New York, NY), 1998.
Venus, Children's Press (New York, NY), 1998.
Bees, Children's Press (New York, NY), 1999.
Butterflies and Moths, Children's Press (New York, NY), 1999.
Cockroaches, Children's Press (New York, NY), 1999.
Jupiter, Children's Press (New York, NY), 1999.
Neptune, Children's Press (New York, NY), 1999.
Pluto, Children's Press (New York, NY), 1999.
Saturn, Children's Press (New York, NY), 1999.
Uranus, Children's Press (New York, NY), 1999.
Caves, Children's Press (New York, NY), 2000.
Geysers, Children's Press (New York, NY), 2000.
Glaciers, Children's Press (New York, NY), 2000.
Valleys and Canyons, Children's Press (New York, NY), 2000.

"ROOKIE READERS" SERIES

Firehouse Sal, illustrated by Ethel Gold, Children's Press (New York, NY), 1996.
Aggie and Will, illustrated by Rebecca McKillip Thornburgh, Children's Press (New York, NY), 1998.
Dinosaurs Dance, illustrated by Patrick Girouard, Children's Press (New York, NY), 1998.
Lightning Liz, illustrated by Brian Floca, Children's Press (New York, NY), 1998.
Nana's Hog, illustrated by Susan Miller, Children's Press (New York, NY), 1998.
What Good Is a Tree?, illustrated by Leo Landry, Children's Press (New York, NY), 1998.
Cowboy Up!, illustrated by Susan Miller, Children's Press (New York, NY), 1999.
Raindrops, illustrated by David J. Brooks, Children's Press (New York, NY), 1999.
Cats!, illustrated by Tom Payne, Children's Press (New York, NY), 2000.
Gatitos!, illustrated by Tom Payne, Children's Press (New York, NY), 2000.
The Long Way Home, illustrated by Terry Sirrell, Children's Press (New York, NY), 2000.
Here Comes Trouble, illustrated by Pable Torrecilla, Children's Press (New York, NY), 2001.
Nana's Fiddle, illustrated by Susan Miller, Children's Press (New York, NY), 2002.

"CORNERSTONES OF FREEDOM" SERIES

The Names Project, Children's Press (New York, NY), 1999.
Angel Island, Children's Press (New York, NY), 2001.

"TALL TALES" SERIES

(Reteller) *Calamity Jane,* illustrated by Judy DuFour Love, Compass Point Books (Minneapolis, MN), 2004.

(Reteller) *Casey Jones,* illustrated by Drew Rose, Compass Point Books (Minneapolis, MN), 2004.

(Reteller) *Davy Crockett,* Compass Point Books (Minneapolis, MN), 2004.

(Reteller) *Molly Pitcher,* illustrated by Patrick Girouard, Compass Point Books (Minneapolis, MN), 2004.

(Reteller) *Captain Stormalong,* illustrated by Chi Chung, Compass Point Books (Minneapolis, MN), 2004.

"ROOKIE CHOICES" SERIES

The Big Beautiful Brown Box, illustrated by Christine Tripp, Children's Press (New York, NY), 2001.

The Big Tree Ball Game, illustrated by Christine Tripp, Children's Press (New York, NY), 2001.

The Messy Lot, illustrated by Christine Tripp, Children's Press (New York, NY), 2001.

Money Trouble, illustrated by Christine Tripp, Children's Press (New York, NY), 2001.

The Noodle Game, illustrated by Christine Tripp, Children's Press (New York, NY), 2001.

The Sparkle Thing, illustrated by Christine Tripp, Children's Press (New York, NY), 2001.

The Pet Show, illustrated by Christine Tripp, Children's Press (New York, NY), 2002.

Unsinkable!, illustrated by Christine Tripp, Children's Press (New York, NY), 2002.

A Flag for All, illustrated by Christine Tripp, Children's Press (New York, NY), 2002.

The Birthday Flowers, illustrated by Christine Tripp, Children's Press (New York, NY), 2002.

The Promise, illustrated by Christine Tripp, Children's Press (New York, NY), 2002.

School Rules, illustrated by Christine Tripp, Children's Press (New York, NY), 2002.

The Sidewalk Patrol, illustrated by Christine Tripp, Children's Press (New York, NY), 2002.

The Cool Cats, illustrated by Christine Tripp, Children's Press (New York, NY), 2003.

Summer Fun, illustrated by Christine Tripp, Children's Press (New York, NY), 2003.

"MAGIC DOOR TO READING" SERIES

Spring Sail, illustrated by R.W. Alley, Child's World (Chanhassen, MN), 2005.

Max's Math Machine, illustrated by Robert Squier, Child's World (Chanhassen, MN), 2006.

Bigger and Smaller, illustrated by Patrick Girouard, Child's World (Chanhassen, MN), 2006.

Elwood's Bath, illustrated by Teri Weidner, Child's World (Chanhassen, MN), 2006.

In the Fall, illustrated by R.W. Alley, Child's World (Chanhassen, MN), 2006.

Loud Larry, illustrated by JoAnn Adinolfi, Child's World (Chanhassen, MN), 2006.

One Summery Day, illustrated by R.W. Alley, Child's World (Chanhassen, MN), 2006.

Rumble Bus, illustrated by Ronnie Rooney, Child's World (Chanhassen, MN), 2006.

Sammy's Something Sweet, illustrated by Kathleen Petelinsek, Child's World (Chanhassen, MN), 2006.

A Shake and a Shiver, illustrated by JoAnn Adinolfi, Child's World (Chanhassen, MN), 2006.

Twelve Plump Cookies, illustrated by Sharon Holm, Child's World (Chanhassen, MN), 2006.

Winter Blanket, illustrated by R.W. Alley, Child's World (Chanhassen, MN), 2006.

Sidelights

Larry Dane Brimner was raised in Kodiak Island, Alaska where his parents began reading him to at a very young age. Introduced to some of the greatest literary giants, including Mark Twain, Ernest Hemingway, and F. Scott Fitzgerald, Brimner was able to read simple sentences by age four and blossomed into an avid bookworm, he read all the children's books in his family's library and eventually began creating his own stories. Brimner attended elementary and high school in Alaska, then moved to California to pursue his baccalaureate degree at San Diego State University. During his undergraduate studies he focused on writing poetry and obtained some success in that genre. Graduating with a degree in literature, Brimner considering becoming a writer but was discouraged by his father. Instead, he began a career in teaching that lasted for twenty years. It was during his time as a teacher that Brimner developed an interest in writing children's books. He left teaching when his first children's book, 1987's *BMX Freestyle*, was published, jump-starting a prolific writing career.

Brimner once explained to *SATA* that his childhood in Alaska inspired his interests in sports, nature, and fiction. "Ever since I was a small child growing up on Kodiak Island, with no television and only sporadic radio reception, I have enjoyed reading and listening to stories," he explained. "My early experience in Alaska must also explain why I'm happiest in a snowy environment, surrounded by nature, and why winter is my favorite season of the year. Unlike most people who seek the sun during the 'gloomy' winter, I love to visit places with stormy weather or snow." "*Animals That Hibernate* and *Unusual Friendships* are both about nature," the author added, "and *Cory Coleman, Grade 2* features a 'winter' sport—ice skating, something I've been doing almost since I started to walk."

Several of Brimner's books introduce young people to sports and provide guides for learning more about them. In *BMX Freestyle* he discusses motocross biking, including chapters on the history of the sport, safety tips, trick techniques, selecting equipment, and directions for building a ramp. Connie Tyrrell Burns, a reviewer for *School Library Journal,* described the book as "well done." *Karate* provides descriptions of various martial-arts styles and moves and discusses their development. A reviewer for *Booklist* decided that readers interested in the martial arts "will be well served by Brimner's introduction." In *Footbagging,* yet another sports book,

Part of the "Rookie Reader" series, Cats *features engaging illustrations by Tom Payne that depict all manner of kitty hijinks.* (Text copyright © 2000 by Larry Dane Brimner. Illustrations copyright © by Tom Payne. Reproduced by permission of Children's Press.)

Brimner explains the background, benefits, and how-tos of footbagging, or hacky-sack, a sport involving the kicking of a small ball or "bag." According to *Young Adults/Children's Reviews,* Brimner's instructions are "clear and encouraging." Another sports-related title, *Snowboarding,* follows the format of Brimner's other sports books: beginners are provided with information ranging from equipment to basic moves. Ann G. Brouse, writing for *School Library Journal,* concluded that "the clarity and thoroughness of this introduction is sure to satisfy the merely curious and serious snowboarding beginners." All of Brimner's sport books are enhanced by bibliographies and/or addresses of sport organizations and associations.

Country Bear's Good Neighbor, Brimner's first work of fiction for children, was described by a *Publishers Weekly* contributor as "a sweet debut." In this story, Country Bear borrows ingredient after ingredient from his neighbor in order to bake a cake. Just when his neighbor, a little girl, decides that Bear has borrowed enough, he brings the baked cake to her house to share. Brimner includes the recipe for "Country Bear's Good Neighbor Cake." According to Anna Biagioni Hart, writing for *School Library Journal,* the "unpretentious and kind" book will be enjoyed by preschoolers and kindergartners. In another "Country Bear" book, *Country Bear's Surprise,* Country Bear fears that the little girl and her friends have forgotten his birthday and are interested only in the private club they have created. Just as Country Bear decides to run away, the little girl surprises him with a birthday party. A recipe for surprise cookies is included with this story, which Kay Weisman, writing for *Booklist,* called a "charmer." *Max and Felix* is also targeted at a young audience. In this work, two frogs capture their comic experiences—ranging from fishing to telling spooky stores—with a camera. According to Marge Loch-Wouters in *School Library Journal,* children will "enjoy spending time" with these frogs.

Brimner is also the author of books for older children. In *Cory Coleman, Grade 2* he tells the story of a boy who invites his class to the ice-skating rink for his birthday party. Although he does not want to invite a boy named Delphinius, who he calls "Dumbphinius," his mother insists that the entire class attend the party. Delphinius does come to the party and attempts to spoil it by knocking children down. Although Cory manages to humiliate Delphinius, the two ultimately become friends. Laura Culberg, reviewing the book for *School Library Journal,* wrote that the novel's resolution is "predictable" yet "believable."

Animals That Hibernate reflects Brimner's enthusiasm for natural subjects. The author illuminates the behavior of animals that sleep (lightly or deeply) through the winter as they store food, prepare a den, and, finally, go to sleep. Although the majority of the book is devoted to mammals, animals included in this examination range from woodchucks to birds and cold-blooded critters. Diane Nunn, a reviewer for *School Library Journal,* explained that "an uncluttered format with frequent subheadings make the information accessible" and that a bibliography, glossary, and index are helpful auxiliaries to the text.

Children are given a humorous story about a young boy's attempt to run away from home in Brimner's *Elliot Fry's Good-Bye,* which *Booklist* contributor Annie Ayres called "a story that most young children will identify with and find reassuring." Throughout the day Elliott is scolded for the things he does: his mother reprimands him for tracking mud into the house, his father tells him he is being too loud, and his sister tattles to his parents when he jumps on the bed. Elliot's tolerance is truly tested when he is informed he will be sharing his room with visiting Uncle Abe. When Elliot replies, "I'm leaving!," he is surprised when his parents begin offering tools to assist in his departure, including snacks and a suitcase. Elliot leaves and makes a short trip around the block, but later decides to return home to his clever parents.

Brimner brings a comforting voice to young readers dealing with sibling rivalry in *The Littlest Wolf.* Little Wolf does not measure up to his older brothers and sisters: he does not run as fast as his siblings, he does not roll in a straight line as they do, and he is no match when it comes to his pouncing abilities. Finally, Little Wolf is set at ease by his father, who reminds the young pup of his uniqueness. Deborah Stevens, writing in the *Bulletin of the Center for Children's Books,* noted that Brimner's "text is reassuring and enjoyably humorous," while a *Publishers Weekly* critic commended the book for its ability to "give fledgling young ones a boost of confidence."

Moving to nonfiction for older readers, in *Letters to Our Children: Lesbian and Gay Adults Speak to the New Generation* Brimner compiles a collection of essays and letters that offer advice and support for gay and lesbian youth. The essays were written by a range of writers; one was penned by an openly gay politician, while another was written by the archbishop of the Ecumenical Catholic Church. Additional contributions came from attorneys, college professors, school teachers, and professional writers. Brimner's common theme is to support teens struggling with their identity as homosexuals, and the book is meant to encourage young adults to love themselves regardless of their sexual orientation. Debbie Carton reviewed the title for *Booklist* and noted that the work is a "warm and supportive collection" that offers a compassionate voice from gay and lesbian adults.

Biographical and Critical Sources

BOOKS

Brimner, Larry Dane, *Elliot Fry's Good-Bye,* Boyds Mills Press (Honesdale, PA), 1994.
Brimner, Larry Dane, *A Migrant Family,* Lerner Publishing (Minneapolis, MN), 1992.

PERIODICALS

Booklist, May 15, 1988, review of *Karate,* pp. 1605-1606; February 15, 1991, Kay Weisman, review of *Country Bear's Surprise,* pp. 1199-1201; March 1, 1994, Annie Ayres, review of *Elliot Fry's Good-Bye,* p. 1267; September 15, 1997, Debbie Carton, review of *Letters to Our Children: Lesbian and Gay Adults Speak to a New Generation,* p. 218.
Bulletin of the Center for Children's Books, July-August, 2002, Deborah Stevenson, review of *The Littlest Wolf,* p. 395.
Kirkus Reviews, January 15, 1988, review of *Footbagging,* pp. 120-121.
New York Times Book Review, January 17, 1993, Henry Mayer, review of *A Migrant Family.*
Publishers Weekly, May 13, 1988, review of *Country Bear's Good Neighbor,* p. 272; December 6, 1993, review of *Elliot Fry's Good-Bye,* p. 73; March 11, 2002, review of *The Littlest Wolf,* p. 71.

School Library Journal, September, 1987, Connie Tyrell, review of *BMX Freestyle,* p. 186; December, 1989, Anne G. Brouse, review of *Snowboarding,* p. 106; November, 1990, Laura Culberg, review of *Cory Coleman, Grade 2;* October, 1988, Anna Biagioni Hart, review of *Country Bear's Good Neighbor,* p. 115; March, 1993, Marge Lock-Wouters, review of *Max and Felix,* p. 171; July, 1991, Diane Nunne, review of *Animals That Hibernate,* p. 77.

ONLINE

Boyds Mills Press Web site, http://www.boydsmillspress.com/ (April 10, 2006), "Larry Dane Brimner."
Children's Author Fest Web site, http://www.authorfest.org/ (April 10, 2006), "Larry Dane Brimner."
Larry Dane Brimner Home Page, http://www.brimner.com (April 10, 2006).*

* * *

BROWN, Jo 1964-

Personal

Born 1964. *Education:* University of Nottingham, B.A.; University of Manchester, M.A.

Addresses

Home—Brighton, England. *Agent*—c/o Author Mail, 18 Tichborne St., Brighton, East Sussex BN1 1UR, England. *E-mail*—jo@jo-brown.co.uk.

Career

Graphic artist, author, and illustrator. Has worked on projects involving advertising, animation, packaging, toy design, and greeting cards.

Writings

SELF-ILLUSTRATED

Where's My Mommy?, Tiger Tales (Wilton, CT), 2002.
If Dogs Wore Clothes, Campbell/Macmillan (New York, NY), 2002.
Little Rabbit Goes out to Play, Tango, 2002.
Pirate Jam, Gingham Dog Press (Columbus, OH), 2003.
Hoppity Skip Little Chick, Tiger Tales (Wilton, CT), 2005.

Adaptations

Where's My Mommy? was adapted for audio cassette, read by Jane Gabbert, Scholastic (New York, NY), 2003.

Sidelights

Graphic artist Jo Brown has written and illustrated several picture books for small children. Her earliest work, *Where's My Mommy?,* tells the story of newly hatched Little Crocodile, who is searching for his mother. He first comes across a blue monkey, a tiger, an elephant, and a zebra. They ask him to make various sounds and motions that prove how differently they are made. When Little Crocodile finally discovers his mother, he tells her that he has been making friends. The story is illustrated with colorful images of geometrically styled animals.

Two reviewers found a strong similarity between Brown's book and P.D. Eastman's *Are You My Mother?* According to Piper L. Nyman in *School Library Journal,* the result is "not highly original." A *Publishers Weekly* critic, in contrast, remarked that Brown's world is "considerably more benevolent" than that of the earlier story, and the reviewer enjoyed the "free-wheeling body language" of the animals.

Pirate Jam is the story of two failed pirates: Fredbeard and Little Jim. The two friends flunk out of pirate school and are left to find occupations of their own making. Their habit of collecting things that wash up on the beach ultimately gives them the materials and inspiration to set themselves up in the jam-making and knitting businesses, which both turn profitable. *Bulletin of the Center for Children's Books* contributor Deborah Stevenson praised the story's "comic detail."

Brown tells a story about the companionship of friends and siblings in her *Hoppity Skip Little Chick.* The title character in this tale is sent out to play by his mother, who is occupied with warming the eggs in her nest. Little Chick is thrilled to play with the geese, a lamb, a pony, and a piglet in the barnyard. In the course of the morning, he makes a game of jumping, running, bouncing, and rolling with these friends. To his surprise, he returns home to find new brothers and sisters to play with.

The story and its illustrations had plenty of charm for reviewers, who admired the vivid activity captured in both of these aspects of the book. A *Children's Bookwatch* writer described the picture book as "gently written and colorfully illustrated," and *School Library Journal* contributor Kathleen Kelly MacMillan recommended the book as a "terrific read-aloud for toddler storytime."

Biographical and Critical Sources

PERIODICALS

Bulletin of the Center for Children's Books, May, 2003, Deborah Stevenson, review of *Pirate Jam,* p. 352.
Children's Bookwatch, June, 2005, review of *Hoppity Skip Little Chick.*
Kirkus Reviews, March 1, 2005, review of *Hoppity Skip Little Chick,* p. 284.
Publishers Weekly, February 18, 2002, review of *Where's My Mommy?,* p. 95.

School Library Journal, July, 2002, Piper L. Nyman, review of *Where's My Mommy?,* p. 84; September, 2003, Susan Pine, review of *Pirate Jam,* p. 175; May, 2005, Kathleen Kelly MacMillan, review of *Hoppity Skip Little Chick,* p. 77.

ONLINE

Jo Brown Home Page, http://www.jo-brown.co.uk (September 13, 2005).*

* * *

BROWN, Ruth 1941-

Personal

Born May 20, 1941, in Tiverton, England; daughter of Hughbert Niels (a company executive) and Dorothy Alice (Wicks) Antonsen; married Kenneth James Brown (an artist and illustrator), August 29, 1964; children: Hogan, James. *Education:* Attended Bournemouth College of Art, 1957-59; Birmingham College of Art, degree (with first-class honors), 1961; Royal College of Art, M.A., 1964. *Politics:* Liberal. *Hobbies and other interests:* Gardening, walking the dog in the countryside, reading, traveling, visiting antique shops, cooking.

Addresses

Home—Bath, England. *Agent*—c/o Author Mail, Andersen Press, Ltd., Random House, 20 Vauxhall Bridge Rd., London SW1V 2SA, England.

Career

Author and illustrator, 1979—.

Awards, Honors

Shortlisted for Kate Greenaway Medal, British Library Association, 1988, for *Ladybird, Ladybird* and 1996, for *The Tale of the Monstrous Toad; Redbook* Children's Book Award, 1988, for *Blossom Comes Home.*

Writings

FOR CHILDREN; SELF-ILLUSTRATED UNLESS OTHERWISE NOTED

Crazy Charlie, Andersen (London, England), 1979, reprinted, 1998.
A Dark, Dark Tale, Dial (New York, NY), 1981, published with Arabic translation by Azza Habib, Andersen (London, England), 1998.
If at First You Do Not See, Andersen (London, England), 1982, Holt (New York, NY), 1983.
The Grizzly Revenge, Andersen (London, England), 1983.
The Big Sneeze, Lothrop (New York, NY), 1985, reprinted, Andersen (London, England), 2002.
Our Cat Flossie, Dutton (New York, NY), 1986, reprinted, Andersen (London, England), 2004.
Our Puppy's Holiday, Andersen (London, England), 1987, published as *Our Puppy's Vacation,* Dutton (New York, NY), 1987.
Ladybird, Ladybird, Andersen (London, England), 1988, published as *Ladybug, Ladybug,* Dutton (New York, NY), 1988.
I Don't Like It!, Andersen (London, England), 1989, Dutton (New York, NY), 1990.
The World That Jack Built, Andersen (London, England), 1990, Dutton (New York, NY), 1991.
The Four-Tongued Alphabet: An Alphabet Book in Four Languages, Andersen (London, England), 1991, published as *Alphabet Times Four: An International ABC,* Dutton (New York, NY), 1991.
The Picnic, Dutton (New York, NY), 1992.
One Stormy Night, Andersen (London, England), 1992, Dutton (New York, NY), 1993.
Copycat, Dutton (New York, NY), 1994.
(Reteller) *Greyfriars Bobby,* Andersen (London, England), 1995, published as *The Ghost of Greyfriar's Bobby,* Dutton (New York, NY), 1996.
The Tale of the Monstrous Toad, Andersen (London, England), 1996, published as *Toad,* Dutton (New York, NY), 1997.
Baba, Andersen (London, England), 1997, published as *Cry Baby,* Dutton (New York, NY), 1997.
A Mad Summer Night's Dream, Andersen (London, England), 1998, Dutton (New York, NY), 1999.
One Little Angel, Andersen (London, England), 1998, published as *The Shy Little Angel,* Dutton (New York, NY), 1998.
Holly: The True Story of a Cat, Andersen (London, England), 1999, Holt (New York, NY), 2000.
Snail Trail, Crown (New York, NY), 2000.
The Happy Frog, Red Fox (London, England), 2001.
Ten Seeds, Knopf (New York, NY), 2001.
Lion in the Long Grass, illustrated by Ken Brown, Andersen (London, England), 2002.
Helpful Henry, Andersen (London, England), 2002.
Ruggles, Anderson (London, England), 2003.
The Christmas Mouse, Red Fox (London, England), 2003.
The Winter Garden, Andersen (London, England), 2004.
Night-Time Tale, Andersen (London, England), 2005.
Imagine, Andersen (London, England), 2006.

ILLUSTRATOR

James Herriot, *The Christmas Day Kitten,* St. Martin's Press (New York, NY), 1986.
James Herriot, *Bonny's Big Day,* St. Martin's Press (New York, NY), 1987.
James Herriot, *Blossom Comes Home,* St. Martin's Press (New York, NY), 1988.
James Herriot, *The Market Square Dog,* St. Martin's Press (New York, NY), 1989.
James Herriot, *Oscar, Cat-about-Town,* St. Martin's Press (New York, NY), 1990.

James Herriot, *Smudge's Day Out,* Michael Joseph (London, England), 1991, published as *Smudge, the Little Lost Lamb,* St. Martin's Press (New York, NY), 1991.
(With Peter Barrett) James Herriot, *James Herriot's Animal Storybook,* Michael Joseph (London, England), 1992, published as *James Herriot's Treasury for Children,* St. Martin's Press (New York, NY), 1992.
Jeanne Willis, *In Search of the Hidden Giant,* Andersen (London, England), 1993, published as *In Search of the Giant,* Dutton (New York, NY), 1994.
Frances Thomas, *Mr. Bear and the Bear,* Andersen (London, England), 1994, Dutton (New York, NY), 1995.
Toby Forward, *The Christmas Mouse,* Andersen (London, England), 1996, published as *Ben's Christmas Carol,* Dutton (New York, NY), 1996.
Hiawyn Oram, *The Wise Doll: A Traditional Tale,* Andersen (London, England), 1997, published as *Baba Yaga and the Wise Doll: A Traditional Russian Folktale,* Dutton (New York, NY), 1998.

ILLUSTRATOR; "YOU AND ME" STORYBOOK SERIES

Judith Miles, *The Three Little Pigs,* Longman (London, England), 1979.
Barbara Parker, *The Three Bears,* Longman (London, England), 1979.
Mary Harris, *The Black and White Cat,* Longman (London, England), 1979.
Judith Miles, *The Ugly Duckling,* Longman (London, England), 1979.
Francesca Zeissl, *King Gargantua,* Longman (London, England), 1981.
Barbara Parker, *Town Mouse, Country Mouse,* Longman (London, England), 1981.

Adaptations

Several of Brown's books have been adapted for audiocassette.

Sidelights

Ruth Brown has written and illustrated numerous children's books, which have won her fans in both in her native England and North America. Known for her delicate use of watercolors, her particular love of cats, and her realistic and atmospheric representations of rural life, she has been particularly praised for her richly textured and colored artwork. "I'm very lucky to earn my living by writing and illustrating books," Brown once told *SATA.* "It means I can work at my own pace in my own time and in my own house. Sometimes I work very hard—seven days a week—and then when I've finished a book I can take a little time off before I start the next one." Among the many original picture books Brown has created are *Toad, Ten Seeds,* and *Mad Summer Night's Dream,* the last praised by *Booklist* contributor John Peters as "a lighthearted romp, depicted with [Brown's] characteristically sweeping brushstrokes." In a review of *Baba*—published in the United States as *Cry Baby*—about a pesky baby sister, Angela Redfern wrote in *School Librarian:* "you come to Ruth Brown's books with high expectations. You know she will write about something that matters."

Born in England in 1941, Brown grew up in Germany and in Bournemouth, England. After five years of arts studies, she married fellow illustrator Ken Brown and began a family. In 1979 she published her first children's book, *Crazy Charlie.* The story of a voracious crocodile who becomes less intimidating after his teeth fall out, the book was well received in England, and its 1983 publication in the United States introduced the author to U.S. audiences. Christine C. Seibold, writing in *School Library Journal,* noted that "children will identify with Charlie's longing for attention, and will cheer when he finally learns it's better to smile than growl." Seibold also commented on the "bold double-spread watercolor illustrations . . . rich in jungle colors and detail."

"The very hardest part of my job is thinking of good ideas," Brown once noted to *SATA.* "The writing is the next most difficult thing and doing the illustrations is the most fun." In creating her stories, she takes inspiration from the most commonplace of events. A fly lands on the nose of a sleeping farmer in *The Big Sneeze,* and sets off a chain reaction of accidents when it causes the dozing agrarian to sneeze. A *Junior Bookshelf* contributor called Brown's artwork for this book "delightfully evocative," while Moira Small noted in *Books for Keeps* that Brown "has produced a visual treat in this wonderful picture book . . . and a lesson in logic for small people!"

Familiar inspirations such as nursery rhymes and the alphabet serve as inspiration for several books by Brown. *The World That Jack Built* employs "the old cumulative Jack verse for a picture book about the environment," according to *Booklist* writer Hazel Rochman. Two contrasting valleys—one verdant and pristine, the other industrial and polluted—combine with the traditional format to bring home the author/illustrator's conservation message in what *Magpies* reviewer Cynthia Anthony described as a "powerful book." *Alphabet Times Four: An International ABC* (published in England as *The Four-Tongued Alphabet: An Alphabet Book in Four Languages*) goes beyond the bounds of traditional A-B-C books by spelling out words in four different languages—English, Spanish, French, and German—that happen to begin with the same letter. Hearne, writing in the *Bulletin of the Center for Children's Books,* noted that "teachers, librarians, and parents will find this a long-term, broad-based aesthetic investment." Reviewing the British edition, a *Junior Bookshelf* critic called Brown's book "beautifully pictured, in richly coloured and mysterious, imaginative paintings."

Animals of all sorts have provided Brown with one of her richest sources of inspiration. In *A Dark, Dark Tale* a black cat finds its way across a dark moor to a gloomy castle and then to a darkened corner of a mysterious room. "Brown's rich acrylic paintings are all shadows and cobwebs," noted *Booklist* contributor Ilene Cooper, adding that *A Dark, Dark Tale* "will work well as a read-aloud with young listeners." Featuring another feline, her book *Our Cat Flossie* follows a house cat through a typical day that includes favorite haunts and favorite pastimes. "Brown is, quite obviously, gone on cats," Christina Olson remarked in a *School Library Journal* review of the book, adding that her "softly colored portraits" of the beloved pet "are charming" and enhance "a book that is simple—fulfillingly so." Chris Powling, writing in *Books for Keeps,* called *Our Cat Flossie* a "straightforward charmer." Praised for its "masterfully painted, realistic" illustrations by a *School Library Journal* reviewer, *Holly: The True Story of a Cat* follows as an abandoned coal-black kitten brings meaning to the holiday festivities of an English family. Based on Brown's own experience, the book features a simple text, while the author/illustrator's obvious understanding of the "cuddly, wily and sometimes standoffish ways of felines" will win points with cat lovers, in the opinion of a *Publishers Weekly* contributor.

Moving from cats to dogs, Brown serves up the adventures of a Labrador puppy in *Our Puppy's Vacation,* which Kristi Thomas Beavin called "visually appealing" in *School Library Journal,* and Betsy Hearne deemed "well worth the trip!" in her review for the *Bulletin of the Center for Children's Books.* In *One Stormy Night* the reader is presented with another dog's-eye view of life, this time a stormy night. Readers worry as a lonely dog enters the gates of a scary manor, searching for shelter from the severe weather. When the storm clears in the morning, the white dog has been transformed: it appears as a carved figure sitting guard on a tomb at a nearby church. A *Junior Bookshelf* critic concluded a review of the book by stating that "Brown knows her animals and her architecture, and she captures the muted tones of night with great skill."

Other popular animal and nature titles from Brown include *Ladybird, Ladybird* (released in the United States as *Ladybug, Ladybug*), *The Picnic,* and *Ten Seeds.* The ladybird or ladybug of the first book is the subject of a Mother Goose rhyme which Brown adapts into something of an environmental message, expanding the rhyme to include the animals and plants of the countryside. "It is Brown's lush, dramatically staged illustrations that add real weight to the poem," noted Phyllis Wilson in *Booklist.* Margery Fisher wrote in *Growing Point* that "there is an unobtrusive lesson in natural history implied in the pages of this expressive picture-book."

Humans venturing into the countryside unwittingly threaten disaster for the rabbits, mice, and moles inhabiting an underground burrow near a picnic site in *The Picnic,* while in *Ten Seeds* Brown weaves a simple counting lesson into a story about life in a backyard vegetable garden. "Brown's talent for illustrating nature is admirably displayed here," commented Judy Constantinides in a *School Library Journal* review of *The Picnic,* while Kristina Lindsay remarked in *Magpies* that the author/illustrator's artwork is "superb, with her delicate watercolours highlighting the stark difference between the bright daylight outside and dark burrow underground." In *Ten Seeds* Brown creates what a *Horn Book* contributor cited as a "marvelous opportunity to discuss plant life cycles and survival," as ten sunflower seeds are planted and through the works of slugs, mice, moles, and other garden visitors only a single flower opens, revealing a wealth of new seeds. Brown's detailed watercolors introduce young readers to the life cycle "with accuracy and charm," according to *School Library Journal* reviewer Patricia Pearl Dole.

Moving to literature, Brown retells the tale of a loyal dog in *The Ghost of Greyfriar's Bobby* and tips her hat to British writer Charles Dickens in a mousey version of *Ben's Christmas Carol,* a holiday classic penned by Toby Forward. In *The Ghost of Greyfriar's Bobby* two modern-day children, tourists in Edinburgh, Scotland, take readers back in time when they happen upon a fountain commemorating a dog called Bobby who was buried in a nearby churchyard. They—and the reader—learn, through a bit of magical flashback, of the loyalty of the dog that followed its master to his grave and then lingered nearby for fourteen years until it died as well. "Atmospheric prose and beguiling full-spread watercolors unfold Bobby's life with his master, Old Jock," commented a reviewer in *Publishers Weekly.* Lisa S. Murphy, writing in *School Library Journal,* noted that "Brown's masterful watercolors paint an inviting picture of both the town of Edinburgh and the gorgeous Scottish countryside," and deemed the book a "beautiful retelling of a hard-to-find legend." From a loyal dog, Brown shifts her focus to a stingy mouse in illustrating *Ben's Christmas Carol,* casting Ben the mouse as Ebeneezer Scrooge. *Ben's Christmas Carol* was heralded by several critics, Susan Dove Lempke writing in *Booklist* that the book's "sumptuous" paintings display London "in all its moods—from spooky and grimy to celebratory."

With *The Tale of the Monstrous Toad*—also published simply as *Toad*—Brown moves from the sumptuous to the grotesque. As Brown's text makes clear, *Toad* is the tale of a "toad odorous, foul and filthy, and dripping with venomous fluid." Toad's very ugliness is his defense, however: when he wanders into the jaws of a large predator, he is quickly spit back out again. Deborah Stevenson, reviewing the book for the *Bulletin of the Center for Children's Books,* wrote that it "seems a bit unfair to turn the toad's natural defenses into such a condemnatory judgment . . . about his personal charms, but the story trips along rhythmically nonetheless." Focusing on Brown's artwork for the book, Caroline Ward commented in *School Library Journal* that, "from the wart-encrusted end paper to the browns and greens of the slimy mire, the fluid watercolor illustrations aptly depict the setting."

As part of her work creating illustrations for stories by other writers, Brown has taken paintbrush in hand to illustrate several stories by beloved veterinarian-turned-writer James Herriot, providing atmospheric and lovingly detailed artwork that enhances and often transcends the usual bounds of book illustration. Reviewing her illustrations for Herriot's *The Market Square Dog*, for example, a *Publishers Weekly* reviewer remarked that "Brown's softly shaded watercolors recall an England of an earlier era, a place of cozy stone cottages and country gardens." Other books by Herriot that have been transformed into picture-book classics with the help of Brown's detailed watercolor illustrations include *Oscar, Cat-about-Town, Smudge, the Little Lost Lamb,* and *The Christmas Day Kitten.*

Biographical and Critical Sources

PERIODICALS

Booklist, December 1, 1981, Ilene Cooper, review of *A Dark, Dark Tale*, p. 494; March 1, 1991, Hazel Rochman, review of *The World That Jack Built*, p. 1397; October 1, 1994, Ellen Mandel, review of *Copycat*, p. 331; September 1, 1996, Susan Dove Lempke, review of *Ben's Christmas Carol*, p. 1; July, 1997, p. 1822; January 1, 1998, Hazel Rochman, review of *Baba Yaga and the Wise Doll: A Traditional Russian Folktale*, p. 818; October 1, 1998, Helen Rosenberg, review of *The Shy Little Angel*, p. 334; November 1, 1998, Phyllis Wilson, review of *Ladybug, Ladybug*, p. 479; June 1, 1999, John Peters, review of *A Mad Summer Night's Dream*, p. 1838; September 1, 2000, Hazel Rochman, review of *Holly*, p. 129; May 15, 2001, Hazel Rochman, review of *Ten Seeds*, p. 1754.

Books for Keeps, May, 1986, Chris Powling, review of *Our Cat Flossie*, p. 27; May, 1992, p. 27; May, 1993, Moira Small, review of *The Big Sneeze*, pp. 7, 36; September, 1997, p. 20.

Bulletin of the Center for Children's Books, October, 1987, Betsy Hearne, review of *Our Puppy's Vacation*, p. 23; March, 1991, pp. 159-160; November, 1991, Betsy Hearne, review of *Alphabet Times Four: An International ABC*, pp. 57-58; September, 1996, p. 6; March, 1997, Deborah Stevenson, review of *Toad*, p. 2442; December, 2000, review of *Holly*, p. 136.

Growing Point, July, 1988, Margery Fisher, review of *Ladybird, Ladybird*, p. 5013.

Horn Book, January-February, 1986, p. 54; January-February, 1987, p. 46; March-April, 1998, Lauren Adams, review of *Baba Yaga and the Wise Doll*, p. 227; September, 2001, review of *Ten Seeds*, p. 570.

Junior Bookshelf, December, 1982, review of *If at First You Do Not See*, p. 218; August, 1985, review of *The Big Sneeze*, p. 172; December, 1991, review of *The Four-Tongued Alphabet: An Alphabet Book in Four Languages*, p. 238; February, 1993, review of *One Stormy Night*, p. 11.

Kirkus Reviews, November 15, 1981, review of *A Dark, Dark Tale*, p. 1403; September 15, 1991, p. 1230.

Magpies, March, 1991, Cynthia Anthony, review of *The World That Jack Built*, p. 26; July, 1993, Kristina Lindsay, *The Picnic*, p. 27; March, 2002, review of *Ten Seeds*, p. 26.

New York Times Book Review, March 14, 1993, p. 18.

Publishers Weekly, May 13, 1983, review of *If at First You Do Not See*, p. 57; October 13, 1989, review of *The Market Square Dog*, p. 51; July 5, 1993, p. 70; August 22, 1994, review of *Copycat*, p. 54; December 12, 1994, p. 62; March 11, 1996, review of *The Ghost of Greyfriar's Bobby*, p. 63; September 30, 1996, p. 89; January 12, 1998, review of *Baba Yaga and the Wise Doll*, p. 58; September 28, 1998, review of *The Shy Little Angel*, p. 57; June 7, 1999, review of *Mad Summer Night's Dream*, p. 82; November 13, 2000, review of *Holly*, p. 103.

School Librarian, August, 1997, Angela Redfern, review of *Baba*, pp. 129-130; winter, 2002, review of *Lion in the Long Grass*, p. 185; summer, 2003, review of *Helpful Henry*, p. 73.

School Library Journal, September, 1983, Christine C. Seibold, review of *Crazy Charlie*, p. 102; November, 1986, Christina Olson, review of *Our Cat Flossie*, pp. 72-73; January, 1988, Kristi Thomas Beavin, review of *Our Puppy's Vacation*, p. 63; March, 1993, Judy Constantinides, review of *The Picnic*, p. 171; March, 1995, p. 187; August, 1996, Lisa S. Murphy, review of *The Ghost of Greyfriar's Bobby*, p. 133; March, 1997, Caroline Ward, review of *Toad*, p. 149; February, 1998, p. 79; October, 1998, review of *The Shy Little Angel*, p. 40; October, 2000, review of *Holly*, p. 57; July, 2001, Patricia Pearl Dole, review of *Ten Seeds*, p. 73.

Times Educational Supplement, July 18, 1997, p. 35.

ONLINE

Andersen Press Web site, http://www.andersenpress.co.uk/ (April 27, 2006), "Ruth Brown."*

* * *

BUTLER, M. Christina 1934-

Personal

Born December 11, 1934, in Scarborough, North Yorkshire, England; daughter of Harold Cautley (a hotel proprietor and engineer) and Mabel (Manners) Tutill; married William Anthony Butler (a political agent), August 23, 1958; children: Katharyn Charlotte, Frances Emma. *Education:* Attended St. Joseph's Convent. *Politics:* Conservative. *Religion:* Church of England (Anglican). *Hobbies and other interests:* Music, swimming, walking, travel, reading.

Addresses

Home—West Bank, Wold Newton Hall, Driffield, East Riding, Yorkshire YO25 3YF, England. *Agent*—c/o Author Mail, Little Tiger Press, 1 The Coda Ctr., 189 Munster Rd., London SW6 6AW, England.

Career

Leeds General Infirmary, Leeds, England, state-registered nurse, 1953-57; Halifax Infirmary, Sheffield, England, worked in Outpatient's Casualty Department, 1958-60, district nursing sister, 1960-65. Playgroup supervisor, 1973-76; preschool nursery supervisor, 1977-84, 1987. Served on various village committees; governor of local primary school, 1973-77, 1989—; local church warden.

Member

Fine Arts Society.

Writings

Can I Live with You?, illustrated by Meg Rutherford, Macdonald Picture Books (Hove, England), 1988, published as *Can I Stay with You?,* Dial (New York, NY), 1988.

Too Many Eggs, illustrated by Meg Rutherford, David Godine (London, England), 1988.

Where Are My Bananas?, Macdonald Picture Books (Hove, England), 1989.

Stanley in the Dark, illustrated by Meg Rutherford, Simon & Schuster (Hemel Hempstead, England), 1990.

Picnic Pandemonium, illustrated by Margaret Rutherford, George Stevens, 1991.

The Dinosaur's Egg, illustrated by Val Biro, Simon & Schuster (Hemel Hempstead, England), 1992.

Mole in a Hole (and Bear in a Lair), illustrated by Meg Rutherford, Simon & Schuster (Hemel Hempstead, England), 1993.

Archie the Ugly Dinosaur, illustrated by Val Biro, Barron's (Hauppauge, NY), 1996.

The Dinosaurs' Dinner, illustrated by Val Biro, Macdonald Young (Hove, England), 1997.

Big Bad Rex, illustrated by Val Biro, Macdonald Young (Hove, England), 1999.

Who's Been Eating My Porridge?, illustrated by Daniel Howarth, Little Tiger (Wilton, CT), 2004.

One Snowy Night, illustrated by Tina Macnaughton, Good Books (Intercourse, PA), 2004.

Snow Friends, illustrated by Tina Macnaughton, Good Books (Intercourse, PA), 2005.

Also author of children's serials and short stories for local radio.

Sidelights

British writer M. Christina Butler draws from her love of nature and her fond memories of farm life in many of her books for younger readers. In *One Snowy Night* a young hedgehog worries that he has no gifts for his many best friends; *Snow Friends* features a cast of animal characters—Bear, Otter, and Rabbit—as they band together to make the best snowman ever; and *Can I Stay with You?* follows a tiny bird after he falls out of his safe nest and must make his way home. In *Who's*

M. Christina Butler takes a new twist on a traditional tale in Who's Been Eating My Porridge?, *featuring illustrations by Daniel Howarth.* (Text copyright © 2004 by M. Christina Butler. Illustrations copyright © 2004 Daniel Howarth. Reproduced by permission of Tiger Tales.)

Been Eating My Porridge? a young bear's struggle at the dinner table due to his refusal to eat his porridge is resolved by his imaginative mom. Praising the illustrations by Daniel Howarth, Andrea Tarr wrote in *School Library Journal* that in *Who's Been Eating My Porridge?* Butler spins "a pleasant tale, complete with a mild surprise at the end.

Butler was born in Scarborough, a seaside resort in North Yorkshire. While she was still young, her family moved to a small village, and these rural surroundings provided her with memories that she would later draw upon in writing her books for young children. "At a time when farming embraced a rich variety of activities that young people could take part in, I was fortunate enough to have a farmer's daughter as my best friend," she once recalled to *SATA*. "From the age of about eight years old, weekends and holidays were spent on the farm. There was so much to do. We devised our own games—had secret codes, maps, and dens. Our constant companions were dogs and horses."

Spending most of her time out of doors did not leave Butler much time for reading when she was young, although she recalls being read to by her mother. The stories of Hans Christian Andersen were among her favorites: "*The Little Match Girl . . .* never failed to have us both in tears long before the end," recalled the writer.

"I loved art but was never drawn to long essay writing," Butler admitted, adding that she "was, however, extremely happy at school." When she turned eighteen, she enrolled at Leeds General Infirmary in West Yorkshire, where she obtained her state registration as a nurse after four years of study. Following graduation, she married William Anthony Butler, and it was his busy career that prompted Butler to begin her own career as a children's book author. "As my husband was often attending evening meetings, [I] began writing children's stories. For years I wrote for local radio; short stories and serials, but always cherished the hope of being published," Butler once explained. The many hours she spent reading aloud after the birth of her two daughters were followed by several years spent working with other children as the supervisor of a nursery school. Butler became familiar with the wide variety of books available for young children and grew interested in the idea of writing children's picture books. In 1987, *Can I Stay with You?*, her first book, was published. Designed as a novelty picture book, it is the story of a little bird who tries to find a new home after he accidentally falls out of the family nest. Other books by Butler include *Too Many Nests*, *Stanley in the Dark*, and *Big Bad Rex*, the last illustrated by Val Biro.

Several of Butler's characters are based on people she recalls from her childhood spent on the farm. "Mrs. Bear in *Too Many Eggs* is my farming friend's mother—the best cook in the world who never used a recipe in her life," she explained. "The mouse in *Stanley in the Dark* is a memory of long walks over the field in the dark to fasten the poultry houses, surrounded by the sounds and shadows of the night, some rather scary."

"The picture-book format is my ideal medium," Butler once explained. "With an interest in art—and not being particularly disposed to writing long tracts of text—I find the combination of moving the story on in the pictures and with a minimum of words fascinating." "To be able to write stories for young children that captivate, stimulate, entertain, and inform in an humorous way and leave them wanting more is my overriding ambition," the author/illustrator continued. "There is something very special about a group of wide-eyed four year olds listening intently to a story."

Biographical and Critical Sources

PERIODICALS

Horn Book, July, 1990, p. 36.
Kirkus Reviews, August 1, 2004, review of *Who's Been Eating My Porridge?*, p. 738; October 1, 2005, review of *Snow Friends,* p. 1077.
School Library Journal, February, 1989, p. 66; January, 2005, Andrea Tarr, review of *Who's Been Eating My Porridge?*, p. 88; November, 2005, Amelia Jenkins, review of *Snow Friends,* p. 83.
Times Educational Supplement, March 11, 1988, p. 24; March 29, 1991, p. 23.

C

CAMPER, Cathy 1956-

Personal
Born 1956, in Madison, WI. *Ethnicity:* "Arab-American." *Education:* A.M.L.S. (library science). *Hobbies and other interests:* Fossilized insects, martial arts films, swimming, running, exploring, music, making art out of seeds and toy robots out of "junk."

Addresses
Home—Portland, OR. *Agent*—c/o Author Mail, Simon & Schuster, 1230 Avenue of the Americas, New York, NY 10020. *E-mail*—cfastwolf@hotmail.com.

Career
Librarian and author. Minneapolis Public Library, Minneapolis, MN, librarian until 2005; currently librarian in Portland, OR. *Sugar Needle*, co-editor; member of board of *Mizna* (Arab-American literary journal), 2000-05. Freelance writer and lecturer.

Writings
Bugs before Time: Prehistoric Insects and Their Relatives, illustrated by Steve Kirk, Simon & Schuster (New York, NY), 2002.

Contributor of articles, short fiction, and artwork to periodicals, including *Cicada, Cricket, Wired, Mizna, Boy Trouble, Other Voices, Musician, Utne Reader, Sugar Needle,* and *Giant Robot.* Contributor of reviews to periodicals, including *School Library Journal, Kirkus Reviews, Five Owls,* and *Women's Review of Books.*

Work in Progress
A trilogy of novels for young adults: *Circle A, Land of Nod,* and *Beautiful Mistakes.*

Sidelights
An interest in paleontology, along with her work as a librarian and book reviewer for periodicals such as *School Library Journal* and *Kirkus Reviews,* helped inspire Cathy Camper to write the children's book *Bugs before Time: Prehistoric Insects and Their Relatives.* She has worked hard to promote alternative materials and ideas via her writing, and in libraries, and to support Arab-American culture. In addition to writing, Camper lectures on insect matters to school and library groups, is a first-degree black belt in tae kwon do, and has been creating "seed art"—pictures made from various seeds—since the late 1980s. Her colorful work, featuring political and cultural figures ranging from civil-rights activist Malcolm X to television's Xena the Warrior Princess, as well as animal images, has been a tradition at the Minnesota State Fair since 1989.

Bugs before Time provides young readers with an informative and entertaining look at the evolution of insects since prehistoric times. In addition, the book examines several related topics, such as how fossils are formed and the manner in which Earth's tectonic plates have shifted over time. Illustrator Steve Kirk's bright illustrations, along with a colorful time line that accompanies the story, help to engross readers even further. *Bugs before Time* "is sure to entrance budding entomologists and surprise dinophiles with the Arthropoda's long evolutionary history," commented Patricia Manning in a review for *School Library Journal.* Kay Weisman, writing in *Booklist,* also thoroughly enjoyed Camper's publishing debut, stating that the book "will be popular with dinosaur enthusiasts who are ready to branch out to other prehistoric species." A *Kirkus Reviews* critic predicted that Camper's "irresistible" "title will fly off the shelves and send shivers of delight."

Biographical and Critical Sources

PERIODICALS

Booklist, March 15, 2002, Kay Weisman, review of *Bugs before Time: Prehistoric Insects and Their Relatives,* p. 1252.
Kirkus Reviews, March 1, 2002, review of *Bugs before Time,* p. 330.

Cover of Cathy Camper's Bugs before Time, *featuring artwork by Steve Kirk.* (Text copyright © 2002 by Cathy Camper. Illustrations copyright © 2002 by Steve Kirk. Reproduced by permission of Simon & Schuster Books for Young Readers, an imprint of Simon & Schuster Children's Publishing Division.)

School Library Journal, May, 2002, Patricia Manning, review of *Bugs before Time,* p. 166.
Science Books & Films, November, 2002, review of *Bugs before Time,* p. 564.

ONLINE

Cathy Camper Home Page, http://www.cathycamper.com (April 11, 2006).
Children's Literature Network, http://www.childrensliteraturenetwork.org/ (April 11, 2006), "Cathy Camper."
Crop Art Gallery Web site, http://www.cropart.com/ (April 11, 2006), "Cathy Camper."

* * *

CAREY, Charles W., Jr. 1951-

Personal

Born June 16, 1951, in Norfolk, VA; son of Charles (an electronics engineer) and Jean Carey; married Deborah Lane (a registered nurse), June 15, 1974; children: Billy, Beth, Jeff, Diana. *Ethnicity:* "Euro-American." *Education:* University of Virginia, B.A. (English), 1973; Virginia Tech, M.A. (history), 1995. *Politics:* Democrat. *Religion:* Roman Catholic. *Hobbies and other interests:* Canoeing, kayaking, miniature wargaming.

Addresses

Home—1102 Biltmore Ave., Lynchburg, VA 24502.
E-mail—historian@centralva.net.

Career

Freelance writer, 1996—. Adjunct history instructor at colleges, including Central Virginia Community College, 1995-2004, Lynchburg College, 1997-2001, Virginia Tech, 2003—, Roanoke College, 2003—, and Radford University, 2004.

Member

Virginia Social Science Association.

Awards, Honors

Writing fellow, American Council of Learned Societies, 1996-98; Spur Award finalist for Best Western Juvenile Nonfiction, Western Writers of America, 2003, for *The Mexican War.*

Writings

George Washington Carver, Child's World (Chanhassen, MN), 1999.
The Emancipation Proclamation, Child's World (Chanhassen, MN), 2000.
American Inventors, Entrepreneurs, and Business Visionaries, Facts on File (New York, NY), 2002.
The Mexican War: "Mr. Polk's War," Enslow Publishers (Berkeley Heights, NJ), 2002.
(Editor) *Life under Soviet Communism,* Greenhaven Press (San Diego, CA), 2003.
Eugene V. Debs: Outspoken Labor Leaders and Socialist, Enslow Publishers (Berkeley Heights, NJ), 2003.
(Editor) *Castro's Cuba,* Greenhaven Press (San Diego, CA), 2004.
(Editor) *The Kennedy Assassination,* Greenhaven Press (San Diego, CA), 2004.
African-American Political Leaders, Facts on File (New York, NY), 2004.
(Editor) *The American Revolution,* Greenhaven Press (San Diego, CA), 2004.
Living through the Korean War, Greenhaven Press (San Diego, CA), 2006.
American Scientists, Facts on File (New York, NY), 2006.

Contributor to books, including *Macmillan Encyclopedia of World Slavery,* Simon & Schuster, 1998; *American National Biography,* Oxford University Press, 1999; *New Encyclopedia of American Scandal,* Facts on File, 2001; *Encyclopedia of American Political History,* CQ Press, 2001; *Invisible Giants: Fifty Americans Who Shaped the Nation but Missed the History Books,* edited by Mark C. Carnes, Oxford University Press, 2002; and *Dictionary of Historical Documents,* Facts on File, 2003. Contributor to periodicals, including *Virginia Social Science Journal.*

Work in Progress

African Americans in Science, for ABC-Clio.

Sidelights

Charles W. Carey, Jr., told *SATA:* "I knew I wanted to write for a living when I was ten years old, but I didn't actually start until I was in my forties. I always wanted to write the Great American Novel until I realized I wrote lousy fiction. But in graduate school I discovered that I could write pretty good history, and I've been dong it ever since."

Biographical and Critical Sources

PERIODICALS

Booklist, November 1, 2002, review of *American Inventors, Entrepreneurs, and Business Visionaries,* p. 522; July, 2004, review of *African-American Political Leaders,* p. 1860.
Choice, February, 2003, L. Kong, review of *American Inventors, Entrepreneurs, and Business Visionaries,* p. 965; July-August, 2004, N.M. Allen, review of *African-American Political Leaders,* p. 2024.
School Library Journal, January, 2003, review of *The Mexican War: "Mr. Polk's War,"* p. 150; October, 2003, Elizabeth Talbot, review of *Life under Soviet Communism,* p. 184; November, 2004, Doris Losey, review of *Castro's Cuba,* p. 160.

* * *

CARHEDEN, Görel Kristina
See NÄSLUND, Görel Kristina

* * *

CARNEY, Mary Lou 1949-

Personal
Born 1949; married; husband's name Gary; children: two. *Education:* Olivet Nazarene University, B.A.; Valparaiso University, M.A.

Addresses
Home—272 E. 1225 N., Chesterton, IN 46304.

Career
Author of inspirational and devotional works and editor. *Guideposts for Kids,* editor; public speaker.

Writings

RELIGIOUS AND INSPIRATIONAL WRITINGS FOR YOUNG PEOPLE, EXCEPT AS NOTED

There's an Angel in My Locker: Devotionals for Junior Highers, Zondervan Books (Grand Rapids, MI), 1986, 2nd edition published as *Angel in My Locker: Devotions for Junior Highers,* 1992.
Angel in My Backpack, Zondervan Books (Grand Rapids, MI), 1987, 2nd edition published as *Angel in My Backpack: Summer Camp Devotions for Junior Highers,* 1992.
Angel in My Attic: Devotions for Junior High Girls, Zondervan Books (Grand Rapids, MI), 1988.

Bible Knock Knocks and Other Fun Stuff, illustrated by Charlie Cox, Abingdon Books (Nashville, TN), 1988.
Jump Right In, illustrated by Stephen DeStefano, Guideposts Publishers (Carmel, NY), 1989.
Make a Wish, F.H. Revell (Tarrytown, NY), 1991.
Dear Wally, I've Got This Problem, illustrated by Susan Scruggs and Charles Cox, F.H. Revell (Tarrytown, NY), 1991.
Too Tough to Hurt, Zondervan Books (Grand Rapids, MI), 1991, revised edition published as *Wrestling with an Angel: A Devotional Novel for Junior Highers,* 1993.
How Do You Hug an Angel?: A Devotional Novel for Junior Highers, Zondervan Books (Grand Rapids, MI), 1993.
(Editor) *Absolutely Angels: Poems for Children and Other Believers,* illustrated by Viqui Maggio, Wordsong/Boyds Mills Press (Honesdale, PA), 1998.
The Power of Positive Thinking for Teens (based on *The Power of Positive Thinking* by Norman Vincent Peale), Ideals Publications (Nashville, TN), 2002.
Tyler Timothy Bradford and the Birthday Surprise (picture book), illustrated by Shari Warren, Gingham Dog Press (Columbus, OH), 2005.
Dr. Welch and the Great Grape Story (picture book), illustrated by Sherry Meidel, Boyds Mills Press (Honesdale, PA), 2005.

FOR ADULTS

Bubble Gum and Chalk Dust: Prayers and Poems for Teachers, Abingdon Press (Nashville, TN), 1982.
A Month of Mondays: Prayers and Poems for the Monday Morning Homemaker Blues, Abingdon Press (Nashville, TN), 1984.
Heart Cries: Prayers of Biblical Women, Abingdon Press (Nashville (TN), 1986.
Spiritual Harvest: Reflections on the Fruit of the Spirit, Abingdon Press (Nashville, TN), 1987.

Sidelights

Mary Lou Carney is the writer of numerous devotional books for children, including *Angel in My Locker: Devotions for Junior Highers, Angel in My Backpack: Summer Camp Devotions for Junior Highers,* and *Angel in My Attic: Devotions for Junior High Girls,* in addition to inspirational works such as *Wrestling with an Angel: A Devotional Novel for Junior Highers.* With the 1998 title *Absolutely Angels: Poems for Children and Other Believers,* she edited works on the theme of angels as protectors from amateurs as well as writers such as Emily Dickinson. Writing for *School Library Journal,* Peg Solonika called the anthology an "uneven hodgepodge of angel-themed poetry" but also felt that the "simple structures filled with optimism and a sincere belief in angels" might appeal to some children. For Susan Dove Lempke, reviewing the same collection in *Booklist,* the "poetry is pleasant if not transcendent" and is paired with "charming, whimsical" illustrations.

Carney turned to less devotional topics with her picture book *Tyler Timothy Bradford and the Birthday Surprise.* Here the eponymous protagonist remembers too late that it is his teacher's thirtieth birthday, and each child was supposed to bring a collection of thirty items to share with the teacher. As he frets and walks toward school, he nibbles on a chocolate cupcake, crumbs of which fall to the sidewalk and attract a troop of ants. The ants continue to follow the young boy to school, thirty of them taking up residence in an ant farm at the back of the class right on cue for him to present to his teacher. While Linda Staskus, reviewing the title in *School Library Journal,* allowed that the book might be employed as a "supplement [to] a unit on number sets," she also complained of the "contrived" and "incredible" ending to the tale.

With the picture book *Dr. Welch and the Great Grape Story,* Carney relates the story of how, in 1869, Dr. Thomas Bramwell Welch, a small-town New Jersey dentist, invented the nonfermented grape juice product that is still known by his name. In Carney's version, Welch was inspired by a desire to make a nonalcoholic alternative to communion wine. Hope Morrison, writing in *Bulletin of the Center for Children's Books,* noted that the book is short on the science of how Welch managed to avoid fermentation of his grapes, but concluded that there is "something inspiring about the age-old story of the common man rising in his ranks." Voicing the same objections regarding the lack of science in the book, a critic for *Kirkus Reviews* nonetheless called Carney's book an "intriguing tale." Higher praise came from Vicki Arkoff, writing in *MBR Bookwatch.* Arkoff commended the "lively prose" in Carney's "remarkable true story of grape juice's journey from idea to invention," and Patricia Manning, writing in *School Library Journal,* called *Dr. Welch and the Great Grape Story,* a "story to be enjoyed while sipping cool grape juice."

Biographical and Critical Sources

PERIODICALS

Atlanta Journal-Constitution, December 19, 1998, Julie Bookman, review of *Absolutely Angels: Poems for Children and Other Believers,* p. E4.
Booklist, November 1, 1998, Susan Dove Lempke, review of *Absolutely Angels,* p. 496; May 1, 2005, Jennifer Locke, review of *Dr. Welch and the Great Grape Story,* p. 1588.
Bulletin of the Center for Children's Books, June, 2005, Hope Morrison, review of *Dr. Welch and the Great Grape Story,* p. 431.
Children's Bookwatch, June, 2005, review of *Dr. Welch and the Great Grape Story.*
Kirkus Reviews, March 1, 2005, review of *Dr. Welch and the Great Grape Story,* p. 284.

MBR Bookwatch, March, 2005, Vicki Arkoff, review of *Dr. Welch and the Great Grape Story.*

School Library Journal, November, 1998, Peg Solonika, review of *Absolutely Angels,* p. 103; November, 2004, Linda Staskus, review of *Tyler Timothy Bradford and the Birthday Surprise,* p. 92; July, 2005, Patricia Manning, review of *Dr. Welch and the Great Grape Story,* p. 86.

ONLINE

Directory of Indiana Children's Authors and Illustrators Web site, http:// www.statelib.lib.in.us/ (September 12, 2005), "Carney, Mary Lou."*

* * *

CARTER, David A. 1957-

Personal
Born March 4, 1957, in Salt Lake City, UT; son of H. Craig (a draftsperson) and Lavon (a homemaker; maiden name, Gill) Carter; married Noelle Lokvig (an illustrator and author), August 10, 1985; children: Molly, Emma. *Education:* Attended Utah State University. *Hobbies and other interests:* Skiing, travel, gardening, tennis.

Addresses
Home and office—14009 Sheridan Ct., Auburn, CA 95603. *E-mail*—PopArt123@aol.com.

Career
Graphic designer and advertising illustrator, c. late 1970s; Intervisual Communications, Inc., California, artist, paper engineer, and book designer until 1987; freelance author and illustrator of children's books, 1987—.

Writings

SELF-ILLUSTRATED

What's in My Pocket?, Putnam (New York, NY), 1989.
Surprise Party, Grosset & Dunlap (New York, NY), 1990.
(With Lynette Ruschak) *Snack Attack: A Tasty Pop-Up Book,* Simon & Schuster (New York, NY), 1990.
Playful Pandas, National Geographic Society (Washington, DC), 1991.
In a Dark, Dark Wood, Simon & Schuster (New York, NY), 1991, published as *In a Dark, Dark Wood: An Old Tale with a New Twist,* Simon & Schuster (New York, NY), 2002.
Jingle Bugs, Simon & Schuster (New York, NY), 1992.
Opposites, Simon & Schuster (New York, NY), 1993.
Colors, Simon & Schuster (New York, NY), 1993.
Counting, Simon & Schuster (New York, NY), 1993.
I'm Shy, Simon & Schuster (New York, NY), 1993.
(With Roger Smith) *In and Out,* Simon & Schuster (New York, NY), 1993.
Says Who?, Simon & Schuster (New York, NY), 1993.
(With James Diaz) *The Elements of Pop-Up: A Pop-Up Book for Aspiring Paper Engineers,* Simon & Schuster (New York, NY), 1999.
Flapdoodle Dinosaurs: A Colorful Pop-Up Book, Simon & Schuster (New York, NY), 2001.
Who Took the Cookie from the Cookie Jar?: Fun Flaps and Pop-Up Surprises, Scholastic (New York, NY), 2002.
Glitter Critters: David Carter's Pop-Up Book, Piggy Toes Press (Los Angeles, CA), 2003.
(With James Diaz) *Let's Make It Pop-Up,* Simon & Schuster (New York, NY), 2004.
One Red Dot, Simon & Schuster (New York, NY), 2005.
Woof! Woof!, Simon & Schuster (New York, NY), 2006.
Blue 2, Simon & Schuster (New York, NY), 2006.

SELF-ILLUSTRATED; "BUGS" SERIES

How Many Bugs in a Box?, Simon & Schuster (New York, NY), 1988.
More Bugs in Boxes, Simon & Schuster (New York, NY), 1990.
Alpha Bugs, Simon & Schuster (New York, NY), 1994.
Love Bugs, Simon & Schuster (New York, NY), 1995.
Feely Bugs, Simon & Schuster (New York, NY), 1995, published in a reduced size edition, 2005.
Bugs in Space, Simon & Schuster (New York, NY), 1997.
Finger Bugs Love Bug, Simon & Schuster (New York, NY), 1997.
Bugs at Play, Simon & Schuster (New York, NY), 1997.
Bugs at Work, Simon & Schuster (New York, NY), 1997.
Busy Bugs, Lazy Bugs, Simon & Schuster (New York, NY), 1997.
Bugs on the Go, Simon & Schuster (New York, NY), 1997.
Stinky Bugs, Simon & Schuster (New York, NY), 1998.
Bed Bugs: A Pop-Up Bedtime Book, Simon & Schuster (New York, NY), 1998.
The Twelve Bugs of Christmas: A Pop-Up Christmas Counting Book, Simon & Schuster (New York, NY), 1999.
Giggle Bugs: A Lift-and-Laugh Book, Simon & Schuster (New York, NY), 1999.
Easter Bugs: A Springtime Pop-Up, Simon & Schuster (New York, NY), 2001.
Chanukah Bugs: A Pop-Up Celebration, Simon & Schuster (New York, NY), 2002.
Peekaboo Bugs: A Hide-and-Seek Book, Simon & Schuster (New York, NY), 2002.
Halloween Bugs: A Trick-or-Treat Pop-Up, Simon & Schuster (New York, NY), 2003.

AND ILLUSTRATOR, WITH WIFE, NOELLE CARTER

I'm a Little Mouse, Holt (New York, NY), 1990.
Merry Christmas, Little Mouse: A Scratch-the-Scent and Lift-the-Flap Book, Holt (New York, NY), 1993.
Peek-a-Boo Little Mouse: A Pat & Play Lift-the-Flap Book, Holt (New York, NY), 1993.
The Nutcracker: A Pop-Up Adaptation of E.T.A. Hoffman's Original Tale, Simon & Schuster (New York, NY), 2000.
Little Mouse's Christmas, Piggy Toes Press (Los Angeles, CA), 2003.

ILLUSTRATOR, DESIGNER, AND/OR PAPER ENGINEER

(With Dick Dudley) Joan Knight, *Journey to Egypt,* illustrated by Piero Ventura, Viking Kestrel (New York, NY), 1986.
Peter Seymour, *Sleeping Beauty,* illustrated by John Wallner, Viking Penguin (New York, NY), 1987.
Peter Seymour, *The Three Little Pigs,* illustrated by John Wallner, Viking Penguin (New York, NY), 1987.
Jannat Messenger, *Lullaby and Goodnight: A Bedtime Book with Music,* Aladdin Books (New York, NY), 1988.
Peter Seymour, *How Things Are Made,* illustrated by Linda Griffith, E.P. Dutton (New York, NY), 1988.
Seymour Simon, *How to Be an Ocean Scientist in Your Own Home,* Lippincott (Philadelphia, PA), 1988.
Peter Seymour, *What's in the Jungle?,* Holt (New York, NY), 1988.
Peter Seymour, *If Pigs Could Fly,* Child's Play, 1988.
Tony Ross, *The Pop-Up Book of Nonsense Verse,* Random House (New York, NY), 1989.
Karen E. Lotz, *The First Christmas: With Four Classic Nativity Ornaments,* illustrated by Joyce Patti, Dutton Children's Books (New York, NY), 1990.
Peter Seymour, *What's in the Prehistoric Forest?,* Holt (New York, NY), 1990.
Peter Seymour, *What's in the Deep Blue Sea?,* Holt (New York, NY), 1990.
Olive A. Wadsworth, *Over in the Meadow: An Old Counting Rhyme,* Scholastic (New York, NY), 1992.
Peter Seymour, *What's in the Cave?,* Holt (New York, NY), 1995.
Grace Maccarone, *Cars, Cars, Cars,* Scholastic (New York, NY), 1995.
Peter Seymour, *What's at the Beach?,* Holt (New York, NY), 1995.
Sarah Weeks, *Noodles: A Pop-Up Book,* HarperCollins (New York, NY), 1996.
Mary Serfozo, *There's a Square: A Book about Shapes,* Scholastic (New York, NY), 1996.
(With David Pelham) Michael Foreman, *Ben's Box: A Pop-Up Fantasy,* Piggy Toes Press (Kansas City, MO), 1997.
Deborah Nourse Lattimore, *I Wonder What's under There?: A Brief History of Underwear,* Browndeer Press (San Diego, CA), 1998.
Alan Benjamin, *Curious Critters: A Pop-Up Menagerie,* Simon & Schuster (New York, NY), 1998.
Sarah Weeks, *Who's under My Hat?,* Harcourt (New York, NY), 2005.
Sarah Weeks, *Ruff! Ruff! Where's Scruff?,* Harcourt (New York, NY), 2006.

Sidelights

David A. Carter is the author or illustrator of several dozen pop-up books for young children, several written with his wife, author and illustrator Noelle Carter. His works have won praise for their clever tactile surfaces and appealing shapes and colors. As Carter once told *SATA:* "I am often asked by children where I get my ideas for books. I have spent many hours contemplating this question and I still do not have the answer." As a child, Carter recalled, "I would play outside all day, spending hours on end in the fields around my home, lifting up rocks and boards in search of bugs. It was always very exciting to lift up the rocks because I never knew what I would find. . . . Lifting something to find a bug was one of my greatest thrills as a child and that is exactly what I had created, unconsciously, in *How Many Bugs in a Box?*"

How Many Bugs in a Box? is one of many titles by Carter that uses insects as a theme to enchant preschoolers. This debut was published in 1987, the same year Carter left his publishing job to become a freelance writer, illustrator, and paper engineer. *How Many Bugs in a Box?* is a counting lesson, with successive page spreads depicting a different type and number of insects, such as "seven space bugs." A *Publishers Weekly* reviewer found it rich in "startlingly bright illustrations" that might easily entice young readers.

After working or collaborating on several other books, Carter returned to the insect world with the 1990 title *More Bugs in Boxes.* Here, he presents a series of questions that lead young readers into guessing the contents of each box. The bugs revealed are, like the pages themselves, drawn in vivid colors and also boast interesting textures; spitfire flies are silvery, for instance, while basketball bugs possess a rubbery texture. Anne Connor, reviewing the book for *School Library Journal,* called *More Bugs in Boxes* an "engineering feat" with "sometimes amazing effects."

Carter's "Bugs" books have been among his most popular titles, and they range in theme from holidays to activities and games to jokes. In *Giggle Bugs: A Lift-and-Laugh Book* readers must pull open flaps to reveal "punchlines to fifty-eight bug-related jokes," according to a reviewer for *Publishers Weekly. The Twelve Bugs of Christmas: A Pop-Up Christmas Counting Book* parodies the traditional holiday carol; there are boxes to unwrap on each spread and "inside each box is a new bug surprise," wrote a *Publishers Weekly* reviewer. Using the same technique for *Easter Bugs: A Springtime Pop-Up,* Carter "conceal[s] his whimsical 'bugs' behind Easter egg-shaped flaps." *Chanukah Bugs: A Pop-Up Celebration* features creatures hiding in dreidels and

Cover of David A. Carter's interactive holiday offering, Chanukah Bugs. (Copyright © 2002 by David A. Carter. Reproduced by permission of Little Simon, an imprint of Simon & Schuster Children's Publishing Division.)

among the latke, "combining humor with handsome graphics" according to Susan Patron in *School Library Journal.*

Carter has also won praise for other works that play upon children's fascination with the animal kingdom. His 1989 book for preschoolers, *What's in My Pocket?,* employs a series of five animals whose heads pop up as the pages are turned. His text poses questions that lead the reader to open another flap on each page, a pocket for the creature that, when lifted, shows what the animal's favorite food is: the rabbit has a carrot, the mouse hides cheese, and so forth. A reviewer for *Junior Bookshelf* found that "the animals have distinctive characters" and, "altogether, there are many things to notice and plenty of movement" in *What's in My Pocket?* Reviewing the work for *Bulletin of the Center for Children's Books,* Zena Sutherland admired Carter's talent for "nice composition and bright color in pictures with no clutter."

Flapdoodle Dinosaurs: A Colorful Pop-Up Book finds members of the early animal kingdom popping up in a modern setting. Shrunk to small enough so that they fit into pickle jars or loaves of bread, all the dinosaurs are hidden behind flaps to pop out at young readers. A *Publishers Weekly* critic found the book to be "just plain fun." *Who Put the Cookie in the Cookie Jar?* uses the same technique, though this one hides miniature thieves in large cookie jars, giving the traditional rhyme "a new twist" according to a *Publishers Weekly* critic.

Working to create new and different "kinetic sculpture," Carter designed and created *One Red Dot,* telling an interviewer for the Powells Books Web site: "With this book, I want you to touch the art." A combination counting book and seek-and-find game, *One Red Dot* reveals paper sculptures with a different number of features on each page, as well as one red dot hidden somewhere on each sculpture. The "graphically bold pop-up book . . . entices readers" to hunt for the single red dot, according to Lisa Gangemi Krapp in *School Library Journal.* Bao Ong, writing in *Newsweek,* reported that the book is designed for "children of all ages," and Lolly Robinson wrote in *Horn Book* that many adult "pop-up aficionados" will appreciate the abstract designs. Robinson also felt that with *One Red Dot,* "Carter pulls out all the stops in a veritable catalog of paper-engineering effects."

Along with pop-up sculptures and lift-the-flap puzzles, Carter has created *Woof! Woof!,* a guessing-game book featuring die-cut holes for readers to feel as well as look at. At the beginning of the book, the shapes have little meaning, but by the end the geometric patterns have become dogs. "The graphical simplicity combines with the touch-and-feel feature to create a perfectly delightful interactive mystery," wrote a contributor to *Kirkus Reviews.*

With his wife, author and illustrator Noelle Carter, Carter has also created titles such as *I'm a Little Mouse.* This story centers on a young mouse who has become lost; he then goes about introducing himself to other animals by explaining that he has fuzzy gray fur and a long tail. In response, the other creatures describe their unique characteristics to him, such as "slippery shiny skin" or "long shaggy hair." Carter creates unusual simulations of such textured surfaces, thus reinforcing his story's text. "Preschoolers will want to touch the mouse and his perky pals again and again," wrote a reviewer for *Publishers Weekly.*

In addition to his solo works, Carter has also collaborated with other authors, such as Mary Serfozo, with whom he created 1996's *There's a Square: A Book about Shapes,* and Peter Seymour, with whom Carter has worked for several years. One of Seymour and Carter's joint efforts, *What's in the Deep Blue Sea?,* offers an unusual strategy: a young tiger stalks through the jungle on his way to the water, where he looks down to see a pair of whiskers, much like his own, appraising him. Throughout the pages, animals hide behind lift-up flaps, and like many books in the pop-up genre, the story's grand finale is designed to electrify young imaginations. In a review of *What's in the Deep Blue Sea?* a *Publishers Weekly* contributor called Carter's images "luxuriant" and commended "the use of dark, saturant color and dry over dry painting to create stunning spreads."

James Diaz and Carter collaborated on a nonfiction instructional book for young artists on designing pop-up art. *The Elements of Pop-Up: A Pop-Up Book for Aspiring Paper Engineers* "is more than a how-to manual on pop-ups," according to Lolly Robinson in a review of the work for *Horn Book.* Robinson noted that the authors describe "the geometry and physics of paper engineering" and the math concepts used in their creation, "explaining the usefulness of kinetic energy." Featuring

A collection of paper sculptures is hidden in Carter's One Red Dot. (Copyright © 2005 by David A. Carter. Reproduced by permission of Little Simon, an imprint of Simon & Schuster Children's Publishing Division.)

the art of both creators, *The Elements of Pop-up* is as much about science as it is about art, and also provides a section on the history of pop-up books. The pair have continued their educational series with *Let's Make It Pop-Up*.

As Carter once told *SATA*, while he "cannot explain the creative process" that produces his books, the "link between my childhood curiosities and thrills and my books has something to do with where my ideas come from. My goal in creating a book is to engage this natural curiosity, to entertain with surprise and silliness and whenever possible to educate, because for me the end result of curiosity is learning.

"The term interactive has become popular in reference to computer software. Pop-up books are also interactive; of course to a big kid like myself the term interactive is nothing more than a big word for play. I believe children learn by playing. One of the things that I like most about pop-up books is that a child who may not be reading yet can interact, or play, with the book. My hope is that this will draw the young reader into the book and hopefully into reading in general.

"If my books can entertain and excite a child who is not a reader, and draw him or her into books and reading, then I have accomplished my goal."

Biographical and Critical Sources

PERIODICALS

Booklist, January 15, 1995, p. 937; December 15, 1999, Ilene Cooper, review of *The Elements of Pop-Up: A Pop-Up Book for Aspiring Paper Engineers,* p. 786; December 1, 2000, review of *The Nutcracker: A Pop-Up Adaptation of E.T.A. Hoffman's Original Tale,* p. 728.

Bulletin of the Center for Children's Books, October, 1989, Zena Sutherland, review of *What's in My Pocket?,* p. 30; January, 1992, p. 120.

Horn Book, January, 2000, Lolly Robinson, review of *The Elements of Pop-Up,* p. 94; November-December, 2005, Lolly Robinson, review of *One Red Dot,* p. 703.

Junior Bookshelf, February, 1990, review of *What's in My Pocket?,* p. 23.

Kirkus Reviews, September 15, 2005, review of *One Red Dot,* p. 1023; February 1, 2006, review of *Woof! Woof!,* p. 129.

Newsweek, September 26, 2005, Bao Ong, "Pop Culture Phenomenon," p. 9.

Publishers Weekly, December 11, 1987, review of *How Many Bugs in a Box?,* p. 62; October 12, 1990, review of *What's in the Deep Blue Sea?,* p. 62; January 11, 1991, review of *I'm a Little Mouse,* p. 100; January 15, 1996, p. 461; May 25, 1998, p. 92; December 21, 1998, review of *Stinky Bugs,* p. 69; July 5, 1999, "Naturally Interactive," p. 73; September 27, 1999, review of *The Twelve Bugs of Christmas,* p. 54; September 25, 2000, review of *The Nutcracker,* p. 76; February 19, 2001, review of *Easter Bugs,* p. 63; December 17, 2001, review of *Flapdoodle Dinosaurs,* p. 93; August 12, 2002, "Otherworldly Tips," p. 302; March 1, 2004, "Pop (up) Culture," p. 71.

School Library Journal, August, 1990, Anne Connor, review of *More Bugs in a Box,* p. 126; February, 1991, p. 74; December, 1995, p. 85; October, 2002, review of *Chanukah Bugs,* p. 58; November, 2005, Lisa Gangemi Krapp, review of *One Red Dot,* p. 89.

Tribune Books (Chicago, IL), February 26, 2006, Mary Harris Russell, review of *Woof! Woof!,* p. 7.

ONLINE

Harcourt Trade Publishers Web site, http://www.harcourtbooks.com/ (April 26, 2006), profile of and interview with Carter.

Powells Books Web site, http://www.powells.com/ (August 26, 2006), interview with Carter.

*   *   *

CONEY, Michael G. 1932-2005
(Michael Greatrex Coney, Mike Coney)

OBITUARY NOTICE— See index for *SATA* sketch: Born September 28, 1932, in Birmingham, England; died of lung cancer November 4, 2005, in Saanichton, British Columbia, Canada. Accountant, hotelkeeper, government official, and author. Coney worked a variety of jobs in his lifetime, but is remembered by readers as a science-fiction novelist and winner of the British Science Fiction Award. After graduating from King Edward's School in his native Birmingham, he worked as a clerk and accountant from the 1950s through the early 1960s. A three-year break as a tenant landlord was followed by more accountancy work at Peplow Warren Fuller until 1969. At that time, Coney decided to move with his wife to Antigua, where they managed a hotel for three years. Their last move came in 1973, when they immigrated to Victoria, British Columbia, Canada, and Coney took a job as a management specialist for the British Columbia Forest Service. He would later co-author a book based on his work experience titled *Forest Adventure: A Guide to the British Columbia Forest Museum* (1985). Coney's attempts to break into writing began in the 1960s, when he started submitting science-fiction tales to *New Worlds* magazine. His first stories proved too radical for the editor's taste, so he began writing science fiction that often took place in future dystopias. These tales found wider acceptance, and soon he was able to publish his first novel, *Mirror Image* (1972); not long afterwards, he won the British Science Fiction Award for *Brontomek!* (1976). In 1983, Coney began his "Song of the Earth" series, which involves high-concept ideas such as alternate realities existing within a multiverse. Coney retired from the forest service in 1989; his last books include *A Tomcat Called Sabrina* (1992) and *No Place for a Sealion* (1992). In his last months he suffered from lung cancer caused by asbestos poisoning. When he learned he was dying, he released three additional, unpublished novels on the Internet, where they were made available to fans free of charge.

OBITUARIES AND OTHER SOURCES:

PERIODICALS

Guardian (London, England), December 1, 2005, p. 37.
Independent (London, England), November 14, 2005, p. 36.

* * *

CONEY, Michael Greatrex
See CONEY, Michael G.

* * *

CONEY, Mike
See CONEY, Michael G.

* * *

CUMMINGS, Priscilla 1951-

Personal
Born April 13, 1951, in Ludlow, MA; daughter of Robert (a farmer and chemistry/physics teacher) and Brenda

Priscilla Cummings (Photograph reproduced by permission.)

(a homemaker) Cummings; married John W. Frece (an educational research foundation administrator), September 17, 1983; children: William Frece, Hannah Frece. *Education:* University of New Hampshire, B.A. (English literature), 1973. *Hobbies and other interests:* Reading, playing piano, taking walks.

Addresses
Home—3026 Aberdeen Rd., Annapolis, MD 21403. *E-mail*—priscummings@comcast.net.

Career
Holyoke Transcript-Telegram, Holyoke, MA, newspaper reporter, 1973-75; *Hartford Courant,* Hartford, CT, newspaper reporter, 1975-76; *Richmond News Leader,* Richmond, VA, newspaper reporter, 1976-82; magazine editor and writer, 1982-85; writer of children's books, 1986—.

Member
Society of Children's Book Writers and Illustrators, Children's Book Guild of Washington, DC.

Awards, Honors
Journalism awards from United Press International (UPI) News Editors of New England, National Federation of Press Women, and Virginia Press Association; Virginia Journalist of the Year, UPI, 1980; Arthur J.

Blaney Award, 1982; Pick of the List, American Booksellers Association, 1997, and Maryland Black-eyed Susan Book List, 1999-2000, both for *Autumn Journey;* International Literacy Award, Metro-Washington Association for Childhood Education, 2001, for "Chadwick the Crab" books; Notable Children's Book selection, American Library Association (ALA), 2002, for *A Face First;* Children's Choice designation, Children's Book Council/International Reading Association, and New York Public Library Books for the Teen Age designation, both 2005, and ALA Best Books for Young Adults designation, 2006, all for *Red Kayak;* books named to various state reading lists.

Writings

PICTURE BOOKS; "CHADWICK THE CRAB" SERIES

Chadwick the Crab, illustrated by A.R. Cohen, Tidewater Publishers (Centreville, MD), 1986.
Chadwick and the Garplegrungen, illustrated by A.R. Cohen, Tidewater Publishers (Centreville, MD), 1987.
The Chadwick Coloring Book, illustrated by A.R. Cohen, Tidewater Publishers (Centreville, MD), 1988.
Chadwick's Wedding, illustrated by A.R. Cohen, Tidewater Publishers (Centreville, MD), 1989.
Chadwick Forever, illustrated by A.R. Cohen, Tidewater Publishers (Centreville, MD), 1993.
Meet Chadwick and His Friends, illustrated by A.R. Cohen, Tidewater Publishers (Centreville, MD), 1999.

PICTURE BOOKS

Oswald and the Timberdoodles, illustrated by A.R. Cohen, Tidewater Publishers (Centreville, MD), 1990.
Sid and Sal's Famous Channel Marker Diner, illustrated by A.R. Cohen, Tidewater Publishers (Centreville, MD), 1991.
Toulouse: The Story of a Canada Goose, illustrated by A.R. Cohen, Tidewater Publishers (Centreville, MD), 1995.
Chesapeake ABC, illustrated by David Aiken, Tidewater Publishers (Centreville, MD), 2000.
Chesapeake 1 2 3, illustrated by David Aiken, Tidewater Publishers (Centreville, MD), 2002.
Chesapeake Rainbow, illustrated by David Aiken, Tidewater Publishers (Centreville, MD), 2004.
Santa Claws: The Christmas Crab, illustrated by Marcy Dunn Ramsey, Tidewater Publishers (Centreville, MD), 2006.

NOVELS

Autumn Journey, Dutton (New York, NY), 1997.
A Face First, Dutton (New York, NY), 2001.
Saving Grace, Dutton (New York, NY), 2003.
Red Kayak, Dutton (New York, NY), 2004.
What Mr. Mattero Did, Dutton (New York, NY), 2005.

Author's novels have been translated into Korean and German.

Sidelights

A former journalist, Priscilla Cummings first tried her hand at writing for young readers in 1986 with the picture book *Chadwick the Crab.* A blue crab who calls the Chesapeake Bay home, Chadwick and his other animal friends are featured in several books about the crustacean, introducing children to the importance of preserving the marine environment from pollution. The author's stories about the crab's adventures have proved popular in the Maryland region, with the "Chadwick the Crab" series selling over 300,000 copies.

Though many of Cummings' books are set on the Chesapeake Bay, she grew up on a dairy farm in western Massachusetts. "Even as a little girl, I enjoyed writing about animals," she recalled on the *Children's Book Guild Web site.* "Often, I illustrated those stories and made them into little books. Writing was something I did for fun." It was something she enjoyed so much, in fact, that she once had more than twenty pen pals from around the world. Cummings followed her dreams of writing and became a newspaper reporter, then moved to magazine writing and editing. When she moved to Maryland, she began learning about blue crabs, which interest inspired her to begin the "Chadwick the Crab" series. Along with the "Chadwick" books, Cummings has written several picture books featuring the Chesapeake Bay, and others featuring different animal characters.

After publishing several picture books, Cummings added a new dimension to her literature career, authoring novels for older readers, including *Autumn Journey* and *A Face First.* In an interview with *Washington Post* contributor Holly Smith, she confided that this transition was not easy. "I'm embarrassed to say this, but parts of *Autumn Journey* were written almost ten years before the book was published." Despite this slow start, however, the author persisted with her longer fiction, publishing *Autumn Journey* in 1997 and *A Face First* four years later. In describing Cummings' efforts, Smith claimed that "some authors write children's books with lovable characters and straightforward text. Others create complex novels that connect with tough-to-reach adolescents. A few can do both. Priscilla Cummings is one of them."

Described as presenting "true strength of character and respect for both family and the natural world" by *School Library Journal* contributor Susan Oliver, *Autumn Journey* follows the story of eleven-year-old Will Newcomb as his father loses his job and the family must leave their Maryland home and move in with relatives. Despite the extra chores, the fifth grader enjoys living on his grandfather's farm, but his parents' constant fighting disturbs him. When his grandfather suffers a heart attack, Will fears that his family will fall apart, a concern

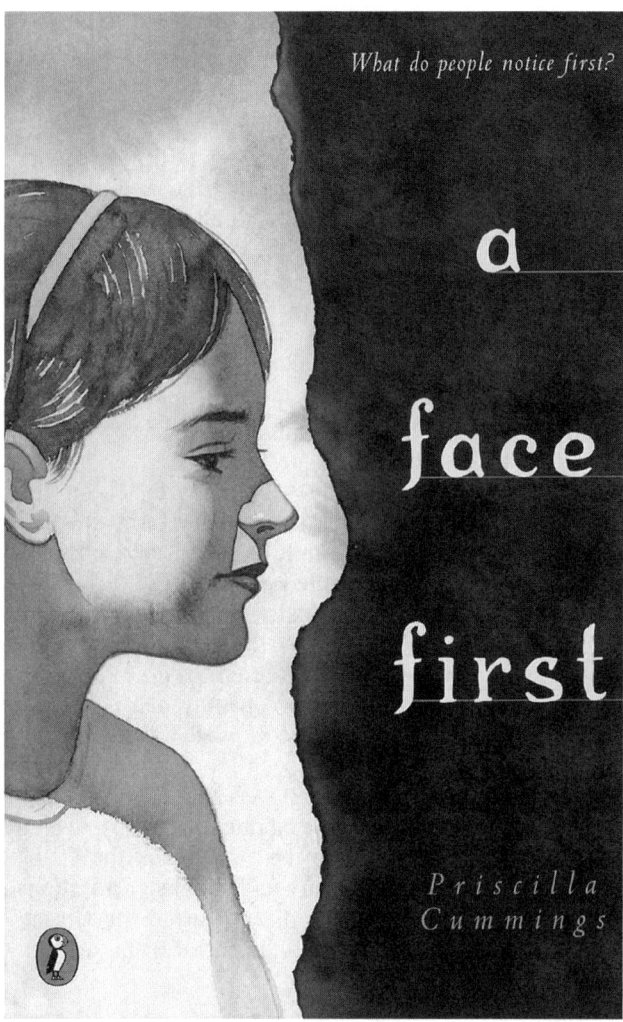

Cover of Cummings' A Face First, *featuring artwork by Goro Sasaki.* (Copyright © 2001 by Priscilla Cummings. Published by Puffin Books. Cover illustration copyright © Goro Sasaki/Bernstein and Andriulli, Inc. Reproduced by permission.)

that intensifies after his father temporarily disappears. A Canada goose Will shoots but cannot bring himself to kill ultimately teaches the boy about perseverance, as he nurses the wounded creature back to health. Writing in *Kirkus Reviews,* a critic found *Autumn Journey* "less a tale of unmitigated woe than a beautifully told, uplifting story about the power and strength of family."

A Face First deals with a different type of tragedy in its focus on twelve-year-old Kelley, who suffers severe burns to her face, hands, and leg during a car accident. As her memory of the events preceding the accident return, Kelley realizes her mother's carelessness caused the crash and begins to blame the woman for the disfigurement. Forced to wear protective coverings, including a plastic pressure face mask, to help her skin heal, the sixth grader retreats into her own private world, rejecting efforts by family and friends to help comfort her. However, with the support of other burn victims, Kelley begins to realize that she is not alone in her suffering and starts working to accept the changes in her life. Critics noted Cummings' extensive knowledge of medical treatment for burn victims, evidenced in the author's descriptive passages of Kelley's time spent in the hospital. However, according to *School Library Journal* critic Cindy Darling, the author "really shines in showing the careful balance of push, pull, and nurturing that must be maintained by the dedicated medical staff." *Booklist* reviewer Carolyn Phelan remarked that this "knowledgeable but compassionate tone rings true," going on to call *A Face First* "a thoughtful read that will encourage empathy."

Another novel for young people, *Saving Grace* is set during the Great Depression, when eleven-year-old Grace is placed in a charity shelter until her family can afford to take care of her and her siblings. That Christmas, Grace is taken in by a wealthy family, and when the Hammonds announce that they may want to adopt her, Grace must decide whether to go back to her family and hope for better times or to stay where she is. "The realistic historical detail is an integral part of the family drama," wrote Hazel Rochman in her *Booklist* review. A *Kirkus Reviews* contributor also noted Cummings' attention to the time period, writing: "The vivid rendition of the Depression era makes this a valuable addition to the genre."

Red Kayak is a novel for older readers in which thirteen-year-old Brady befriends the DiAngelos, a well-off tourist family whose members the local Chesapeake Bay community view as outsiders. When some of Brady's friends play a prank that results in the death of the DiAngelos's three-year-old son, the teen feels responsible; while he does not want to betray his friends, he wants to do what is right. "Cummings has created a multifaceted story that is as much about the families and life in the Chesapeake as it is about a prank gone awry," wrote Vicki Reutter in *School Library Journal,* while a *Kirkus Reviews* contributor found the novel to be a "well-written, sometimes gripping story." As Anne O'Malley noted in her *Booklist* review, "Brady's ultimate decision is both anguished and well reasoned, making for a realistic conclusion."

Similarly written for young teens, *What Mr. Mattero Did* tells the story of three seventh graders who accuse their school music teacher of sexual abuse. Mr. Mattero's own daughter, Melody, is in eighth grade; the story is told half from her perspective and details what the accusation does to her family. The other half is told from the viewpoint of Claire, one of the accusers. Knowing the truth of what happened—that Mr. Mattero is innocent—Claire begins to question her own actions, as well as those of her friends. Jennifer Hubert, reviewing the novel for *Booklist,* considered *What Mr. Mattero Did* "an age-appropriate introduction to a difficult topic," and a *Publishers Weekly* reviewer concluded: "Riveting and timely, this shocking slice-of-life drama is sure to keep pages turning." Jeffrey Hastings wrote in *School Library Journal* that "Cummings has crafted an engrossing and thought-provoking tale involving sensitive, real-life issues."

Cummings once told *SATA:* "When children at school ask me what advice I have for them, as future authors, I tell them they should be reading at every opportunity: books, magazines, newspapers. I tell them to write—not just stories, but poems, letters, journal entries, essays—whatever. And I tell them this: they should be learning to watch and listen.

"As a newspaper reporter for ten years, I learned that standing back to watch and listen often gave me as much compelling information as asking a question or demanding an answer. As an author, I have discovered that standing back to watch and listen gives me many of the valuable details that bring a character to life and drive a story forward.

"When I was on the burn unit of a local hospital researching my novel, *A Face First,* I stood back to become the eyes and ears of my character, Kelley, a twelve-year-old burn victim, slowly recovering in a hospital bed. Outside the window, I saw how 'the traffic never stopped.'In the book, I wrote: 'At two, three, four o'clock in the morning, headlights came and went steadily in the darkness. Like a pulse, Kelley couldn't help but think. Life outside the hospital went on: People got in their cars, buckled themselves in, and went places, even if it was just to pick up shirts at the cleaners or get a gallon of milk at the 7-Eleven or order a meatball sub at Jerry's.'

"Inside the hospital, I listened to a burn patient cry as he struggled to eat a canned pear, and heard the sounds of a Medivac helicopter landing outside the window to deliver another patient into the emergency room entrance below. Both of these details also become part of Kelley's story.

"Standing back to watch, and listen, for the telling detail has been just as important to me as watching for the right ideas, and listening to my heart and mind for the story to emerge."

Biographical and Critical Sources

PERIODICALS

Booklist, February 1, 2001, Carolyn Phelan, review of *A Face First,* p. 1052; May 15, 2003, Hazel Rochman, review of *Saving Grace,* p. 1665; September 1, 2004, Anne O'Malley, review of *Red Kayak,* p. 106; July, 2005, Jennifer Hubert, review of *What Mr. Mattero Did,* p. 1915.
Bulletin for the Center of Children's Books, February, 2001, review of *A Face First,* p. 220; October, 2004, Deborah Stevenson, review of *Red Kayak,* p. 66.
Kirkus Reviews, June 1, 1997, review of *Autumn Journey,* p. 871; June 1, 2003, review of *Saving Grace,* p. 801; September 1, 2004, review of *Red Kayak,* p. 862; July 15, 2005, review of *What Mr. Mattero Did,* p. 788.
Kliatt, September, 2004, review of *Red Kayak,* p. 6.
Publishers Weekly, August 11, 1997, Claire Rosser, review of *Autumn Journey,* p. 402; January 22, 2001, review of *A Face First,* p. 325; August 29, 2005, review of *What Mr. Mattero Did,* p. 57.
School Library Journal, February, 1987, Hayden E. Atwood, review of *Chadwick the Crab,* p. 66; October, 1997, Susan Oliver, review of *Autumn Journey,* p. 132; February, 2001, Cindy Darling, review of *A Face First,* p. 117; June, 2003, review of *Saving Grace,* p. 137; September, 2004, Vicki Reutter, review of *Red Kayak,* p. 202; August, 2005, Jeffrey Hastings, review of *What Mr. Mattero Did,* p. 126.
Voice of Youth Advocates, February, 2001, Mary E. Heslin, review of *A Face First,* p. 421; October, 2003, review of *Saving Grace,* p. 302; August, 2005, Rollie Welch, review of *What Mr. Mattero Did,* p. 214.
Washington Post, July 5, 2001, Holly Smith, "Maturing with Her Audience."

ONLINE

Cornell Maritime Press Web site, http://www.cornellmaritimepress.com/ (April 8, 2006), profile of Cummings.
Children's Book Guild Web site, http://www.childrensbookguild.org/ (December 14, 2001), "Pricilla Cummings."

Cover of Cummings' 2005 novel What Mr. Mattero Did. (Copyright © 2005 by Priscilla Cummings. Published by Dutton Children's Books. Cover photograph copyright © 2005 by Getty Images.)

D

DALE, Anna 1971-

Personal
Born 1971, in England. *Education:* Kent University, B.A. (history); M.A. (writing for children), 2002. *Hobbies and other interests:* Walking with her dog, conservation work, swimming.

Addresses
Home—Southampton, England. *Agent*—c/o Author Mail, Bloomsbury Publishing, 36 Soho Square, London W1D 3QY, England.

Career
Novelist. Works part time at a bookshop.

Awards, Honors
Carnegie Medal longlist inclusion, 2004, for *Whispering to Witches.*

Writings

Whispering to Witches, Bloomsbury (New York, NY), 2004.
Dawn Undercover, Bloomsbury (New York, NY), 2005.

Adaptations
Dale's books have been adapted as audiobooks.

Sidelights
Anna Dale loved to tell stories as a child, and that hobby, along with her love of children's literature, has followed her into adulthood. When a temporary job at a book shop following college became something more

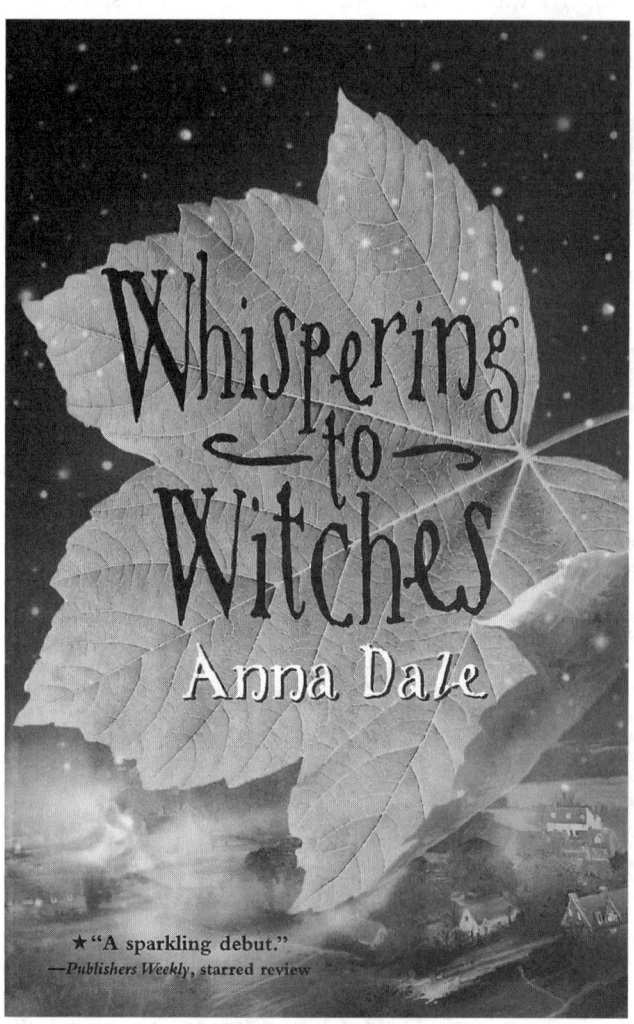

Cover of Anna Dale's Whispering to Witches, *featuring artwork by Melvyn Grant.* (Text copyright © 2004 by Anna Dale. Illustrations by Melvyn Grant. Published by Bloomsbury Children's Books. Reproduced by permission.)

permanent, Dale was inspired by her daily involvement with both children's books and their readers to do some writing of her own. Her first novel, *Whispering to Witches,* came out of her coursework toward a master's degree in creative writing and was actually written over a span of two months. While her more recent work has been less hurried, Dale has devised a useful strategy to combat writers' block. "If I'm struggling with a particularly troublesome sentence," she explained in an interview for the Bloomsbury Web site, "I find the consumption of chocolate an absolute necessity."

A fantasy involving a threat to British witchery, *Whispering to Witches* introduces Joe Binks, a twelve year old who becomes caught up with a coven of rather confused witches while taking the train from school to visit his mother and stepfather for Christmas break. He befriends Twiggy, the youngest of the five members of the Deadnettle Coven, and through her becomes aware of a plot by the diabolical Logan Dritch to rid Earth of its spell-casting population through use of a powerful hex. Dritch has acquired the hex by stealing page 513 from the powerful witches' reference, *Mabel's Book,* and the Deadnettles now hope to regain the missing text, with Joe's help. Comparing *Whispering to Witches* to J.K. Rowling's "Harry Potter" books, a *Publishers Weekly* contributor wrote that the author "nimbly ties together the spidery threads of her story in a beguiling denouement," while in *Booklist* Kay Weisman praised Dale's story as "tightly plotted and with enough twists and turns to keep readers on their toes." "Dale has fun creating the witch universe . . . and imbues it with some clever spells and tricks," according to *Rambles* online reviewer Celeste Miller, the critic dubbing *Whispering to Witches* a "light and exciting tale."

From fantasy, Dale turns to the mystery genre in *Dawn Undercover*. In this middle-grade story, eleven-year-old Dawn Buckle longs for excitement, but because of her drab dress and unremarkable appearance she is often overlooked by everyone around her. Dawn's nondescript nature ultimately serves her well, however; while leaving school one day, she is recruited for a super-secret spy organization, undergoes super-secret-spy training, and then embarks on her super-secret spy mission: to travel to a small village and track down a fellow spy named Angela who has mysteriously vanished while on the trail of the evil Murdo Meek. While noting that Dale starts her story off slowly, a *Publishers Weekly* contributor cited the author's "ample humor" and quaint British references, concluding that the "complex" plotting of *Dawn Undercover* incorporates "false leads and tangles that will keep kids guessing." "Dawn's growth in self-esteem and confidence is believable," wrote Cindy Dobrez in a *Booklist* review of Dale's novel, adding that the book's "secondary characters are unique."

Biographical and Critical Sources

PERIODICALS

Booklist, November 15, 2004, Kay Weisman, review of *Whispering to Witches,* p. 601; March 1, 2005, Traci

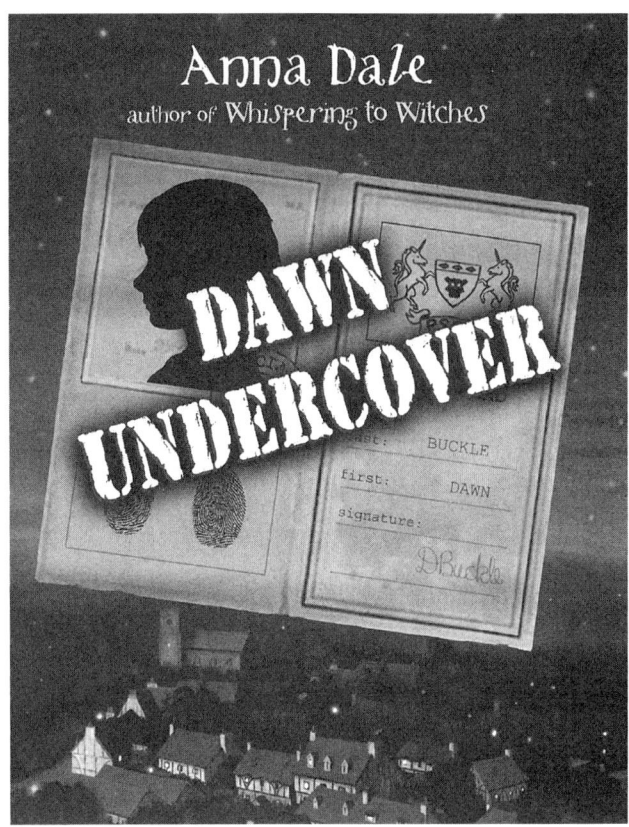

Cover of Dale's Dawn Undercover, *featuring artwork by Melvyn Grant.* (Text copyright © 2005 by Anna Dale. Illustrations by Melvyn Grant. Published by Bloomsbury Children's Books. Reproduced by permission.)

Todd, review of *Whispering to Witches* (audio version), p. 1218; October 15, 2005, Cindy Dobrez, review of *Dawn Undercover,* p. 50.

Kirkus Reviews, October 1, 2004, review of *Whispering to Witches,* p. 958; October 15, 2005, review of *Dawn Undercover,* p. 1135.

Kliatt, Carol Reich, review of *Whispering to Witches* (audio version), p. 58.

Publishers Weekly, October 4, 2004, review of *Whispering to Witches,* p. 88; December 20, 2004, "Flying Starts," p. 30; January 10, 2005, review of *Whispering to Witches,* p. 24; November 14, 2005, review of *Dawn Undercover,* p. 69.

School Library Journal, November, 2004, Elaine E. Knight, review of *Whispering to Witches,* p. 140; February, 2005, Cindy Lombardo, review of *Whispering to Witches* (audio version), p. 76.

ONLINE

Bloomsbury Web site, http://www.bloomsbury.com/childrens/ (May 1, 2006), "Anna Dale."

Rambles Online, http://www.rambles.net/ (February 5, 2005), Celeste Miller, review of *Whispering to Witches.*

DALEY, Michael J. 1959-

Personal

Born September 18, 1959, in Worcester, MA; son of Dermot Jerome (a utility foreman and truck driver) and Phyllis Mary (a homemaker; maiden name, DeMatteo) Daley; married Katherine Jessie Haas (a writer), April 25, 1981. *Education:* Dartmouth College, B.A. (English), 1981. *Hobbies and other interests:* Tinkering and construction, Scottish dancing, wine making, renewable energy, citizen activism.

Addresses

Home—367 Lettieri Rd., Westminister, VT 05346. *E-mail*—mjdaley@sover.net.

Career

Writer and educator. Grocery manager, c. early 1980s; yarn mill spinning fram operator, mid-1980s-1991; Great New England Energy Show, coordinator, 1989-94, publisher, 1995-96; energy lobbyist, 1996-99.

Member

Society of Children's Book Writers and Illustrators, Vermont Citizens Campaign for Health, New England Coalition, Electric Auto Club of America, American Solar Energy Society.

Awards, Honors

Rhode Island Children's Book Award nomination, 2007, for *Space Station Rat*.

Writings

At Home with the Sun: Solar Energy for Young Scientists, Professor Solar Press, 1995.
Nuclear Power: Promise or Peril?, Lerner Publications (Minneapolis, MN), 1997.
Amazing Sun Fun Activities, illustrated by Buckley Smith, Learning Triangle Press (New York, NY), 1998.
Choose Your Own Future Adventure Game, Northeast Sustainable Energy Assn., 1998.
Getting around without Gasoline, Northeast Sustainable Energy Association, 2002.
Space Station Rat, Holiday House (New York, NY), 2005.
Shanghaied to the Moon, G.P. Putnam's Sons (New York, NY), 2007.

Contributor to periodicals, including *St. Anthony Messenger, Momentum, Youth Update, America,* and *Religion Teacher's Journal.*

Sidelights

Michael J. Daley was born in Worcester, Massachusetts, and grew up in nearby Millbury, until his family moved first to the Berkshires and then to Vermont, where he now makes his home. His life-long love of science, machines, tinkering, and science fiction have informed his books for both children and adults with a unique spirit. In *At Home with the Sun: Solar Energy for Young Scientists,* for example, he provides young readers with directions for a Pizza Box Solar Oven, a popular project because the oven is fun to build, and because Daley's directions include the recipe for solar s'mores. In addition to his writing, Daley ha s presented energy issues to over 25,000 children throughout New England.

With *Space Station Rat,* Daley moves into fiction, spinning a futuristic story about a boy named Jeff who lives with his parents on a space observation station. The only young person on the station, Jeff is usually in the way or in trouble of one sort or another. Then adventure enters his life when he decides to help his robotic nanny in the task of finding a space-station stowaway: a rodent who is chewing on and damaging the station's electrical wiring. Unknown to Jeff, the rat Nanny is hunting is not a normal rodent: an escaped lab rat, the creature is actually a smart, technologically proficient creature that has been trained to wiretap and retrieve confidential information. Rat has also been taught to communicate on a computer keyboard, as Jeff learns when he begins receiving e-mails from the tiny typist. In Daley's novel, rat and boy learn to trust each other, thwart Nanny's efforts to destroy the rodent, and become friends despite their odd circumstances.

Chris Sherman, writing in *Booklist,* enjoyed *Space Station Rat,* writing that "short, snappy sentences, appealing characters, and tension between Nanny and Jeff combine with constant threats of ship malfunctions and Rat's struggle to survive to create a fast-paced story sure to please science fiction buffs." Elaine E. Knight, a reviewer for *School Library Journal,* called the book "a thoughtful and satisfying adventure for middle grade science-fiction fans," and a *Kirkus Reviews* critic predicted that "science geeks will enjoy the details of life on a space shuttle."

Daly told *SATA:* "In my fiction I want the readers to fell like they've visited outer space. In my novel *Shanghaied to the Moon* readers will take a journey to the moon in a space shuttle and re-live some of the perils and beauty faced by pioneering astronauts.

"I write my books in a five-by-five-foot tower room, on a solar-powered laptop computer. This keeps me well-acquainted with the cramped conditions in spaceships and space stations!"

Biographical and Critical Sources

PERIODICALS

Booklist, November 1, 1997, Chris Sherman, review of *Nuclear Power: Promise or Peril?,* p. 459; August, 2005, Chris Sherman, review of *Space Station Rat,* p. 2026.

Cover of Michael J. Daley's Space Station Rat, *featuring artwork by Ashley Mims.* (Text copyright © 2005 by Michael J. Daley. Jacket art copyright © 2005 by Ashley Mims. Reproduced by permission of Holiday House, Inc.)

Bulletin of the Center for Children's Books, July-August, 2005, review of *Space Station Rat.*
Kirkus Reviews, June 1, 2005, review of *Space Station Rat,* p. 635.
School Library Journal, January, 1998, Linda Wadleigh, review of *Nuclear Power,* p. 122; August, 2005, Elaine E. Knight, review of *Space Station Rat,* p. 126.

* * *

D'AMICO, Carmela

Personal
Married Steve D'Amico (an artist); children: Olivia.

Addresses
Home—Seattle, WA. *Agent*—c/o Author Mail, Arthur Levine Books, Scholastic, Inc., 557 Broadway, New York, NY 10012.

Career
Children's book author and freelance writer.

Awards, Honors
Washington State Book Award, Oppenheim Toy Portfolio Gold Seal, *Child* magazine Best Book of the Year award, and Book Sense pick, all 2004, and Pacific Northwest Bookseller's Association Book Award, 2005, all for *Ella the Elegant Elephant;* Oppenheim Toy Portfolio Gold Seal award, 2005, for *Ella Takes the Cake.*

Writings

Ella the Elegant Elephant, illustrated by husband, Steve D'Amico, Arthur Levine (New York, NY), 2004.
Ella Takes the Cake, illustrated by Steve D'Amico, Arthur Levine (New York, NY), 2005.
Ella Sets the Stage, illustrated by Steve D'Amico, Arthur Levine (New York, NY), 2006.

Contributor to periodicals.

Adaptations
Ella the Elegant Elephant was adapted as a video with book, Spoken Arts, 2005.

Work in Progress
A young-adult novel; an adult novel; more books for children.

Sidelights
Working with her husband, illustrator Steve D'Amico, Carmela D'Amico introduces readers to an engaging animal character in the books *Ella the Elegant Elephant* and *Ella Takes the Cake.* Ella, the smallest pachyderm on Elephant Island, is facing the first day of school with some nervousness. However, the gift of a beautiful red hat that once belonged to her grandmother gives the shy youngster the confidence to face the unknown. Wearing the hat to school, Ella takes some teasing from school bully Belinda Blue, but sticks to her right to be different, earning the respect of her fellow students and the nickname Ella the Elegant Elephant. Praising the picture book as "winsome," a *Kirkus Reviews* writer added that "the true message" of *Ella the Elegant Elephant* "is Ella's remarkable ability to remain true to herself." "With its charming and whimsical cartoons and simple design, this offering seems like a picture book from an earlier era," noted Rachel G. Payne in *School Library Journal,* citing as comparisons the "Babar" books by Jean de Brunhoff and Ludwig Bemelmans' "Madeleine" stories.

Ella also stars in *Ella Takes the Cake,* as well as in *Ella Sets the Stage,* both of which return readers to Little Village, on Elephant Island. The precocious young elephant helps her mother at the family bakery in *Ella Takes the Cake,* as the task of delivering a special layer cake in her wagon draws Ella into adventure. Praising

Featuring illustrations by husband, Steve D'Amico, Ella Takes the Cake *presents Carmela D'Amico's engaging story about a little elephant who wants to help.* (Copyright © 2005 by Carmela and Steven D'Amico. Reprinted by permission of Arthur A. Levine Books, an imprint of Scholastic Inc.)

Steve D'Amico for his "detailed, richly colored" illustrations, *Booklist* contributor Ilene Cooper added that "take-charge" Ella is a "charming" protagonist who "makes the story her own." Praising the story for its focus on resolve and responsibility, *School Library Journal* contributor Donna Cardon cited *Ella Takes the Cake* for its "personality and charm," and its "sunny Mediterranean" setting.

Biographical and Critical Sources

PERIODICALS

Booklist, November 1, 2004, Shelle Rosenfeld, review of *Ella the Elegant Elephant,* p. 488; August, 2005, Ilene Cooper, review of *Ella Takes the Cake,* p. 2022.

Kirkus Reviews, August 15, 2004, review of *Ella the Elegant Elephant,* p. 804; August 15, 2005, review of *Ella Takes the Cake,* p. 912.

Publishers Weekly, October 4, 2004, review of *Ella the Elegant Elephant,* p. 87.

School Library Journal, November 1, 2004, Rachel G. Payne, review of *Ella the Elegant Elephant,* p. 96; September, 2005, Donna Cardon, review of *Ella Takes the Cake,* p. 168.

ONLINE

Scholastic Web site, http://books.scholastic.com/teachers/authorsandbooks/ (May 18, 2006), "Carmela D'Amico."*

D'AMICO, Steve

Personal
Married; wife's name Carmela (an author); children: Olivia.

Addresses
Home—Seattle, WA. *Agent*—c/o Author Mail, Arthur Levine Books, Scholastic, Inc., 557 Broadway, New York, NY 10012.

Career
Children's book illustrator.

Awards, Honors
Washington State Book Award, Oppenheim Toy Portfolio Gold Seal, *Child* magazine Best Book of the Year award, and Book Sense pick, all 2004, and Pacific Northwest Bookseller's Association Book Award, 2005, all for *Ella the Elegant Elephant; Ella the Elegant Elephant* included in Society of Illustrators Original Art Show collection; Oppenheim Toy Portfolio Gold Seal award, 2005, for *Ella Takes the Cake.*

Illustrator
Carmela D'Amico, *Ella the Elegant Elephant,* Arthur Levine (New York, NY), 2004.
Carmela D'Amico, *Ella Takes the Cake,* Arthur Levine (New York, NY), 2005.
Carmela D'Amico, *Ella Sets the Stage,* Arthur Levine (New York, NY), 2006.

Adaptations
Ella the Elegant Elephant was adapted as a video with book, Spoken Arts, 2005.

Work in Progress
Illustrating more books for children, with wife, Carmela D'Amico.

Sidelights
For Sidelights essay, see entry on Carmela D'Amico.

Biographical and Critical Sources

PERIODICALS

Booklist, November 1, 2004, Shelle Rosenfeld, review of *Ella the Elegant Elephant,* p. 488; August, 2005, Ilene Cooper, review of *Ella Takes the Cake,* p. 2022.

Kirkus Reviews, August 15, 2004, review of *Ella the Elegant Elephant,* p. 804; August 15, 2005, review of *Ella Takes the Cake,* p. 912.

Publishers Weekly, October 4, 2004, review of *Ella the Elegant Elephant,* p. 87.

School Library Journal, November 1, 2004, Rachel G. Payne, review of *Ella the Elegant Elephant,* p. 96; September, 2005, Donna Cardon, review of *Ella Takes the Cake,* p. 168.

ONLINE

Scholastic Web site, http://books.scholastic.com/teachers/authorsandbooks/ (May 18, 2006), "Steve D'Amico."*

E

EDWARDS, Wallace 1957(?)-

Personal
Born c. 1957, in Canada. *Education:* Ontario College of Art (now Ontario College of Art and Design), degree (illustration), 1980.

Addresses
Home—Yarker, Ontario, Canada. *Agent*—c/o Don Sedgwick, 1603 Italy Cross Rd., Petite Riviere, Nova Scotia B0J 2P0, Canada.

Career
Illustrator, author, and artist. Commercial artist, beginning mid-1980s. *Exhibitions:* Paintings exhibited throughout Canada and the United States.

Awards, Honors
Governor General's Award for Children's Literature—Illustration, and *ForeWord* magazine Book-of-the-Year Gold Award, both 2002, and Children's Choice Award for Beginning and Young Readers, International Reading Association, and Ruth Schwartz Children's Book Award for Best Picture Book shortlist, both 2003, all for *Alphabeasts;* Great Book Award, Canadian Toy Testing Council, Ruth and Sylvia Schwartz Children's Book Award for Best Picture Book, and Amelia Frances Howard-Gibbon Illustration Award, Canadian Library Association, all 2005, all for *Monkey Business;* Governor General's Award for Children's Literature finalist, 2005, for *Mixed Beasts.*

Writings

SELF-ILLUSTRATED

Chez Zoo, Doubleday Canada (Toronto, Ontario, Canada), 2001.
Alphabeasts, Kids Can Press (Tonawanda, NY), 2002.
Monkey Business, Kids Can Press (Tonawanda, NY), 2004.

OTHER

(Illustrator) Kenyon Cox, *Mixed Beasts; or, A Miscellany of Rare and Fantastic Creatures,* compiled by Professor Julius Duckworth O'Hare, Esq, revised edition, Kids Can Press (Tonawanda, NY), 2005.

Work in Progress
The X-Tinct Files and *Under the Big Top,* both for Kids Can Press.

Sidelights
As a teenager, Canadian artist and writer Wallace Edwards covered pages of his school notebooks with cartoon drawings rather than notes. While it did not win him a spot on the high-school honor roll, that same tendency earned Edwards respect from his instructors after he became a student at the Ontario College of Art. Moving from cartoons to still life, he became interested in animal studies after viewing the wildlife drawings by one of his teachers, Paul Young. Edwards's obsessive nature was soon channeled into similar work, and hundreds of drawings for clients ranging from the Metropolitan Toronto Zoo to Canadian environmental agencies have been the result. Edwards' highly acclaimed books for children also share this inspiration: *Alphabeasts* and *Monkey Business* are noted for the author/artist's incredibly detailed drawings of animals, each creature set within an incongruous setting that allows readers to use their own imaginations to connect the images into a narrative. In addition, his illustrations for a new edition of Kenyon Cox's lyrical 1904 work *Mixed Beasts; or, A Miscellany of Rare and Fantastic Creatures* allows Edwards to conjure up such creatures as the Camelephant, Bumbleweaver, and Creampuffin. "I don't want there to be a story," the author/artist noted in describing his books to *Quill & Quire* interviewer Josh Knelman. "Kids make up their own stories."

Canadian author/illustrator Wallace Edwards creates fascinating images, each of which tell a unique story, in his 2002 project Alphabeasts. (Text and illustrations © 2002 by Wallace Edwards. Used by permission of Kids Can Press Ltd., Toronto.)

Alphabeasts collects the watercolor paintings Edwards completed while weaning himself off a cable-television addiction that was taking up far too much of his free time. Completed over a year and a half, the book allowed the artist to indulge his imagination and playfully juxtapose images to create a thought-provoking whole. In each picture, animals with names from A to Z appear amid colorful surroundings that reveal surprises, puzzles, and a hidden key. Noting Edwards' "sense of wit," a *Publishers Weekly* contributor characterized the illustrations as providing "an explosion of color and pattern," while *Booklist* critic Michael Cart deemed the work "faintly surreal" and compared the work to *Animalia* by Australian author/illustrator Graeme Base. "Imagine a slightly dilapidated Victorian house occupied solely by animals and you have the premise," explained Cart, although Carol Schene wrote in *School Library Journal* that "there is an art deco tone in the rich and varied patterns" that appear throughout the book's pages. Praising the award-winning work as "well done and full of surprises," Denise Parrott noted in *Resource Links* that Edwards "demonstrates a good knowledge of how to present art to kids in a vibrant, fun manner."

While *Alphabeasts* collects letters, *Monkey Business* collects twenty-six idioms: expressions, such as "sweet tooth" and "can of worms," that cannot be translated into another language literally. In each watercolor illustration, Edwards creates a literal depiction of the idiom in question: for example, the titular "monkey business" is illustrated by a monkey engaged in a business accounting operation. Monkeys are also concealed within other illustrations, providing observant readers with a challenge. In a *Canadian Review of Materials* appraisal, Dave Jenkinson noted that "Edwards' illustrations are full of detail and merit many viewings in order to 'see' how much is actually there," while in *Publishers Weekly* a critic noted that Edwards' "deadpan text" humorously contrasts against "multilayered illustrations that are at once humorous and absurd." Noting the usefulness of the book for teachers, Ilene Cooper added in a *Booklist* review that *Monkey Business* can be savored for "the richness of both the art and our language," and is useful for English classes as well as "creative writing and art studies."

Regarding the praise that has been heaped on his work during his short career as a book illustrator, Edwards remains pragmatic. "I just tried to draw the book I wish I'd had as a kid," he told Knelman. "I still have a very kid mentality. Strangely, it's also what pleases the adult in me." He has found creating illustrations with children in mind to be a perfect fit; as Edward explained on the *Ontario College of Art and Design Web site*, "I like the idea that children look carefully at pictures, and in many ways I think that children are the best audience to create for. I am always amazed at their creativity, which inspires and delights me."

Biographical and Critical Sources

PERIODICALS

Booklist, November 1, 2002, Michael Cart, review of *Alphabeasts,* p. 500; November 1, 2004, Ilene Cooper, review of *Monkey Business,* p. 477.
Kirkus Reviews, September 1, 2004, review of *Monkey Business,* p. 863.
Quill & Quire, August, 2002, Gwyneth Evans, review of *Alphabeasts;* February, 2003, Josh Knelman, "Call of the Wild: Animals Cast a Spell on Illustrator Wallace Edwards."
Publishers Weekly, September 2, 2002, review of *Alphabeasts,* p. 74; October 4, 2004, review of *Monkey Business,* p. 86.
Resource Links, December, 2002, Denise Parrott, review of *Alphabeasts,* p. 5.
School Library Journal, December, 2002, Carol Schene, review of *Alphabeasts,* p. 121; September, 2004, Steven Engelfried, review of *Monkey Business,* p. 186.

ONLINE

Canadian Review of Materials Online, http://www.umanitoba.ca/cm/ (January 31, 2003), Wayne Serebrin, review of *Alphabeasts;* (October 1, 2004) Dave Jenkinson, review of *Monkey Business;* (October 28, 2005) Valerie Neilsen, review of *Mixed Beasts.*

Ontario College of Art and Design Web site, http://www.ocad/on.ca/ (April 27, 2006), "Wallace Edwards."

Suite 101 Web site, http://www.suite101.com/ (April 25, 2006), Irene Tanner-Yuen, "Improbabilities in Wallace Edwards' *Monkey Business*" and "A Pen and Pencil Menagerie: Wallace Edwards' *Alphabeasts.*"*

* * *

ERICSSON, Jennifer A. 1957-

Personal

Born November 21, 1957; daughter of William A. and Eileen (McAuliffe) Barber; married 1981 (divorced 2001); chilren: Annie Beth. *Education:* University of Rhode Island, B.S. (human development, conseling, and family relations), 1979. *Hobbies and other interests:* Reading, taking long walks, watching movies, building gingerbread houses, creating stained glass pieces, traveling.

Addresses

Home—Concord, NH. *Agent*—c/o Author Mail, Adams Media Corporation, 57 Littlefield St., Avon, MA 02322. *E-mail*—jaericsson@aol.com.

Career

Freelance children's writer. Baker Free Library, Bow, NH, children's librarian.

Member

Society of Children's Book Writers and Illustrators (New England chapter), New Hampshire Writers' Project.

Awards, Honors

Children's Choice Award, International Reading Association/Children's Book Council, 1993, for *No Milk!*; American Booksellers Association Pick of the List, 1996, for *The Most Beautiful Kid in the World;* Elizabeth Yates Award.

Writings

No Milk!, illustrated by Ora Eitan, Tambourine Books (New York, NY), 1993.

The Most Beautiful Kid in the World, illustrated by Susan Meddaugh, Tambourine Books (New York, NY), 1996.

Gingerbread Houses for Kids, illustrated by Beth L. Blair, White Birch (Concord, NH), 1998.

(With Beth L. Blair) *The Everything Kids' Puzzle Book: Mazes, Word Games, Puzzles & More! Hours of Fun!,* Adams (Avon, MA), 2000.

She Did It!, illustrated by Nadine Bernard Westcott, Farrar, Straus (New York, NY), 2002.

(With Beth L. Blair) *The Everything Kids' Halloween Puzzle & Activity Book: Hours of Spine-Tingling Fun!,* Adams (Avon, MA), 2003.

(With Beth L. Blair) *The Everything Kids' Christmas Puzzle & Activity Book: Hours of Holiday Fun!* Adams (Avon, MA), 2003.

Out and about at the Bakery, illustrated by Anne McMullan, Picture Window Press (Minneapolis, MN), 2003.

Home to Me, Home to You, illustrated by Ashley Wolff, Little, Brown (New York, NY), 2005.

(With Beth L. Blair) *The Everything Kids' Gross Puzzle & Activity Book: Hours of Disgusting Fun!,* Adams (Avon, MA), 2005.

(With Beth L. Blair) *The Everything Kids' Crazy Puzzle Book: Wild and Wacky Puzzles to Mix up the Fun!,* Adams (Avon, MA), 2005.

(With Beth L. Blair) *The Everything Kids' Pirates Puzzle & Activity Book: Set Sail into a Treasure Trove of Fun!,* Adams (Avon, MA), 2006.

Entrepreneur Magazine's Pocket Guides: How to Sell Collectibles on eBay, Entrepreneur Press (Irvine, CA), 2006.

I Take a Piece of Chalk, illustrated by Michelle Shapiro, Roaring Brook (New Milford, CT), 2007.

Sidelights

Children's librarian Jennifer A. Ericsson is the author of several picture books as well as coauthor of a number of puzzle and activity books for young readers with collaborator Beth L. Blair. Covering such topics as a city boy learning how to milk a cow, sibling rivalry, and a child missing her mother while the woman is away on business, Ericsson's picture books often use humor to explore realistic situations. When not writing children's books, Ericsson often visits schools and offers workshops on picture book writing. She makes her home in Concord, New Hampshire.

In her debut, *No Milk!,* Ericsson tells the story of a young boy who tries everything he can think of to get a cow to produce milk, from saying "please" to throwing a temper tantrum. "Ericsson comically delivers a refreshingly different message . . .: it's finding how that does the trick," wrote a *Publishers Weekly* critic. Michele Landsberg, writing in *Entertainment Weekly,* called the book "amusing," and other critics and readers agreed; *No Milk!* was chosen for the Children's Choice Award by the International Reading Association and the Children's Book Council.

In *The Most Beautiful Kid in the World* young Annie wants to choose a better outfit to celebrate her grandmother's birthday than the one her mother chooses for her. As Mom prepares for the party, Annie pulls out a more festive assortment of clothing, topping off her new look with an improvised make-up made of peanut butter. When she makes her entrance at the party her new look is a hit; as it turns out, Grandmother has a similar fashion sense. "Ericsson has a canny appreciation of the girl's wish to look genuinely stunning (and

A working parent's temporary absence from the family is the focus of Jennifer A. Ericsson's Home to Me, Home to You, *illustrated by Ashley Wolff.* (Text copyright © 2005 by Jennifer A. Ericsson. Illustrations by Ashley Wolff. Published by Little, Brown & Company. Reproduced by permission of the illustrator.)

to stay out of her mother's line of vision)," wrote a *Publishers Weekly* contributor. According to Ilene Cooper in *Booklist,* "children will appreciate both Annie's determination to do things her way and her exuberance while doing them."

Four sisters each blame the others for everything that goes wrong in their house in *She Did It!* When their mother reaches the end of her tolerance and sends them to their room, the siblings team up and cooperate to clean up the house. Calling the book "fast-paced and witty," a *Kirkus Reviews* contributor noted that Ericsson's rhyming text keeps the tale "bustling along right up to its satisfying conclusion." Hazel Rochman, writing in *Booklist,* added that "the rhyme, with noisy words that sound like their meaning, is great for reading out loud." According to *School Library Journal* critic Gay Lynn Van Vleck, "Even children without siblings will grow fond of this mischievous but loving family."

Ericsson covers the topic of parents who must travel on business in her picture book *Home to Me, Home to You.* Here each two-page spread features a mother and child going through their day as the mother travels home from a business trip. Parallels, such as the mother napping on an airplane while her child naps at home, help to show how both characters are thinking about each other, despite the distance. A *Kirkus Reviews* contributor considered *Home to Me, Home to You* a "compassionate story." According to Martha Topol in *School Library Journal,* "this title will provide comfort to readers who are faced with separation from a parent," while *Booklist* critic Julie Cummins dubbed the story "a realistic snapshot of a now-common family situation."

Biographical and Critical Sources

PERIODICALS

Booklist, March 1, 1993, Julie Corsaro, review of *No Milk!,* p. 1234; September 15, 1996, Ilene Cooper, review of *The Most Beautiful Kid in the World,* p. 246; February 15, 2002, Hazel Rochman, review of *She Did It!,* p. 1019; September 1, 2005, Julie Cummings, review of *Home to Me, Home to You,* p. 144.

Bulletin of the Center for Children's Books, October, 1996, review of *The Most Beautiful Kid in the World,* p. 57.

Children's Bookwatch, October, 2005, reveiw of *Home to Me, Home to You.*

Entertainment Weekly, June 18, 1993, Michele Landsberg, review of *No Milk!,* p. 70.

Horn Book, September-October, 1993, Lolly Robinson, review of *No Milk!,* p. 583.

Kirkus Reviews, January 15, 2002, review of *She Did It!,* p. 104; July 1, 2005, review of *Home to Me, Home to You,* p. 734.

Reading Teacher, October, 1994, review of *No Milk!,* p. 153.

Publishers Weekly, February 8, 1993, review of *No Milk!,* p. 85; June 24, 1996, review of *The Most Beautiful Kid in the World,* p. 59; June 1, 1998, review of *No Milk!,* p. 65; May 22, 2000, review of *The Everything Kids' Puzzle Book: Mazes, Word Games, Puzzles & More! Hours of Fun!,* p. 95; January 14, 2002, review of *She Did It!,* p. 59

School Library Journal, June, 1993, Elizabeth Hanson, review of *No Milk!,* p. 74; October, 1996, Virginia Opocensky, review of *The Most Beautiful Kid in the World,* p. 92; March, 2002, Gay Lynn Van Vleck, review of *She Did It!,* p. 176; August, 2005, Martha Topol, review of *Home to Me, Home to You,* p. 94.

Teacher Librarian, February, 2003, review of *She Did It!,* p. 42.

* * *

ERMATINGER, James W. 1959-

Personal

Born 1959. *Education:* San Diego State University, B.S. (biology), 1980, M.A. (ancient history), 1982; Indiana University, Ph.D. (ancient history), 1988.

Addresses

Office—Department of History, Southeast Missouri State University, One University Plaza, MS 2960, Cape Girardeau, MO 63701. *E-mail*—jermatinger@semo.edu.

Career

Educator and writer. Earlham College, Richmond, IN, instructor in history, 1988; Wright State University, Dayton, OH, instructor in history, 1989; Kearney State College, Kearney, NE, instructor in history, 1989-91; University of Nebraska at Kearney, assistant professor, then professor of history, 1991-95; Lourdes College, Sylvania, OH, professor of history, 1995-01; Southeast Missouri State University, Cape Girardeau, professor of history and chair of department, 2001—.

Member

Association of Ancient Historians, American Numismatic Society, American Historical Association, American Society of Papyrologists, American Philological Association.

Awards, Honors

University of Nebraska at Kearney research services council grant, 1990-93, 1994-95, and summer research fellowship, 1993; Distinguished Faculty Award, Honors Program, University of Nebraska at Kearney, 1995; Lourdes College summer grant, 1999; National Endowment for the Humanities grant.

Writings

The Economic Reforms of Diocletian, Scripta Mercaturae (St. Katharinen), 1996.
The Decline and Fall of the Roman Empire ("Greenwood Guides to Historic Events of the Ancient World" series), Greenwood Press (Westport, CT), 2004.

Contributor to numerous publications, including *American Journal of Numismatic* and *Historia.*

Biographical and Critical Sources

PERIODICALS

Choice, October, 2005, review of *The Decline and Fall of the Roman Empire.*
Reference & Research Book News, February, 2005, review of *The Decline and Fall of the Roman Empire,* p. 43.
School Library Journal, August, 2005, Joanne K. Cecere, review of *The Decline and Fall of the Roman Empire,* p. 142.

ONLINE

Southeast Missouri State University Web site, http://www4.semo.edu/ (April 11, 2006), "James W. Ermatinger."*

F

FEIFFER, Kate 1964-

Personal
Born 1964, in New York, NY; daughter of Jules (a writer and cartoonist) and Judy (a writer) Feiffer; married Chris Alley (a civil engineer), September, 1996; children: Madeline. *Education:* Sarah Lawrence College, B.A.

Addresses
Home—Oak Bluffs, Martha's Vineyard, MA. *Office*—c/o Author Mail, Simon & Schuster, 1230 Avenue of the Americas, New York, NY 10020. *E-mail*—katefeiffer@adelphia.net.

Career
Television producer and author. J.B. Pictures, New York, NY, former picture researcher and editor; television work in Boston, MA, beginning 1991, including researcher and associate producer for nationally syndicated talk show and associate producer of films for *Frontline;* WHDH-TV, Boston, political producer and producer of news program *Reallife*. Freelance writer and publicist, 1998—. Artist-in-residence for elementary schools, producing news programs with children.

Member
Authors Guild.

Writings
Double Pink, illustrated by Bruce Ingman, Simon & Schuster Books for Young Readers (New York, NY), 2005.

Producer and writer of documentary films, including *Matzo and Mistletoe*. Author of column "Kate's Column" for *Martha's Vineyard* magazine.

Work in Progress
Several children's books, including one in collaboration with father, illustrator Jules Feiffer, forthcoming 2007.

Sidelights
Starting her career as a Boston-based television producer, Kate Feiffer eventually exchanged her fast-paced city lifestyle for a low-key life on Martha's Vineyard. Her career as a freelance writer and full-time mom allowed Feiffer to find an outlet for her whimsical humor in children's books, and her first effort, *Double Pink,* was published in 2005. The story was inspired by Feiffer's own daughter, Madeline; in the book a girl named Madison is absolutely obsessed with the color pink. Even as a toddler, pink was a priority, and toys, clothes, and Madison's room all had to be pink. From preference, Madison's craving for pink has since moved to obsession, but when the girl takes things too far and colors even her self bright pink, she is swallowed up in the pink world she has created and even her mother cannot find her amid all the pinkness. Illustrator Bruce Ingman captures the humor in Feiffer's story; according to *New York Times Book Review* contributor Penelope Green he "careens happily over the edge when the story does, painting a raucous fuchsia delirium." Green went on to praise Feiffer for her "economy of style and understated wit," commenting that it is reminiscent of the author's father, noted cartoonist and writer Jules Feiffer. Catherine Threadgill, writing in *School Library Journal,* joked that "young readers are likely to identify with Madison, and a few might even be tickled-well, you know," and a *Kirkus Reviews* predicted that "little girls . . . will enjoy Madison's over-the-top exploration of this favorite shade."

Biographical and Critical Sources

PERIODICALS

Cape Cod Times, January 20, 2006, C.K. Wolfson, "Vineyard Author's Children's Book Wins Raves."

Kirkus Reviews, October 15, 2005, review of *Double Pink,* p. 1136.

New York Times Book Review, December 4, 2005, Penelope Green, review of *Double Pink,* p. 60.

Publishers Weekly, November 7, 2005, review of *Double Pink,* p. 72.

Martha's Vineyard Times, December 1, 2005, Perry Garfinkel, "Feiffers in the Pink."

School Library Journal, November, 2005, Catherine Threadgill, review of *Double Pink,* p. 90.

Vineyard Gazette, October 25, 2005, Julia Rappaport, "Colored in Shades of Pink."

ONLINE

Kate Feiffer Home Page, http://katefeiffer.com (April 11, 2006).

* * *

FLUTSZTEJN-GRUDA, Ilona 1930-

Personal

Born 1930, in Varsovie, Poland; immigrated to Canada, 1968; children: three. *Education:* College degree (chemistry), 1966.

Addresses

Home—Quebec, Canada. *Agent*—c/o Author Mail, Sumach Press, 1415 Bathurst St., Ste. 202, Toronto, Ontario M5R 3H8, Canada. *E-mail*—gruda@videotron.ca.

Career

University of Quebec, Trois-Rivières, Quebec, Canada, professor of chemistry, 1968-91; writer. Affiliated with Polish Jewish Heritage Foundation.

Writings

Quand les grands jouvaient à la guerre,, Actes Sud Junior, 1999, translated from the Polish by Sarah Cummins as *When Grownups Play at War: A Child's Memoir,* Sumach Press (Toronto, Ontario, Canada), 2005.

L'aïeule (novel), translated from the Polish by Joanna Gruda, Éditions David (Ottawa, Ontario, Canada), 2004.

Sidelights

When Grownups Play at War: A Child's Memoir is Ilona Flutsztejn-Gruda's account of her experiences living in eastern Europe during World War II. At age nine, Flutsztejn-Gruda and her family fled from their home in Warsaw, Poland in the wake of the Nazi invasion, and

Cover of Ilona Flutsztejn-Gruda's When Grownups Play at War, *a World War II memoir first published in French in 1999.* (By Ilona Flutsztejn-Gruda. Translated by Sarah Cummins. Sumach Press, 2005. Reproduced by permission.)

after a grueling six-year journey, finally settled on a collective farm in Uzbekistan where they learned to adapt to a rural lifestyle. The author recounts the hardships of this forced relocation as well as of the anti-Semitism that was so prevalent during the war years. She also shares the emotional toll on her family; her mother, for example, carried a terrible guilt over the fact that her own sister had to be left behind in Poland due to illness. When the Flutsztejn family returned to their native Poland, all their relatives had vanished and no record of them remained.

Noting that Flutsztejn-Gruda's account of her family's "leave-taking . . . is most memorable," Hazel Rochman wrote in a *Booklist* review that *When Grownups Play at War* "speaks with immediacy about a refugee child's trauma and survival." Andrea Belcham, writing in the *Montreal Review of Books,* commented that "Flutsztejn-Gruda advances her narrative at a rapid pace, with only the sparest of passages devoted to self-reflection, though her attention to the physical details of the foreign lands and situations that she and her family encounter are astute."

After completing her college degree, Flutsztejn-Gruda immigrated to eastern Canada, and taught chemistry at the University of Quebec for over two decades. She wrote her memoir, in Polish, shortly after retiring from her university post, and has also gone on to pen a novel which is published in French. "I always told my story of wartime survival to my family—first to my children and then to my grandchildren," she commented to Stuart Nulman for the Canadian *Jewish Tribune.* In addition to publishing her own story of survival, Flutsztejn-Gruda has also been an active participant in the Polish Jewish Heritage Foundation, helping other Holocaust survivors record their stories. "It is very important to get as many remaining Holocaust survivors as possible to write about their experiences and to give witness to this tragic period in history," she told Nulman.

Biographical and Critical Sources

BOOKS

Flutsztejn-Gruda, Ilona, *When Grownups Play at War: A Child's Memoir,* translated by Sarah Cummins, Sumach Press (Toronto, Ontario, Canada), 2005.

PERIODICALS

Booklist, October 1, 2005, Hazel Rochman, review of *When Grownups Play at War,* p. 46.
Montreal Review of Books, winter, 2006, Andrea Belcham, "The Will to Live."

ONLINE

Canadian Review of Materials, http://www.umanitoba.ca/ (April 11, 2006).
Jewish Tribune Online, http://www.jewishtribune.ca/ (April 11, 2006), Stuart Nulman, "From Poland to Uzbekistan."
Sumach Press Web site, http://www.sumachpress.com/ (April 11, 2006).*

* * *

FORDE, Catherine 1961-

Personal

Born 1961; children: two sons. *Hobbies and other interests:* Reading, swimming, jogging, calking, skiing, music.

Addresses

Home—Glasgow, Scotland. *Agent*—c/o Author Mail, Egmont, 239 Kensington High St., London W8 6SA, England. *E-mail*—info@catherineforde.co.uk.

Career

Educator and writer. Collins (publisher), former lexicographer; secondary school teacher in Scotland.

Awards, Honors

Blue Peter "Book I Couldn't Put Down" designation shortlist, and British Book Trust Teenage Book Award shortlist, both 2004, and Grampian Book Award, 2005, all for *Fat Boy Swim;* North Lanarkshire Book Award shortlist, Calderdale Teenage Book Award shortlist, Leicestershire Book of the Year shortlist, Renfewshire Teenage Book Award shortlist, Angus Award shortlist, and Scottish Arts Council award, all 2005, all for *SKARRS.*

Writings

Think Me Back, House of Lochar (Colonsay, Scotland), 2001.
The Finding, House of Lochar (Conosay, Scotland), 2002.
Fat Boy Swim, Egmont (London, England), 2003, Delacorte Press (New York, NY), 2004.
SKARRS, Egmont (London, England), 2004.
I See You Baby . . . , Barrington Stoke (Edinburgh, Scotland), 2005.
The Drowning Pond, Egmont (London, England), 2005.
Firestarter, Egmont (London, England), 2006.

Work in Progress

The novel *Tug of War.*

Sidelights

Scottish writer Catherine Forde worked as a secondary-school English teacher until making the transition to children's book author. Publishing her first book in 2001, Forde earned particular praise two years later, when her young-adult novel *Fat Boy Swim* was released. Also released in the United States, the novel introduces fourteen-year-old Jimmy, a Scottish boy who is sorely overweight and known around school as "Fat Boy Fat." Asthmatic and chronically bullied by classmates, Jimmy has little to feel upbeat about, and his down-in-the-dumps attitude worries his overly protective mother for posing a direct threat to the teen's health. Fortunately, his upbeat Aunt Pol is a proactive force in Jimmy's life and she helps him sustain a sense of humor. When Jimmy meets a local priest nicknamed GI Joe, he takes to heart the man's encouragement that he take up swimming and cooking. In the water, Jimmy discovers a natural talent and learns that he is capable of changing his life. Meanwhile, a love interest bubbles to the surface in his cooking class.

Fat Boy Swim was praised by several critics for its realistic portrayal of a troubled teen. While noting that Forde is "a bit heavy-handed" in defending her young protagonist, *Booklist* Gillian Engbert added that the novel's "messy ending is satisfyingly realistic; despite his newfound swimming talent . . . Jim still has complicated, unresolved questions about who he wants to be." A *Kirkus Reviews* critic called the novel "warm and full of vivid imagery," while Francisca Goldsmith stated in *School Library Journal* that "each character is developed and interesting."

Forde has continued her writing career with the young-adult novels *The Drowning Pond* and *Firestarter,* the former a mix of supernatural and frustrated adolescent angst that a *Bookseller* contributor dubbed "bleakly uncompromising" and full of "historical parallels." She discussed her craft in an interview posted on the Egmont Books Web site, noting: "I always promised myself I'd write a book some day, but didn't actually start writing properly until my younger son started school. . . . Sick of doing more housework to keep myself busy, I sat down at the computer and I haven't stopped writing since." "I enjoy putting characters in difficult situations or involving them in conflict to see how they will develop," Forde added. "Things that have happened in my own life can creep into my writing demanding to be relived or explored, and people who are important to me often become characters in my story."

Biographical and Critical Sources

PERIODICALS

Booklist, September 1, 2004, Gillian Engberg, review of *Fat Boy Swim,* p. 110; Feburary 1, 2005, Anna Rich, review of *Fat Boy Swim,* p. 988.
Kirkus Reviews, September 1, 2004, review of *Fat Boy Swim,* p. 864.
School Library Journal, September, 2004, Joel Shoemaker, review of *Fat Boy Swim,* p. 204; February, 2005, Francisca Goldsmith, review of *Fat Boy Swim,* p. 76.

ONLINE

Catherine Forde Home Page, http://www.catherineforde.co.uk (April 11, 2006).
Egmont Web site, http://www.egmont.co.uk/ (April 11, 2006), "Catherine Forde."*

* * *

FOX, Aileen 1907-2005
(Aileen Mary Henderson)

Cover of Catherine Forde's **Fat Boy Swim,** *featuring artwork by Edward Schnurr.* (Text copyright © 2003 by Catherine Forde. Illustrations by Edward Schnurr. Published by Delacorte Press. Used by permission of Random House Children's Books, a division of Random House, Inc.)

OBITUARY NOTICE— See index for *SATA* sketch: Born July 29, 1907, in London, England; died November 21, 2005, in Exeter, England. Archaeologist, educator, and author. Fox was an accomplished archeologist best known for her research and excavations of Roman settlements in the southwestern United Kingdom. After completing an M.A. in English in 1932 at Newnham College, Cambridge, she decided that working at an archaeological dig might be interesting. With the help of Roman art scholar Jocelyn Toynbee, arrangements were made for her to assist on an excavation in Richborough, Kent. This was just after World War II, and the area was still in ruins from German bombings. Fox saw this as an advantage, for the area had already, in essence, been dug up by the Nazis. She enthusiastically worked on uncovering the Roman ruins there, publishing her findings in *Roman Exeter: Excavations in War-Damaged Areas, 1945-1947* (1952). Her research also led to an appointment in 1947 as lecturer in archaeology at the University of Exeter, where she would teach until 1972. After this first experience on a dig, Fox concentrated on Roman settlements in the area, learning that, contrary to previous beliefs, the influence of the Roman Empire had extended very far into Cornwall. Though Roman ruins remained her specialty, Fox also conducted research extending back into prehistoric times and forward into the Middle Ages. After retiring from Exeter, she taught at the University of Aukland for a year as a visiting lecturer. In New Zealand she became interested in the native Maori tribes and conducted archaeological research on them, as well. This resulted in such books as *Prehistoric Maori Fortifications in the North Island of New Zealand* (1976) and *Tiromoana Pa, Te Awanga: Hawke's Bay Excavations, 1974-75* (1978). Among her other publications are a children's book written with Alan Sorrell titled *Roman Britain* (1961), the scholarly *South-West England* (1964; revised edition, 1973), and the autobiography *Aileen: A Pioneering Archaeologist* (2000).

OBITUARIES AND OTHER SOURCES:

BOOKS

Fox, Aileen, *Aileen: A Pioneering Archaeologist,* Leominster Gracewing, 2000.

PERIODICALS

Independent (London, England), December 16, 2005, p. 38.
Times (London, England), December 21, 2005, p. 48.

G

GAFFNEY, Timothy R. 1951-

Personal
Born April 12, 1951, in Dayton OH; son of Elmer (a former Department of Defense employee) and Clara (a homemaker; maiden name, Stoddard) Gaffney; married Jean Buckle (a librarian), January 22, 1977; children: Kimberly, Christine, Mark, Matthew. *Education:* Ohio State University, B.A., 1974. *Politics:* Democrat. *Religion:* Presbyterian.

Addresses
Office—433 S. 5th St., Miamisburg, OH 45342-2940. *E-mail*—tgaffney@coxohio.com.

Career
Journalist and writer. *Piqua Daily Call,* Piqua, OH, reporter, 1974-78; *Kettering-Oakwood Times,* Kettering, OH, reporter, 1978-79; *Dayton Daily News,* reporter, beginning 1979, military affairs reporter, beginning 1985.

Member
Dayton Newspaper Guild (former member of executive board), Experimental Aircraft Association, Aircraft Owners and Pilots Association, Women in Aviation International.

Awards, Honors
AOPA Max Karant Award for aviation reporting, 1998.

Writings

NONFICTION

Jerrold Petrofsky: Biomedical Pioneer, Children's Press (Danbury, CT), 1984.
Kennedy Space Center, Children's Press (Danbury, CT), 1985.
Chuck Yeager: First Man to Fly Faster than Sound, Children's Press (Danbury, CT), 1986.
Edmund Hillary: First to Climb Mt. Everest, Children's Press (Danbury, CT), 1990.
(With Scott Montgomery) *Back in Orbit: John Glenn's Return to Space,* Longstreet Press, 1998.
Air Safety: Preventing Future Disasters, Enslow (Berkeley Heights, NJ), 1999.
Secret Spy Satellites: America's Eyes in Space, Enslow (Berkeley Heights, NJ), 2000.
Air Show Pilots and Airplanes, Enslow (Berkeley Heights, NJ), 2001.
Amazing Agricultural Aircraft, Enslow (Berkeley Heights, NJ), 2001.
Hurricane Hunters, Enslow (Berkeley Heights, NJ), 2001.

Contributor to periodicals, including *Boys' Life.*

FICTION

Grandpa Takes Me to the Moon, illustrated by Barry Root, Tambourine, 1996.
Wee and the Wright Brothers, illustrated by Bernadette Pons, Henry Holt (New York, NY), 2004.

Author of blog *Air City.*

Sidelights
Timothy R. Gaffney is an Ohio-based journalist who has translated his long-time interest in space exploration and aircraft into a library of books geared for younger readers. His nonfiction books, which include *Secret Spy Satellites: America's Eyes in Space, Hurricane Hunters,* and *Back in Orbit: John Glenn's Return to Space,* as well as biographies of notable individuals such as test pilot Chuck Yeager, mountain-climber Sir Edward Hillary, and Dr. Jerrold Petrofsky, whose research into the electronic stimulation of human muscles resulted in a means by which those suffering from pa-

ralysis could regain movement. Gaffney has also ventured into fiction with the picture books *Grandpa Takes Me to the Moon* and *Wee and the Wright Brothers*. Praising *Hurricane Hunters* for its "informative" discussion of the aircraft used by the government's Weather Reconnaissance Squadron, NASA, and the National Oceanic and Atmospheric Association, *School Library Journal* contributor Patricia Manning cited Gaffney's "careful research." Inspired by Gaffney's meeting with astronaut James Irwin, one of the first men to walk on the moon, *Grandpa Takes Me to the Moon* relates an imaginative bedtime story about a trip skyward that "makes a momentous and remote event engagingly accessible" to younger children, according to a *Publishers Weekly* reviewer.

In *Wee and the Wright Brothers* Gaffney takes readers back to 1903 and introduces them to a tiny mouse living in the Wright brothers' bicycle shop in Dayton, Ohio. Wee publishes a local mouse newspaper and wants to cover the brothers' newfangled flying machine. A dedicated reporter, Wee stows away in the pocket of Orville Wright's jacket on just the right day and experiences the famous initial flight first hand. *Wee and the Wright Brothers* "makes a good introduction to the inventors for wee ones," commented Harriett Fargnoli in a *School Library Journal* review, while in *Booklist* Carolyn Phelan praised the book's "cheerful tone," as well as its "intrepid hero, and the ability to convey information without making it ponderous."

Gaffney once told *SATA*: "I have had a lifelong interest in writing. My interests in space and exploration were sparked by such books as *Have Spacesuit—Will Travel* by Robert Heinlein, everything by Arthur C. Clarke, the television show *Sea Hunt*, and *The Silent World* by Jacques Cousteau. I enjoy the sounds that words make and the pictures they can evoke in one's mind.

"My interest in aviation was probably inevitable. I was born in Dayton, the home of the Wright Brothers, who invented the airplane and established the principles of flight. My mother and father worked at old Wright Field in the 1930s and 1940s, the Air Force's center for aeronautical research and development. My parents encouraged reading and I feasted on books about dinosaurs (*Lost World*, by Arthur Conan Doyle), adventure (*The Silent World*, by Cousteau, *Kon Tiki*, by [Thor] Heyerdahl), and space (the 'Tom Swift' series, as well as all books by Heinlein and Clarke).

"I was good at writing but bad at math, so instead of becoming a scientist I became a newspaper reporter, which allowed me to write and draw a weekly paycheck. In 1985 I became the military affairs reporter for the *Dayton Daily News*; as a result, I have interviewed many aviation pioneers and astronauts. I have had unusual opportunities to fly in blimps, biplanes, bombers and fighters." Gaffney, a private pilot, recalled one particular opportunity with pride: "At the Dayton Air Show in 1990, officials of the Soviet Union's Mikoyan design bureau granted my request to fly in one of the Soviet Union's most advanced fighters, the MiG-29." This experience made Gaffney the first newspaper reporter to fly in such an advanced Soviet jet.

Biographical and Critical Sources

PERIODICALS

Booklist, September 1, 2004, Carolyn Phelan, review of *Wee and the Wright Brothers,* p. 131.
Bulletin of the Center for Children's Books, October, 1996, review of *Grandpa Takes Me to the Moon,* p. 58.
Instructor, October, 1996, review of *Grandpa Takes Me to the Moon,* p. 68.
Kirkus Reviews, August 15, 2004, review of *Wee and the Wright Brothers,* p. 805.
New York Times Book Review, January 5, 1997, review of *Grandpa Takes Me to the Moon,* p. 22.
Publishers Weekly, July 22, 1996, review of *Grandpa Takes Me to the Moon,* p. 241.
Reading Teacher, March, 1998, review of *Grandpa Takes Me to the Moon,* p. 504.
School Library Journal, September, 1996, Kathy East, review of *Grandpa Takes Me to the Moon,* p. 178; February, 2000, William C. Schadt, review of *Air Safety: Preventing Future Disasters,* p. 131; February, 2002, Patricia Manning, review of *Hurricane Hunters,* p. 144; December, 2004, Harriett Fargnoli, review of *Wee and the Wright Brothers,* p. 108.

ONLINE

Writers.net, http://www.writers.net/writers/ (April 11, 2006), "Timothy Gaffney."

* * *

GEORGE, Jean
See GEORGE, Jean Craighead

* * *

GEORGE, Jean Craighead 1919-
(Jean George)

Personal
Born July 2, 1919, in Washington, DC; daughter of Frank Cooper (an entomologist) and Mary Carolyn (Johnson) Craighead; married John Lothar George January 28, 1944 (divorced, 1963); children: Carolyn Laura, John Craighead, Thomas Luke. *Education:* Pennsylvania State University, B.A., 1941; attended Louisiana State University, Baton Rouge, 1941-42, and University of Michigan. *Politics:* Democrat. *Hobbies and other interests:* Painting; field trips to universities and laboratories of natural science, modern dance, white-water canoeing.

Jean Craighead George. (Photograph by Ellan Young Photography. Reproduced by permission of Jean Craighead George.)

Addresses

Home—Chappaqua, NY. *Agent*—c/o Author Mail, HarperCollins, 10 E. 53rd St., 7th Fl., New York, NY 10022. *E-mail*—jeangeorgemail@aol.com.

Career

Writer and journalist. International News Service, Washington, DC, reporter, 1941-43; Washington Post and Times-Herald, Washington, DC, reporter, 1943-46; *Pageant* magazine, New York, NY, artist, 1946-47; Newspaper Enterprise Association, New York, NY, artist and reporter, 1946-47; teacher in Chappaqua, NY, 1960-68; Reader's Digest, Pleasantville, NY, staff writer, 1969-74, roving editor, 1974-80.

Member

PEN, League of Women Voters, Dutchess County Art Association.

Awards, Honors

Aurianne Award, American Library Association (ALA), 1956, for *Dipper of Copper Creek;* Newbery Honor Book, ALA, Notable Book citation, ALA, 1960, International Hans Christian Andersen Award honor list, International Board on Books for Young People (IBBY), 1962, Lewis Carroll Shelf citation, 1965, and George G. Stone Center for Children's Books Award, 1969, all for *My Side of the Mountain;* named Woman of the Year, Pennsylvania State University, 1968; Claremont College award, 1969; Eva L. Gordon Award, American Nature Study Society, 1970; *Book World* First Prize, 1971, for *All upon a Stone;* Newbery Medal, ALA, National Book Award finalist, American Association of Publishers, German Youth Literature Prize, West German section of IBBY, and Silver Skate, Netherlands Children's Book Board, all 1973, and one of ten best American children's books in two hundred years listing, Children's Literature Association, 1976, all for *Julie of the Wolves;* School Library Media Specialties of South Eastern New York Award, 1981; Irvin Kerlan Award, University of Minnesota, 1982; University of Southern Mississippi Award, 1986; Grumman Award, 1986; Washington Irving Award, Westchester Library Association, 1991; Reading Is Fundamental Award, 1995; Knickerbocker Award for Juvenile Literature, School Library Media Section of New York Public Library Association; Children's Book Guild Award for Nonfiction, Children's Book Guild/*Washington Post,* 1998, for "an author or author-illustrator whose total work has contributed significantly to the quality of nonfiction for children"; Notable Children's Books list, *New York Times,* 1999, for *Frightful's Mountain;* Jeremiah Ludington Award, 2003; Key Award nomination, 2005; *My Side of the Mountain* selected a New York Librarians book to represent the state at National Book Festival, 2005; Grumman Award.

Writings

WITH HUSBAND JOHN LOTHAR GEORGE; SELF-ILLUSTRATED JUVENILE FICTION

Vulpes, the Red Fox, Dutton (New York, NY), 1948.
Vison, the Mink, Dutton (New York, NY), 1949.
Masked Prowler: The Story of a Raccoon, Dutton (New York, NY), 1950.
Meph, the Pet Skunk, Dutton (New York, NY), 1952.
Bubo, the Great Horned Owl, Dutton (New York, NY), 1954.
Dipper of Copper Creek, Dutton (New York, NY), 1956.

SELF-ILLUSTRATED JUVENILE FICTION

The Hole in the Tree, Dutton (New York, NY), 1957.
Snow Tracks, Dutton (New York, NY), 1958.
My Side of the Mountain, Dutton (New York, NY), 1959.
The Summer of the Falcon, Crowell (New York, NY), 1962.
Red Robin, Fly Up!, Reader's Digest (Pleasantville, NY), 1963.
Gull Number 737, Crowell (New York, NY), 1964.
Hold Zero!, Crowell (New York, NY), 1966.
Water Sky, Harper (New York, NY), 1987.
On the Far Side of the Mountain, Dutton Children's Books (New York, NY), 1990.

The Tarantula in My Purse: And 172 Other Wild Pets, HarperCollins (New York, NY), 1996.
Tree Castle Island, HarperCollins (New York, NY), 2002.
Charlie's Raven, Dutton (New York, NY), 2004.

JUVENILE FICTION

Coyote in Manhattan, illustrated by John Kaufmann, Crowell (New York, NY), 1968.
All upon a Stone, illustrated by Don Bolognese, Crowell (New York, NY), 1971.
Who Really Killed Cock Robin?: An Ecological Mystery, Dutton (New York, NY), 1971.
Julie of the Wolves, illustrated by John Schoenherr, Harper (New York, NY), 1972.
All upon a Sidewalk, illustrated by Don Bolognese, Dutton (New York, NY), 1974.
Hook a Fish, Catch a Mountain: An Ecological Spy Story, Dutton (New York, NY), 1975, published as *The Case of the Missing Cutthroats: An Ecological Mystery,* HarperCollins (New York, NY), 1996.
Going to the Sun, Harper (New York, NY), 1976.
The Wentletrap Trap, illustrated by Symeon Shimin, Dutton (New York, NY), 1978.
The Wounded Wolf, illustrated by John Schoenherr, Harper (New York, NY), 1978.
River Rats, Inc., Dutton (New York, NY), 1979.
The Cry of the Crow, Harper (New York, NY), 1980.
The Grizzly Bear with the Golden Ears, illustrated by Tom Catania, Harper (New York, NY), 1982.
The Talking Earth, Harper (New York, NY), 1983.
Shark beneath the Reef, Harper (New York, NY), 1989.
One Day in the Tropical Rain Forest, illustrated by Gary Allen, Crowell (New York, NY), 1990.
The Missing Gator of Gumbo Limbo: An Ecological Mystery, HarperCollins (New York, NY), 1992.
The First Thanksgiving, illustrated by Thomas Locker, Philomel Books (New York, NY), 1993.
The Fire Bug Connection: An Ecological Mystery, HarperCollins (New York, NY), 1993.
Dear Rebecca, Winter Is Here, illustrated by Loretta Krupinski, HarperCollins (New York, NY), 1993.
Julie, illustrated by Wendell Minor, HarperCollins (New York, NY), 1994.
Animals Who Have Won Our Hearts, illustrated by Christine Herman Merrill, HarperCollins (New York, NY), 1994.
Acorn Pancakes, Dandelion Salad, and 38 Other Wild Recipes, illustrated by Paul Mirocha, HarperCollins (New York, NY), 1995.
To Climb a Waterfall, illustrated by Thomas Locker, Philomel Books (New York, NY), 1995.
Everglades, illustrated by Wendell Minor, HarperCollins (New York, NY), 1995.
There's an Owl in the Shower, illustrated by Christine Herman Merrill, HarperCollins (New York, NY), 1995.
Julie's Wolf Pack, illustrated by Wendell Minor, HarperCollins (New York, NY), 1997.
Look to the North: A Wolf Pup Diary, illustrated by Lucia Washburn, HarperCollins (New York, NY), 1997.
Arctic Son, illustrated by Wendell Minor, Hyperion Books for Children (New York, NY), 1997.
Dear Katie, the Volcano Is a Girl, Hyperion Books for Children (New York, NY), 1998.
Elephant Walk, Disney Press (New York, NY), 1998.
Giraffe Trouble, Disney Press (New York, NY), 1998.
Gorilla Gang, Disney Press (New York, NY), 1998.
Rhino Romp, Disney Press (New York, NY), 1998.
Frightful's Mountain, Dutton Children's Books (New York, NY), 1999.
Incredible Animal Adventures, Harper Trophy (New York, NY), 1999.
Morning, Noon, and Night, HarperCollins (New York, NY), 1999.
Snow Bear, Hyperion Books for Children (New York, NY), 1999.
Nutik, the Wolf Pup, illustrated by Ted Rand, HarperCollins (New York, NY), 2000.
Nutik and Amaroq Play Ball, illustrated by Ted Rand, HarperCollins (New York, NY), 2000.
Lonesome George, illustrated by Wendell Minor, HarperCollins (New York, NY), 2001.
Autumn Moon, HarperTrophy (New York, NY), 2001.
Winter Moon, HarperTrophy (New York, NY), 2001.
Frightful's Daughter, illustrated by Daniel San Souci, Dutton (New York, NY), 2002.
Spring Moon, HarperTrophy (New York, NY), 2002.
Summer Moon, HarperTrophy (New York, NY), 2002.
Cliff Hanger, illustrated by Wendell Minor, HarperCollins (New York, NY), 2002.
Fire Storm, illustrated by Wendell Minor, HarperCollins (New York, NY), 2003.
Snowboard Twist, illustrated by Wendell Minor, HarperCollins (New York, NY), 2004.
Luck: The Story of a Sandhill Crane, illustrated by Wendell Minor, HarperCollins (New York, NY), 2006.

NONFICTION

Spring Comes to the Ocean (juvenile), illustrated by John Wilson, Crowell (New York, NY), 1966.
(Self-illustrated) *Beastly Inventions: A Surprising Investigation into How Smart Animals Really Are* (juvenile), McKay, 1970, published as *Animals Can Do Anything,* Souvenir Press, 1972.
Everglades Wildguide, illustrated by Betty Fraser, National Park Service, 1972.
(With Toy Lasker) *New York in Maps, 1972/73,* New York Magazine, 1974.
(With Toy Lasker) *New York in Flashmaps, 1974/75,* Flashmaps, 1976.
The American Walk Book: An Illustrated Guide to the Country's Major Historical and Natural Walking Trails from New England to the Pacific Coast, Dutton (New York, NY), 1978.
The Wild, Wild Cookbook: A Guide for Young Foragers (juvenile), illustrated by Walter Kessell, Crowell (New York, NY), 1982.
Journey Inward (autobiography), Dutton (New York, NY), 1982.
(Self-illustrated) *How to Talk to Your Animals* (also see below), Harcourt (New York, NY), 1985.

(Self-illustrated) *How to Talk to Your Dog* (originally published in *How to Talk to Your Animals*), Warner (New York, NY), 1986, illustrated by Sue Truesdell, HarperCollins (New York, NY), 2000.

(Self-illustrated) *How to Talk to Your Cat* (originally published in *How to Talk to Your Animals*), Warner (New York, NY), 1986, illustrated by Paul Meisel, HarperCollins (New York, NY), 2000.

"THIRTEEN MOONS" SERIES; JUVENILE NONFICTION

The Moon of the Bears, illustrated by Mac Shepard, Crowell (New York, NY), 1967.
The Moon of the Owls, illustrated by Jean Zallinger, Crowell (New York, NY), 1967.
The Moon of the Salamanders, illustrated by John Kaufmann, Crowell (New York, NY), 1967.
The Moon of the Chickarees, illustrated by John Schoenherr, Crowell (New York, NY), 1968.
The Moon of the Fox Pups, illustrated by Kiyoaki Komoda, Crowell (New York, NY), 1968.
The Moon of the Monarch Butterflies, illustrated by Murray Tinkelman, Crowell (New York, NY), 1968.
The Moon of the Wild Pigs, illustrated by Peter Parnall, Crowell (New York, NY), 1968.
The Moon of the Mountain Lions, illustrated by Winifred Lubell, Crowell (New York, NY), 1968.
The Moon of the Deer, illustrated by Jean Zallinger, Crowell (New York, NY), 1969.
The Moon of the Alligators, illustrated by Adrina Zanazanian, Crowell (New York, NY), 1969.
The Moon of the Gray Wolves, illustrated by Lorence Bjorklund, Crowell (New York, NY), 1969.
The Moon of the Moles, illustrated by Robert Levering, Crowell (New York, NY), 1969.
The Moon of the Winter Bird, illustrated by Kazue Mizumura, Crowell (New York, NY), 1969.

"ONE DAY" SERIES; JUVENILE NONFICTION

One Day in the Desert, illustrated by Fred Brenner, Harper (New York, NY), 1983.
One Day in the Alpine Tundra, illustrated by Walter Gaffney-Kessell, Harper (New York, NY), 1984.
One Day in the Prairie, illustrated by Bob Marstall, Harper (New York, NY), 1986.
One Day in the Woods, Harper (New York, NY), 1988.

OTHER

(Author of introduction and contributor) *Marvels and Mysteries of Our Animal World,* Reader's Digest Association, 1964.
(Illustrator) John Johnson Craighead, *Hawks, Owls, and Wildlife,* 1969.
(Editor with Ann Durell and Katherine Paterson) Aliki, *The Big Book for Our Planet,* Dutton Children's Books (New York, NY), 1993.

Also author of play *Tree House,* music by Saul Aarons. Contributor of articles on natural history and children's literature to periodicals, including *Horn Book, Audubon, Reader's Digest, National Wildlife,* and *International Wildlife.* Consultant for science books.

George's manuscripts are held in the Kerlan Collection at the University of Minnesota, Minneapolis.

Adaptations

My Side of the Mountain was adapted as a film starring Teddy Eccles and Theodore Bikel, Paramount, 1969. *Julie of the Wolves* was adapted as a recording, read by Irene Worth, Caedmon, 1977; as a film; and as a musical with music by Chris Kubie. *One Day in the Woods* was adapted as a musical video, with music by Fritz Kramer and Kubie, Kunhardt Productions, 1989; and as a musical, with music by Kubie, HarperCollins Audio, 1997. *On the Far Side of the Mountain* and *Frightful's Mountain* were recorded as an audiocassette by Recorded Books, 1995. Other books adapted for audiocassette include *Charlie's Raven,* Recorded Books, 2004.

Work in Progress

A novel titled *The Last Polar Bear,* about the threat to the poles posed by global warming.

Sidelights

Newbery Medal winner Jean Craighead George has made nature the center of her fiction and nonfiction work in a career spanning over half a century of writing and illustrating that includes over one hundred books. In her novels, picture books, and books of fact, George gives young readers many fascinating glimpses into the natural world, earning a reputation as "our premier naturalist novelist," according to *New York Times Book Review* contributor Beverly Lyon Clark. Writing first with her husband and more recently alone, she has penned studies of animals, such as *Dipper of Copper Creek,* as well as adventures featuring young people learning to survive in wilderness, like *My Side of the Mountain, Julie of the Wolves,* and *Charlie's Raven,* the first two of which inspired several sequels. Her books are distinguished by authentic detail and a blend of scientific curiosity, wonder, and concern for the natural environment, all expressed in a manner critics have described as both unsentimental and lyrical. As Karen Nelson Hoyle observed in *Dictionary of Literary Biography,* George "elevates nature in all its intricacies and makes scientific research concerning ecological systems intriguing and exciting to the young reader."

Born in Washington, DC, to a family of naturalists, George was destined to develop an early love of nature. Her father was an entomologist, her mother was a lover of nature and of storytelling, and her twin brothers were also drawn to the outdoors and contributed articles to major magazines about falconry while still in high school. Her twin brothers were a hard act for George to follow, and while growing up she was as adept on the softball field as she was on a mountain trail. George graduated from Pennsylvania State University in 1941, studying science and English. Thereafter she studied art at Louisiana State University and pursued graduate work at the University of Michigan.

George met her future husband, John Lothar George, during World War II; the couple married four months after their first meeting. Three children were soon born, and after the war John worked on his dissertation on birds and taught at various colleges, including Vassar. George's first six books were written in collaboration with her husband; each book characterizes a different animal. These early books "are best represented," according to Hoyle, by *Dipper of Copper Creek,* which "interweaves facts about the life cycle of the water ouzel with the tale of prospector Whispering Bill Smith and his grandson Doug's yearning for independence." Winner of the Aurianne Award in 1956, *Dipper of Copper Creek* set the tone for much of George's literary output through its informed and sensitive blendings of fact and fiction.

One of her first major solo efforts was *My Side of the Mountain,* a book that had been growing in her mind for some time before she put pen to paper. Using the woods lore she learned while on camping trips with her father and brothers along the Potomac River, George thought up a character and plot device to present such information. A survival story about a teenage boy who runs away to the woods and lives off the land for a year, *My Side of the Mountain* won a number of awards, including a Newbery Honor, and widespread praise. The first-person account describes thirteen-year-old Sam Gribley's self-sufficient wilderness life in detail, including the hollowed-out tree that becomes his home, his capture and training of the female peregrine falcon he names Frightful, and his various woodland recipes. Equipped with a pen knife, a ball of cord, an ax, and forty dollars, Sam whittles a fish hook out of a green twig, constructs a tent from hemlock boughs, and makes snowshoes from ash saplings and deer hide. His year in the woods is considered by some critics the ultimate survival tale for youngsters. Writing in *Horn Book,* Karen Jameyson commented on the book's premise: "When Sam explains, in his determined, quietly exuberant way, that he has decided to leave his New York City home . . . to go to live on the old Gribley land in the Catskill Mountains, the plan sounds a bit cockamamie. It also sounds mighty appealing." Zena Sutherland, writing in the *Bulletin of the Center for Children's Books,* called the novel "amazing and unusual," as well as "absorbing reading."

So appealing is its premise that *My Side of the Mountain* has become a modern classic. It was adapted for a movie in 1969 and has also inspired two highly popular sequels, 1990's *On the Far Side of the Mountain* and 1999's *Frightful's Mountain,* as well as the 2002 picture book *Frightful's Daughter.* In *On the Far Side of*

Illustrated by Daniel San Souci, Frightful's Daughter *is a picture-book sequel to George's popular novel* My Side of the Mountain. (Text copyright © 2003 by Jean Craighead George. Illustrations copyright © 2002 by Daniel San Souci. All rights reserved. Used by permission of Dutton Children's Books, a division of Penguin Young Readers Group, a member of Penguin Group (USA) Inc.)

the Mountain Sam's peregrine falcon, Frightful, has been seized by a conservation officer as an endangered species, and Sam's sister Alice then goes missing. Reviewing an audio version of the book, Edith Ching noted in *School Library Journal* that George's "attention to detail continues to be important" in this novel, and concluded that the book "is a narrative for all ages." With *Frightful's Mountain* the point of view shifts from humans to wildlife. The book opens with Frightful, Sam's peregrine, held by poachers, and the bird can think of only one thing: returning somehow to Sam. Sam's sister Alice is instrumental in freeing Frightful, but then the falcon must make its own way back to Sam. "George builds the suspense in a third-person narration that most often takes the falcon's perspective," noted a reviewer for *Publishers Weekly,* the critic adding that details such as peregrine migratory, mating, and nesting habits "are seamlessly woven into the plot." Praising the title in the *New York Times Book Review,* Mary Harris Russell commented that *Frightful's Mountain* "is a novel that will change the way you look at the world."

The falcon's story is continued for younger children in *Frightful's Daughter.* Enhanced by Daniel San Souci's detailed paintings, George's story recounts the plight of peregrine chick Oksi as she learns the ways of the wild and the dangers posed by some humans in order to survive. Almost caught by poachers, Frightful's young, independent-minded offspring is cared for by Sam until it is time to return to the wild, in a book that a *Kirkus Reviews* writer cited as an effective "means of introducing children to Sam Gribley's intriguing world."

The popularity of *My Side of the Mountain* could not have come at a better time for George, who divorced in 1963 and set about earning a living as a single parent by her writing. She also pursued her love of nature, turning her home in Chappaqua, New York, into something of a zoo with hundreds of wild animals living in her house and backyard, among them owls, robins, mink, seagulls, and even tarantulas. The success of *My Side of the Mountain* helped, as did a job with *Reader's Digest* from 1969 to 1982. Several other juvenile novels followed, including *Gull Number 737, Hold Zero!,* and *Coyote in Manhattan,* as well as the popular nonfiction series, "Thirteen Moons," which features a different animal for each of the new moons of the year's lunar calendar. Sutherland noted in a *Bulletin of the Center for Children's Books* review of series installment *The Moon of the Fox Pups* that George "writes of the animal world with knowledge and enthusiasm, her descriptions of wild life untainted by melodrama or anthropomorphism." The thirteen books in the series were reissued in 1993 with new illustrations.

One summer in the late 1960s George and her younger son, Luke, made a journey to Alaska, and this trip strongly shaped her novel *Julie of the Wolves*. The two had gone to Barrow to learn about wolf behavior from a scientist doing a study there, but they also got some unplanned lessons in native Inuit culture. George met a young Inuit woman from whom she learned a great deal about native life. The young woman also inspired the character of George's heroine. From the scientists studying wolves, George learned that humans are able to communicate with wolves and learn wolf language. One female wolf actually communicated back to the author. "When she answered back," George recalled on her home page, "I knew that I wanted to write a book about a little girl who is lost on the tundra and saves her life by communicating with wolves. So I did."

Julie of the Wolves tells the story of the adventures of an Inuit teen who becomes lost on the tundra while running away from an unhappy marriage. When her father disappears on a hunting expedition, Miyax—also known by the English name Julie—is adopted by relatives. At age thirteen she marries so she can leave her foster home. Although her husband is slow-witted and the marriage is little more than a formality, Miyax is content to live with his family. His forceful attempt to have sex with her, however, frightens her and she leaves him. Remembering her California pen pal's repeated invitations to visit, Miyax sets out across the tundra. When she loses her way in the barren land, she survives by learning how to communicate with a wolf pack and is befriended by the lead wolf in the pack whom she names Amaroq. Julie's knowledge of Inuit ways is also crucial, although gradually she begins to understand that the old ways are dying.

Reviewers were enthusiastic about the novel. Hoyle called *Julie of the Wolves* "George's most significant book," and wrote that the novel's "plot, character development, and setting are epic in dimension." Writing in *School Library Journal,* Alice Miller Bregman described the book as "compelling," and commented further that "George has captured the subtle nuances of Eskimo life, animal habits, [and] the pain of growing up, and combines these elements into a thrilling adventure which is, at the same time, a poignant love story." Reviewing *Julie of the Wolves* for the *New York Times Book Review,* James Houston observed that the novel "is packed with expert wolf lore, its narrative beautifully conveying the vastness of tundra as well as many other aspects of the Arctic." Though Houston questioned the reality of such a connection between human and wolf, he concluded that readers "slowly come to think of these wolves as dear friends." Writing in *Horn Book,* Virginia Haviland lauded the work as a "book of timeless, perhaps even of classic dimensions." Awards committees took a similar view, nominating the book for many prizes, and the novel won the prestigious Newbery Medal among other honors.

George revisits her characters in *Julie,* a 1994 sequel that begins only minutes after the ending of *Julie of the Wolves,* as well as in the 1997 novel *Julie's Wolf Pack,* a story told almost totally from the perspective of the wolves. In *Julie* the Inuit girl returns to her family's village, Kangik, only to discover that her long-estranged father, Kapugen, has married a white woman and left the old ways behind. In fact, readers learn that he is the one who shot Amaroq from a plane at the end of the previous novel. Julie struggles to save her beloved wolves and also falls in love with a young Siberian man, Peter Sugluk. "This one will go like hotcakes, both to new readers and old fans of the prequel," commented Susan Dunn in a *Voice of Youth Advocates* review of *Julie*. Dunn concluded that book is both "an excellent adventure story" and a novel that supplies a "delicious taste of a nontraditional lifestyle and personality." Writing in the *New York Times Book Review,* Hazel Rochman observed that "what's glorious is the lyrical nature writing. . . . George's sense of the place is so instinctive and so physically precise that the final Edenic vision of natural world order restored . . . is like a ringing song of triumph."

With *Julie's Wolf Pack* the focus shifts to the pack, now led by Kapu, the new alpha male. Constantly challenged by a loner wolf named Raw Bones, Kapu must prove himself to the pack, while rabies looms as another enemy. Though many reviewers felt the third novel lacks the dramatic tension of the first two, largely because Julie is peripheral to the plot, Carrie Eldridge, writing in *Kliatt,* thought George's "obvious knowledge of her subject matter is admirable and resonates throughout the story." Speaking with Karen Williams in the *Christian Science Monitor,* George explained her affinity for wolves: "I am intrigued that their society is very much like ours—with leaders (alphas), vice presidents (betas), and cabinet members. They all have talents, and the wolf pack recognized them. I love their devotion to each other. They stay together partly for economic reasons, but mainly because of their deep affection and loyalty."

George has written about the Arctic in other novels, as well, most notably in *Water Sky* and *The Wounded Wolf.* She has also looked at nature in the continental United States with ecological mysteries such as *Hook a Fish, Catch a Mountain: An Ecological Spy Story* (republished as *The Case of the Missing Cutthroat*), *Who Really Killed Cock Robin?: An Ecological Mystery, The Fire Bug Connection: An Ecological Mystery,* and *The Missing 'Gator of Gumbo Limbo;* and with adventures tales such as *Going to the Sun,* set in the Rocky Mountains; *River Rats, Inc.,* dealing with white-water rafting; *The Wentletrap Trap,* set on Bimini; and *The Cry of the Crow,* set in the Florida Everglades. Another novel set in the Everglades is *The Talking Earth.* More environmental issues are dealt with in *There's an Owl in the Shower,* in which an out-of-work logger's son takes in a baby owl only to discover that it is a species of spotted owl that has cost his father his job.

While illustrating many of her books for children, George frequently teams up with talented artists such as Wendell Minor, Thomas Locker, Ted Rand, and Daniel San Souci in producing her nature-filled books. Among her collaborations with Minor is *Arctic Son,* a "picture-book ode to the Arctic," according to a reviewer for *Publishers Weekly.* A chronicle of the birth and early years of George's grandson, the book is a "warm, positive story of life in the Far North," wrote Mollie Bynum in *School Library Journal.* In *Morning, Noon, and Night,* another collaboration with Minor, George portrays the activities of a variety of animals from dawn on the East Coast to sundown on the West. The Arctic spring is captured in *Snow Bear,* which tells of an Inuit girl who goes out on a hunt and encounters a bear cub. Patricia Manning, reviewing *Snow Bear* for *School Library Journal,* commented that "the simple, pleasing text is accompanied by luminous watercolors that faithfully record this charming (if improbable) chance meeting." Teaming up with Locker, George has also produced *The First Thanksgiving* and *To Climb a Waterfall,* and has created a series of picture books as companion volumes to Disney's *Animal Kingdom.*

George teamed with Rand to produce two picture-book adaptations of *Julie's Wolf Pack.* In *Nutik, the Wolf Pup* and *Nutik and Amaroq Play Ball* Julie's younger brother Amaroq is put in charge of a hungry wolf pup that has been orphaned in the wild. While the pair quickly become the best of friends, Amaroq realizes that at some point his new playmate will have to be returned to the

Cover of George's Tree Castle Island, *featuring artwork by Wendell Minor.* (Text copyright © 2003 by Jean Craighead George. Cover art © 2002 by Wendell Minor. Cover © 2003 by HarperCollins Publishers, Inc. Used by permission of HarperCollins Publishers.)

pack. Praising Rand's paintings in *Nutik, the Wolf Pup* for their ability to "capture the affection between boy and pup," *Booklist* contributor Linda Perkins also cited George's work in "skillfully telescop[ing]" a subplot of her novel "into a picture book with heart-tugging appeal."

Also featuring illustrations by Minor, *Tree Castle Island* is characteristic of George in its focus on a resourceful young person's ability to survive in the wild. The novel finds fourteen-year-old Jack staying with his Uncle Hamp in Florida while Jack's parents travel to Europe. Building his own canoe, he explores the Okefenokee Swamp near his uncle's house. After several days of exploring, Jack discovers that he cannot return home because of a blockage that has formed in the river; the current is now running the wrong way. Deciding to wait the situation out, the teen makes his way to an island in the middle of the swamp, where he builds a makeshift tree house for protection. A stray dog named Dizzy wanders onto the scene and becomes the boy's companion, followed by a local boy named Jake who, in a twist of fate, ultimately changes Jack's life forever. Carolyn Phelan, writing in *Booklist,* praised George's choice of the Okefenokee Swamp as "a well-developed, original setting." The book's ending, wrote a critic for *Kirkus Reviews,* is "a pleasant and satisfying surprise."

George researched *Tree Castle Island* by exploring the 700-square miles of the Okefenokee Swamp with her fourteen-year-old nephew and two granddaughters. She based Jack's island tree house on an old legend about Paradise Island, a beautiful island deep in the swamp where the mysterious "Sun Daughters" are said to live. "Although Jack doesn't find Paradise Island," George told Deborah Hopkinson in an online interview for *BookPage,* "he does make an important discovery about his own past."

Another story inspired by the author's research trips with family members, *Charlie's Raven* introduces readers to thirteen-year-old Charlie, who worries about his naturalist grandfather as the man recovers from a debilitating heart attack. After learning from his Teton Sioux friend Singing Bird that ravens have the ability to help the sick heal, Charlie captures a young raven chick he names Blue Sky. Hiding his true motives and unsure whether a bird with such a bad reputation can actually work for good, he declares that the bird is part of a research project. As Charlie's grandfather teaches the teen how to care for and observe the bird, he truly does seem to heal, and the experience also creates a strong bond between the man and his grandson. As Charlie learns about the bird, he begins to understand the duality of nature; as a *Kirkus Reviews* writer noted, "there aren't true dividing lines between good and bad in the natural world." Kay Weisman, reviewing *Charlie's Raven* in *Booklist,* called the book "a satisfying family story," while in *Publishers Weekly* a critic wrote that George "weaves threads of Native American lore and scientific fact into a moving story." While noting that the novel contains an overabundance of not-quite-believable occurances, Ellen Fader wrote in *School Library Journal* that young readers "will close the book with a healthy respect for the natural world."

Throughout her writing career, George has blended scientific accuracy with her love of nature and her ability to convey that love through telling detail, dramatic narrative, and likeable, realistic characters. As she noted on her home page, despite the distractions of modern culture, "Children are still in love with the wonders of nature, and I am too. So I tell them stories about a boy and a falcon, a girl and an elegant wolf pack, about owls, weasels, foxes, prairie dogs, the alpine tundra, the tropical rain forest. And when the telling is done, I hope they will want to protect all the beautiful creatures and places." Discussing her life as a writer during an online chat posted at the New York Public Library Web site, George exclaimed: "I just love it. I have a perfect life where I read, I go out into the wilderness and camp. I meet scientists and learn about their studies of wild animals and then I come home and I sit at my computer, close my eyes and start creating the world I have seen. Then I get up and make supper!"

Biographical and Critical Sources

BOOKS

Beacham's Guide to Literature for Young Adults, Volumes 2, 4, Beacham Publishing (Osprey, FL), 1990.

Cary, Alice, *Jean Craighead George,* Learning Works (Santa Barbara, CA), 1996.

Children's Literature Review, Volume 1, Thomson Gale (Detroit, MI), 1976.

Contemporary Literary Criticism, Volume 35, Thomson Gale (Detroit, MI), 1985.

Dictionary of Literary Biography, Volume 52: *American Writers for Children since 1960: Fiction,* Thomson Gale (Detroit, MI), 1986.

Gallo, Donald R., editor, *Speaking for Ourselves: Autobiographical Sketches by Notable Authors of Books for Young Adults,* National Council of Teachers of English (Urbana, IL), 1990.

George, Jean Craighead, *Journey Inward,* Dutton (New York, NY), 1982.

St. James Guide to Young-Adult Writers, 2nd edition, St. James Press (Detroit, MI), 1999.

Viguers, Ruth Hill, *A Critical History of Children's Literature,* revised edition, Macmillan (New York, NY), 1969.

Writers for Young Adults, Scribner (New York, NY), 1997.

PERIODICALS

Booklist, May 15, 1993, p. 1693; July, 1993, p. 1970; August, 1994, p. 2064; April 15, 1995, p. 1505; August, 1995, p. 1966; September, 1995, p. 77; November 15, 1996, Carolyn Phelan, review of *The Tarantula in My Purse: And 172 Other Wild Pets,* p. 581; August, 1998, p. 2014; December 1, 1998, p. 670; August, 1999, p. 2063; September 1, 1999, Linda Perkins, review of *Frightful's Mountain,* p. 132; February 1, 2001, Linda Perkins, review of *Nutik, the Wolf Pup,* p. 1055; May 15, 2001, Carolyn Phelan, review of *Nutik and Amaroq Play Ball,* p. 1757; March 15, 2002, Carolyn Phelan, review of *Tree Castle Island,* p. 1255; September, 2002, Julie Cummins, review of *Frightful's Daughter,* p. 136; December 1, 2003, Ilene Cooper, review of *Fire Storm,* p. 684; August, 2004, Kay Weisman, review of *Charlie's Raven,* p. 1933; October 15, 2004, GraceAnne A. DeCandido, review of *Snowboard Twist,* p. 410.

Bulletin of the Center for Children's Books, June, 1960, Zena Sutherland, review of *My Side of the Mountain,* p. 161; July-August, 1968, Zena Sutherland, review of *The Moon of the Fox Pups,* p. 174; January, 1972, p. 74; April, 1995, pp. 275-275; July, 2001, review of *Nutik, the Wolf Pup,* p. 408.

Christian Science Monitor, September 25, 1997, Karen Williams, "Talking with Wolves, Then Writing about Them," p. 82.

Horn Book, January-February, 1973, Virginia Haviland, review of *Julie of the Wolves,* pp. 54-55; July-August, 1989, Karen Jameyson, "A Second Look: *My Side of* the Mountain," pp. 529-531; November-December, 1989, pp. 808-810; November-December, 1994, p. 730; January-February, 1998, p. 71; March-April, 2000, p. 209.

Kirkus Reviews, May 1, 2002, review of *Tree Castle Island,* p. 654; May 15, 2002, review of *Cliff Hanger,* p. 732; August 15, 2002, review of *Frightful's Daughter,* p. 1223; August 15, 2003, review of *Fire Storm,* p. 1972; September 1, 2004, review of *Charlie's Raven,* p. 865.

Kliatt, September, 1995, p. 62; May, 1996, p. 8; July, 1996, p. 52; July, 1999, Carrie Eldridge, review of *Julie's Wolf Pack,* p. 16; May, 2003, Claire Rosser, review of *Tree Castle Island,* p. 16.

New York Times Book Review, January 21, 1973, James Houston, review of *Julie of the Wolves,* p. 8; May 10, 1987, Beverly Lyon Clark, review of *Water Sky,* p. 26; May 20, 1990, p. 42; November 13, 1994, Hazel Rochman, review of *Julie,* p. 27; November 16, 1997, p. 58; November 21, 1999, Mary Harris Russell, review of *Frightful's Mountain,* p. 28.

Publishers Weekly, September 20, 1993, p. 32; January 23, 1995, p. 70; April 28, 1997, p. 77; July 21, 1997, review of *Arctic Son,* p. 200; May 25, 1998, p. 92; May 31, 1999, p. 96; October 18, 1999, review of *Frightful's Mountain,* p. 83; May 7, 2001, p. 249; April 29, 2002, review of *Cliff Hanger,* p. 69; September 15, 2003, review of *Fire Storm,* p. 67; October 4, 2004, review of *Charlie's Raven,* p. 88.

School Library Journal, January, 1973, Alice Miller Bregman, review of *Julie of the Wolves,* p. 75; February, 1993, p. 97; September, 1994, p. 176; June, 1995, p. 100; September, 1995, p. 163; May, 1996, Edith Ching, audio review of *On the Far Side of the Mountain,* p. 75; June, 1996, p. 122; November, 1997, Mollie Bynum, review of *Arctic Son,* pp. 81-82; March, 1999, p. 174; April, 1999, p. 94; September, 1999, Patricia Manning, review of *Snow Bear,* p. 182; January, 2001, Debra Bogart, review of *Frightful's Mountain,* p. 74; March, 2001, Catherine T. Quattlebaum, review of *Nuttik the Wolf Pup,* p. 208; May, 2002, Faith Brautigam, review of *Tree Castle Island,* p. 152; September, 2002, Margaret Bush, review of *Frightful's Daughter,* p. 192; December, 2002, Dorian Chong, review of *Frightful's Daughter,* p. 96; November, 2003, Linda Ludke, review of *Fire Storm,* p. 94; September, 2004, Ellen Fader, review of *Charlie's Raven,* p. 205; November, 2004, Rebecca Luhman, review of *Snowboard Twist,* p. 103.

Teaching PreK-8, May, 1994, Diane Winarski, "The Dynamic Environment of Jean Craighead George."

Voice of Youth Advocates, December, 1994, Susan Dunn, review of *Julie,* p. 272; August, 1996, p. 156; April, 1998, p. 42; February, 2000, p. 110; March, 2001, Catherine T. Quattlebaum, review of *Nutik, the Wolf Pup,* p. 208; July, 2001, Sally R. Dow, review of *Nutik and Amaroq Play Ball,* p. 81.

ONLINE

BookPage, http://www.bookpage.com/ (May 15, 2006), Deborah Hopkinson, interview with George.

Jean Craighead George Home Page, http://www.jeancraigheadgeorge.com (May 15, 2006).

New York Public Library Summer Reading Web site, http://summerreading.nypl.org/ (August 17, 2004), "Transcript of Live Chat with Jean Craighead George."

OTHER

All about the Book!: A Kid's Video Guide to "Julie of the Wolves" (DVD), Tim Podell Productions, 2002.

A Talk with Jean Craighead George (DVD), Tim Podell Productions, 1991.

Storyteller: A Year with Jean Craighead George (DVD), Craighead Environmental Research Institute, 2005.*

*   *   *

GERBER, Merrill Joan 1938-

Personal

Born March 15, 1938, in Brooklyn, NY; daughter of William (an antique dealer) and Jessie (Sorblum) Gerber; married Joseph Spiro (a college teacher), June 23, 1960; children: Becky Ann, Joanna Emily, Susanna Willa. *Education:* Attended University of Miami, 1955; University of Florida, B.A., 1959; Brandeis University, graduate study, 1959-60, M.A., 1980. *Religion:* Jewish.

Addresses

Office—Division of the Humanities and Social Sciences, 228-77, California Institute of Technology, Pasadena, CA 91125. *E-mail*—mjgerber@caltech.edu.

Career

Pasadena City College, Pasadena, CA, creative writing lecturer, 1980-89; California Institute of Technology, Pasadena, creative writing lecturer, 1989—. Former editor, Houghton Mifflin Co., Boston, MA; lecturer at many writers' conferences, including those at University of California, University of Florida, and Pasadena City College; has taught creative writing at California State University at Los Angeles, University of Redlands.

Awards, Honors

Wallace Stegner fiction fellowship to Stanford University, 1962-63; residency grant, Yaddo Writers' Colony, 1981; Andrew Lytle Fiction Prize, *Sewanee Review,* 1985, for "At the Fence"; short fiction award, *Fiction Network,* 1985, for "Hairdos"; O. Henry Award, Doubleday, 1986, for "I Don't Believe This"; Pushcart Editors' Book Award for literary distinction, 1990, for *King of the World;* Harold U. Ribalow Prize for best English-language book of fiction on a Jewish theme, *Hadassah* magazine, 1992, for *The Kingdom of Brooklyn;* named Alumna of Outstanding Achievement, University of Florida, 1997; McGiniss-Ritchie prize, *Southwest Review,* 2001, for "Anna Passes On"; *Anna in the Afterlife* chosen a best novel of 2002, *Los Angeles Times.*

Merrill Joan Gerber (Photograph reproduced by permission.)

Writings

NOVELS

An Antique Man, Houghton Mifflin (Boston, MA), 1967.
Now Molly Knows, Arbor House (New York, NY), 1974.
The Lady with the Moving Parts, Arbor House (New York, NY), 1978.
King of the World, Pushcart (Wainscott, NY), 1990.
The Kingdom of Brooklyn, Longstreet Press (Atlanta, GA), 1992.
Anna in the Afterlife, Syracuse University Press (Syracuse, NY), 2002.
Glimmering Girls: A Novel of the Fifties, University of Wisconsin Press (Madison, WI), 2005.

SHORT STORIES

Stop Here, My Friend, Houghton Mifflin (Boston, MA), 1965.
Honeymoon, University of Illinois Press (Champaign, IL), 1985.
Chattering Man: Stories and a Novella, Longstreet Press (Atlanta, GA), 1991.
This Old Heart of Mine: The Best of Merrill Joan Gerber's Redbook Stories, Longstreet Press (Athens, GA), 1993.
Anna in Chains, Library of Modern Jewish Literature series, Syracuse University Press (Syracuse, NY), 1998.
This Is a Voice from Your Past: New and Selected Stories, Ontario Review Press (Princeton, NJ), 2005.

YOUNG-ADULT FICTION

Please Don't Kiss Me Now, Dial (New York, NY), 1981.
Name a Star for Me, Viking (New York, NY), 1983.
I'm Kissing as Fast as I Can, Fawcett (New York, NY), 1985.
The Summer of My Indian Prince, Fawcett (New York, NY), 1986.
Also Known as Sadzia! The Belly Dancer!, Harper (New York, NY), 1987.
Marry Me Tomorrow, Fawcett (New York, NY), 1987.
Even Pretty Girls Cry at Night, Crosswinds (Don Mills, Ontario, Canada), 1988.
I'd Rather Think about Robby, Harper (New York, NY), 1988.
Handsome as Anything, Scholastic (New York, NY), 1990.

OTHER

Old Mother, Little Cat: A Writer's Reflections on Her Kitten, Her Aged Mother . . . and Life (nonfiction), Longstreet Press (Atlanta, GA), 1995.
Botticelli Blue Skies: An American in Florence, University of Wisconsin Press (Madison, WI), 2002.
Gut Feelings: A Writer's Truths and Minute Inventions, University of Wisconsin Press (Madison, WI), 2003.

Also author of *Old Mother, Little Cat* (e-book); contributor to books, including *Prize Stories: The O. Henry Awards 1986,* edited by William Abrahams, Doubleday (New York, NY), 1986, and *The Best American Mystery Stories 1998.* Contributor of short stories and essays to periodicals, including *American Scholar, Chattahoochee Review, Commentary, Family Circle, Ladies' Home Journal, Mademoiselle, McCall's, New Yorker, Redbook, Salmagundi, Sewanee Review, Southwest Review,* and *Woman's Day.* Also contributor of articles on writing to *The Writer* and *Writer's Digest.*

Sidelights

"Merrill Joan Gerber is not one to be pushed into a corner," wrote Lisa See Kendall in *Publishers Weekly.* Gerber has published collections of short stories, novels, and young-adult titles, as well as guides for writers, a travel memoir, and personal essays. She began writing stories and essays when she was seven years old, and her first published piece of work, a poem, appeared in *The Writer* when she was eighteen. She began selling stories to magazines such as the *New Yorker* and *Redbook.* Over the course of her career, Gerber published more short stories in *Redbook* than any other contributor to that magazine. However, her publication record has not always won her recognition. Gerber is a "seriously underrated and often-overlooked writer," according to *Booklist* reviewer Margaret Flanagan in her review of *This Is a Voice from Your Past: New and Selected Stories.*

Gerber's early stories and novels described daily life of American women who accepted their roles as wives and mothers. In 1990 she published *King of the World,* a book she she felt was "her best work to date," according to Kendall. "You can only tell some of the story in teen books or *Redbook*," Gerber told Kendall. "But you get to a point where you say you're going to tell all you know. You're going to reveal certain pains, resentments, and angers." It took Gerber years to find a publisher, but when the book was finally published by Pushcart Press, it received Pushcart's Editor's Book Award. A *Booklist* reviewer called it "a powerful, sad, and haunting tale of love and madness."

After *King of the World*, Gerber published three books with Longstreet Press: *Chattering Man: Stories and a Novella* (stories), *This Old Heart of Mine: The Best of Merrill Joan Gerber's Redbook Stories*, and *The Kingdom of Brooklyn*, a novel that tells the story of Issa, who grows up during and just after World War II. A reviewer for *Publishers Weekly* called the last-named work "a brutally candid, semiautobiographical novel" and praised Gerber's writing, noting that "her wry purity of style packs psychological dynamite."

Anna in Chains follows the life of Anna Goldman, an old woman who tries to maintain herself first in her own apartment, then a retirement home, and finally in a nursing home. The novel was dubbed "a wonderfully wry look at the outrageous indignities of old age" by a reviewer for *Publishers Weekly*. *Anna in the Afterlife* takes place in the four days between Anna's death and her burial, a period that allows her to uncover secrets of her past and gain a deeper understanding of her life before she departs into eternity.

As the author once told *SATA*: "During my fourteenth year, my father gave me a very large bound book, a blank publisher's 'dummy' to use as a diary. Its title was nothing less dramatic than *Mutiny on the Bounty*—on its cover was a sailing vessel, embossed, its sails at full tilt, its hull crashing about on a stormy sea. What better diary imaginable in which to record the passions of the teen years? What metaphor *could* be better?" Drawing on these diary entries, during the 1980s Gerber penned several novels for teens, among them *The Summer of My Indian Prince*, *Marry Me Tomorrow*, and *Even Pretty Girls cry at Night*. "Now that I have survived those years (if one ever does)," the author once noted, "and have observed and sometimes helped as my three daughters passed through their teen years, I know there is no other time of life when experience is so intense, awareness so piercingly sharp, hope so hopeful, and love so tender. Likewise, never again is pain so painful, or despair so agonizing." While writing her young-adult novels, Gerber explained that she was able "to re-enter, re-create, and . . . reinterpret some of those most significant experiences. Communicating with young readers going through those times, and offering them perhaps some calming reassurance, as well as some perspective on their passage, is one of the great satisfactions of writing YA books."

Old Mother, Little Cat: A Writer's Reflections on Her Kitten, Her Aged Mother . . . and Life is a memoir about Gerber's mother's long stay in a nursing home at the same time that Gerber discovers a kitten living under her house. The kitten's energy and love of life stands in contrast to her mother's dying, and the two stories play out against each other. "Gerber has done an excellent job of conveying her mother's strength and humanity," wrote a reviewer for *Publishers Weekly*.

Botticelli Blue Skies: An American in Florence "presents an absolutely delightful travel memoir," according to Margaret Flanagan in *Booklist*. The book describes the semester Gerber and her professor husband lived for three months in Florence. Alison Hopkins, writing for *Library Journal* called the book "an absorbing account of life in another country."

Gerber describes her fiction writing processes in *Gut Feelings: A Writer's Truths and Minute Inventions*. Denise J. Stankovics, writing in *Library Journal*, praised Gerber's ability to "cleverly blend . . . memoir and invention to illustrate how an author's life influences her literary output." A critic for *Kirkus Reviews* called the entries in the collection "refined, concise, often emotionally wringing vignettes."

Biographical and Critical Sources

PERIODICALS

Booklist, November 15, 2002, Margaret Flanagan, review of *Botticelli Blue Skies: An American in Florence,* p. 565; March 1, 2005, Margaret Flanagan, review of *This Is a Voice from Your Past,* p. 1136.

Kirkus Reviews, March 1, 2003, review of *Gut Feelings: A Writer's Truths and Minute Inventions,* p. 360; January 15, 2005, review of *This Is a Voice from Your Past,* p. 71; March 15, 2005, review of *Glimmering Girls: A Novel of the Fifties,* p. 305.

Library Journal, September 15, 2002, Alison Hopkins, review of *Botticelli Blue Skies,* p. 83.

Los Angeles Times, May 7, 1988.

Los Angeles Times Book Review, December 18, 1985.

New York Times Book Review, December 15, 1985.

Publishers Weekly, July 25, 1991, review of *Chattering Man,* p. 38; August 3, 1992, review of *The Kingdom of Brooklyn,* p. 61; November 8, 1993, Lisa See Kendall, "Merrill Joan Gerber: A Veteran of the Short Story (and More) Collects Some of Her Strongest Stories," pp. 54-55; September 25, 1995, review of *Old Mother, Little Cat: A Writer's Reflections on Her Kitten, Her Aged Mother . . . and Life,* p. 38; November, 25, 2002, review of *Botticelli Blue Skies,* p. 56.

Shofar, winter, 2003, review of *Anna in the Afterlife,* p. 202.

Washington Post Book World, November 17, 1985.

ONLINE

California Techical College Web site, http://www.its.caltech.edu/ (May 6, 2006), "Merrill Joan Gerber."

Autobiography Feature

Merrill Joan Gerber

Merrill Joan Gerber contributed the following autobiographical essay to *SATA*:

A FEW WORDS

They had lost so many by the time I was born. My mother had lost her father and her brother. My grandmother had lost her first husband, her second husband, and her son. My aunt, who lived with us, had (also) lost her father and her brother. By the time I was five, my mother had, in addition, lost her nephew and her stillborn son; my aunt (if you count the dead baby) had lost two nephews; and my grandmother, likewise, two grandsons. Each counted her own losses fully; the overlap seemed merely to increase the number of snatched-away souls. Their combined ghostly mass in our home was cumulative and oppressive. The women who raised me hovered about me in fear and mourning. The awareness of loss-sustained and loss-yet-to-come was my first impression of the nature of life.

My household was volatile: my mother explosive, my father conciliatory (he had to be), my aunt and grandmother (who lived upstairs while I lived with my parents downstairs) acting as buffers or mediators or simply "flies on the wall." There was no telling what a day would bring. I spent my childhood in a heightened state of awareness, the better to predict when to take cover, or to guess from what quarter the explosion would come. At times I would try to hide from it, at others I would decide how to cause it. I took it all in. I made my judgments, assessments, drew my conclusions. I didn't let down my guard very often—they all depended on me to keep things going. I ran from the downstairs to the upstairs to the downstairs, checking the positions and states of mind of the major players, keeping the house in balance.

I knew I was pivotal, an important property. My aunt, single, childless, wanted me, and perhaps wanted my father, too. My mother, who had me, was gifted with little patience. They all coveted me, fought over me, bargained for me, courted me. My sister wasn't born till I was seven, so I had their undiluted attention for years. And they had mine.

My fiction does, of course, take a good deal of its energy from this early life, but I have worked on my art in my fiction, and here, in these pages, I want to discuss the origins of that life and its surroundings. I have always paid close attention to my family history, ab-

Merrill Joan Gerber, age three, with father, William Gerber, in Brooklyn, 1941. (Reproduced by permission.)

sorbed every detail of what happened and to whom it happened and when it happened and why it happened and how each person felt about it. All this was extremely important to me, though I can't say exactly why. I don't think my mother cared two hoots about the "old country." It was better forgotten, as far as she was concerned, but I believe what happened there and how it affected our household is what formed me into the person and writer I became.

My mother had very little use for the immigrant relatives who—with their poor diction, crude thinking, and vulgar behavior—caused her to feel embarrassment and disgust. I don't think my father did much reflecting on the meaning of life (he was too busy trying to earn a living). My grandmother was an uncomplicated, practical woman from Poland, busy cooking and cleaning, and grieving her losses on the bench in front of our house. It may have been my aunt, my mother's younger sister—the one who was the wallflower, the one who never left the house, the one who was too delicate to work out in the world, the one who believed she would meet the love of her life, if she was meant to, while putting out the garbage, the one who said my father should have married her and not my mother—whose influence was so powerful. So little happened to her that she held a magnifying glass to each tiny act that in any way related to her, replayed in her mind every careless remark of a neighbor or relative, relived each gesture of a schoolmate or a girlfriend. She knew all the family tragedies, romances, accidents, suicides, and scandals— and regaled me with their details. She remembered every word some young man or another had ever said to her (or, more to the point, to my mother). She held grudges forever. She remembered slights and rehearsed them every day. She was meticulous in her recollections, particularly if they concerned my mother who always denied, and does to this day, what her sister remembered about her. My aunt saw significance in everything. As did I.

Part One

My mother's mother, Beckie Panker Sorblum, had come to America in steerage from Kutno, Poland, at the age of twenty-one. She was courted by her handsome first husband, Davis Josephthal, who told her that he spoke seven languages and had been an aristocrat in Europe. In fact, he had left a wife and daughter behind in Europe, which he neglected to tell her. He soon abandoned my grandmother, too, and she was forced by circumstance to put her two small children, Eva and Sam, into an orphanage. She found work as a midwife during the years she was going through the formal requirements to attain her "get" (Jewish divorce). When she finally did, she learned that her husband had died in a diabetic coma shortly after leaving her.

Through acquaintances, as was the way in those days, she met my grandfather, a tailor eleven years her junior, named Morris Sorblum (although before passing through customs on Ellis Island, his name had been "Sauerbach"). Soon after their marriage they had two children: my mother, Jessie Sorblum, born November 28, 1907, and my aunt, Yetta Sorblum, born June 10, 1910. They lived briefly on the lower east side of New York, then moved to an apartment at 613 East 138th Street in the Bronx where they paid a rent of $38 a month for five rooms. My grandfather's employer, who owned a women's garment factory, also owned the apartment house in which the family lived—so that whatever my grandfather earned at work, he paid back to his boss in rent. The two sisters, Jessie and Yetta, went to PS 9, the school where my mother got her first look at the genteel, cultured life of her (gentile) teachers. She aspired to education, to speaking the English language in beautiful tones. She told me many times of her greatest humiliation: when she met her

"Grandparents Beckie and Morris Sorblum with my mother, Jessie, age three, and my aunt Yetta (later named Greta), age one," about 1918. (Reproduced by permission.)

first-grade teacher in the street, the teacher did not seem to recognize her. My mother said to her: "Oh dear, teacher don't know me." Immediately, she was aware of her grammatical error and was shamed by it. By the passion and frequency with which she told this story, I know she was haunted by this lapse all her life. At graduation from eighth grade, she won the "gold medal for academic excellence." As she stood in the darkened audience to go up to the stage to receive it, the boy who was in competition with her for the medal muttered to her as she passed him by, "Just wait till I get you outside." Many Jewish parents, who had left their homes and families and crossed an ocean to seek education and a better life for their offspring, demanded and expected that their children bring home academic honors. (I don't think this was the case in my mother's home, however. My grandmother, Beckie, was a mild-mannered simple person who had no knowledge of book-learning or desire for it. If anyone yearned for education, it was my mother. At the time I write this, she is eighty-six years old and living, paralyzed, in a nursing home and still she cherishes her gold medal. Last year, when my daughter Joanna passed her orals in comparative literature at Yale, my mother asked me to give it as a gift to her.)

When my mother was seven, her parents noticed that she spent much of her time "playing piano" on the edge of the kitchen table. They arranged to buy her an upright piano and weekly piano lessons. She devoted herself to practicing and was soon playing the music of Chopin, Mozart, and Beethoven. When her mother's parents, Fanny (Feygele) and Israel Panker, came to the United States from Poland, they lived for a time with my grandmother's sister, Sarah Panker Weisgrow. When Fanny took ill, she moved into the Bronx apartment to be nursed by my grandmother. Her bed was placed in front of the piano, denying my mother access to her precious hours of practice time. My mother told me she did not have charitable thoughts about the old woman whose smell was unpleasant and whose bed blocked her way to the piano. Not long after that, my mother was at a party and remembers feeling an icy sensation come over her. She knew something dreadful had happened, and when she got home, she learned that her grandmother had died.

Her father's parents, David Ichiel and Elka Hyah Sorblum, came to America, too, when their children could arrange to care for them, but my mother could not speak Yiddish (and refused to learn it) so she had almost no communication with them.

In 1924, when the sisters were fourteen and sixteen, the family moved from the Bronx to Brooklyn.

Author's mother, age thirteen, at eighth grade graduation, wearing gold medal for academic excellence. (Reproduced by permission.)

(My aunt told me very recently that the reason for their move was that my mother was ashamed of their living quarters, that after one of her dates took her home and expressed surprise that she "lived in such a dump" she demanded of my grandfather that they move to a classier place. "She always got what she wanted.") The small two-story house they bought (for $9,999) at 405 Avenue O in Brooklyn was hardly a castle (though I grew up there and thought it was. My novel, *The Kingdom of Brooklyn,* is set there).

My grandfather made his living studying the fashions in windows of department stores, and then copying them in sample patterns he made for his employer. In his nights at home, he sewed stylish clothes for his daughters. My mother was always proud to be well dressed.

He also had a great love for opera, and especially for the singer Enrico Caruso. Buying the cheapest tickets to the Metropolitan Opera House, he frequently took my mother with him, and together they stood in the back of the theater to watch the performances. On his Victrola at home, he played the great operas and instructed her in the highlights of their melodrama.

At some point my mother was faced with the choice of attending one of two high schools: Hunter, which offered an academic program, or Roosevelt, which offered a commercial course. Because she had a girlfriend going to Roosevelt who begged her to go there, my mother agreed—and once there, found herself bored and impatient. (As my aunt made clear not long ago, eager to set the record straight once again, "Your mother thought she knew more than her teachers.")

My mother dropped out of high school and took a brief business course after which she went to work for a law firm. She had gotten the job by stating she'd had previous legal experience. On her first day there, when a man came into the office and asked for "the process server," she commenced to look in the drawers of her desk, thinking it must be something like a cake server. (She told this story without amusement; being humiliated as a result of her ignorance was intolerable to her.)

A year after the family moved to the house in Brooklyn, my mother's half brother, Sam Josephthal, was drowned at sea. He had served in the infantry during World War I, and after the war he lived with the family in the Brooklyn house, contributing not only a thousand dollars of the two-thousand-dollar down payment but also helping with the mortgage payments. Eva was married by then, to Eddie Sherman, a prizefighter. They also lived in a house in Brooklyn with their three sons: my cousins Irving, Henry, and Fred. As the story was told all the years I was growing up, Sam went fishing one stormy Yom Kippur night in 1925—went fishing with a "bad lot" of friends on a night when a good Jewish son should have been in shul—and was lost when his boat sank in the waters off Coney Island.

(Sixty years after his disappearance, my aunt Eva, sitting with me in 1985 on the porch of her retirement hotel in Miami Beach, told me the truth that had never been told to my grandmother or my mother or my aunt. Sam's boat had, in fact, been gunned down by the Coast Guard. On that stormy night in the Prohibition year of 1925, he and his friends had been bootlegging whiskey over the high seas.)

After his disappearance, my mother, only eighteen, was required to take on the grisly job of visiting the morgue to look at the faces of drowned men in the hopes of identifying her brother. (He was never found and, seven years later, the family was allowed to collect on his thousand-dollar life insurance policy.)

In 1929, only four years after Sam's drowning, my grandfather, Morris Sorblum, died at the age of forty-eight. His death occurred due to suffocation brought on by the swelling of the floor of his mouth. His severe throat pain had been misdiagnosed over the phone by a neighborhood doctor who dismissed it as "only a sore throat" and refused to make a house call. My mother called him a second time, in desperation, when my grandfather claimed his pain was so severe he was going to throw himself out the window. The doctor said he was "just high-strung and of a nervous temperament" and "tended to exaggerate." My mother finally called for an ambulance. As they carried my grandfather down the stairs, he looked at my mother who was standing at the foot of the stairs just outside the door. As he passed her by he admonished her to "button up your coat." He died in the ambulance on the way to the hospital.

His illness was later identified as Ludwig's angina, a disease that was often fatal before the advent of antibiotics. After his death (on March 15, which would be the date of my birth nine years later) my mother called the local doctor who had refused to come and see her father. She threatened to kill him. Within weeks, he had closed his practice and moved out of the neighborhood.

My grandmother, who had a poor command of English (she spoke mainly Yiddish) was faced with finding a way to pay off the mortgage. My mother was already working. Her sister, Yetta, who in high school had changed her name to Yvonne, Yvette, and finally to Greta, began to bake cookies at home and box them for my mother to take with her to her office building in Manhattan to sell to fellow workers. My mother told me she hated carrying greasy cardboard boxes (the grease stained the fine clothes that her father had sewn for her). My mother by then was earning $41 a week, an unusually high salary for those times, and was working for two New York state senators, Elwood M. Raybenold and Charles E. Scribner. So impressed were they with her competence and intelligence that they offered to send her to law school at night while she continued to work for them during the day. She was flattered and considered the offer seriously, but finally had to decline. There were not enough hours in the day and night to do all she would have had to do.

*

In 1933, my aunt Greta gave a party at the Brooklyn house, to which my father came along (or more likely was "dragged along") as the buddy of one of my aunt's friends. He was brought, the story goes, as the date for my aunt. Uneasy in the crowd of strangers in the house, he wandered out to the front porch and sat there alone in the dark, smoking his pipe. This is where he first saw my mother, who was coming home from a date with a young lawyer. (I've heard many versions of this meeting and it was one of my earliest inspirations for the use of family history in my fiction.)

My parents married on November 10, 1934, in a wedding that took place in the house on Avenue O. (My father's mother was against this marriage, having the belief that her three sons should not marry before their two sisters were married. Neither of my father's sisters seemed destined to make an early marriage, and eventually all the brothers took wives while "the girls" were still single.)

My mother and father, as newlyweds, lived on in the house with my aunt and grandmother. (They were given the large, upstairs front bedroom, while my grandmother and aunt shared a bed in the back room. It wasn't till my sister was born that the house was converted into an upstairs and a downstairs apartment.) My father took upon himself the duties of supporting my grandmother and aunt (my mother continued to work, as well) and did whatever work came his way. His first job was as a sales clerk in the men's pajama department of Loeser's Department Store.

My father's history—like my mother's—was about struggle and survival. His mother, Fanny Goldstein Gerber, had five children: Lillian, Nat, William (this was my father's American name, but he was called Velvel Gerber in elementary school, and sometimes Meyer Wolf), Mac, and Pauline. Fanny had to accept the charity of her brother, Harry Goldstein, after her husband, my paternal grandfather Abraham Gerber—so the story goes—was hit on the head by a falling hammer while working in the navy yards and wasn't "right in the head" afterward. I never met him, nor did my mother, although she often packed boxes of goodies and sweets for my father and his brothers to take to him when they went off on Sunday afternoons to visit him in what must have been the insane asylum. (None of the brothers and sisters would ever discuss his illness with me, not then and not when I was an adult.)

My grandmother Fanny lived upstairs in her brother Harry Goldstein's house on Eighty-sixth Street in Bensonhurst; Harry ran a profitable neighborhood liquor

"In the house of my father's uncle Harry Goldestein in Bensonhurst: father, me (age five), mother, Grandmother Beckie Sorblum, and Aunt Greta," 1944. (Reproduced by permission.)

store with his brothers. Only my father's eldest brother, Nat, was given (or took for himself) the opportunity to go to college. He later became rich and successful in the oil business and moved to Park Avenue in Manhattan, where he and his wife, Bertha, and their children, Iris and Eddie, lived in high style. Each of the other Gerber siblings made his way as best he could. None of them, I think, aside from my Uncle Nat, finished high school.

I know my father did not even finish sixth grade. After he married my mother, he plunged into one business venture after another. In 1956, he traveled to Cleveland with her to look into a business venture he'd heard was promising: servicing crane machines and pinball machines in bars and roadhouses. The crane machine was actually a form of gambling. It had a claw hand which reached into a pile of "prizes" each time a player deposited a coin. Occasionally the claw would grasp a toy, a cheap wristwatch, or some other object, and drop it into a chute, from which it would slide out to the patron. People seemed to love playing them and my father had high hopes for this business. He planned to set up a series of these machines in New York, but they were soon destined to be pronounced illegal by Governor Thomas Dewey, who ordered that all crane machines in the city be dumped in the East River.

My mother wrote letters home from Cleveland, testifying to the rare pleasure of being alone with my father. On November 10, 1936, their second anniversary, she wrote:

Dear Mom and Gretch—

Your lovely card duly arrived . . . Will brought me a lovely one & a grand corsage of gardenias. We went to see the only show in town, *Naughty Marietta*—orchestra—tenth row . . . After we left Will drove home in what seemed a strange direction, and then pulled up in a sinister-looking block with Negroes all over the place. I hadn't expected to be taken anywhere else, but there we were at Cedar Gardens, the Cotton Club of Cleveland. It was a strange and nice experience . . . a really nice place, all Negro entertainers and mighty good ones. We stayed for two floor shows—both different—and got home at 3 . . .

Anyhow, we had a grand and glorious evening—and I know you'll be glad.

In another letter written home to Brooklyn, February 25, 1937, my mother says:

Maybe I'll do some work on my scrapbook this afternoon. Though I have some silk underwear needs ironing . . . and Will's shorts need sewing together . . . Soon my Willyum will be home . . . so long now while I beautify myself.

This period away was one of the few times my parents had alone together for the next fifteen years. I was conceived in Cleveland and born in Brooklyn on March 15, 1938.

My father, always willing to try again, began to work on a series of inventions. He perfected (or so he thought), among other things, a wooden hockey game with twirling hockey sticks, a plastic device called "Stand-A-Plate" (which didn't stand up—all the plates tipped over and broke), and in the fifties he wanted to take a patent on a Coney Island-type ride called "The Merry-Go-Bob"—named for myself and my sister, Barbara.

In 1943, my father and mother decided to leave my grandmother and aunt in Brooklyn for a few months and take a trip to Miami Beach, a place in which my father had always dreamed of living. It was wartime; soldiers were on the beach and occupying most of the hotels. My father opened a small business cutting records for soldiers who, before they shipped out, wanted to send messages home to their wives and mothers.

My mother found herself pregnant during this time, and it was also in these months in Florida that we learned (from a newspaper my mother opened one morning where she read the "Missing in Action" list) about the disappearance of Henry, my aunt Eva's middle son (who was born exactly—to the day—twenty years earlier than I was, on March 15, 1918). He had always wanted to be a flier and had enlisted in the air corps to train as a pilot. While he was in training, he wrote home often, sending pictures of himself in flight gear to his mother and little presents for me. (I still have his gold Air Corps wings.) One letter from April 27, 1942, reads:

Dear Folks,

Flew like an angel yesterday. Things are getting tougher. I'm really learning how to twist that plane around the skies . . . I like flying upside down best of all.

On the sixth of February 1943, he was shot down in a mission over New Guinea. My aunt Eva was sent this letter by her son's commanding officer:

Merrill, age four, with cousin Henry Sherman, the flier who was shot down in World War II, 1942. (Reproduced by permission.)

Dear Mrs. Sherman:

How it pains me to write you this, the saddest duty of my life. Your son was a fine young man, a good friend of mine. I knew of his devotion to you. . . All I can do now is tell you what we know happened on the 6th day of February, 1943. On that day we took a flight of our ships to Uau, New Guinea. Six in all. Over the Uau airport we were attacked by about forty Zeros and some Bombers. Henry was flying a ship called *Early Delivery*. The Zeros came in fast and four were diving at Henry's ship. He went near the port in a turn and from then on—no one is sure. It's not anything to help your feelings, but the Japs lost 26 in this fight to (I am sorry to say) our one. In this land of thousands of miles of jungles, mountains, and God knows what, anything is possible. But all we can do is look and try to find his ship.

My mother, pregnant in Florida at the time of Henry's disappearance, found herself increasingly unable to eat, and was constantly nauseated. In Brooklyn, my aunt Greta received a letter addressed to my father from the government that threatened him with the draft if he didn't get a job in a defense plant. My parents decided to return quickly to Brooklyn. After the long and arduous train ride, my mother—upon arrival home—hemorrhaged and lost the baby who would have been my brother. My father did get a job in a defense plant that manufactured airplane wings, but he was awkward and during some mechanical operation he damaged a number of plane parts. Although he also cut himself badly, he was suspected of sabotage, and the incident was carefully investigated.

Not long after we returned to Brooklyn, my aunt Greta saw an article in the newspaper titled "Lindy over Shangri-La" in which she read that Charles Lindbergh had flown over a mountaintop in New Guinea and had seen three U.S. planes, which had made emergency landings and were stranded there. She wrote a letter to Lindbergh in care of the Ford Motor Company and told him of Henry's disappearance. She expressed the hope that perhaps her nephew was a survivor of one of those forced landings. Could Lindbergh possibly help her?

Lindbergh responded personally. Our family still has the letter. In it, Lindbergh told my aunt that the newspaper report that he had seen an isolated place in New Guinea where several planes had made forced landings was untrue. He offered her his deepest sympathy and concern for her nephew who had been reported missing. He added that he wished he had information that would be of value to her. He signed it personally.

Even so, Henry's mother, my aunt Eva, never gave up hope that Henry would come home. She convinced herself that the term "missing in action" might well mean that Henry had been taken prisoner by natives in the jungles of New Guinea and one day would free himself and come home. She cherished this wish just as my grandmother never gave up hope that her drowned son might not have drowned at all, but would one day come walking home. My grandmother, in the years after Sam's disappearance, consulted fortune-tellers and went to seances to try to contact Sam's spirit. She left the lights burning in our house day and night for years after he was lost at sea.

(My aunt Eva died at the age of ninety-two in 1987, never knowing the fate of her son. Two years after her death, Henry's body was found by gold prospectors in New Guinea who unearthed a transport plane that had crashed into the side of a mountain. Henry was discovered in the pilot's seat with four of his buddies also in the plane, all of them skeletons, all of them still wearing their dog tags. He was buried with military honors, a war hero, at Arlington National Cemetery, attended by his only surviving brother, Fred Sherman.)

At the war's end, my sister, Barbara, was born on February 17, 1945. My father opened an antique shop at 33 Hansen Place, Brooklyn. He stocked it, to begin with, with the contents of a trunk he bought at an auction. He called the store "Gerber's Jewelry Exchange" (later "Gerber's Antiques") and it became the source—under one guise or another—of our family's income from that time on.

In our house on Avenue O, my aunt Greta, who had learned beauty skills by assisting a neighborhood beautician named Edith Lee, opened a small beauty shop in an upstairs bedroom. Women came and went all day. I often sat nearby as she cut hair and filed nails, and I listened to the women tell the stories of their lives.

When I was ten, my grandmother, who was then seventy-seven, seemed to take a sudden turn for the worse. Coming home from school, I would often find a doctor at her side, treating her for spasms of chest pain, for dizziness and shortness of breath. My aunt and mother leaned over her, waiting to see if she would live or die. Their anxiety indicated to me constantly (as if I hadn't already noticed this) that life was a dangerous and ultimately fatal business. Likewise, when my father was late coming home (he often went on "calls" to buy antiques for his store), my mother, aunt, and grandmother watched out the window for his car, conjecturing about whether he'd been shot in a holdup, killed in a car accident on the icy streets, or abducted for ransom. I went to sleep on many nights expecting never to see my father again.

On the other hand, my father had a genial, relaxed nature and a supreme talent for enjoying life. When he wasn't working, he sat in the sun smoking his pipe, or he played with the dog, or went fishing. I was always aware that the women in my life regarded this playful enjoyment of life as foolish and irresponsible: to be anxious and to be worried were the only important acts of existence; the rest was time wasted.

I am told I rarely smiled as a child. At some point, my mother, who composed coy jingles and rhyming verse nearly every day of her life, wrote a note and left it at my place at the table: *"If smiles she won't hoard, I'm pretty sure she'll get a reward!"* I was insulted and humiliated by the criticism, and not at all amused.

*

I discovered early that reading books was the best way to find out what life was really about. Like Saul Bellow, who said that "fiction is news from existence," I found that fiction told me more about truth than truth did. Fiction was the telling of secrets. From fiction I learned about romantic love, about passion, about the details of childbirth. I learned that life was not, for everyone, exactly as it took place in my house. Such revelations gave me hope for my own future. Books also provided a retreat from the noisy, intrusive demands of a crowded household.

The first television set did not arrive in my neighborhood till I was twelve years old—and when I went to a neighbor's house to watch it, most often I saw Milton Berle cavorting about in a dress! I was always glad to return to my books.

My father used to take me to the Brooklyn Public Library every Friday evening, and I'd come home with a huge armful of books. Because he also bought out "estates" for his antique business, he often brought home cartons of books for me, and I'd arrange them in tall piles beside my bed. The "best" books were at the bottom, to be saved for last. These were "Nancy Drew"

"*Father in his store, 33 Hansen Place, Brooklyn,*" *about 1946.* (Reproduced by permission.)

mysteries and books about collies. I made a rule for myself that I had to read all the books, even the ones about the Civil War and medical diseases. I didn't have to read *all* of every book, but I had to give each one a fair chance. I got up an hour early to read before school. Sometimes there were duplicates; my father always urged me to give the extra book away to a friend. He didn't understand that two books were twice the treasure; also that I had no worthy friends.

My mother had an affinity for only one book: the dictionary. She spent hours teaching me to rhyme. Her vocabulary was exceptional, her typing skills superb, and as always she spent hours at the piano. Sometimes she played songs to which my father sang along ("Old Folks at Home," "White Christmas," "Danny Boy") though she generally felt it was beneath her to be an "accompanist" or to play "popular" music. I was not inclined to enjoy piano lessons much myself but found myself fascinated with the typewriter keyboard, and, in fact, won the typing medal at my high school graduation. The pleasure of writing, for me, still includes the pleasure of typing.

The first poems I wrote were about the women who came to my aunt's beauty parlor: *My aunt has a customer, her name is Sadie, I like her very very much, for she is a nice lady.* In the same series was this poem: *I have a friend Allen, scarlet fever he has, he likes music very much, especially jazz.* In 1951, when I was thirteen, a boy from my class invited me to the movies, and I still have the manuscript of the story I wrote, called "First Date." One section reads: *I was in the middle of my top lip when the doorbell rang. There went my lipstick, down my chin.*

Around this time, I (undoubtedly with my mother's help) wrote a jingle that was published in my eighth grade school magazine, at PS 238. It began:

Seven a.m., the alarm starts in beepin'
And I start to think "What a swell day for sleepin'"—
Hurry and eat, get dressed on the double,
If I am late there'll be plenty of trouble.

I don't think my heart was ever in any of these "cute" efforts. My mother, who had a strong penchant for rhyme, oversaw and directed my creative output, which clearly expressed more of my mother's talents than mine. She excelled at singsong rhymes and wrote skits for the PTA, for the Girl Scouts (some of her rhymes were set to music and performed at my school), and she published amusing verse in the local newspapers. I came across one she wrote in 1966 which is titled "Supermarket" and begins:

My confusion is great
I fear for my fate
My marketing's become such a chore,
One needs a degree
At least Ph.D.
To cope with the problems past that door.

I was embarrassed by her flip facility, and besides—I had darker thoughts, more ominous things than she had (or was willing to express) to write about.

Merrill, age thirteen, on eighth-grade graduation day in the garden at 405 Avenue O with sister, Barbara, mother, and father, 1951. (Reproduced by permission.)

In 1952, when I was fourteen and my sister seven, my parents moved to Miami Beach and left my aunt and grandmother behind in the house in Brooklyn. (In 1949, my aunt had married Alex Mitchell, a cabinet-maker, who had three grown children from a previous marriage.) My sister and I had been sick so often during the bitter winters (I had pneumonia four times before I was fourteen) that a doctor recommended to my parents that they consider moving with us to a milder climate. My father, who had always wanted to live in Florida, was eager to move, and my mother finally felt able to break away from her mother and sister. She craved, and was going to get, at long last, some privacy and a life of her own with her family.

I started tenth grade at Miami Beach High School and joined a Young Judea club whose leader made a great impression on me. I had a new nickname now—of all things, "Merry"—and I arrived in Florida ready to live a transformed life. From the gray skies of Brooklyn, I now looked out upon the pastel blues and greens of ocean and palm trees. My parents were in high spirits for a short time, having hopes, once again, for success in business. Miami Beach High School offered a different world from the dangerous high school I'd gone to in ninth grade where so many of the young Italian boys carried switchblades. In the new school, whose students were mostly Jewish, there was an innocence and an air of cheerful trust in the world. Of course, these were the naïve fifties—we believed we'd encounter no obstacles as we made our way into the future.

However, almost at once, my father trusted the wrong man and lost our family's fortune. My mother was furious with him; she had to get a job as a typist to keep a roof over our heads. Their hostility did not make life simple, living as we did, the four of us, in a one-bedroom apartment.

I was writing quite a bit then, partly to escape the confines of our small quarters, and partly to explore the new emotions I was feeling. Many of my early stories were deeply romantic, if not totally sentimental. (One story I recall from this period was about two palm trees that grew side by side and which were downed in a hurricane. When the storm subsided, it was discovered that—wonder of wonders—their roots were intertwined!)

In Miami Beach, which my parents felt was a "safe place," I was free to take the bus downtown to the library near the ocean, and there I sometimes met my new classmates from the high school. (It was in the stacks of this library that I encountered my first flasher.) The novels I'd read had taught me that fiction was permitted to contain secrets that could never be spoken of. This freedom, possible only in writing, was, or could be, one of the few freedoms I could claim. I decided I would write my own stories, I would tell the secrets of my heart.

*

I met my future husband—Joseph Spiro—when I was fifteen. This event is recorded in my diary as follows:

> Sunday, March 7, 1954: Today I went on a Young Judea picnic . . . this one is only a week and a day away from my birthday. I met the leader . . . and he is as wonderful as Irma says. He makes you like him the minute you meet him. The boys were the same as usual, but I got to talking with Joe Spiro and he is very nice. I had seen him looking in the store window yesterday—but I hadn't even said Hello to him. Anyway he stayed with me most of the time and when they played ball he knew I didn't want to play, so he offered to take a walk with me.

"The store" was the hole-in-the-wall place my father had rented in the lobby of the Roberts Hotel on Flagler Street in downtown Miami and where he conducted (for a time, till some inevitable failure caused him to move on) a watch-repair business. I would sometimes go there with him on Saturdays and help him wind the watches. It was outside this store that Joe Spiro waited each week to take a bus to his piano lesson. (A pianist! How this would please my mother, I thought.) I eventually loaned him a book of duets and suggested that one day we play together. Later I wrote in my diary: *What a woman won't do for a man!*

The diary was a grand thing my father had given me while we were still in Brooklyn—a book as big in size as the edition of *Gone with the Wind* I read when I was thirteen—a printer's dummy bound in gray cloth with the title on the spine announcing: *The Heritage of the Bounty*. On the front of the book was an engraving of an old sailing ship with its sails raised and engorged with wind. Inside my father had written:

"To Merry, a book to enter happy & interesting events, Dad." (In my eighth grade autograph book he had written "Look up, aim high, you'll get there by and by.")

Merrill, age seventeen, with Joe Spiro, Miami Beach, 1955. (Reproduced by permission.)

Writing in this diary gave me the sense that I was actually writing a book. On April 24, 1954, I entered this note: *Well, at least if I don't ever write a book I can say I did. This could sort of be called my autobiography.* On a prior page I had written: *I hate Chemistry and Gym. School is getting to be a pain. It's raining now. I wonder if I'm like Emily Dickinson. After I die this whole book may be published. God forbid!! Oh well—back to my term paper.*

At some level, I already saw myself as a writer. I filled the whole diary (and spent much of my time hiding it from my sister). The ecstasies and disappointments recorded therein are cause for embarrassment now, but at the time there were matters so serious and private going on that I wrote about them in shorthand (which I was learning then. Every girl of my generation was advised, indeed, commanded, to take typing and shorthand). Of course, I can no longer decipher those entries now.

(The habit of diary writing, which developed into the more serious form of journal keeping, and later included the recording of all my dreams, became a daily habit of my life. To date I have filled fifteen manuscript boxes with typewritten journal entries and have also recorded thousands of dreams, from the early 1950s onward. The comfort of wrapping words around thoughts and images is pleasure, necessity, and sustenance for me.)

When Joe Spiro graduated from high school in 1954, he went on to college at the University of Florida in Gainesville, four hundred miles to the north of Miami. I planned to follow him there the next year when I graduated. Unfortunately, and to my dismay, I won a scholarship to the University of Miami, and found myself—at the beginning of my freshman year—starting college there, miserable about being separated from Joe. College for girls in the mid-fifties was a generally miserable experience, in any case. Though we were not consciously aware of the oppressiveness of the times as we lived through them (it's astonishing now how much abuse one is willing to accept as "necessary"), freshman girls who lived in the dormitories were treated virtually as prison inmates. Girls had to be in by 9 p.m., and a flashlight check was taken every night to certify that each girl was in her proper bed.

I had registered to take a writing class with Fred Shaw, a popular teacher and a columnist for the *Miami Herald* who held his class in the evening in a local coffee shop. In order for me to get permission to be out after 9 p.m., I had to petition the Dean of Women Students and beg for the privilege to take the class. All freshmen were required to wear little beanies and to obey orders of upperclassmen. Any infraction of their silly rules would bring upon one a summons to "Honor Court." Punishment for breaking a rule required hours of service doing ridiculous things. I had no heart for this, especially when I was stopped and "arrested" for not wearing my beanie and told I had to appear in court for a "trial." I broke down in tears more than once when talking on the phone to my parents. I begged to be allowed to go to the University of Florida. They couldn't fail to recognize how miserable I was, and they did understand how badly I wanted to be with Joe. Finally they agreed that I could transfer to the state college at the end of the term.

*

In February 1956, I triumphantly took what was called the "milk train" to Ocala, Florida, where Joe Spiro met me at the station. There in Gainesville, in the beautiful, rural environment of the north Florida woods, I had the good fortune to meet the great writing teacher of my life, Andrew Lytle. One of the original Agrarians at Vanderbilt University and a close friend of Allen Tate, Lytle was then just finishing his novel *The Velvet Horn*. His workshop had (and still has) legendary standing. It was in his class that I first understood I had a serious calling. He taught stories of his favorite writers, among them James Joyce, Flannery O'Connor, and Katherine Anne Porter. Our writing class met at night in a rickety wooden structure. Mr. Lytle would arrive, smiling, his glasses strung around his neck on a black grosgrain ribbon. His colleague and loyal disciple Smith Kirkpatrick (a novelist who also taught a class in writing) always sat in an old armchair at Lytle's left hand.

Before discussing the students' stories, Mr. Lytle liked to read one of his own favorites to us. He was an inspired actor, and any story he read took on the dimension of theater. I can still see his face as he began reading Flannery O'Connor's "A Good Man Is Hard to Find." Mr. Lytle's eyes sparkled with the thrills he knew were coming. Now and then he could not contain himself and would burst out laughing as he read one perfect comic line after another. On other nights he showed a more somber demeanor; when he read James Joyce's "The Dead" in class, Mr. Lytle became very serious, indeed. I still have the notes I took on the night of April 16, 1959 (I found them in the pages of our textbook, Gordon and Tate's *The House of Fiction*). Here are a few of the comments I took down that night:

Parts 1 and 2: Gabriel is in his last and sinning state. Part 3: Gabriel is regenerated.

The supernatural appears only through the natural.

The three fates (the three muses) are the three women—virgins—completed—living in death.

Asceticism and debauchery are both forms of death, one by denial, one by excessive use.

Age is dead youth.

The head is the upper phallus.

Trappist monks don't speak.

In the end we all come to earth.

This kind of talk was heady stuff to a girl who, before college, had read widely in *Seventeen* magazine and thought she aspired to publish there.

Each night when class ended, the women students had to race back to the dorms to get in by curfew, which at Gainesville was an hour later than at the University of Miami. We were aware Mr. Lytle often stayed to talk with the men after class, but the women did not have such privileges. I knew that Mr. Lytle liked to visit the male students in their rooms and talk with them about life and art late into the night. The men in our class boasted of this—and I was jealous.

One day I took courage and asked to have a private conference with Mr. Lytle. I'd been writing a story whose direction and meaning I hadn't the faintest sense of. It seemed sad enough and dense enough to be "artistic"; I thought he and I should talk about it. Mr. Lytle invited me to come to his study at his house in Gainesville; he told me he rose before dawn to work, and asked that I arrive in the early morning, about eight. I distinctly remember walking to his house in the chill woodsy morning. Fall leaves were underfoot, and the sun was newly up. I carried my story under my arm—never before had I felt so *serious*; I was a serious writer, on my way to have a talk with the great master.

Merrill with Andrew Lytle (left) and Smith Kirkpatrick at an event honoring Andrew Lytle, De Kalb College, Georgia, 1989. (Reproduced by permission.)

Mr. Lytle showed me the carved wooden chair in his study; he pointed out the *ouroboros* on it; it was his favorite symbol—the snake eating its own tail. I indicated my story, which Mr. Lytle had already read, and asked him to help me figure out what it was "about."

He thought for a moment. Then he said, "Merrill, there is only one way to write: you must follow the thread back into the labyrinth; there and only there you will find the meaning." (His advice was never less cryptic than this, in all the years I studied with him. Somehow, though, he gave his students reason to believe they had the gifts to conquer the riddle of those labyrinths and come out the other side.)

One afternoon I met Mr. Lytle on campus. "I trust you have a story to read in class tonight," he said. "I'm counting on you."

"Oh yes, I have one," I said.

"Good, I'm looking forward to it." I watched him walk away, feeling extreme panic. It was 2 p.m. I had exactly five hours in which to invent and write a story. I went to my room and began typing. By 6:45 that evening I had written a twelve-page story. Mr. Lytle read it in class that night and it was well received. He told me he was much taken with it, and that the following week, when he was leaving for New York to meet with his editor, he intended to bring this story, himself, directly to the offices of the *New Yorker*. I cannot recount my state of mind during his absence. I believe I didn't sleep, barely ate. All week I waited for a telegram! None came. And when I saw Mr. Lytle in class after his trip, he seemed to have no special news for me. In fact, he gave me no signal at all. After class I tapped his arm, trembling. "Mr. Lytle. What did the *New Yorker* say?" "The *New Yorker*? Oh my! I forgot about that."

During my years in Lytle's class, I had begun sending out stories with great determination and seriousness in the hopes of publication. I sent a great many stories to *Seventeen* magazine and eventually I no longer received their standard rejection letter but graduated to what was (I suppose) meant to be a more encouraging version: "Your story has passed first reading and we are holding it for further consideration." This kind of reply meant I entered a much higher level of anxiety and hope, and when the final turndown came, which it always did, the blow was fierce. (In fact, *Seventeen* magazine did not publish a story of mine till I was fifty-four years old!) However, in 1957, they notified me that one of my stories had been chosen as an "honorable mention" in their fiction contest, and they sent me a ten-dollar check and a silver "17" charm, which I still have in my jewel box.

When at the library, where I should have been studying for my classes, I haunted the periodical shelves instead, reading the short stories in every new literary journal as it arrived. I was writing poetry, then, too—and sending it off to magazines. One day, in 1956, when I was eighteen, I arrived in the library and found a poem of mine in *The Writer* magazine, a poem about a squirrel. (I no longer wrote poetry in rhymed stanzas!) I learned my poem had won a prize, a book of poetry by Elizabeth Bishop.

My yearning for publication was powerful; I was indefatigable in sending out my work again and again. These were also the years during which *Mademoiselle* magazine offered "guest editorships" to young women with writing talent. Sylvia Plath won one of these which took her to New York. Years later, as it turned out, the managing editor with whom she worked at *Mademoiselle,* Cyrilly Abels (who also figured as a character in her novel *The Bell Jar*) became my literary agent. Though I never made it as a *Mademoiselle* guest editor, I did learn that in 1959 I was a runner-up in the *Mademoiselle* College Fiction Contest, the same year Joyce Carol Oates was named the winner. Any small validation just set me on a more determined path toward my goal. I was busy reading Thomas Wolfe, and books about his great editor Maxwell Perkins. Like me, Thomas Wolfe had lived in Brooklyn (for a time, anyway) and he had died in 1938, the year I was born. I cherished the conceit that I had been born to replace him, and would in time, so to speak, step into his shoes. I, too, would have a Maxwell Perkins for my editor.

After Joe Spiro graduated from the University of Florida, he spent some time at the University of Michigan and a period in the Air Force reserve. He then received a National Defense Education Act fellowship to study history at Brandeis University in Waltham, Massachusetts. More than willing to follow him, I too had applied for a scholarship there, but I hadn't gotten one, so there was nothing for me to do but carry on with my education where I could afford to—which meant staying in Gainesville to pursue a graduate degree in English at the University of Florida.

In the fall of 1960, Joe drove me from Miami Beach to Gainesville and we bid one another good-bye. He drove away on the next leg of his journey to Massachusetts, and I (in a fair state of dejection) began to prepare to teach a freshman class and take my own courses for the M.A. degree. The day after Joe left, my mother phoned me from home to say I had received a telegram from Brandeis: someone had refused a fellowship and funds were now available for me if I still wanted the scholarship. The grant was mine—all I had to do was call Brandeis and accept.

I was beside myself with confusion. I had already committed myself to my rented room and promised my services to the university. I went to Andrew Lytle with my desperate dilemma. He suggested that I search my soul (that cloudy labyrinth) and do what was necessary. When he saw the answer in my face, he led me to his green Cadillac, drove me to his bank, loaned me enough money to buy a plane ticket to Boston, rounded up some students to help me pack and who would drive me to the airport. He kissed me good-bye and wished me Godspeed.

I still have in my bookcase my cherished copy of his novel *The Velvet Horn,* in which he had written: *"To Merrill Joan Gerber—who has great promise as an artist. Andrew Lytle, Christmas, 1957."* At this writing, Andrew and I have corresponded for thirty-four years. In the summer of 1992, when I visited him at his log cabin in Monteagle, Tennessee, he (at the age of ninety!) made lunch for me with greens he had grown in his own garden.

*

By the time I entered Brandeis University as a graduate student, I was certain I would have a life as a writer. Only a few universities at that time actually had departments of creative writing, Stanford and Iowa being the main ones. I had earlier applied to the Iowa Writing Program with a letter of reference from Andrew Lytle, and though I had received an invitation from Paul Engle, his offer ($300) was too small to take me very far. My parents, not wanting me to go to so cold and so faraway a place as Iowa, did not offer any financial help. Besides, Joe Spiro was at Brandeis, and that's where I truly wanted to be.

While a student at Brandeis, I fulfilled the requirements for a master's degree in English, taking courses in Samuel Johnson, in Robert Frost, in Whitman and Dickinson, in D.H. Lawrence. I remember my shock at how backward I seemed and how lacking my education seemed to be when the first professor I encountered asked us to list the names of five well-known literary critics. I didn't know one name. Some of my classmates, having done their undergraduate work at Ivy League colleges, could easily reel off a list. My second major embarrassment concerned the title I gave to the master's paper I wrote on Samuel Johnson: I called it "The Friendly Giant." And, if I am not mistaken, I turned in to Professor Milton Hindus a paper on Emily Dickinson fastened together with a pink ribbon! Even so, he told me then (and affirmed this again just recently) that it was the best paper he had ever received from a graduate student. In like manner, I received considerable praise for my paper on D.H. Lawrence's "The Fox."

Still, I was not really cut out to be a scholar. On the side, so to speak, I was also writing short stories, many of which dealt with my recently completed teenage years (I was twenty-two the year I attended Brandeis). I submitted these stories to popular magazines for young women and to one in particular called *Datebook* magazine. To my delight, an editor named Art Unger began to buy and publish them. At this time, I also acquired a New York agent, Sterling Lord. One snowy day I went into New York to meet him so we could discuss "my career strategy." He encouraged me to continue writing teen stories, and eventually sold many of these stories to *Datebook* for $100 each (with a 10 percent commission for himself). Toward the end of my first year at Brandeis, having completed the course work for the M.A. degree (but not having taken the orals), I applied for a fellowship to go on toward the Ph.D. Irving Howe, then the head of the English department, spoke to me about my application: he told me, in so many words, that I was "only a girl and only a writer" and although I had grades and qualifications good enough to receive one of their fellowships, there were men he felt needed them more than I did. The year was 1960; men were still unselfconscious about making remarks of this kind to women. Howe's clear dismissal (of my sex, of my talent, and of me) took care of my hopes for staying on in graduate school. After my conversation with him, I decided not to take my oral exams. I expected I would fail, and I didn't wish to be further humiliated.

(Twenty years later, in 1981, I appealed to Brandeis University for the opportunity to complete my degree. With the intervention of my professor, Milton Hindus, it was arranged that I would take the M.A. written exam [orals were no longer required for the master's degree] at a college in California where the exam could be monitored. I did, in fact, write a three-hour exam on the subject: "How is *To the Lighthouse* a book about growing up?" I passed, happily, and received my master's degree.)

In 1961, however, after I left Brandeis, I went in another direction. Since Joe Spiro and I were planning to marry (which we did, on June 23, 1960), I began looking for a job in the Boston environs where we planned to live while he stayed on at Brandeis working on his degree in the History of Ideas. (Our first apartment was in an attic at 14 1/2 Prentiss Street, Cambridge, Massachusetts.) I was hired as an editorial assistant by Houghton Mifflin Publishers and spent a year working in the educational department on Tremont Street, but I frequently made visits to the trade offices at 2 Park Street, where the "real writing" was being set into print. Philip Roth had just published *Goodbye, Columbus, and Five Short Stories* with Houghton Mifflin, and I read and re-read his collection, marveling at his honesty in writing about family life. I think he gave me courage to take certain risks, although I was already well on my way to alienating my relatives even at that time.

During that year at Houghton Mifflin, I sat at my desk at a window that overlooked the golden dome of the State House and the green expanse of Boston Common, and I imagined the stories I wanted to write. Since my husband was applying to various colleges for a job for the following fall, I also applied for something new and promising: a Wallace Stegner fiction fellowship at Stanford University in California. We had no clear sense of where the future would take us: we were open to all possibilities.

Just as in some of my duller college lecture classes I sometimes started to write stories in my notebook instead of taking class notes, that year at Houghton Mifflin, on lunch hours and on days there was not much work, I managed to make notes for a story or two. I finished one story called "The Cost Depends on What You Reckon It In," which was about an old woman in a Brooklyn nursing home. (My grandmother had been in a home such as this.) Written from the point of view of the old woman's daughter who visits her three times a day, the story (as it has turned out) proved to be an exploration of the subject of old age, which I was to treat extensively in much of my later work.

My agent, Sterling Lord, who had been selling my teen stories to *Datebook,* wrote me after he read it that I'd best stick to what worked, and urged me not to write this sort of story, which he described to me as "maudlin."

Outraged (an emotion I have experienced a good deal in my many years of having my work rejected), I decided to dismiss my agent. I did so, and went ahead and submitted the story on my own to *Mademoiselle* magazine. Just at that time, I was called on by my employer to account for some error regarding a piece used in one of their anthologies for which proper acknowledgment had not been made. The anthology, which I had edited, had been previously worked on by a former employee, who, as far as I understood the situation, had made the original error. Still, the repercussions at the publishing house were serious (was there a lawsuit threatened?) and the result was that I was dismissed from a job I didn't care for all that much. As fortune would have it, during my very first week of being out of work, I received a letter from *Mademoiselle* offering to buy my story "The Cost Depends on What You Reckon It In." Jubilant, I realized that I was the real thing: an unemployed writer. Furthermore, *Mademoiselle* was famous for publishing the early works of many great writers. I was on my way.

And there was another piece of news, as well. I learned, just about that time, that I was going to be a mother!

Part Two

In late April of 1962, I was in the ninth month of my first pregnancy. Three days before my baby was due to be born, I received a telegram from Wallace Stegner in California telling me I had been chosen to receive the Stegner fiction fellowship and he looked forward to seeing me at Stanford in the fall. He offered his congratulations to me!

Being big as a battleship and on course for only one destination, I had completely forgotten that I'd applied for the fellowship. The news threw me into a turmoil; while my husband and I folded the newly washed virgin diapers (we had been advised to wash them no less than six times before use), we debated the wild possibility that we might accept my prize and go west. Joe had just been offered his first job, at Boston University, and I had forgotten (I hoped temporarily) in the dizzying demands of the last weeks of pregnancy, that I was (or wanted to be) a writer.

We could not fail to see, however, that an opportunity was upon us; we knew it would never come again. We knew it would change our lives. We decided, in the vernacular of these times, to go for it.

Robert Stone and Ed McClanahan were Stegner fellows with me that year (1962) and we met for the first time at a welcoming reception at Mary and Wallace Stegner's home. I had brought our infant daughter (Becky Ann Spiro, born May 3, 1962) to the party and laid her on the Stegners' bed, surrounded by pillows. When I arrived in the living room, the first thing I saw was a large, framed portrait of Wallace Stegner on the wall, and, an instant later, the man himself moved toward me through the crowd, *straight* toward me, looking directly at me. Tall, fair-haired, extraordinarily handsome, he extended his hand to me, and greeted me with great warmth and kindness. I went slightly weak in the knees, realizing that I had really come to this place, that I had crossed the country, left family behind, come west with a two-month-old infant and barely any money but the $2,500 which I was to receive from the fellowship and on which our small family would have to survive for the year. Yet—seeing his smile at that moment—I knew this day would mark our lives in some important way.

The fiction workshop became (along with my new baby) the center of my world. I had every hope that the Stegner workshop would stir my energies in new and wondrous ways. We met once a week on the Stanford campus, in the Jones Room of the main library, along with other members of the advanced writing class. Seated around a large oval table, we offered up for criticism the efforts we'd worked on all week. What motivated us as we sat at home trying to write was the knowledge that the others were at their typewriters typing away, and that Wally Stegner would be listening to our words and sometimes reading them aloud so that we could listen to our own rhythms.

Though Stegner could perceive in an instant the flaws in a piece of fiction (the weak link, the parts we'd

Author with Stegner fellows: Robert Stone (back) and Ed McClanahan, Stanford University, 1963. (Reproduced by permission.)

hurried over, the emotions we didn't understand and tried to sail past, the sloppy construction of a sentence or the misfit of even one word), he preferred to keep silent at first, to remain in the background and allow the class to thrash out their differences. Only when he observed we were not even close, had missed the fatal flaw, did he step forward and offer his advice.

The first story I wrote in his workshop was "about" a young woman who gives birth to a daughter and whose mother comes to stay with her in order to help out ("A Daughter of My Own," in *Stop Here, My Friend*). The experience turns out to be a nightmare. I felt safe writing this story (a revelation of intimate family dynamics as well as an exposé of some dangerously raw hatreds) three thousand miles from my mother, nowhere near the scene of the crime, among supportive strangers. Wally Stegner made it clear that in his workshop we were free of constraints of conscience (not of literary conscience!), and free of the forms that protected us in ordinary society. Good artistic taste was the measure, not good taste. Here, in the workshop, we could let it all out, say it the way we saw it, take great risks as long as we said it well, said it honestly, said it powerfully. And *never* (he stressed) were we to assume that the narrator or protagonist was one and the same as the author. At least we had that much protection.

Stegner seemed to have an aversion to following (or having us follow) any theoretical or philosophical principles relating to the writing of fiction. He often said "I don't know what I think till I see what I say."

He wanted us to sit down and unite—and only afterward turn on our "editing" mind, see what we'd produced, and go about shaping it, ordering it, and refining it.

(Andrew Lytle, by contrast, had taken his position at the head of the workshop table as the acknowledged master of the craft and laid down certain rules he expected us to observe—rules about point of view, about the nature of "enveloping action" as it related to "action proper.")

The story I wrote in Stegner's workshop about the mother and daughter (which was, of course, "fiction") was received in class with enormous enthusiasm and very few criticisms. I remember Wally standing at the side of the room, smiling enigmatically as if he knew all along I was going to pull it off. Buoyed up by my success among my peers, I asked if the story was ready to send off into the great maw of the literary marketplace. We discussed "markets" at that time (Wally knew a fair amount about the "selling" end of the writing business and was willing to share information with us, whereas Andrew Lytle always felt it unseemly to discuss the commercial aspects of writing when "art" should be our primary concern).

I decided to send my story off to *Redbook* magazine and within days I heard from them that they wanted to buy it! This was triumph, indeed—to be able to walk into class and report to those who had been present at its birth, so to speak, that the creature was not only viable, but salable! (It did not occur to me till much later that eight million copies of it would find its way into drugstores and doctors' waiting rooms, and that my mother would be certain to see it!) Wally was suitably proud of my sale, but cautious. Caution was his byword: *"Don't get too puffed up, don't get too confident, don't get too sure of yourself. The next story will be just as hard to write, maybe harder. It probably won't sell. You can't keep your eye on the marketplace, you have to keep it on the work. The rest comes, or it doesn't come—but that's not the focus."*

Chastened, and fortified for the blow certain to come, I wrote my second story, "We Know That Your Hearts Are Heavy," about the funeral of an uncle. I sent it to the *New Yorker* and they bought it. By return mail. Those in the workshop looked at me with some suspicion, I felt. But no, I had no agent, I had no connections, I had no reputation. My ship had merely come in. This was easy! All I had to do from now on was type for a few hours a day, and someone would publish it. I was jubilant. Wally Stegner did not caution me again but he made it clear I should restrain myself. He knew the ways of the world. He knew this was like the passing of a comet, it happened only every century or so.

But I was not the only fellow for whom the comet appeared. That year Houghton Mifflin awarded Bob Stone their literary fellowship. Because he had no phone, one of their editors called me. They entrusted me with the news and asked me to get it to Bob. My husband and I hurried over to his little rented house and I fairly banged the door down with excitement. When I told him about his award, we danced around together on the rickety wooden porch in jubilation.

I did my writing in our little Stanford Village two-room apartment (in what used to be an army barracks), on a manual typewriter supported on a plank laid across two tall wooden crates. Joe, who was homebound and baby-sitting, had decided to build a harpsichord out of a kit. (He deserves special acknowledgment, I think, since this was not yet the era of house-husbands and liberated wives.) While I was writing my stories, he kept the baby's supplemental bottle warming on one burner of the stove, and he melted lead in a tin pot on the other in order to weight the keys on the harpsichord.

We bought an old car and found that we could get free clothes for the baby at the Trading Post—a used clothing exchange near the laundry machines in the center of Stanford Village. We liked living in the converted barracks among other married students, many of whom had babies who became acquainted with our daughter. (I tried to forgive the university for denying us campus housing when we first arrived; the secretary in the housing office had claimed it was the rule to give apartments in Stanford Village only to married *male* students with families, but after she saw the infant in my arms, and after I said I intended to write an angry letter to the president of the university—for what other power did I have but that in my pen?—she reconsidered, made some phone calls, and allowed that she could stretch the rules and give us space. The rent was $52 a month, including utilities. On that scale, we could just about make ends meet.)

*

We often gathered at the Stegners' home, which was in a wooded and secluded area of Los Altos Hills. Theirs had been the only house on their road until recently. The Stegners seemed troubled as others gradually built on the neighboring hillsides and crowded the landscape with buildings and visible wires. From their patio, they pointed out to us the growing scars on the landscape.

Illustrious visitors sometimes dropped in. Malcolm Cowley was there one evening and—distracted from his discourse on literature—he got down on the floor to play with my baby daughter, delighting in her resemblance to his own grandchild. Wally was relaxed with us, always cordial and kind. The parties at the Stegners' house were of the classic sort: wonderful food, serious conversation, the sharing of good literature, good music. But I felt his pulling back from what was happening, in a general sense, on campus. The sixties were taking hold in a big way. We knew of other types of parties going on around Palo Alto. Drugs were bursting onto the scene. I had heard the stories about Ken Kesey but hadn't met him yet. There were rumors of amazing and wild goings-on in the vicinity of a street known as Perry

Lane. Wally seemed a little uncomfortable with the turn the world was taking. As a man who respected the earth and its natural glories, he also respected and cherished the workings of his mind—he wanted nothing to do with turning on and tuning out. He clearly wished to be present in his unaltered consciousness at all times, to witness the process that went on within; to observe the scenes that took place without, especially in the natural world.

Joe and I let the psychedelic world spin on its merry way, finding our own world colorful enough, with the new baby to keep us delighted and entertained, with my stories falling onto the page in rapid and splendid prose (or so I thought), and with his harpsichord taking shape, slowly, in a corner of the living room, its angular walnut sides gleaming with wood wax, its strings being strung, its plectra being cut and fine-tuned with an X-acto knife.

Even though I was the only female fellow, I made myself available to talk shop with the male fellows at our various social gatherings, but inevitably, given the nature of that era, I would find myself out of the circle and would drift away to talk with the wives of the men; Bob Stone's wife, Janice, had a little girl, and Ed McClanahan's wife, Kit, also had a daughter, and both women (a year or two ahead of me in the raising of children) had much advice for me. The men had other concerns; Bob was writing what was to become his novel *A Hall of Mirrors,* and Ed was in the process of working on his book about a fatal school bus accident. I was still heady with the success of my two sales, and it seemed the world was getting rosier every day.

One morning we heard a bulletin on the radio that the United States government had learned there were missiles sighted in Cuba. Furthermore, many reserve units (and they named them, including Joe's Air Force reserve unit) were being called into service.

War! How could such a threat come into our cozy den, where literature and music and stuffed teddy bears were the gods, and where our golden-haired little daughter had begun to show signs of awareness, language, humor? Within a matter of days, my husband was packed and gone away to Hamilton Air Force Base north of San Francisco, and I was left alone, with a car I couldn't drive, with a little baby for whom I was solely responsible, and with my typewriter on a plank for company and consolation.

Everyone in the writing program heard the news and knew of my plight. Kit and Janice offered to baby-sit for me on the days of the workshop, Mary Stegner called and offered her help; Wally took it in stride. Writers had to face these matters head-on, and with a stoic attitude. Even if my husband were called away to war in Cuba, I'd manage somehow. I had the goods to cope. I had a good mind. I was here at Stanford as proof of that, wasn't I? Negotiating these roadblocks was one of the challenges of life.

Wally's message fortified me, reminded me to try to study every aspect of each experience, to try to make sense of it. I wrote another story, and another. Nothing seemed to lessen my energy for writing that year. Joe, still not knowing if he'd be sent to Cuba, was able to come home on weekends, and take away with him parts of the harpsichord to work on at the base. (He was trained in the operation of the Teletype, but not much was going on in Teletype operations at the time.)

One day I came home from class to find in the mail a letter from a major Boston publisher. It contained an offer for my first book of stories! The terms made me heady with joy: they would give me an advance of $150, on the condition that—after my book was completed and in their hands—if they didn't like it, they could reject it and I would return to them half of the advance.

Given my recent successes, I had no doubt that they would like it and publish it. I could almost feel the book in my hands. I called Wallace Stegner and told him I had to see him, at once, at once. I was levitating. Gravity seemed to have no effect on me. Wally said he would meet me at the library within the hour. I don't remember how I got to campus—I may have flown on my own wings.

Wally greeted me with his wise, patient smile. I always responded to his presence by feeling a burst of inner confidence, and I think the other fellows did, too. Because his standards were so high, for himself and for us, we seemed to be able to call up our deepest resources to satisfy his expectations. I felt certain the news I was flying to tell him would delight him, and I was pleased to demonstrate to him that he had not made a mistake in his judgment by choosing me for the fellowship.

I held out the letter from the publisher. He read it once, twice. He examined it seriously. He rubbed his chin. He looked at the second page of the letter, which was a miniature contract. If I signed on the solid line, we had a deal.

"You just tell them you're sorry," Wally said to me. "You appreciate their interest, but you have other irons in the fire."

"But I don't!" I cried.

"But you will," he said.

"But aren't they a big publishing house? Aren't they respectable?"

"Their offer isn't respectable," Wally said. "They want you to give them *half* back if they don't like the book? Half of $150?"

"Oh," I said. "I guess that isn't very good then."

"You hold out for what you're worth," Wally instructed me. And in his eyes I could see my worth blooming, like a flower taking on color and beauty.

Before the year was out, I had an offer from another Boston publisher for nearly fifteen times the amount of the first offer—with *no* conditions and no suggestion that they "might not like it."

Wally and I corresponded for thirty years after those fine days, and, when my second daughter, Joanna, was a student at Stanford, we visited him and Mary at their home. We laughed about my streak of astounding good luck in the early weeks of my fellowship, and I certified that my pile of rejections would now be able to give any writer a run for his money.

When I sent Wally a copy of my fifth novel, *The Kingdom of Brooklyn,* he wrote these words to me: "You've done it this time . . . You've worked very long and hard, and you're a finished artist now. And I don't mean 'done with.' Mary and I both read the book with fascination. So will many others, the more the merrier. We're very happy about this one."

(In April of 1993, Wallace Stegner died at the age of eighty-four from injuries sustained in an auto accident that occurred in New Mexico, where he was driving to receive an honor for his work.)

Part Three

After our year at Stanford, Joe and I spent two years in Riverside, California, where Joe taught history at the University of California at Riverside. On January 17, 1965, our second daughter, Joanna Emily Spiro, was born. Joe accepted a job teaching history at Pasadena City College, and we moved to Monterey Park, California.

My parents and Joe's parents had moved to California from Florida by then, and it seemed we were situated for life now in the West. In 1965, my first book of stories, *Stop Here, My Friend,* was published by Houghton Mifflin (the same publishing house that had fired me in 1961), and I was invited to teach writing at the University of Redlands, in Redlands, California, in the fall of the year. In August of 1965, my father was diagnosed with lymphocytic leukemia. In his brief period of remission, because he didn't want me to have to drive a long distance alone, he drove with me once a week from Monterey Park to Redlands, where he waited while I taught my class. My father died at the age of fifty-six on December 7, 1965. (For seventeen years longer, my mother continued to run the antique store, "Gerber's Antiques," on Melrose Avenue in Los Angeles, that she and my father had opened in 1963.)

From the time of my first sale to *Redbook* in 1962, I understood that it was possible to write, in many different tones, the family stories which interested me. "A Daughter of My Own," published in 1964, was the first of a series of "lighter" stories that I wrote for *Redbook* over the next twenty-seven years. In them, Janet and Danny and their three daughters travel through the arc of family life, from the time before the birth of the first child to the day the youngest goes away to college and beyond, when Janet and Danny are once again alone with each other.

After we moved to Monterey Park, my third daughter, Susanna Willa Spiro, was born on May 1, 1967. In

Merrill and Joe with daughters Susanna (three months), Joanna (two years), and Becky (five years), Monterey Park, California, 1967. (Reproduced by permission.)

the years that I was home with my three little girls, all born within a five-year period, writing these stories kept me sane and challenged. Women of my generation raising children in the sixties did not, in general, go to work. *Redbook* welcomed my interpretation of American motherhood and paid me generously. A first sale in those days of the early sixties brought a thousand dollars. (I believe that's still their range of payment now, thirty years later.) I stress that the stories were "American"—meaning that any specific rendition of Jewish family life was definitely not welcome. "Ethnic" fiction was not being written (or was, but was not readily published) in those days. Not only did I publish stories in *Redbook* in the sixties and onward through 1991, but also in the *New Yorker* (two of my stories were published there in the early sixties, but none were accepted after my editor, Rachel MacKenzie, died), in the *Ladies' Home Journal,* in *Family Circle,* in *Good Housekeeping,* in *McCall's,* and in *Woman's Day.* During the same period, my "literary" stories were accepted by the *Virginia Quarterly Review,* the *Sewanee Review,* the *Atlantic, Shenandoah, Prairie Schooner,* and other quarterlies. A number of these won prizes, including "At the Fence," which won the Andrew Lytle Fiction Prize for the best story in the *Sewanee Review* in 1985, and "I Don't Believe This," first published in the *Atlantic* and chosen for *Prize Stories: The O. Henry Awards 1986*.

Eventually, I sold *Redbook* forty-two stories (I was told I hold the record of having sold more stories to *Redbook* than any single author) and in 1993, Longstreet Press published a collection of twenty-five of these related stories about Janet and Danny, titled *This Old Heart of Mine: The Best of Merrill Joan Gerber's Redbook Stories*.

Not until I was described in a review as a "women's magazine" writer did I ever see myself in this light. Just as when I spoke to my children I used a manner of speaking appropriate to their ages, so would I write in a mode appropriate to the level of my purpose and intent. (Cynthia Ozick once remarked of me that I have "many arrows in my quiver.") I have learned, from hard experience, that the literary world does not think well of a writer who publishes in popular magazines. In 1967, when my novel *An Antique Man* was published by Houghton Mifflin, *Time* magazine sent a photographer to my home. He stayed all day, had me serve him lunch, asked me to change my clothing three times, and led me to believe *Time* intended to cover my book in a serious way. Cover it they did (they ran a review, but used no photograph), and the phrase I remember all these years later is the reviewer's remark to the effect that "Gerber, who writes for the women's magazines, makes it all come out right in the end."

For the last twenty-five years I have applied for Guggenheim grants and National Endowment for the Arts grants but have received neither. As an agent once told me, "You fall between the stools," and indeed, I believe that a writer is taken less seriously if she writes in different voices and modes. In the early eighties, my friend and correspondent Norma Klein suggested that I write for young-adult readers since I knew intimately the voices and souls of teenagers. In the 1980s I wrote nine novels for teenagers.

From the time of my first published work in 1956, I have written steadily and published stories or books every year. I teach occasionally at writers' conferences, and in 1980 began teaching a class in fiction writing at Pasadena City College, where I taught until 1990. In 1981, I spent a month at Yaddo Writers' Colony in Saratoga Springs, New York. In 1989, I accepted a position as lecturer in creative writing at the California Institute of Technology, where I still teach part-time now in 1994.

In looking back over these years of being a writer, I have a sense that my "formative years" came to a close, in a literal sense, after my years in the Stegner workshop. Before that time, the elements were busy arranging themselves into the formula that was to turn me into a writer. After becoming a "grown-up"—a wife and mother who settled in one place—I simply pursued my calling, continuing to observe, to think, to write.

My other literary history, of publishers and agents, of triumphs and disappointments, of acceptances and rejections, is quite another story, perhaps one to be told at another time.

What I do see from this vantage point is that certain patterns have emerged which should not (but sometimes do) seem surprising. Though I always knew I was a Jewish girl from Brooklyn, I never defined myself as "a Jewish writer"—perhaps because I never had a Jewish teacher, mentor, or model who encouraged me to stake my claim, or perhaps because I did not live in any formal Jewish community. Fate conspired to have me study the literature of the South (in the South) with Andrew Lytle, and the literature of the West (in the West) with Wallace Stegner.

However, my sense of myself as a Jewish writer was happily and forcefully confirmed when I received, for my novel *The Kingdom of Brooklyn* in 1993, the Harold U. Ribalow Prize given by *Hadassah* magazine "for literary excellence for a work of fiction on a Jewish theme" (and whose judges were Elie Wiesel, Anne Roiphe, and Louis Begley). This prize, and the Editors' Book Award bestowed on *King of the World* in 1989 by Bill Henderson of Pushcart Press "to celebrate an important and unusual book of literary distinction," have been supports to stand against when the tides of rejection (the given of any writer's life) tend to come in hard and strong.

I have made my home in California; Joe and I live in Sierra Madre in the house we bought twenty-six years ago, near the foothills of the San Gabriel Mountains. Our daughters are followers "of the book" (one is a librarian and two are in graduate school studying literature).

I sometimes wonder how our lives would have turned out had Joe and I stayed in New York. (Both of us were born in Brooklyn.) Many of my close friends are writers who live in New York. I have had long and intimate correspondences with New York writers Cynthia Ozick, Lynne Sharon Schwartz, and Norma Klein (who died in 1989).

Have I written even a semblance of my autobiography in these pages? As Wallace Stegner suggested in his essay for this series, a writer's autobiography occurs regularly in his fiction. The facts, as we remember them, are not always as they were, and in many cases after we shape them to our artistic ends, we lose the "truth" entirely. I think the advantage is that we may emerge with a greater truth. I have used my own "facts of life" in my work in many ways and I have told many stories in many voices. Which story is the true story? Which voice is the true voice? I don't think the writer could begin to tell you the answer.

Merrill Joan Gerber contributed the following update to *SATA* in 2005:

Merrill Joan Gerber and her husband, Joe Spiro, 2003. (Reproduced by permission.)

A Few More Words. . .

About My Life

"They had lost so many by the time I was born." With these words, I began my autobiographical essay for this series, which was published nearly a dozen years ago. In the intervening years, my models for life, my mother and her sister, the women who introduced me to fear and loss, have been lost to me as well.

I see now, in my sixty-seventh year, how primed I was as a young child to be attentive to loss and death and how my inclination to write about these powerful experiences has continued to expand over the years. When I was not yet twenty-five, I published my first story in *Mademoiselle* ("The Cost Depends on What You Reckon It In") based on a visit I took to a nursing home in Brooklyn when I was twelve. My aunt Greta took me there to visit my grandmother after she had been paralyzed by a stroke. Before then, my grandmother had lived upstairs with my aunt in our family home. The memory of what I saw that day, in a time when nursing homes were far less regulated than they are now, haunted me all through my childhood.

In the story I wrote for *Mademoiselle,* I took the voice of the woman I imagined my aunt to be. I defined the old woman's suffering and the indignities she endured. I told of the refusal of the nursing home owner to call a doctor when she was in severe pain, and the incredible error, after her death, of her almost being buried in the wrong grave.

My mother's old age and death possessed my adult imagination, much as I had been obsessed with my grandmother's when I was a child. History, which alarmingly repeated itself, caused not only my grandmother a paralyzing stroke, but also my mother and her sister. The duties of caring for the two women fell to me for more than a decade.

In 1995 I published my first memoir, *Old Mother, Little Cat: A Writer's Reflections on Her Kitten, Her Aged Mother . . . and Life.* This book had begun as a journal I kept each day after visiting my mother at the nursing home. Though totally lucid, she was paralyzed and fed by a feeding tube. Each day we talked about her impossible situation ("This is living?" she asked me one day) and each day she told me she wished to die. No matter what I did to encourage her, entertain her, comfort her, hold her and love her, she maintained that her life was essentially over.

At about this same time, a stray Manx kitten appeared under our house and we adopted him into our lives. I began to record his antics, his beauty, and the warmth and fun we experienced in his presence. A metaphoric balance seemed to occur, between his youth and joyful growth into life and my mother's illness and descent toward death. The two tales, intertwined, became the book, *Old Mother, Little Cat: A Writer's Reflections on Her Kitten, Her Aged Mother . . . and Life.*

My mother's presence was enormous in my life—not only in her dying years, but also during the years of her widowhood after my father's death from leukemia at the age of fifty-six. In those years, my mother phoned me several times each day and poured her tales of woe—and sometimes her adventures—into my ears. I had begun writing stories about such a bereaved heroine—stories about the life of an old woman living on her own in the Fairfax area of Los Angeles. When my aunt Greta moved from the east coast to California with her second husband, she also called me daily, and insisted on recounting the details and miseries of her life. Both sisters were experts at complaining. Though I was trying to inhabit my own life as a writer, as a wife and mother, and as a teacher of fiction writing at the California Institute of Technology, the agonies of my mother and aunt lived in my mind much of the time.

In 1998 I published *Anna in Chains,* a series of stories based on a character named Anna whose essence had sprung from my mother but joined up with a spirit who spoke partly in her voice, partly in mine, and with an added tone of irony and wit and sometimes even of humor. Anna's sister, named Gert in the stories, had her say in many of the situations. By the book's end, Anna had been demoted from living independently in an apartment, to living in a retirement home and, finally, at the end of the line, to living in the dreaded nursing home. In the book's last story, "Anna in Chains," she reflects on how to kill herself.

Anna makes a valiant effort at suicide by wedging herself behind a piano in the nursing home's chapel, hoping to starve herself to death, but she is discovered there and returned to one more long engagement with life.

My own mother died on New Year's Eve in 1997—at the age of ninety. With her passing, I thought my literary connection to my mother had finally ended. It seemed to me that all her stories had been told, both in the real-life memoir *Old Mother, Little Cat,* and in the fictional leap to a more intense realm in *Anna in Chains.*

With grandson Jacob. (Reproduced by permission.)

However, I realized I was not yet finished with my subject. After her death, my mother's history came back to me in new guises, in ways that only I knew, or in new perspectives that only I saw. I thought the fictional Anna should be made privy to these insights I was having.

Thus, in 2002, I published *Anna in the Afterlife,* a group of connected stories that the publisher, Syracuse University Press, called "a novel." Anna is present in this book during the four days between her death and burial—and during this time she reflects on the her children and their fates, on her romance with her beloved husband, on her sister's suicide attempt, on her brother's mysterious disappearance in the 1920s, and she reviews in person the goings-on (with her ironic commentary) of her own death and burial. *Anna in the Afterlife* was selected as one of the best novels of 2002 by the *Los Angeles Times.* With this book, my mother's powerful voice ceased speaking to me, or so it seems to me at the time of this writing.

*

In 1996 I had taken a leave of absence from my caretaking of the old women to accompany my husband to Italy, where he was leading a group of students from Pasadena City College for a three-month period of study in Florence.

I had not wanted to go with him; I had not wanted to leave my mother for that long a time. I went to the nursing home, where she lay paralyzed and on a feeding tube, and asked her what I should do.

"You can't wait for me, I could live to be a hundred. Go and do what you have to do. I'll just be here. And if something happens. . . . don't come back."

"Meaning?"

"Meaning if I die, don't come back."

Reluctantly, I traveled to Italy. I suffered severe (but sometimes thrilling) culture shock, which I recorded in daily e-mails home to my three daughters. When I returned home and reread my e-mails, I realized I had written the basic outline for a book about this experience. I had also taken hundreds of photographs during our stay in Italy, each reflecting some event that moved me (and almost none of them taken in churches or museums!). I wrote a travel memoir, *Botticelli Blue Skies: An American in Florence,* which was published by University of Wisconsin Press in 2002.

In 2003 I attended a reading by Joyce Carol Oates at Occidental College in Los Angeles. We had met briefly, many years before, and, when she saw me there, she mentioned how much she had admired my story "This Is A Voice From Your Past" (first published in the *Chattahoochee Review* and later in *The Best American Mystery Stories 1998*).

A month later I received a letter from her, asking if I might be interested in publishing a volume of "new and selected stories" with *Ontario Review Press,* which Oates runs with her husband, Ray Smith.

Together she and I chose, from twenty-five stories, thirteen that would be in the book (including a new one I had written, "Dogs Bark," which now is the closing story of the volume). *This Is a Voice from Your Past,* which became the title of the book, was published in 2005.

In 2004 a university library archivist asked me about my archive and if I might be interested in placing my papers with a library. I began to take stock of the enormous weight of papers in my home—all those filled closets and file cabinets and storage boxes and bookshelves. After I began hauling out my papers (journals, and manuscripts and letters and dreams), I started to sort them. I realized I had everything, including my high school diary. I had every letter I wrote to my mother from Girl Scout camp, every letter she wrote to me, in camp, in college, when I was a young mother at Stanford, and for all the years after, till she moved, with my father and sister, to be near us in California. What's more, she somehow owned every letter she had written to *her* mother. We each saved everything, and when my mother died, I became keeper of all our written words, including the notebooks of pain and suffering she wrote during her seven years, paralyzed and on a feeding tube, in the nursing home.

In 1961, the year after I was married and living in Boston, she wrote from Florida: "Merrill, we have a few cartons or trunks or tons (sez Daddy) with the Merrill Joan Gerber writings from yesteryear. What shall we do with the stuff? If we only had an attic, a basement, or Madison Square Garden. Dad says if we buy a Greyhound bus we will take them for you to peruse. We love you dearly, but what shall we do with the stuff, moving around as we do???"

With grandson Adam. (Reproduced by permission.)

Whatever I may have replied, my mother kept every piece of paper, hers, mine and ours, and now they're all here in my house in California—in my office, on tables in my living room, my dining room, and all over the empty bedrooms of my children. The boxes include my piano lesson notebook from 1949, when I was eleven, with my weekly assignments of scales and pieces to practice. I have the program from the Carnegie Chamber Music recital hall where my piano teacher, Miss Gwendlyn Haber, performed on June 12, 1947.

Many of the boxes contain letters from my writer-friends, some now famous, some now dead, some still plying their trade as I am, writing their books, still exchanging news with me of their disappointments, their struggles, and their passion to write. For years, in some cases for decades, we wrote each other often, sometimes once or twice a week, on real paper, and mailed these letters in envelopes, with stamps on them. Now most of us have succumbed to e-mail.

Cynthia Ozick and I have corresponded for twenty-one years. We first met at a reading she did at Claremont in 1983—and had a brief exchange about the first book review she ever did, which happened to be of my first book of stories, *Stop Here, My Friend.* I reminded her it was a negative review; she protested that it could not have been! She wrote these words to me on February 18, 1983: *"I didn't remember anything negative in that long-ago review! Hence my mention of it. I have no copy of it, and wonder what it said. If it said something hurtful, that* feels *strange: because all these years I have kept your name as a writer of great gifts."* I sent her the review from *Midstream,* June 1965, and we began our long, passionate exchange of letters. On April 22, 1983, she wrote: *"Well, I can see that you & I can talk for a lifetime. So let's do that. If I am West, I'll come to see you . . . If you are East, come to see me."* (I have been East to see her, and stayed in her home.) When my novel, *The Kingdom of Brooklyn,* won the Hadassah Ribalow Prize in 1993, she spoke at the ceremony in New York along with Lynne Sharon Schwartz.

I've had decades-long correspondences with my teachers—with Andrew Lytle, the great writing teacher at the University of Florida, and with Wallace Stegner, who chose me for the Stegner fiction fellowship at Stanford. Both are now dead though their words still reverberate in my mind. Lytle told me early on that I had "the gift" and reminded me not to worry about a "presumed lightness of appearance on the scene." Stegner, after he read *The Kingdom of Brooklyn* in 1992, wrote me that I'd "done it this time" and that "you're a finished artist now." He assured me he didn't mean I was "done with" but that the book was "splendid and painfully honest."

Honesty has always been at the heart of my need to write. When Professor Mario Materassi, whom I met in Florence, interviewed me about my mode of working, I told him that "in polite society we just talk on the surface, and I couldn't live on that surface. So I had to go home and write what I felt and saw." In fact, that is what I have continued to do in all of my work.

We still live in the house we bought in 1968 in Sierra Madre, California. I continue to teach fiction writing at the California Institute of Technology. My husband and I are now grandparents—a new, awesome stage of life that brings more joy, playfulness, and wonder than I could have imagined.

GOODE, Diane 1949-
(Diane Capuozzo Goode)

Personal

Born September 14, 1949, in Brooklyn, NY; daughter of Armand R. and Paule (Guerrini) Capuozzo; married David A. Goode (an author and professor), May 26, 1973; children: Peter. *Education:* Attended École des Beaux Arts, Aix-en-Provence, France, 1971-72; Queens College of the City University of New York, B.F.A., 1972.

Addresses

Home—33 Prospect Ave., Watchung, NJ 07069-5029.

Career

Children's book illustrator and writer, 1975—. Substitute teacher in New York, NY, public schools, 1972-73; University of California, Los Angeles, teacher of a studio workshop on children's book illustration, 1976-79. *Exhibitions:* Exhibitor at museums, colleges, and libraries, including Metropolitan Museum of Art, 1982; Denver Public Library, 1985; Krasl Art Center, 1987; Mount Holyoke College Art Museum, 1991-92; Cedar Rapids Museum of Art, 1998-2001; Keene State Gallery; Simmons College Art Gallery; Dromkeen Children's Literature Collection; Richmond Library; and University of Southern Maine. Work included in permanent collection at Kerlan Collection.

Awards, Honors

Southern California Council on Literature for Children and Young People award for illustration, 1976, for *The Selchie's Seed* and *Little Pieces of the West Wind*, and 1979, for *Dream Eater;* Caldecott honor book award, American Library Association (ALA), 1983, for *When I Was Young in the Mountains;* Parents' Choice Award, 1985, for *Watch the Stars Come Out*, and 1986, for *I Go with My Family to Grandma's; Redbook* Top-Ten Children's Picture Books designation, 1985, for *Watch the Stars Come Out;* Best Children's Books of the Year designation, Child Study Children's Book Committee, 1987, for *I Go with My Family to Grandma's,* and 1989, for *I Hear a Noise;* Picks of the List, American Bookseller, for *Where's Our Mama?, Diane Goode's American Christmas, The Diane Goode Book of American Folk Tales and Songs, Watch the Stars Come Out,* and *I Go with My Family to Grandma's;* Notable Children's Trade Books in the Field of Social Studies designation, National Council of Social Studies/Children's Book Council (CBC), for *The Diane Goode Book of American Folk Tales and Songs, Watch the Stars Come Out, I Go with My Family to Grandma's,* and *When I Was Young in the Mountains;* Notable Book designation, ALA, for *Tattercoats: An Old English Tale, Watch the Stars Come Out,* and *When I Was Young in the Mountains;* Teachers' Choice award, National Council of Teachers of English, for *Watch the Stars Come Out* and *When I Was Young in the Mountains;* Library of Congress Children's Book of the Year designation, for *When I Was Young in the Mountains;* Children's Choice citation, International Reading Association/CBC, for *The Unicorn and the Plow;* Storytelling World award, 1998, for *Diane Goode's Book of Giants and Little People;* Society of Illustrators Certificate of Merit; named English-Speaking Union Ambassador of Honor.

Writings

SELF-ILLUSTRATED

I Hear a Noise, Dutton (New York, NY), 1988.

Where's Our Mama?, Dutton (New York, NY), 1991.

Mama's Perfect Present, Dutton (New York, NY), 1996.

The Dinosaur's New Clothes, Blue Sky (New York, NY), 1999.

(Reteller) *Cinderella: The Dog and Her Little Glass Slipper,* Blue Sky (New York, NY), 2000.

Tiger Trouble!, Blue Sky (New York, NY), 2001.

Monkey Mo Goes to Sea, Blue Sky (New York, NY), 2002.

Thanksgiving Is Here!, HarperCollins (New York, NY), 2003.

Mind Your Manners!, Farrar, Straus & Giroux (New York, NY), 2005.

The Most Perfect Spot, HarperCollins (New York, NY), 2006.

FOR CHILDREN

The Diane Goode Book of American Folk Tales and Songs, compiled by Ann Durell, Dutton (New York, NY), 1989.

Diane Goode's American Christmas, Dutton (New York, NY), 1990.

Diane Goode's Book of Silly Stories and Songs, Dutton (New York, NY), 1992.

Diane Goode's Christmas Magic: Poems and Carols, Random House (New York, NY), 1992.

The Little Books of Nursery Animals (contains *The Little Book of Cats, The Little Book of Farm Friends, The Little Book of Mice,* and *The Little Book of Pigs*), Dutton (New York, NY), 1993.

Diane Goode's Book of Scary Stories and Songs, Dutton (New York, NY), 1994.

Diane Goode's Book of Giants and Little People, Dutton (New York, NY), 1997.

ILLUSTRATOR

Christian Garrison, *Little Pieces of the West Wind,* Bradbury (New York, NY), 1975.

Shulamith Levey Oppenheim, *The Selchie's Seed,* Bradbury (New York, NY), 1975, revised edition, Harcourt (New York, NY), 1996.

Christian Garrison, *Flim and Flam and the Big Cheese,* Bradbury (New York, NY), 1976.

Flora Annie Steele, *Tattercoats: An Old English Tale,* Bradbury (New York, NY), 1976.

(And translator) Madame de Beaumont, *Beauty and the Beast,* Bradbury (New York, NY), 1978.

Christian Garrison, *The Dream Eater,* Bradbury (New York, NY), 1978.

Emoeke de Papp Severo, translator, *The Good-Hearted Youngest Brother* (translation of the Hungarian folktale "A joszivu legenyke"), Bradbury (New York, NY), 1981.

Louise Moeri, *The Unicorn and the Plow,* Dutton (New York, NY), 1982.

Cynthia Rylant, *When I Was Young in the Mountains,* Dutton (New York, NY), 1982.

Diane Goode's Little Library of Christmas Classics (contains "The Nutcracker," "Christmas Carols," "The Fir Tree," and "The Night before Christmas"), Random House (New York, NY), 1983.

J.M. Barrie, *Peter Pan,* edited by Josette Frank, Random House (New York, NY), 1983.

Carlo Collodi, *The Adventures of Pinocchio,* Random House (New York, NY), 1983.

Amy Ehrlich, adapter, *The Random House Book of Fairy Tales,* Random House (New York, NY), 1985.

Riki Levinson, *Watch the Stars Come Out,* Dutton (New York, NY), 1985.

Deborah Hautzig, *The Story of the Nutcracker Ballet,* Random House (New York, NY), 1986.

Riki Levinson, *I Go with My Family to Grandma's,* Dutton (New York, NY), 1986.

(Reteller) Julian Hawthorne, *Rumpty-Dudget's Tower,* Knopf (New York, NY), 1987.

(And translator) Charles Perrault, *Cinderella,* Knopf (New York, NY), 1988.

Noel Streatfeild, *Ballet Shoes,* Random House (New York, NY), 1991.

Noel Streatfeild, *Theater Shoes,* Random House (New York, NY), 1994.

Lloyd Alexander, *The House Gobbaleen,* Dutton (New York, NY), 1995.

Robert Louis Stevenson, *A Child's Garden of Verses,* Morrow (New York, NY), 1998.

Cynthia Rylant, *Christmas in the Country,* Blue Sky (New York, NY), 2002.

Margaret Wise Brown, *Christmas in the Barn,* HarperCollins (New York, NY), 2004.

Cynthia Ryland, *Alligator Boy,* Harcourt (New York, NY), 2007.

Books illustrated by Goode have been translated into Spanish.

Sidelights

Diane Goode is an award-winning author-illustrator of children's books who is noted for her anthologies of folktales and songs, as well as for whimsical picture books. Some of her stories, such as *Where's Our Mama?, Mama's Perfect Present,* and *Monkey Mo Goes to Sea,* are original tales, while others, such as *Cinderella: The Dog and Her Little Glass Slipper* and *The Dinosaur's New Clothes,* recast old stories in a fresh and humorous setting. The versatile Goode has also paired her illustrations with the writings of other authors to create works such as the Caldecott honor book *When I Was Young in the Mountains* as well as beautifully illustrated renditions of such classics as *Peter Pan, Beauty and the Beast, The Night before Christmas,* and *A Child's Garden of Verses.* Based on an 1802 school primer listing the rules for proper dinner-table behavior, Goode's self-illustrated *Mind Your Manners!* showcases her humor and sense of fun as she transforms dour pronouncements such as "Stuff not thy mouth so as to fill thy cheeks" into what *Booklist* critic Jennifer Mattson deemed a "comic, pictorial narrative" showing an elegantly dressed family of the times gleefully engaging in "precisely the opposite of everything the text prescribes, to the disgust and dismay of their captive dinner guests.

"When I was a child I loved books and art," Goode once told *SATA.* "Reading allowed me to escape into the reality of others, and drawing let me create my own. My father was of Italian descent, and my mother was French. My brother and I enjoyed the richness of

Diane Goode depicts an Appalachian childhood in her illustrations for Cynthia Rylant's 1982 Caldecott Honor-winning picture book **When I Was Young in the Mountains.** (Text copyright © 1982 by Cynthia Rylant. Illustrations copyright © 1982 by Diane Goode. Published by Puffin Books. All rights reserved. Used by permission of Dutton Children's Books, a division of Penguin Young Readers Group, a member of Penguin Group (USA) Inc.)

both cultures. We traveled to Europe every summer from the time we were infants, visiting family and the great cathedrals and museums of the world. These early impressions helped shape my appreciation for life and art. I was bedazzled by Michelangelo's *Pieta*. Could marble be warm and luminous? Could monumental forms be at once tender and powerful? Man's creative ability seemed staggering. I saw the works of Da Vinci, Rembrandt, Botticelli, Lautrec, Monet, Manet, Cezanne, and all the great artists. I was awestruck. I was in love with art!

"I have been drawing ever since I can remember, but my formal education began at Queens College in art history. I soon switched to fine arts, where I tried my hand at everything: drawing, painting, sculpture, etching, and color theory. I took a year off to study at the École des Beaux Arts in Aix-en-Provence. It was an artist's dream.

"After graduating, I taught high school for a year, putting together a portfolio at night. In my blissful ignorance of publishing, I had decided to illustrate children's books. It was just as well that I was so naive, or else I would have been too afraid to try. As luck would have it, I was contracted to illustrate my first picture book in 1973. I was twenty-four then and knew nothing at all about commercial art. Since I was living in California, my New York publisher taught me color separation over the phone!"

Goode's first illustration project was *The Selchie's Seed,* by Shulamith Oppenheim, and her success here provided her with the opportunity to create artwork for texts by other authors. Moving to more classic works, she began to illustrate anthologies of traditional tales, such as *Diane Goode's Little Library of Christmas Classics,* which contains such popular Christmas tales as "The Fir Tree," "The Night before Christmas," and "The Nutcracker," as well as several well-known Christmas carols. "This small, gaily decorated slipcase holds four books that Goode has illustrated in extremely pretty, full-color, animated holiday scenes," noted a reviewer for *Publishers Weekly*. George A. Woods observed in the *New York Times* that the "star of this package . . . is Diane Goode, whose illustrations lend just the right accompanying note to each book."

Goode's illustrated retellings of oft-told tales and verses won the admiration of critics and readers alike. Her adaptation of Julian Hawthorne's *Rumpty Dudget's Tower* brought praise from Jeanne Marie Clancy in *School Library Journal:* "Goode's colorful cross-hatched illustrations for her adaptation enhance the story and capture the spirit of the characters, especially the mischievous Rumpty-Dudget." A *Booklist* reviewer commented that the "beauty and wit of Goode's well-composed artwork will draw readers into the rather old-fashioned tale," while *Horn Book* critic Margaret A. Bush concluded that Goode's "fine execution of both text and illustration breathes new life into the old story, making it freshly accessible as an old-fashioned fairy tale, eminently suited for reading aloud." Goode's illustrations have also been credited with attractively interpreting Robert Louis Stevenson's collection *A Child's Garden of Verses*. *School Library Journal* critic Robin L. Gibson asserted that the artist "applies her characteristically charming illustrations to Stevenson's poems with appealing results." Gibson went on to observe that Goode "captures the exuberance of childhood in many pictures."

Much of Goode's creative energy has focused on anthologies. In *Diane Goode's Book of Scary Stories and Songs* she collects works featuring ghosts and goblins from around the world. *Horn Book* contributor Nancy Vasilakis dubbed the book a "welcome addition to the Halloween or storytelling shelves." A *Publishers Weekly* reviewer, noting that the funny stories "are rather tame," assured readers that the book "will be appreciated more for its rich multicultural flavor than for its fright value." With *Diane Goode's Book of Giants and Little People* the author/illustrator deals with the theme of the "triumph of a small but clever hero over a gigantic adversary," according to *Booklist* reviewer Julie Corsaro. Working once again with tall tales and folktales from around the world, Goode puts together a smorgasbord of stories. Corsaro went on to note that "Goode's elegant watercolors bring it all together, her appealing cartoon-style art displaying a penchant for the compelling contrast between big and small." A *Publishers Weekly* critic felt that these stories of giants and little people add to Goode's "stable of stellar collections." "With this blithely spirited book," concluded the reviewer, "Goode has done it again . . . and that's no exaggeration."

Goode expanded her role from illustrator and reteller to author/illustrator of original stories in 1988 with *I Hear a Noise,* and has gone on to write and illustrate several more titles. A reviewer for *Junior Bookshelf* deemed her authorial debut "a joyously funny book," adding that, "In its high spirits, its high humour, the book is entirely original." *I Hear a Noise* is a story without narrative; it employs only dialogue and art to address the familiar childhood fear of bedtime fiends. Like many little boys, the hero, lying in bed, complains that he hears a noise. While his mother tries to comfort him, a green dragon swoops in, snatches them up, and flies off with mother and son in tow. Back at its castle, the monster's siblings argue over these human trophies, until the mother dragon breaks up the squabbling and insists that the captives be returned to their home. Goode "puts an amusing new twist on the well-worn subject of monsters at bedtime," declared a *Kirkus Reviews* critic. A reviewer for *Booklist* called the book a "gloriously spine-tingling thriller," adding that the author/illustrator's "engagingly expressive creatures . . . will leave youngsters clamoring for yet one more read of this soft-edged, bedtime chiller."

Goode's French heritage and travels have inspired the popular picture books *Where's Our Mama?* and *Mama's Perfect Present.* In the first title, two children become separated from their mother at the Gare d'Orsay train station in Paris. Aided by a kindly French gendarme, the brother and sister set out to find their beautiful mother, treking from one place to the next. All the while, the illustrations reveal the "lost" mother in one corner of the crowded page; finally the two children see her, as well. Set early in the twentieth century, *Where's Our Mama?* was written in tribute to Goode's own mother. A writer for *Kirkus Reviews* observed that the book is reminiscent of a Russian folktale and called it "a charming transformation of a story that deftly dramatizes the child's-eye view of a most important person." *Horn Book* reviewer Mary M. Burns concluded her enthusiastic review by stating that "the book is as gallic as a shrug, as logical as Pascal, and as winning as a song by Maurice Chevalier. A witty, wonderful production. C'est magnifique!"

"Mayhem? Mais Oui! The rosy-cheeked children who searched Paris high and low in *Where's Our Mama?* are back," celebrated a *Publishers Weekly* reviewer regarding *Mama's Perfect Present.* Now accompanied by their dachshund, Zaza, who leaves destruction in its wake, the two siblings are searching for the perfect birthday gift for their beloved mother. Not surprisingly, each place they visit is in turn visited with chaos as a result of their rambunctious dog. A *Publishers Weekly* critic promised that this sequel "will leave young readers chuckling at Zaza's exploits and everyone else chuckling an appreciative ooh-la-la." Mary M. Burns asserted in *Horn Book:* "This is a true picture story, with the understated text serving as a straight-faced, innocent commentary on the action, which is visualized through careful manipulation of line, deft shading, and delicate hatching." In a *Booklist* review, Ilene Cooper commented that "the story is clever and full of fun, but it is really the pictures that make this come alive."

Other picture books by Goode include *Tiger Trouble!* which finds a boy and his pet tiger, Lily, threatened with eviction from their city apartment after their new cat-hating landlord moves in upstairs. Fortunately, Lily soon proves her worth when robbers appear, giving an upbeat ending to what a *Kirkus Reviews* writer called a "fanciful and cheerily outlandish tale." Praising the story's nostalgic 1930s setting, *School Library Journal* contributor Bina Williams noted that "Goode's fetching watercolors are delightful and luminous," while in *Booklist* Ilene Cooper wrote that the story's "multiethnic cast of kids is endearing, [and] the New York setting bristles with activity." Set in a similar era, *Monkey Mo Goes to Sea* finds a boy paired with another unusual pet, this time a monkey. Visiting his grandfather for lunch on a luxurious ocean liner docked nearby, Bertie and his pet Mo do their best to behave, with humorous results. The impish Mo "will endear himself to youngsters as they will recognize . . . much of themselves in his well-intentioned" antics, predicted Rosalyn Pierini in *School Library Journal,* while Cooper wrote that Goode's "well-structured book has a sly story that's as strong as the illustrations."

Goode shows that she is not afraid to give tradition friendly tug with books such as *The Dinosaur's New Clothes* and *Cinderella: The Dog and Her Little Glass Slipper.* With *The Dinosaur's New Clothes* she provides Hans Christian Andersen's classic story with "a prehistoric makeover," according to a *Publishers Weekly* critic. Goode recasts the royals of the original version as a gaggle of pompadoured dinosaurs holding court at the French palace of Versailles, while a Tyrannosaurus rex—king of all dinosaurs—stars as the fashion-conscious emperor. "It's all good silly fun," concluded the critic, "a light parody of Andersen's send-up of gullibility and greed." A pack of hounds step into key roles in Goode's revisionist "Cinderella," and "silly images abound," according to a *Publishers Weekly* writer. Scruffy canines with powdered wigs fill the royal ballroom, dresses are patterned with paw prints, and "Goode works dog motifs into her luminous paintings with amusing frequency."

As Goode explained of her work to *SATA,* "When you depend on pure line for expression, the slightest variation in length or thickness of the line of the mouth, the

Goode presents a whimsical retelling of Hans Christian Anderson's well-known fable in **The Dinosaur's New Clothes,** *published in 1999.* (Text and illustrations copyright © 1999 by Diane Goode. Reprinted by permission of The Blue Sky Press, an imprint of Scholastic Inc.)

angle of an eyebrow, the sweep of a tail, the pose of a foot, changes the mood of the entire illustration. I often do the same small character over and over until the line is right, until I can just dash it off and it seems to come alive. My theme for this new approach is 'less is more.'

"In a successful picture book, illustration and text should move together like perfectly attuned partners in a dance. The illustrations not only support, but can serve as a counterpoint to the text. If I've done it right, the effort should not be evident, it should look easy and natural. It's an exciting process."

"Working in the field of children's literature has been a great joy," the author/illustrator once noted. "How lucky to be able to do the work I love and also contribute in some small way to the lives of our children. How lucky to find in my work the two things I've cherished since childhood: art and books."

Biographical and Critical Sources

BOOKS

Cummins, Julie, editor, *Children's Book Illustration and Design,* PBC International, 1992.

PERIODICALS

Booklist, January 15, 1988, review of *Rumpty Dudget's Tower,* p. 862; December 1, 1988, review of *I Hear a Noise,* pp. 647-648; October 1, 1994, p. 321; July, 1996, Ilene Cooper, review of *Mama's Perfect Present,* p. 1824; September 15, 1997, Julie Corsaro, review of *Diane Goode's Book of Giants and Little People,* p. 237; November 1, 2000, GraceAnne A. DeCandido, review of *Cinderella: The Dog and Her Little Glass Slipper,* p. 543; October 1, 2001, Ilene Cooper, review of *Tiger Trouble!,* p. 325; March 15, 2002, Ilene Cooper, review of *Monkey Mo Goes to Sea,* p. 1256; October 15, 2003, Ilene Cooper, review of *Thanksgiving Is Here!,* p. 418; November 15, 2005, Jennifer Mattson, review of *Mind Your Manners!,* p. 49.

Bulletin of the Center for Children's Books, September, 1991, p. 10; December, 1996, p. 136.

Five Owls, September-October, 1991, p. 9.

Horn Book, March-April, 1988, Margaret A. Bush, review of *Rumpty Dudget's Tower,* pp. 199-200; September, 1988, p. 615; November-December, 1991, Mary M. Burns, review of *Where's Our Mama?,* pp. 727-728; September, 1992, p. 592; January-February, 1995, Nancy Vasilakis, review of *Diane Goode's Book of Scary Stories and Songs,* p. 75; November-December, 1996, Mary M. Burns, review of *Mama's Perfect Present,* pp. 723-724; March-April, 2002, Mary M. Burns, review of *Monkey Mo Goes to Sea,* p. 202; November-December, 2002, Mary M. Burns, review of *Christmas in the Country,* p. 738.

Junior Bookshelf, April, 1989, review of *I Hear a Noise,* p. 61; June, 1992, p. 102.

Kirkus Reviews, July 1, 1988, review of I Hear a Noise, p. 973; August 1, 1991, review of *Where's Our Mama?,* p. 1010; September 1, 2001, review of *Tiger Trouble!,* p. 1290; November 1, 2002, review of *Christmas in the Country,* p. 1625; August 1, 2003, review of *Thanksgiving Is Here!,* p. 1017; October 15, 2005, review of *Mind Your Manners!,* p. 1138.

New York Times, December 4, 1983, George A. Woods, review of *Diane Goode's Little Library of Christmas Classics,* pp. 77-79.

New York Times Book Review, April 19, 1992, p. 16; January 19, 1997, p. 24.

Publishers Weekly, September 2, 1983, review of *Diane Goode's Little Library of Christmas Classics,* p. 80; July 29, 1988, p. 230; June 29, 1992, p. 61; September 7, 1992, p. 67; July 4, 1994, review of *Diane Goode's Book of Scary Stories and Songs,* p. 60; September 2, 1996, review of *Mama's Perfect Present,* p. 129; July 28, 1997, review of *Diane Goode's Book of Giants and Little People,* p. 73; June 28, 1999, review of *The Dinosaur's New Clothes,* p. 78; August 7, 2000, review of *Cinderella,* p. 95; February 25, 2002, review of *Monkey Mo Goes to Sea,* p. 66; September 22, 2003, review of *Publishers Weekly,* p. 65.

School Library Journal, January, 1988, Jeanne Marie Clancy, review of *Rumpty Dudget's Tower,* p. 66; February, 1989, p. 69; September, 1992, p. 215; September, 1994, p. 207; September, 1996, p. 178; November, 1997, p. 107; January, 1999, Robin L. Gibson, review of *A Child's Garden of Verses,* p. 121; September, 2000, Margaret A. Chang, review of *Cinderella,* p. 216; December, 2001, Bina Williams, review of *Tiger Trouble!,* p. 102; March, 2002, Rosalyn Pierini, review of *Monkey Mo Goes to Sea,* p. 187; September, 2003, Andrea Tarr, review of *Thanksgiving Is Here!,* p. 178; November, 2005, Grace Oliff, review of *Mind Your Manners!,* p. 92.

Washington Post Book World, February 9, 1992, p. 11.

ONLINE

Scholastic Web site, http://www.books.scholastic.com/teachers/ (May 18, 2006), interview with Goode.

* * *

GOODE, Diane Capuozzo
See GOODE, Diane

* * *

GORRELL, Gena K. 1946-
(Gena Kinton Gorrell)

Personal

Born July 14, 1946, in Toronto, Ontario, Canada; daughter of John Stobie (an art director) and Laura (a musician) Muir; married W. Peter Gorrell (a manager), May 21, 1966. *Education:* Attended University of Toronto.

Addresses

Agent—c/o Author Mail, Tundra Books, 481 University Ave., Ste. 900, Toronto, Ontario M5G 2E9, Canada. *E-mail*—gorrell@netrover.com.

Gena K. Gorrell (Photo by Dianne Last, 2000.)

Career

Lester & Orpen Dennys (publisher), Toronto, Ontario, Canada, editor, 1978-91; freelance editor and writer. Toronto Police, volunteer constable in marine unit, 1991-2005; volunteer first-aid instructor for St. John Ambulance, 1991-2003.

Awards, Honors

Parents' Choice Award, 1997, for *North Star to Freedom;* Norma Fleck Award for Outstanding Nonfiction for Children shortlist, 1999, and New York Public Library Books for the Teen Age selection, and Canadian Children's Book Centre Choice, both 2000, all for *Catching Fire;* New York Public Library Books for the Teen Age selection, and Norma Fleck Award, both 2001, and Hackmatack Children's Choice Book Award shortlist, 2002, all for *Heart and Soul;* American Society for the Prevention of Cruelty to Animals Henry Bergh Children's Book Award, 2004, for *Working like a Dog.*

Writings

Stories of the Witch Queen, illustrations by N.R. Jackson, Peppermint Press (Cavan, Ontario, Canada), 1985.

North Star to Freedom: The Story of the Underground Railroad, foreword by Rosemary Brown, Stoddart (Toronto, Ontario, Canada), 1996, Delacorte Press (New York, NY), 1997.

Catching Fire: The Story of Firefighting, Tundra Books (Toronto, Ontario, Canada), 1999.

Heart and Soul: The Story of Florence Nightingale, Tundra Books (Toronto, Ontario, Canada), 2000.

Working like a Dog: The Story of Working Dogs through History, Tundra Books (Toronto, Ontario, Canada), 2003.

Sidelights

Canadian writer Gena K. Gorrell moved into writing after working for many years as a book editor and researcher. Drawing on her curiosity and her personal interests, she has produced a number of highly praised nonfiction titles that range from biographies and social history to *Catching Fire: The Story of Firefighting.* Inspired by Gorrell's experiences in emergency services as a volunteer police officer and first-aid instructor, *Catching Fire* reveals the history of firefighting, the job of fire investigators, and the scientific background necessary to battle fires and discusses the many different dangers modern firefighters must confront during the course of their dangerous but necessary job.

Man's best friend earns his reputation for a good reason, as Gorrell shows in *Working like a Dog: The Story of Working Dogs through History.* Evolved from wolves, dogs have skills that have aided mankind throughout the centuries, such as their ability to scent out danger, retrieve game during a hunt, herd livestock, guard against predators, and pull sleds. Beginning with an outline of dog history and evolution, Gorrell introduces readers to modern canine heroes, including a yellow lab that works as a guide dog for the blind, the search-and-rescue dogs that aided firefighters and police during the 9/11 tragedy, and dogs that are trained to nose out everything from illegal drugs to dangerous snakes to hidden caches of fish. Winner of the American Society for the Prevention of Cruelty to Animals' Henry Bergh Children's Book Award, *Working like a Dog* was praised by Anne Chapman Callaghan in *School Library Journal* as "a thoroughly researched and captivating offering," while *Resource Links* contributor Carol-Ann Hoyte dubbed it "fascinating and comprehensive." In *Quill & Quire,* John Wilson wrote that in Gorrell's "splendid, in-depth book . . . even the most fanatical dog lover will discover something new."

North Star to Freedom: The Story of the Underground Railroad and *Heart and Soul: The Story of Florence Nightingale* focus on America's past. *North Star to Freedom* profiles the men and women who, in order to escape slavery in the American south, risked their lives on the dangerous trek north to freedom. Harriet Tubman and Henry "Box" Brown are among the people covered in Gorrell's inspirational book. The English nurse who became known as the "Lady of the Lamp" due to her work reforming hospital care is the subject of the award-winning *Heart and Soul,* a book described by a *Resource Links* contributor as a "compelling biography" that presents "both Florence's passion to help others who were less fortunate and her own 'inner struggles.'" Now considered the founder of modern nursing, Nightingale rejected the prospects of marriage in favor of contributing to society's betterment by studying nursing. In charge of hospital nursing care during the Crimean War, she witnessed the appalling conditions of battlefield medicine and spent the rest of her life battling to improve standards of care. Considered difficult and uncompromising in person, Nightingale nonetheless achieved her goal, as Gorrell shows in a work that "succeeds in separating myth from reality, smoothly crafting a picture of a gifted individual who was also wholly human," according to *School Library Journal* reviewer Cindy Darling Codell.

Gorrell told *SATA*: "How are kids today supposed to learn about their world? The past gets longer and longer—not just literally, but also because we're expected to know more about it than our grandparents were—while much of our emerging knowledge is beyond a lay person's comprehension. I'm concerned that some kids may feel overwhelmed, and may give up trying to understand where we've come from and where we're going, leading to a sense of apathy, futility, and inadequacy.

"My goal in each book is to explain a small corner of the world, focusing on what's interesting and memorable (not all that stuff you forget as soon as you turn the page). I try to put the topic in context, tying it to other times and places. I hope to give kids some of those 'aha!' moments when a piece of the jigsaw suddenly fits into place, and the puzzle of our world seems a little less impenetrable."

Biographical and Critical Sources

PERIODICALS

Booklist, February 15, 1997, Hazel Rochman, review of *North Star to Freedom: The Story of the Underground Railroad,* p. 1012; January 1, 2001, Carolyn Phelan, review of *Heart and Soul: The Story of Florence Nightingale,* p. 944; November 1, 2003, Lauren Peterson, review of *Working like a Dog: The Story of Working Dogs through History,* p. 494.

Bulletin of the Center for Children's Books, February, 1997, review of *North Star to Freedom,* p. 205; May, 1999, review of *Catching Fire: The Story of Firefighting,* p. 314.

Canadian Book Review Annual, 2000, review of *Heart and Soul,* p. 532.

Horn Book, January, 2001, Anita L. Burkam, review of *Heart and Soul,* p. 110.

Publishers Weekly, December 16, 1996, review of *North Star to Freedom,* p. 61.

Quill & Quire, April, 1996, review of *North Star to Freedom,* p. 41; April, 1999, review of *Catching Fire,* p. 35; January, 2001, review of *Heart and Soul,* p. 36; October, 2003, John Wilson, review of *Working like a Dog.*

Resource Links, June, 1997, John Fielding, review of *North Star to Freedom,* p. 229; October, 1999, review of *Catching Fire,* p. 17; February, 2001, review of *Heart and Soul,* p. 22; October, 2003, Carol-Ann Hoyte, review of *Working like a Dog,* p. 22.

School Library Journal, January, 1997, Shirley Wilton, review of *North Star to Freedom,* p. 125; June, 1999, William C. Schadt, review of *Catching Fire,* p. 146; December, 2000, Cindy Darling Codell, review of *Heart and Soul,* p. 161; December, 2003, Anne Chapman Callaghan, review of *Working like a Dog,* p. 167.

Voice of Youth Advocates, February, 1998, review of *North Star to Freedom,* p. 364; February, 2001, review of *Heart and Soul,* p. 441; February, 2004, Michele Winship, review of *Working like a Dog,* p. 510.

ONLINE

Gena K. Gorrell Home Page, http://www.netrover.com/~gorrell/ (May 18, 2005).

Canadian Review of Materials Online, http://www.umanitoba.edu/cm/ (September 5, 2003), review of *Working like a Dog.*

* * *

GORRELL, Gena Kinton
See GORRELL, Gena K.

* * *

GRABER, Janet 1942-

Personal
Born 1942, in Newcastle upon Tyne, England; married second husband Richard Graber; children: three; three stepchildren.

Addresses
Home—Burnsville, MN *Agent*—c/o Author Mail, Marshall Cavendish, 99 White Plains Rd., Tarrytown NY 10591-9001.

Career
Writer. Has worked for London studios of Twentieth Century-Fox.

Member
Society of Children's Book Writers and Illustrators.

Awards, Honors
Distinguished Achievement Award, American Association of Educational Publishers, for short story "Thanksgiving Gumbo."

Writings

I Couldn't Do It without My Group: Secrets of Starting and Running a Successful Writers' Group, Children's Book Insider, 1995.

Jacob and the Polar Bears (picture book), illustrated by Sandra Salzillo-Shields, Moon Mountain Publishing (North Kingstown, RI), 2002.

Resistance (young-adult novel), Marshall Cavendish (New York, NY), 2005.

Also contributor of articles to *School,* the *Newcastle Journal,* London *Evening Standard,* and *Once Upon a Time.*

Work in Progress
A trilogy of young-adult novels, the "Crossland Chronicles."

Sidelights
Janet Graber did not begin her life as an author until she was in her fifties, and she was sixty before she sold her first full-length work, a picture book for children titled *Jacob and the Polar Bears.* The story traces the adventures of a little boy whose hand-me-down pajamas are decorated with a total of 172 polar bears "who only want to go 'swimming, swimming, swimming,' in the 'cold, cold night,'" related John Gessner in *This Week Online.* The first night Jacob wears his semi-new pajamas, the bears come to life and scamper off to wreak havoc. Jacob has to leave his bed and track them down, embarking on a magical voyage. In the process, wrote a reviewer for *BookViews.com,* Jacob finds out "how hard it is to make them behave despite their exuberance."

Resistance, Graber's first novel for young adults, is a story of World War II. Fifteen-year-old Marianne is marooned in occupied France with her mother and deaf younger brother, Michel. Marianne also finds herself caught between her promise to her now-dead soldier father—to protect Michel—and the efforts of her mother and Michel to support the underground French Resistance against their Nazi occupiers. As a further complication, Marianne has to deal with a pair of German officers who live in her house and an injured English soldier living secretly in her woodshed. "Marianne wants only to quit involvement in the Resistance and be safe"; explained a *Kirkus Reviews* contributor, "but where is safety during wartime?" "Slowly, painfully," Carolyn Phelan commented in *Booklist,* "she discovers who is worthy of her trust, how to deal with those who are not, and what risks are worth taking." "This first novel has an edgy excitement," concluded Hope Morrison in the *Bulletin of the Center for Children's Books,* "born of the well-drafted first-person perspective of a young person in the know amidst enormous danger."

Biographical and Critical Sources

PERIODICALS

Booklist, May 15, 2005, Carolyn Phelan, review of *Resistance,* p. 1669.
Bulletin of the Center for Children's Books, June, 2005, Hope Morrison, review of *Resistance,* p. 440.
Kirkus Reviews, March 1, 2005, review of *Resistance,* p. 286.

ONLINE

BookViews.com, http://www.bookviews.com/ (August 31, 2005), review of *Jacob and the Polar Bears.*
Midwest Book Review Online, http://www.midwestbookreview.com/ (August 31, 2005), review of *Jacob and the Polar Bears.*
Moon Mountain Publishing Web site, http://www.moonmountainpub.com/ (August 31, 2005), brief author biography.
This Week Online, http://www.thisweek-online.com/ (October 10, 2002), John Gessner, "Author Draws on Whimsy, Imagination, Perseverance" (interview).
WritingforChildren.com, http://www.writingforchildren.com/ (August 31, 2005), brief author biography.*

* * *

GREEN, John 1978(?)-

Personal
Born c. 1978. *Education:* Graduated from college in 2000.

Addresses
Home—Chicago, IL. *Agent*—c/o Dutton Children's Books Publicity, 375 Hudson St., New York, NY 10014. *E-mail*—john@sparksflyup.com.

Career
Worked as a chaplain in a children's hospital; *Booklist,* Chicago, IL, production editor and book reviewer.

Writings

Looking for Alaska (young-adult novel), Dutton Children's Books (New York, NY), 2005.

Contributor of scripts to radio, including *All Things Considered,* National Public Radio, and to WBEZ, Chicago; contributor to national magazines.

Adaptations
Looking for Alaska has been adapted as a film of the same title, directed by Josh Schwartz, expected 2006.

Work in Progress
An Abundance of Katherines.

Sidelights
John Green worked briefly as a chaplain at a children's hospital following his college graduation, a position he credits with giving him a great deal of insight into the thoughts of teenagers. He then moved on to *Booklist,* starting off as a temp and working his way up to production editor and occasional book reviewer. In addition, he contributes frequently to National Public Radio (NPR)'s *All Things Considered,* and to Chicago NPR affiliate WBEZ. He got his start writing for NPR thanks to a work-related correspondence for *Booklist* with writer Amy Krouse Rosenthal, who had a periodic program on WBEZ. Rosenthal found Green's e-mails entertaining and asked if he had ever written any short pieces that might be suitable for radio. Although he had not, Green claimed to have a few things that were appropriate; he then promptly went home and wrote several brief, humorous articles. Rosenthal selected one of them, "Nine Girls I've Kissed and What I Learned about Them from Google," and aired it. Several additional articles followed, and eventually Green found himself recording a piece for *All Things Considered.* In an interview for *MediaBistro,* Green explained what it's like to write for the radio: "I have no idea what would be good for the air. But I've always read my writing aloud to myself. . . . What I later learned is that when you're writing for the radio, you have to dispense with flashy writing and abundant adjectives in favor of action verbs and funny jokes. Writing for the radio needs to be very, very tight, because people get bored easily."

Green's young-adult novel, *Looking for Alaska,* is about a young man named Miles "Pudge" Halter, who leaves his home in Florida to attend Culver Creek, a boarding school in Birmingham, Alabama. The Alaska in the title is not the state, but a girl Pudge meets in school and who is the driving force of the clique that adopts Pudge. Neither popular nor outgoing at his previous school, Pudge now finds himself part of a colorful group that includes a trailer-park kid with an eerie memory whose name is Chip but goes by the nickname Colonel; a Japanese student named Takumi; a Romanian girl named Lara; and, of course, Alaska. His new friends are brilliant, willing to discuss Edna St. Vincent Millay and W.H. Auden, but they are also troublemakers with a tendency to drink in the woods and smoke in the school bathrooms. This insistence on bucking the system seems intriguing to Pudge, until Alaska's extreme behavior gets her killed in a drunken collision with a police car, an incident that may or may not have been a suicide. Pudge, who has always had a fascination with the last words of famous people, suddenly finds himself facing death on a very personal level.

Peter D. Sieruta, in a review for *Horn Book,* called Green's work a "mature novel, peopled with intelligent characters who talk smart, yet don't always behave that way, and are thus notably complex and realistically portrayed teenagers." A contributor to *Publishers Weekly* remarked that "the novel's chief appeal lies in Miles's well-articulated lust and his initial excitement about being on his own for the first time." *School Library Journal* contributor Johanna Lewis commented that "Miles's narration is alive with sweet, self-deprecating humor, and his obvious struggle to tell the story truthfully adds to his believability." *Bulletin of the Center for Children's Books* critic Deborah Stevenson concluded that "Green gives the time-tested plot of boarding-school maturation its full and considerable due, evoking the substantial appeal of the situation's hothouse intensity, heady independence, and endless possibilities."

Green himself admits that his own boarding school experience was a source of material for the book. In an interview for *PenguinPutnam.com,* he remarked: "I like writing for teenagers because big questions—about love and religion and compassion and grief—matter to teens in a very visceral way. And it's fun to write teenage characters. They're funny and clever and feel so much so intensely."

Biographical and Critical Sources

PERIODICALS

Booklist, March 1, 2005, Ilene Cooper, "Last Words from a First Novelist," interview with John Green, p. 1181.

Bulletin of the Center for Children's Books, February, 2005, Deborah Stevenson, review of *Looking for Alaska,* p. 252.

Horn Book, March-April, 2005, Peter D. Sieruta, review of *Looking for Alaska,* p. 201.

Kirkus Reviews, March 1, 2005, review of *Looking for Alaska,* p. 287.

Kliatt, March, 2005, Paula Rohrlick, review of *Looking for Alaska,* p. 12.

Philadelphia Inquirer, March 30, 2005, Katie Haegele, "Private-School Pranks, Perhaps Worse, in *Looking for Alaska.*"

Publishers Weekly, February 7, 2005, review of *Looking for Alaska,* p. 61; July 25, 2005, "The O.C. Cools off with John Green's YA Novel, *Looking for Alaska,*" p. 8.

School Library Journal, February, 2005, Johanna Lewis, review of *Looking for Alaska,* p. 136.

ONLINE

BookPage.com, http://www.bookpage.com/ (August 30, 2005), "John Green."

Internet Movie Database, http://www.imdb.com/ (August 30, 2005), "John Green."

MediaBistro.com, http://www.mediabistro.com/ (August 30, 2005), "Pop Quiz: John Green."

Penguin Putnam Web site, http://www.penguinputnam.com/ (August 30, 2005), "Q&A with Author John Green."

SparksFlyUp.com, http://www.sparksflyup.com/ (August 30, 2005), "A Shout in the Street: A Bit about John Green."

Teenreads.com, http://www.teenreads.com/ (August 30, 2005), "John Green."*

* * *

GRIESSMAN, Annette 1962-

Personal

Born January 29, 1962, in Princeton, NJ; daughter of John (an electrical engineer) and Phyllis (a secretary) Schumacher; married Detlef Griessman (an electrical engineer), December 22, 1984; children: Alex, Kayla. *Education:* Purdue University, B.S. (electrical engineering), 1984. *Hobbies and other interests:* Reading, gardening, astronomy, "watching good movies, and spending time with my kids."

Addresses

Home—Kokomo, IN. *Agent*—c/o Author Mail, Houghton Mifflin, 222 Berkeley St., Boston, MA 02116-3764. *E-mail*—agriessman@insightbb.com.

Career

Delco Electronics, Kokomo, IN, test engineer, 1984-88; writer.

Member

Society of Children's Book Writers and Illustrators.

Awards, Honors

Polly Bond Award, 1998, for *Jenny's Prayer.*

Writings

Jenny's Prayer, illustrated by Mary Anne Lard, Morehouse Publishing (Harrisburg, PA), 1998.

Gabriel, God, and the Fuzzy Blanket, illustrated by David L. Erickson, Morehouse Publishing (Harrisburg, PA), 2000.

The Fire, illustrated by Leonid Gore, Putnam (New York, NY), 2005.

Like a Hundred Drums, illustrated by Julie Monks, Houghton Mifflin (Boston, MA), 2006.

Work represented in anthologies, including "Tales from the Wonder Zone" series, edited by Julie Czerneda. Contributor of short stories to periodicals, including *Spider.*

Sidelights

When Annette Griessman graduated from Purdue University with a degree in electrical engineering, the thought of drawing on her love of reading and estab-

Cover of Annette Griessman's The Fire, *featuring artwork by Leonid Gore.* (Text copyright © 2005 by Annette Griessman. Illustrations copyright © 2005 by Leonid Gore. All rights reserved. Used by permission of G.P. Putnam's Sons, a division of Penguin Young Readers Group, a member of Penguin Group (USA) Inc.)

lishing a career as a children's book author must have seemed like a long shot. However, after five years spent working as an engineer, Griessman left her job to raise her family, and this choice enabled her to find the time to pursue her writing. Praised for their compelling plots and realistic characters, Griessman's books for young readers include the faith-based picture books *Jenny's Prayer* and *Gabriel, God, and the Fuzzy Blanket*. *The Fire*, which she published in 2005, is a story about a strong family that holds together in the face of trying circumstances.

In *The Fire*, Mama, Pepito, and Maria, the story's narrator, are sitting in the family kitchen one afternoon. Mama is busily making soup, while the two children entertain themselves quietly, when suddenly smoke is seen coming from the hallway. The three run outside in the nick of time, and firemen arrive to try and save their home. As the family watches from a place of safety, flames destroy all the material possessions that used to be part of their lives. Young Maria despairs that everything is gone, while her mother, looking at a photo and at the stuffed teddy bear that she managed to salvage from the burning home, bravely assures her children that everything will be alright; the important thing is that they are safe and together. Griessman's "fine book has a message that could help children experiencing any kind of life-changing disaster," commented Judith Constantinides in *School Library Journal*. "Along with giving firefighters due homage, this rare look at a house fire from the victim's perspective will draw strong reactions—and plenty of discussion—from children," stated a *Kirkus Reviews* critic.

Griessman once told *SATA:* "When I was young, I developed a strange habit—I would read anything. I read books, newspapers, magazines, and when those were in short supply, I turned to receipts, cereal boxes, and soup cans. My collection of books grew to enormous proportions, and I learned to read even faster to get through new ones. My favorite authors couldn't write fast enough to keep me in books. To fill my time I tried a variety of hobbies, but inevitably I found myself bored to tears. It finally occurred to me that maybe I should try writing. By writing, I could not only stay busy, but also tell the kinds of stories I loved to read. It was a wonderful and fateful day. Now I write as obsessively as I read. In another few years, I may even be good at it.

"I am very happy with my success in the children's market so far, as I think children have a great need for good stories. If a child learns to love books when he is young, the habit will stay with him for life, enriching that life with bits of wisdom, humor, joy, and just plain fun."

Biographical and Critical Sources

PERIODICALS

Booklist, October 1, 2005, Julie Cummins, review of *The Fire,* p. 62.
Christian Parenting Today, November, 2000, Lisa Jackson, review of *Gabriel, God, and the Fuzzy Blanket,* p. 87.
Kirkus Reviews, September 15, 2005, review of *The Fire,* p. 1026.
Publishers Weekly, December 14, 1998, review of *Jenny's Prayer,* p. 71.
School Library Journal, November, 2005, Judith Constantinides, review of *The Fire,* p. 93.

ONLINE

Annette Griessman Home Page, http://www.annettegriessman.com (April 11, 2006).

H-J

HANNIGAN, Katherine

Personal
Born in western NY. *Education:* State University of New York, B.S. (mathematics and education), 1987, B.F.A (painting), 1997; Rochester Institute of Technology, M.F.A (painting), 1991.

Addresses
Home—IA. *Agent*—c/o Author Mail, Greenwillow Press/HarperCollins Childrens, 1350 Avenue of the Americas, New York, NY 10019.

Career
Educator and writer. Head Start, former education coordinator; instructor at Rochester Institute of Technology, Rochester, NY, Buffalo State College, Buffalo, NY, and Niagara County Community College, Sanborn, NY; Iowa State University, Ames, instructor in drawing, then assistant professor of art and design, 2001-c.04; full-time writer.

Awards, Honors
Book Sense Book-of-the-Year Honor Book designation, Best Book of the Year designations from *School Library Journal, Publishers Weekly,* and *Child* magazine, and Gold Award, Parents's Choice, all 2005, all for *Ida B . . . and Her Plans to Maximize Fun, Avoid Disaster, and (Possibly) Save the World.*

Writings
Ida B . . . and Her Plans to Maximize Fun, Avoid Disaster, and (Possibly) Save the World, Greenwillow Press (New York, NY), 2004.

Adaptations
Ida B . . . and Her Plans to Maximize Fun, Avoid Disaster, and (Possibly) Save the World was adapted as an audiobook read by Lili Taylor, Books on Tape, 2004.

Work in Progress
Two stories for middle-grade readers.

Sidelights
Growing up in western New York, Katherine Hannigan was constantly surrounded by books, as well as by the rodents adopted as family pets and a succession of stray cats and dogs. With a vivid imagination, she developed a knack for creating stories involving playthings, such as a pair of clay figures she manipulated from behind her second-grade pop-up desk; paper characters cut from Valentine's Day cards; and the dolls populating her closet and who starred in Hannigan's early theatrical performances. Continuing to draw on that imagination as an adult, Hannigan is the author of the entertaining middle-school novel *Ida B . . . and Her Plans to Maximize Fun, Avoid Disaster, and (Possibly) Save the World.*

Before beginning her writing career, Hannigan studied art in New York and obtained bachelor's and master's degrees in painting. After teaching in upstate New York for several years, she moved west, teaching art and design at Iowa State University. While in Iowa, Hannigan once again found inspiration in her surroundings, and she began to develop the title character for her first children's book. *Ida B . . . and Her Plans to Maximize Fun, Avoid Disaster, and (Possibly) Save the World* was still in its draft stage when Hannigan decided to take a writing workshop conducted by children's author Kate DiCamillo in 2002. After Hannigan submitted a chapter from her unpublished work and won the praise of the veteran author, DiCamillo passed along the manuscript to a literary agent and the novel was published by Greenwillow Books in 2004. *Ida B . . . and Her Plans to Maximize Fun, Avoid Disaster, and (Possibly) Save the World* became a *New York Times* bestseller and won numerous accolades from critics.

In an interview with an online *BookBrowse* contributor, Hannigan noted that her title character, Ida B, was developed from "a love of laughter," and "a fondness for

Cover of Katherine Hannigan's Ida B. . . and Her Plans to Maximize Fun, Avoid Disaster, and (Possibly) Save the World, *featuring artwork by Dana Tezarr*. (Text copyright © 2004 by Katherine Hannigan. Jacket art © 2004 by Dana Tezarr/Potonica. Dana Tezarr/Photonica/Getty Images. Published by Greenwillow Books.)

people with a good dose of puckishness in them." Ida B, is indeed, a distinctive and "unforgettable heroine," as *School Library Journal* contributor Faith Brautigam noted, while a *Publishers Weekly* critic dubbed her a "firecracker of a character." In the book nine-year-old Ida B speaks to the trees and the brooks that surround her family farm and spends the majority of her free time making arts and crafts. Home-schooled throughout her life, she is accustomed to freedom and tranquility. Things drastically change, however, when her mother develops cancer and her parents decide to sell a portion of the family's apple grove—which also happens to be Ida B's playground—to help pay medical bills. Matters are exacerbated when Ida B is sent to public school, but it is at this point that the girl decides to deal directly with the changes taking place around her. As pressures mount, she becomes an embittered nine year old and feels as if everything in her life has betrayed her.

Reviewing *Ida B . . . and Her Plans to Maximize Fun, Avoid Disaster, and (Possibly) Save the World*, critics hailed Hannigan for her ability to realistically portray the mind-set of a nine year old. Faith Brautigam, writing in *School Library Journal,* noted that "Ida B is a true character in every sense of the word." Likewise, *Booklist* contributor Ilene Cooper commented on Hannigan's ability to fully capture "the fury children can experience" and "the tenacity with which they can hold on to their anger." Another tactic Hannigan employs can be seen in the resolution of the story, as Ida B begins to appreciate the changes in her life. *Horn Book* contributor Susan Dove Lempke stated that Hannigan "skillfully depicts the slow climb back . . . where Ida B can allow herself to express happiness again."

With her skills in characterization, plot, storyline, and writing style, Hannigan impressed many critics. Cooper noted in *Booklist* that the writer "gets it down brilliantly," while a *Publishers Weekly* reviewer regarded *Ida B . . . and Her Plans to Maximize Fun, Avoid Disaster, and (Possibly) Save the World* as an "insightful, seemingly intuitive first novel." In a similar fashion, a *Kirkus Reviews* critic noted that the book is a "funny debut from a promising new author," while Lempke described Hannigan as "clearly an author to watch."

Biographical and Critical Sources

PERIODICALS

Booklist, September, 2004, Ilene Cooper, review of *Ida B . . . and Her Plans to Maximize Fun, Avoid Disaster, and (Possibly) Save the World,* p. 1924; January 1, 2004, Jennifer Mattson, interview with Hannigan, p. 843.

Horn Book, November-December, 2004, review of *Ida B . . . and Her Plans to Maximize Fun, Avoid Disaster, and (Possibly) Save the World,* p. 709.

Kirkus Reviews, July 15, 2004, review of *Ida B . . . and Her Plans to Maximize Fun, Avoid Disaster, and (Possibly) Save the World,* p. 686.

Publishers Weekly, July 26, 2004, review of *Ida B . . . and Her Plans to Maximize Fun, Avoid Disaster, and (Possibly) Save the World,* p. 55; December 12, 2004, Jennifer M. Brown, "Katherine Hannigan," pp. 30-34.

School Library Journal, August, 2004, Faith Brautigam, review of *Ida B . . . and Her Plans to Maximize Fun, Avoid Disaster, and (Possibly) Save the World,* p. 122.

ONLINE

BookBrowse, http://www.bookbrowse.com/ (April 10, 2006), interview with Hannigan.

HarperChildrens Web site, http://harperchildrens.com/ (April 10, 2006), "Katherine Hannigan."

* * *

HENDERSON, Aileen Mary
See FOX, Aileen

HENRIQUEZ, Emile F. 1937-

Personal
Born April 29, 1937, in New Orleans, LA; son of Manuel V. and Amelia (Arguello) Henriquez; married Mary Ann Barrois (a homemaker), July 21, 1989; children: Emile F., Jr., Amelia Jennings, Daniel, Alfred, Kathy Blohm. *Education:* Attended John McCrady Art School, 1955-60, and Tulane University, 1966-68. *Religion:* Roman Catholic. *Hobbies and other interests:* Travel, exercise, collections, reading, drawing.

Addresses
Home and office—1818 Barrymore St., Slidell, LA 70461.

Career
Illustrator and graphic artist. Boeing Company, New Orleans, LA, graphic illustrator, 1963-74; Schwegmann's Supermarkets, New Orleans, newspaper advertisement coordinator and graphic artist, 1974; Textron Marine and Land Systems, New Orleans, graphic illustrator, 1974-81, chief illustrator, 1981-85, design coordinator, 1985-95; freelance illustrator, 1995—. *Military service:* Louisiana National Guard, 1955-63; became sergeant E5.

Member
Slidell (LA) Art League.

Awards, Honors
First-place award in drawing and watercolor, Slidell Art League, 1971.

Illustrator
(With Lucien C. Barbarin) Denise W. McConduit, *D.J. and the Zulu Parade,* Pelican (Gretna, LA), 1995.
Denise Walter McConduit, *D.J. and the Jazz Fest,* Pelican (Gretna, LA), 1997.
Denise Walter McConduit, *D.J. and the Debutante Ball,* Pelican (Gretna, LA), 2004.
Freddi Williams Evans, *The Battle of New Orleans: The Drummer's Story,* Pelican (Gretna, LA), 2005.

Sidelights
New Orleans-based graphic artist and illustrator Emile F. Henriquez has contributed his artistic talents to several books for younger readers, including *The Battle of New Orleans: The Drummer's Story,* by Freddi Williams Evans. A rhyming tale for budding readers, the story focuses on the U.S. troops fighting under General Andrew Jackson against the British during the War of 1812. Henriquez creates illustrations that are "realistic" according to *School Library Journal* critic Judith Constantinides, and he depicts the Cajun, German, French, Spanish, and Native American men who have all united under General Jackson to defend their home city.

Henriquez recognized his passion for art and drawing at a young age. "I can remember drawing all my life," the illustrator once recalled to *SATA*. "I used comic books for reference until high school, when I was designated my school's official artist. I studied under John McCrady, an excellent regionalist painter of the ash can school. I studied at Tulane University much later. For thirty years I worked as a commercial artist and moonlighted for extra money and experience. I designed truck floats for the Mardi Gras parades in New Orleans and won many awards for them. Some of the commercial techniques and methods I employ were learned in the street and are not taught at most schools. Today, I freelance from a home studio, working on a diversified range of art projects, from calligraphy to graphic design to fine art."

Biographical and Critical Sources

PERIODICALS

School Library Journal, November, 2005, Judith Constantinides, review of *The Battle of New Orleans: The Drummer's Story,* p. 90.

* * *

HILL, Laban Carrick

Personal
Male. *Education:* Bernard M. Baruch College, B.A. (English; cum laude), 1986; Latin and Greek Institute of the City University of New York, certificate (summa cum laude), 1986; Columbia University, M.F.A., 1989.

Addresses
Home—Burlington, VT. *Agent*—Susan Cohen, Writers House, 21 W. 26th St., New York, NY 10010. *E-mail*—labanhill@yahoo.com.

Career
Poet, children's writer, lecturer, and educator. *New Yorker,* New York, NY, senior copywriter and marketing analyst, 1982-86; Sterling Publishing, senior copywriter, 1990-91; Bantam Publishing, New York, NY, senior copywriter, 1991-93; Baruch College, City University of New York, instructor in composition and English as a second language, 1993-94; Eating Well Books, New York, NY, marketing and promotion director, 1994-96; St. Michaels College, lecturer in English and writing, 1994-2000; Vermont College, mentor in M.F.A. program, 2003-05, member of adjunct faculty, 2006; University of Vermont, member of adjunct faculty, 2006. Freelance writer. Volunteer writing and poetry teacher; lecturer to U.S. Embassy in Egypt, 2006. Former co-

editor, *American Letters and Commentary* (literary magazine). Greater Burlington Girls Soccer League, vice president of board of directors, 1997-2003; Flechter Free Library, commissioner, 2003—

Member
PEN, Authors Guild, Author's League of America.

Awards, Honors
Counterpoint Prize first prize, 2001; Parents' Choice Gold Award, and National Book Award finalist, both 2004, both for *Harlem Stomp!;* numerous other award for children's books.

Writings

Monster Dots, Sterling Publishing, 1993.
Clinton Street Crime Wave, Bantam (New York, NY), 1994.
Santa's Surprises, Readers Digest (Pleasantville, NY), 1996.
Bugged Out!, illustrated by Bill Schmidt, Gareth Stevens (Milwaukee, WI), 1997.
Stampede!: Choose Your Own Adventure, Bantam (New York, NY), 1997.
Jonathan Franzen's The Corrections ("Spark Notes"), Spark Publishers (New York, NY), 2003.
Harlem Stomp!: A Cultural History of the Harlem Renaissance, Little, Brown (New York, NY), 2003.
The Spy's Survival Handbook, Scholastic (New York, NY), 2004.
Casa Azul: An Encounter with Frida Kahlo (young-adult novel), Watson-Guptill (New York, NY), 2005.
Napoleon's Sitter (young-adult novel), Watson-Guptill (New York, NY), 2005.
America Dreaming: How Youth Changed America, Little, Brown (New York, NY), 2007.

Contributor of poetry to anthology *Contemporary Poetry of New England* and to periodicals, including *Denver Quarterly, Minetta Review, Strabotomy, Outreach, Onion River Review, Tar River Review, Central Park,* and *American Letters & Commentary.* Contributor of articles to Scribners "American Writers" and "British Writers" series. Contributor to periodicals, including *Counterpoint, Eating Well, Johnson State University Magazine, Vanderbilt,* and *Vermont Quarterly.*

"X-TREME MYSTERIES" NOVEL SERIES

Deep Powder, Deep Trouble, Hyperion (New York, NY), 1998.
Crossed Tracks, Hyperion (New York, NY), 1998.
Rocked Out: A Summer X-Games Special, Hyperion (New York, NY), 1998.
Half Pipe Rip-off, Hyperion (New York, NY), 1998.
Lost Wake, Hyperion (New York, NY), 1998.
Out of Line, Hyperion (New York, NY), 1998.
Spiked Snow, Hyperion (New York, NY), 1998.
Total White Out, Hyperion (New York, NY), 1998.

"CHOOSE YOUR OWN NIGHTMARE" NOVEL SERIES

Watch out for Room 13, illustrated by Bill Schmidt, Gareth Stevens (Milwaukee, WI), 1997.
The Evil Pen Pal, illustrated by Bill Schmidt, Gareth Stevens (Milwaukee, WI), 1998.
The Toy Shop of Terror, illustrated by Bill Schmidt, Gareth Stevens (Milwaukee, WI), 1998.
Welcome to Horror Hospital, illustrated by Bill Schmidt, Gareth Stevens (Milwaukee, WI), 1998.

Work in Progress
Slick, an adult novel set in contemporary Memphis; *Achilles Dead,* an adult novel focusing on the postmodern poetry scene; *Every Man Jack: American Jack Tales; Tipton County,* a nonfiction memoir based on the alleged murder of Hill's grandfather in Tennessee.

Sidelights
Laban Carrick Hill is the author of several titles for young readers and young adults, including illustrated chapter books for early readers, nonfiction and historical fiction for older readers, and novels in the "X-treme Mysteries" series. His highly praised nonfiction title *Harlem Stomp!: A Cultural History of the Harlem Renaissance* was a finalist for the National Book Award for young people's literature. In addition to books, Hill is a published poet. He has also contributed biographical essays to Scribners' "American Writers" and "British Writers" series, and his synopsis and analyses of *The Corrections* by Jonathan Franzen was published as *Jonathan Franzen's The Corrections* for the "Spark Notes" study series.

Harlem Stomp! delves into the Harlem Renaissance, the period from 1900 to 1924 when music, literature, and art surged from the African-American community in Harlem, New York. Covering such noteworthy figures as Booker T. Washington, W.E.B. DuBois, Sgt. Henry Johnson, and Charles Spurgeon Johnson, Hill includes short biographies, analyses of cultural conflicts of the day, and background information on the factors leading up to this cultural awakening. "This compelling history will leave readers familiar or unfamiliar with this high-flying period eager to discover more," wrote a contributor to *Publishers Weekly.* A *Kirkus Reviews* critic considered the book "clearly a labor of love," and Joanne K. Cecere wrote in *School Library Journal* that "the words and images bring this extraordinary period to life." Noting that Hill includes excerpts of "great selections from literature and journalism of the period" in his book, Hazel Rochman commented in her *Booklist* review that, while the biographies occasionally lag, "far livelier are discussions of their works, which show how the writers changed the view of blacks." To help teachers introduce *Harlem Stomp!* to students, the publisher has also provided a downloadable teacher's guide.

Cover of Laban Carrick Hill's Casa Azul, *featuring artwork by Frida Kahlo.* (Text copyright © 2005 by Laban Carrick Hill. Published by Watson-Guptill Publications. Reproduced by permission.)

Hill's historical fiction title, *Casa Azul: An Encounter with Frida Kahlo,* is part of the "Art Encounters" series of historical novels that introduce young-adult readers to famous artists. Drawing on Kahlo's painting "Self Portrait (with Monkey and Hummingbird)" for inspiration, Hill's story centers around two young people—fourteen-year-old Maria Ortiz, and Victor, Maria's younger brother—who are invited to stay in Kahlo's mysterious house, where what is real and what is fantastic are often the very same thing. Other residents of Kahlo's home are Fuland the monkey and Chica the cat, both of whom are able to speak. "In the spirit of Kahlo's life and art, the magical realism is both playful and dark," noted Rochman in a *Booklist* review. Steev Baker, writing in *School Library Journal,* commented that "Hill's short art-history novel accomplishes with style what it is meant to do," while *Magazine of Fantasy and Science Fiction* contributor Charles de Lint deemed the novel "a terrific introduction to magical fantasy and the creative impulse." A *Kirkus Reviews* critic also noted the similarities between the novel and Kahlo's creative work, writing that "Hill's blend of realism, fantasy, and Aztec myth nicely mirrors Kahlo's surreal juxtaposition of real and unreal."

Along with his nonfiction and historical fiction titles, Hills has published several titles for young mystery lovers. The "X-treme Mysteries" center around young sleuths who enjoy such extreme sports as rock climbing, snowboarding, and skate boarding. When their respective sports are endangered by nefarious activities, the kids rise to the challenge to solve the mystery. In *The Spy's Survival Handbook* Hill explores codes and gives helpful hints on how to successfully shake a pursuer and create an effective disguise. "Young secret agents can hone their skills," a *Publishers Weekly* critic commented in a review of the title.

Biographical and Critical Sources

PERIODICALS

Booklist, February 15, 2004, Hazel Rochman, review of *Harlem Stomp!: A Cultural History of the Harlem Renaissance,* p. 1065; October 1, 2005, Hazel Rochman, review of *Casa Azul: An Encounter with Frida Kahlo,* p. 48.
Bulletin of the Center for Children's Books, April, 2004, Elizabeth Bush, review of *Harlem Stomp!,* p. 330.
Kirkus Reviews, November 15, 2003, review of *Harlem Stomp!,* p. 1360; June 15, 2005, review of *Casa Azul,* p. 683.
Kliatt, May, 2005, Janis Flint-Ferguson, review of *Casa Azul,* p. 13.
Magazine of Fantasy and Science Fiction, August, 2005, Charles de Lint, review of *Casa Azul,* p. 27.
Publishers Weekly, December 22, 2003, review of *Harlem Stomp!,* p. 63; June 7, 2004, "Spy vs. Spy," p. 53.
School Library Journal, January, 2004, Joanne K. Cecere, review of *Harlem Stomp!,* p. 148; October, 2004, review of *Harlem Stomp!,* p. S66; September, 2005, Steev Baker, review of *Casa Azul,* p. 204.
Voice of Youth Advocates, February, 2004, Valerie Ott, review of *Harlem Stomp!,* p. 511; April, 2004, "Pure Poetry," p. 16.

ONLINE

Laban Carrick Hill Home Page, http://www.labanhill.com (April 4, 2006).
National Book Foundation Web site, http://www.nationalbook.org/ (April 8, 2006), "Laban Carrick Hill."

* * *

hooks, bell 1952-
(Gloria Jean Watkins)

Personal

Born September 25, 1952, in Hopkinsville, KY; daughter of Veodis and Rosa Bell Watkins. *Education:* Stanford University, B.A., 1973; University of Wisconsin, M.A. 1976; University of California Santa Cruz, Ph.D. (English), 1987.

bell hooks (Photograph by John Pinderhughes, Pinderhughes Photography, Inc. Reproduced by permission.)

Addresses

Home—291 W. 12th St., New York, NY 10031. *Office*—Department of English, Berea College, 101 Chestnut St., Berea, KY 40404.

Career

Social critic, educator, and writer. Yale University, New Haven, CT, assistant professor of Afro-American studies and English, 1980-85; Oberlin College, Oberlin, OH, associate professor of English, 1986-94; City College of New York, professor, then distinguished professor of English, 1995-2004; Berea College, Berea, KY, distinguished professor-in-residence, beginning 2004. Co-founder, *Hambone* literary magazine.

Awards, Honors

American Book Award, Before Columbus Foundation, 1991, for *Yearning: Race, Gender, and Cultural Politics;* Writer's Award, Lila Wallace/*Reader's Digest* Fund, 1994; Image Award nomination, National Association for the Advancement of Colored People, 2001, for *Happy to Be Nappy;* Children's Book of the Year designation, Bank Street College, 2002, for *Homemade Love;* Hurston Wright Legacy Award nomination, 2002, for *Salvation: Black People and Love.*

Writings

FOR CHILDREN

Happy to Be Nappy, illustrated by Chris Raschka, Hyperion (New York, NY), 1998, boardbook edition, Jump at the Sun (New York, NY), 2001.
Homemade Love, illustrations by Shane W. Evans, Hyperion (New York, NY), 2002.
Be Boy Buzz, illustrated by Chris Raschka, Hyperion (New York, NY), 2002.
Skin Again, illustrated by Chris Raschka, Hyperion (New York, NY), 2004.

ADULT NONFICTION

Ain't I a Woman: Black Women and Feminism, South End Press (Cambridge, MA), 1981.
Feminist Theory: From Margin to Center, South End Press (Cambridge, MA), 1984, second edition, 2000.
Talking Back: Thinking Feminist, Thinking Black, Between-the-Lines, 1988.
Yearning: Race, Gender, and Cultural Politics, Between-the-Lines, 1990.
(With Cornell West) *Breaking Bread: Insurgent Black Intellectual Life,* South End Press (Cambridge, MA), 1991.
Black Looks: Race and Representation, South End Press (Cambridge, MA), 1992.
Sisters of the Yam: Black Women and Self Recovery, South End Press (Cambridge, MA), 1993, second edition, 2005.
Outlaw Culture: Resisting Representations, Routledge (New York, NY), 1994.
Teaching to Transgress: Education as the Practice of Freedom, Routledge (New York, NY), 1994.
Changing the Subject: Painting and Prints, 1992-94, Art in General, 1994.
Art on My Mind: Visual Politics, New Press, 1995.
Killing Rage: Ending Racism, Holt (New York, NY), 1995.
Reel to Real: Race, Sex, and Class at the Movies, Routledge (New York, NY), 1996.
Remembered Rapture: The Writer at Work, Holt (New York, NY), 1999.
All about Love: New Visions, Morrow (New York, NY), 2000.
Feminism Is for Everybody: Passionate Politics, South End Press (Cambridge, MA), 2000.
Where We Stand: Class Matters, Routledge (New York, NY), 2000.
Salvation: Black People and Love, Morrow (New York, NY), 2001.
Communion: The Female Search for Love, Morrow (New York, NY), 2002.
Teaching Community: A Pedagogy of Hope, Routledge (New York, NY), 2002.
Rock My Soul: Black People and Self-Esteem, Atria Books (New York, NY), 2003.
We Real Cool: Black Men and Masculinity, Routledge (New York, NY), 2004.

The Will to Change: Men, Masculinity, and Love, Atria Books (New York, NY), 2004.

(With Amalia Mesa-Bains) *Homegrown: Engaged Cultural Criticism,* South End Press (Cambridge, MA), 2006.

Contributor to books, including *Double Stitch: Black Women Write about Mothers and Daughters,* 1992, *Anthology of Contemporary African-American Women Artists,* 1995, *The Masculine Masquerade,* 1995, *An Elliptical Traverse of 20th-Century Art,* 1996, *Spoils of War,* 1997, *Talking about a Revolution,* 1998, and *UpSouth,* 1999. Contributor to periodicals, including *Emerge, Callalo, Utne Reader,* and *Catalyst.*

OTHER

A Woman's Mourning Song (poetry), Writers and Readers, 1992.
Bone Black: Memories of Girlhood, Holt (New York, NY), 1996.
Wounds of Passion: A Writing Life, Holt (New York, NY), 1997.

Sidelights

Considered among the foremost intellectuals of her generation, bell hooks is a social critic and educator who writes about social and cultural topics ranging from racism to feminism to the theory of art and the practice of education. Well known in academic circles for her essays collected in the books *Ain't I a Woman: Black Women and Feminism* and *Yearning: Race, Gender, and Cultural Politics,* among others, hooks has also written movingly of her own childhood in the memoir *Bone Black: Memories of Girlhood,* and of writing in both *Wounds of Passion: A Writing Life* and *Remembered Rapture: The Writer at Work.* Beginning with 1999's *Happy to Be Nappy,* hooks broadened her audience to include younger children, and the picture books she has produced with illustrators Chris Raschka and Shane W. Evans have been commended for instilling young African Americans with cultural pride and self-esteem.

Born Gloria Jean Watkins in 1952, hooks grew up in Kentucky, the daughter of a custodial worker and a homemaker. Poetry was a family-shared interest, and when frequent storms caused power outages, the Watkins family would sit in candlelight and recite poetry to one another. Writing her own poetry at an early age, hooks was also inspired by the writings of Emily Dickinson. While she dreamed about becoming an architect when she grew up, the power of words would ultimately prove more compelling than design, although hooks has discussed both art and design in her nonfiction writing.

Hooks's experiences growing up in a segregated community have caused her to focus predominately on the effects of racism in much of her published work. Additionally, her father's rigid traditional beliefs regarding gender roles made her question, early on, the sexism alive in both the black community and U.S. society at large. Her feminist stance is rooted in the strong female role models that figured largely in her early life; in fact, her adopted name is that of her great grandmother, adopted in order, according to Paula Giddings in *Ms.,* to "honor the unlettered wisdom of her foremothers." Hooks writes the name in the lower case, as she explained to Michel Marriott in the *New York Times,* "to emphasize her message and not herself."

In her first book for children, Happy to Be Nappy, *hooks shines an upbeat light on African-American culture, with illustrations by Chris Raschka.* (Text copyright © 1999 by bell hooks. Illustration copyright © 1999 by Chris Raschka. All rights reserved. Reprinted by permission of Hyperion Books for Children.)

The place of African-American women within the feminist movement of the late twentieth century is the focus of several of hooks's essay collections, including her first, 1981's *Ain't I a Woman.* Begun when its author was nineteen years old, *Ain't I a Woman* takes its title from a speech by the nineteenth-century former slave and abolitionist Sojourner Truth. In this book hooks challenges the minor role black women were given in both the feminist and black liberation movements, and champions the idea of sisterhood among black women. She expands her thesis regarding black feminism in *Feminist Theory* and the essay collection *Talking Back.* A prolific writer, she continued to publish a book per year throughout the 1990s, in addition to her teaching duties, which included serving as distinguished professor of English at the City College of New York. In books such as *Black Looks: Race and Representation* and *Outlaw Culture: Resisting Representations* she takes on cultural and societal shibboleths: studying not only the black woman's place in the scheme of things, but also that of the black intellectual, while also examining the role of the outsider in so-called mainstream society.

Teaching to Transgress, a collection of essays about the power of teaching, was praised as "full of hope and excitement for the possibility of education to liberate and include" by a *Publishers Weekly* critic, while her *Art on My Mind,* a book on the impact of black artists, particularly women, prompted *Booklist* critic Donna Seaman to write that, "As erudite and sophisticated as hooks is, she is also eminently readable, even exhilarating."

Viewed as inspirational reading for teen readers, hooks's autobiographical writings include the childhood chronicle *Bone Black* and her recollections of her college years in *Wounds of Passion.* In *Bone Black* hooks recalls the formative influences on her youth: the black community, strong women, religion, and the local library. Openly discussing her budding sexuality as well as the domestic turbulence in her home, hooks draws an intimate portrait of growing up black in a segregated community. Dottie Kraft, writing in *School Library Journal,* found the book to be a "treasure box of memories" and a "unique autobiography of a contemporary African-American woman," while Seaman wrote in *Booklist* that the memoir, a "lyrical, deeply moving, and brilliantly structured autobiography," showcases hooks's ability "to articulate the sharp, unrelenting anguish of her young self, and her struggle to find comfort and inspiration in books." *Wounds of Passion,* which takes up hooks's life at the point at which she leaves Kentucky to enroll at Stanford and has, at its heart, her prolonged love affair with a man who she spent fifteen years with, was described by Ann Burns in *Library Journal* as an "exceptionally written memoir."

With *Happy to Be Nappy* hooks takes a new direction in her written work, creating a children's picture book that celebrates the unique qualities of blackness. For hooks's young protagonist, her nappy hair is "soft like cotton, / flower petal billowy soft, full of frizz and fuzz." A reviewer for *Publishers Weekly* called the book a "joyous ode to hair" and a "powerful, uplifting and, above all, buoyantly fun read-aloud." In *Booklist* Rochman described the book as "bubbling over with affection, and injecting a strong self-esteem boost for girls." Praising the author's "ebulient, poetic text," Rochman also commended Raschka's "superb" illustrations for "bolstering the theme of individuality."

Described by *Horn Book* critic Susan Dove Lempke as "a celebration of humanity rather than ethnicity," *Skin Again* takes another physical characteristic and brings home the point that beneath our varied shells, all humans are unique. "The skin I'm in is just a covering," hooks's young narrator recites. "It cannot tell my story." Addressing the issue of stereotypes in rhythmic language that will appeal to young children, the book employs "exuberant, playful imagery that will open discussion," according to Rochman. Dubbing *Skin Again* a "verbal and visual celebration" that features Raschka's "impressionistic" art, *School Library Journal* reviewer Grace Oliff praised hooks for her "deft handling of language," noting that it makes the story "gently persuasive rather than didactic."

Building self-esteem, particularly among African-American children, is the unifying theme of hooks's picture books. Described by a *Publishers Weekly* reviewer as a "stunning volume" that "celebrates all things boy," *Be Boy Buzz* once again reunites hooks and Raschka in a pairing of rhyme and delightful artistry. What the *Publishers Weekly* reviewer described as the author's "rhythmic blend of brevity and eloquence" inspires the illustrator's pastel and watercolor portraits depicting a young boy engaging in everything from running and jumping to pouting and dreaming. While noting in her *Black Issues Book Review* article that hooks's "liberal use of Ebonics may prove controversial," Evette Porter nonetheless praised the "sparse narrative" for its ability to convey a range of childhood feelings.

Broadening her scope from the child to the family, *Homemade Love* pairs hooks's verse with Evans' brightly toned artwork to present what a *Kirkus Reviews* contributor described as a "paean to parental unconditional love" that features a "joyful, loving African-American family." Narrated by a young black girl dubbed "girlpie" by her parents, the book shows that mis-steps do not diminish true affection within a loving home. In *School Library Journal* Amy Lilien-Harper praised the book's young protagonist for "exuding happiness and a zest for life," while in *Booklist* Gillian Engberg commended hooks's picture book as "an elemental celebration of children and African-American pride."

Biographical and Critical Sources

BOOKS

Contemporary Black Biography, Volume 5, Thomson Gale (Detroit, MI), 1994.
Contemporary Literary Criticism, Volume 94, Thomson Gale (Detroit, MI), 1994.
Feminist Writers, edited by Pamela Kester-Shelton, St. James Press (Detroit, MI), 1996.
Florence, Namulundah, *Bell Hooks's Engaged Pedagogy: A Transgressive Education for Critical Consciousness,* Bergin & Garvey, 1998.
hooks, bell, *Bone Black: Memories of Girlhood,* Holt (New York, NY), 1996.
hooks, bell, *Happy to Be Nappy,* Hyperion (New York, NY), 1998.
hooks, bell, *Skin Again,* Hyperion (New York, NY), 2004.
hooks, bell, *Wounds of Passion: A Writing Life,* Holt (New York, NY), 1997.

PERIODICALS

Black Enterprise, June, 1992, p. 23.

Black Issues Book Review, November-December, 2002, Evette Porter, "Bell hooks' Be a Boy and Girlpie," p. 42.

Booklist, June 1, 1995, Donna Seaman, review of *Art on My Mind: Visual Politics,* p. 1715; September 15, 1995, Bonnie Smothers, review of *Killing Rage: Ending Racism,* pp. 118, 147; September 15, 1996, Donna Seaman, review of *Bone Black,* p. 189; February 15, 1999, Donna Seaman, review of *Bone Black,* p. 1025; August 19, 1999, Hazel Rochman, review of *Happy to Be Nappy;* November 1, 2002, Hazel Rochman, review of *Be Boy Buzz,* p. 508; February 1, 2003, Gillian Engberg, review of *Homemade Love,* p. 1001; January 1, 2004, Vernon Ford, review of *We Real Cool: Black Men and Masculinity,* p. 796; September 15, 2004, Hazel Rochman, review of *Skin Again,* p. 250.

Bookwatch, July 1989, p. 4; September, 1992, p. 10.

Bulletin of the Center for Children's Books, December, 2002, review of *Be Boy Buzz,* p. 160; February, 2003, review of *Homemade Love,* p. 238; December, 2004, Karen Coats, review of *Skin Again,* p. 171.

Choice, April, 1982, review of *Ain't I a Woman: Black Women and Feminism,* p. 1141; July, 1985, p. 1703.

Essence, July, 1989, p. 20.

Horn Book, November-December, 2004, Susan Dove Lempke, review of *Skin Again,* p. 698.

Kirkus Reviews, April 15, 1995, review of *Art on My Mind,* p. 534; November 15, 1998, review of *Remembered Rapture: The Writer at Work;* September 1, 2002, review of *Be Boy Buzz,* p. 1310; December 1, 2002, review of *Homemade Love,* p. 1769; August 15, 2004, review of *Skin Again,* p. 897.

Library Journal, December 1, 1981, Mary Biggs, review of *Ain't I a Woman,* p. 2326; March 15, 1985, p. 68; December, 1988, p. 126; July, 1992, p. 109; September 15, 1996, Ann Burns, review of *Bone Black,* p. 75; October 1, 1997, Ann Burns, review of *Wounds of Passion,* p. 94; March 15, 2000, Ann Burns, review of *All about Love: New Visions,* p. 112; November 1, 2000, Emily Joy Jones, review of *Where We Stand: Class Matters,* p. 104.

Ms., July, 1983, p. 24; October, 1985, Paula Giddings, review of *Feminist Theory: From Margin to Center,* p. 25.

Multicultural Review, April, 1992; March, 1993, Itibari M. Zulu, review of *Black Looks: Race and Representation,* p. 84.

New Directions for Women, January, 1992, p. 22.

New Statesman, October 22, 1982, p. 31; November 30, 1990, p. 39.

New York Times, November 13, 1997, Michel Marriott, "The Eye of the Storm," pp. F1, F4.

New York Times Book Review, February 29, 1993, D. Soyini Madison, review of *Black Looks,* p. 23; December 18, 1994, p. 27; September 17, 1995, p. 25; December 15, 1996, Thulani Davis, "Native Daughter," p. 32.

Phylon, March, 1983, p. 85.

Political Science Quarterly, spring, 1983, p. 84.

Progressive, March, 1991, p. 42.

Publishers Weekly, November 18, 1988, review of *Talking Back: Thinking Feminist, Thinking Black,* p. 72; November 22, 1991, p. 49; June 15, 1992, p. 95; July 19, 1999, review of *Happy to Be Nappy,* p. 194; September 30, 2002, review of *Be Boy Buzz,* p. 71; November 18, 2002, review of *Homemade Love,* p. 59; November 25, 2002, Robert Fleming, "Feminist Revolutionary Comes down to Earth" (interview), p. 54; November 10, 2003, review of *We Real Cool,* p. 49; October 18, 2004, review of *Skin Again,* p. 62.

Queen's Quarterly, summer, 1990, p. 318; November 7, 1994, review of *Teaching to Transgress: Education as the Practice of Freedom* and *Outlaw Culture: Resisting Representations,* p. 70; September 22, 1997, review of *Wounds of Passion,* p. 64; July 19, 1999, review of *Happy to Be Nappy,* p. 194.

School Library Journal, March, 1997, Dottie Kraft, review of *Bone Black,* p. 217; November, 1999, Karen James, review of *Happy to Be Nappy,* p. 120; December, 2002, Amy Lilien-Harper, review of *Homemade Love,* p. 97; December, 2002, Anna DeWind Walls, review of *Be Boy Buzz,* p. 97; September, 2004, Grace Oliff, review of *Skin Again,* p. 162.

Sight and Sound, June, 1991, p. 36; May, 1997, p. 34.

Village Voice Literary Supplement, June, 1982, p. 10; December, 1992, p. 14; November, 1995, p. 19.

West Coast Review of Books, April, 1982, p. 51.

Women's Review of Books, February, 1985, P. Gabrielle Foreman, review of *Feminist Theory,* p. 3; September, 1991, p. 12; October, 1993, p. 12; March, 1995, p. 10.

ONLINE

Orlo Web site, http://www.teleport.com/~orlo/be4/interview/bellhooks.html (May 10, 2006), interview with hooks.

Shambhala Sun Web site, http://www.shambhalasun.com/ (May 10, 2006), Pema Chödrön, interview with hooks.

OTHER

bell hooks: Cultural Criticism and Transformation (film), Media Center Foundation, c. 1995.*

* * *

JACOBSON, Jennifer
See JACOBSON, Jennifer Richard

* * *

JACOBSON, Jennifer Richard 1958-
(Jennifer Jacobson)

Personal

Born 1958, in NH; married; children: two. *Education:* Harvard University, M.A. *Hobbies and other interests:* Hiking, swimming, skiing, reading.

Addresses

Home—Cumberland, ME. *Agent*—c/o Author Mail, Candlewick Press, 2067 Massachusetts Ave., Cambridge, MA 02140. *E-mail*—jennifer@jenniferjacobson.com.

Career

Writer of books for teachers and for children, 1995—. Sixth-grade teacher, curriculum coordinator, and language arts specialist at various schools in New England; educational consultant.

Awards, Honors

Bank Street's Best Children's Book, Top Ten First Novels of 2001, *Booklist,* both for *Winnie Dancing on Her Own;* Children's Curriculum choice, *School Library Journal,* nominee, Rhode Island Children's Book Award, 2004, both for *Truly Winnie.*

Writings

FOR CHILDREN; AS JENNIFER RICHARD JACOBSON EXCEPT AS NOTED

(As Jennifer Jacobson) *Mr. Lee* (picture book), illustrated by John Agee, Open Court Pub. (Chicago, IL), 1995.
(As Jennifer Jacobson) *Getting to Know Sharks* (nonfiction), Sadlier-Oxford (New York, NY), 1997.
(As Jennifer Jacobson) *A Net of Stars* (picture book), illustrated by Greg Shed, Dial Books for Young Readers (New York, NY), 1998.
Moon Sandwich Mom (picture book), illustrated by Benrei Huang, A. Whitman (Morton Grove, IL), 1999.
Winnie Dancing on Her Own (chapter book), illustrated by Alissa Imre Geis, Houghton Mifflin (Boston, MA), 2001.
Truly Winnie (chapter book), illustrated by Alissa Imre Geis, Houghton Mifflin (Boston, MA), 2003.
Andy Shane and the Very Bossy Dolores Starbuckle (for beginning readers), illustrated by Abby Carter, Candlewick Press (Cambridge, MA), 2005.
Stained (young-adult novel), Atheneum Books for Young Readers (New York, NY), 2005.
Winnie at Her Best (chapter book), illustrated by Alissa Imre Geis, Houghton Mifflin (Boston, MA), 2005.
Andy Shane and the Pumpkin Trick (for beginning readers), Candlewick Press (Cambridge, MA), 2006.

FOR ADULTS; AS JENNIFER RICHARD JACOBSON EXCEPT AS NOTED

How Is My First Grader Doing in School?: What to Expect and How to Help, Simon and Schuster (New York, NY), 1998.
(With Dottie Raymer) *How Is My Second Grader Doing in School?: What to Expect and How to Help,* Simon and Schuster (New York, NY), 1998.
How Is My Third Grader Doing in School?: What to Expect and How to Help, Simon and Schuster (New York, NY), 1999.
The Big Book of Reproducible Graphic Organizers, Scholastic (New York, NY), 1999.
(With Dottie Raymer) *How Is My Fourth Grader Doing In School?: What to Expect and How to Help,* Simon and Schuster (New York, NY), 2000.
(With Dottie Raymer) *How Is My Fifth Grader Doing In School?: What to Expect and How to Help,* Simon and Schuster (New York, NY), 2000.
(With Dottie Raymer) *How Is My Sixth Grader Doing In School?: What to Expect and How to Help,* Simon and Schuster (New York, NY), 2000.
(As Jennifer Jacobson; with Dottie Raymer) *Reading Renaissance Power Lessons: Literature-based Lessons to Teach Reading Skills,* School Renaissance Institute (Madison, WI), 2001.

Sidelights

Jennifer Richard Jacobson is a teacher-turned-writer who has produced titles for parents and educators, such as the popular *How Is My First Grader Doing in School?: What to Expect and How to Help* and its sequels, as well as numerous books for children. Writing for a younger audience, Jacobson has produced award-winning picture books and chapter books, including the "Winnie" books, as well as a young-adult novel, the 2005 *Stained.*

Reviewing her picture book *A Net of Stars,* about how a little girl manages to overcome her fear of heights by riding a Ferris wheel under the stars at night, *Booklist* reviewer Hazel Rochman praised the manner in which Jacobson relates her tale "quietly in the first person." A writer for *Publishers Weekly* was also positive about this "nostalgiac" work, concluding that "young readers conquering anxieties of their own will want to linger over this comforting drama." Jacobson's 1999 picture book, *Moon Sandwich Mom,* provides another learning experience, this time for a young fox who discovers that life isn't really any better at his friends' houses. Kathy Broderick, writing in *Booklist,* observed that Jacobson "does a good job getting this 'grass-is-greener' story to a level little ones can understand."

With *Winnie Dancing on Her Own,* Jacobson moved to chapter books in a story about third-grade Winnie and her friends Zoe and Vanessa. Ballet class threatens the friendship of these three, since Winnie would much rather go to the library than to dance class. Suddenly an outsider to her other friends' growing intimacy, Winnie learns important lessons about herself and her relationship to her widowed father as a result. A critic for *Kirkus Reviews* felt that the author "does a skillful job of showing the heart-wrenching emotions felt by a child left behind by unfeeling friends," and a reviewer for *Publishers Weekly* called this beginning novel an "uplifting tale." Jacobson reprises her youthful protagonist in *Truly Winnie,* a "winning second episode," according to a critic for *Kirkus Reviews.* This time Winnie and her friends go to summer camp, but she is separated from Zoe and Vanessa and must make new friends and avoid the usual gestures of sorrow from others when they learn that her mother is dead. When Winnie tells one white lie to avoid such condolences, she discovers that the lies suddenly multiply and she ends up in trouble. *Booklist* contributor Rochman noted that "young readers will find a lot to talk about; they'll recognize that Winnie's lie is also a wish." Jean Gaffney, reviewing the same title in *School Library Journal,* called it a "satisfying, quick-moving story [that] portrays the fun and challenge of camp life and making new friends."

Jacobson's first young-adult novel, *Stained,* appeared in 2005 and quickly earned positive reviews. This tale of a teenage triangle and sexual abuse by a priest is a "carefully written novel [that] tells how adolescents are vulnerable to sexual abuse," according to *Kliatt* reviewer Claire Rosser. Set in 1975, the novel is told from the point of view of teenager Jocelyn, who has found real affection with Benny, a boy who is new to the neighborhood. Meanwhile Gabe, whom Jocelyn has known since childhood, is acting odder than usual, and then Benny, feeling guilty about his relationship with Jocelyn, begins visiting the local priest and avoiding her. When Gabe suddenly disappears, things come to a head in what a *Publishers Weekly* reviewer described as a "quietly powerful, expertly told tale." Similarly, a contributor for *Kirkus Reviews* called Jacobson's first young-adult offering a "well-written and suspenseful story." Writing in *Horn Book,* Lauren Adams praised Jocelyn's narrative voice as "honest and compelling," and Rosser felt that Jocelyn's narration "grips the reader with her honesty, her confusion, and her growing wisdom."

Biographical and Critical Sources

PERIODICALS

Booklist, June 1, 1998, Hazel Rochman, review of *A Net of Stars,* p. 1779; July, 1999, Kathy Broderick, review of *Moon Sandwich Mom,* p. 1951; September 15, 2001, Hazel Rochman, review of *Winnie Dancing on Her Own,* p. 232; November 15, 2001, Hazel Rochman, review of *Winnie Dancing on Her Own,* p. 567; September 1, 2003, Hazel Rochman, review of *Truly Winnie,* p. 119.
Horn Book, March-April, 2005, Lauren Adams, review of *Stained,* p. 202.
Kirkus Reviews, August 1, 2001, review of *Winnie Dancing on Her Own,* p. 1125; August 1, 2003, review of *Truly Winnie,* p. 1018; March 1, 2005, review of *Stained,* p. 288.
Kliatt, January, 2005, Claire Rosser, review of *Stained,* p. 8.
Publishers Weekly, June 22, 1998, review of *A Net of Stars,* p. 90; August 6, 2001, review of *Winnie Dancing on Her Own,* p. 90; August 25, 2003, review of *Truly Winnie,* p. 66; October 6, 2003, review of *Winnie Dancing on Her Own,* p. 87; February 1, 2005, review of *Stained,* p. 176.
School Library Journal, December, 2001, Elaine Lesh Morgan, review of *Winnie Dancing on Her Own,* p. 104; November, 2003, Jean Gaffney, review of *Truly Winnie,* p. 96; October, 2004, review of *Truly Winnie,* p. S30; March, 2005, Francisca Goldsmith, review of *Stained,* p. 212.

ONLINE

Jennifer Richard Jacobson Home Page, http://www.jenniferjacobson.com (May 30, 2005).*

* * *

JACOBSON, Rick

Personal

Married Laura Fernandez (a musician and illustrator); children: three. *Education:* Alberta College of Art, earned degree (with honors).

Addresses

Home—Toronto, Ontario, Canada. *Agent*—c/o David and Lynn Bennett, 72 Glengowan Rd., Toronto, Ontario M4N 1G4, Canada. *E-mail*—jaco@rogers.com.

Career

Children's author and illustrator and graphic designer. *Exhibitions:* Works (with wife, Laura Fernandez) included in permanent collection of Royal Geographical Society, London, England.

Awards, Honors

(All with Laura Fernandez) Toronto Art Directors Club awards; New York Art Directors Club Award of Excellence; Gold Medal for illustration; Ruth Schwartz Children's Book Award, 1998, for *Jeremiah Learns to Read;* Amelia Francis Howard-Gibbon Book Award, 2002, for *The Magnificent Piano Recital;* Amelia Francis Howard-Gibbon Book Award shortlist, Nautilus Book Awards finalist, 2005, and Hackmatack Award finalist, 2005-06, all for *Picasso.*

Writings

AND ILLUSTRATOR WITH WIFE, LAURA FERNANDEZ

Picasso: Soul on Fire, Tundra (Plattsburgh, NY), 2004.
The Mona Lisa Caper, Tundra (Plattsburgh, NY), 2005.

ILLUSTRATOR

(With Gordon Suavé) Benjamin Evans, *Diary of an Alien: Original Thoughts from the Enterprising Mind of Benjamin Evans,* Storybook (Toronto, Ontario, Canada), 1989.

(With Gordon Suavé) Cheryl Lousley, *Reigad Wai: Original Thoughts from the Enterprising Mind of Cheryl Lousley,* Storybook (Toronto, Ontario, Canada), 1989.

David Strobel, *Crime in 2001: Original Thoughts from the Enterprising Mind of David Strobel,* Storybook (Toronto, Ontario, Canada), 1989.

ILLUSTRATOR, WITH LAURA FERNANDEZ

Nancy Hundal, *I Heard My Mother Call My Name,* HarperCollins (New York, NY), 1994.

Esther Kalman, *Tchaikovsky Discovers America,* Lester Publishing (Toronto, Ontario, Canada), 1994, Orchard (New York, NY), 1995.

Jo Ellen Bogart, *Jeremiah Learns to Read,* Scholastic Canada (Markham, Ontario, Canada), 1997, Orchard (New York, NY), 1999.

Norah McClintock, *Sins of the Father,* Scholastic Canada (Toronto, Ontario, Canada), 1997.

Michael Bedard, *Glass Town,* Atheneum (New York, NY), 1997.

Maxine Trottier, *Prairie Willow,* Stoddart Kids (New York, NY), 1998.

L.M. Montgomery, *Anne of Green Gables,* foreword by Kate Macdonald Butler, Tundra (Plattsburgh, NY), 2000.

Maxine Trottier, *Little Dog Moon,* Stoddart Kids (New York, NY), 2000.

Marilynn Reynolds, *The Magnificent Piano Recital,* Stoddart Kids (Toronto, Ontario, Canada), 2000, Orca (Custer, WA), 2001.

Rukhasana Khan, *King of the Skies,* North Winds Press (Markham, Ontario, Canada), 2001.

Douglas Cowling, *Vivaldi's Ring of Mystery,* North Winds Press (Markham, Ontario, Canada), 2004.

Contributor of illustrations to *Smithsonian, Applied Arts,* and *Artist's* magazine.

Sidelights

Canadian author and illustrator Rick Jacobson and his wife, musician and artist Laura Fernandez, have collaborated on art for more than a dozen picture books. The pair have also worked together in advertising and publishing, and their joint portraits of such notable people as Margaret Atwood, Bill Gates, Sr., and Sir Richard Francis Burton hang in the permanent collection of the Royal Geographical Society in London, England. The pair have provided highly realistic illustrations for new books as well as classics, including a highly lauded edition of L.M. Montgomery's classic *Anne of Green Gables,* published in 2000.

One of Jacobson and Fernandez's early picture books, *Tchaikovsky Discovers America,* features "lush, dramatically lit, romantic illustrations," according to Sarah Ellis in *Horn Book.* Stephanie Zvirin, writing in *Booklist,* commented that "the paintings are splendid," describing them as "dramatic, richly colored, and alive with extraordinary, bright highlights." For *Glass Town,*

Rick Jacobson joins wife and fellow illustrator Laura Fernandez in relating a true story about a famous art theft in **The Mona Lisa Caper.** (Text copyright © 2005 by Rick Jacobson. Illustrations copyright © 2005 by Rick Jacobson and Laura Fernandez. Reproduced by permission of Tundra Books of Northern New York.)

a title written by Michael Bedard about the early lives of England's famous Brontë sisters, the "full-bleed, realistic seascapes . . . give life to" both the real and imaginary settings in the story, according to a critic for *Publishers Weekly.* Ilene Cooper, in *Booklist,* wrote that "the pictures, interestingly executed in a style that is almost photo-realist, will hold readers' attention."

Of the couple's illustrations for *Prairie Willow,* Kay Weisman wrote that their "vibrant, textured paintings . . . highlight the prairie's wide expanses and the family's classic faces." Reviewing *Little Dog Moon* for *School Library Journal,* Wendy Lukehart noted that "illustration and text work together to create, by turn, peace, mystery, and drama." Jacobson and Fernandez's illustrations for *The Magnificent Piano Recital* were honored with the Amelia Frances Howard-Gibbon Award; according to a critic for *School Librarian,* "in the expert hands" of the artists "this tender story . . . truly comes to life."

Along with his illustration work, Jacobson has written several books dealing with prominent artists and art history, each co-illustrated with Fernandez. *Picasso: Soul on Fire* is a biography of famous painter Pablo Picasso; several of Picasso's own paintings are represented, along with new illustrations by Jacobson and Fernandez. According to Anne Hatcher in *Resource Links,* Jacobson's "text is a fantastic introduction to modern art and the life of Pablo Picasso." *Booklist* critic Gillian Engberg commented on the couple's original illustrations, considering them "striking oil portraits." Heather E. Miller, writing for *School Library Journal,* noted that while other books for young readers about Picasso are available, "few have been as accessible to this audience as Jacobson's title." *School Arts* contributor Ken Marantz commented that Fernandez and Jacobson's paintings "are charged with passion," and *Canadian Review of Materials* contributor Ann Stinner noted that "the text and illustrations join forces to convey the whole sensuous, messy process of making art."

The Mona Lisa Caper retells a story of crime and art history from the voice of the famous painting herself. Set in 1911, the middle-grade novel recounts how Vincenzo Perugia made an attempt to "liberate" the Mona Lisa from the Louvre Museum in Paris, intending to take her home to Italy, where she had been created. "The writing is sprightly, and the watercolor artwork superior—realistic, but with touches of whimsy," wrote *Booklist* critic Ilene Cooper. According to a contributor to *Publishers Weekly,* "Jacobson and Fernandez's beautifully drafted watercolors convey a sense of excitement while capturing many details of the era." Stinner considered *The Mona Lisa Caper* "a perfect opportunity to introduce young readers to art history and the real-life adventures of one painting in particular," while *Resource Links* reviewer Anna S. Rinaldis found the "true gem of a book" to be "a brilliant story that is sure to captivate the attention of its readers."

Biographical and Critical Sources

PERIODICALS

Booklist, March 15, 1995, Stephanie Zvirin, review of *Tchaikovsky Discovers America,* p. 1331; August, 1997, Ilene Cooper, review of *Glass Town,* p. 1897; September 15, 1998, Kay Weisman, review of *Prairie Willow,* p. 241; November 1, 2004, Gillian Engberg, review of *Picasso: Soul on Fire,* p. 496; July, 2005, review of *The Mona Lisa Caper,* p. 1925.

Children's Bookwatch, June, 2005, review of *The Mona Lisa Caper.*

Horn Book, March-April, 1995, Elizabeth S. Watson, review of *Tchaikovsky Discovers America,* p. 190; May-June, 1995, Sarah Ellis, review of *Tchaikovsky Discovers America,* p. 372.

Publishers Weekly, August 4, 1997, review of *Glass Town,* p. 75; September 19, 2005, review of *The Mona Lisa Caper,* p. 66.

Resource Links, October, 2004, Anne Hatcher, review of *Picasso,* p. 23; October, 2005, Anna S. Rinaldis, review of *The Mona Lisa Caper,* p. 4.

School Arts, March, 2005, Ken Marantz, review of *Picasso,* p. 72.

School Librarian, October, 2001, "Amelia Frances Howard-Gibbon Award," p. 63.

School Library Journal, March, 2001, Wendy Lukehart, review of *Little Dog Moon,* p. 222; April, 2001, Jane Marino, review of *The Magnificent Piano Recital,* p. 121; December, 2004, Heather E. Miller, review of *Picasso,* p. 132; August, 2005, Wendy Lukehart, review of *The Mona Lisa Caper,* p. 98.

Studio, May-June, 1992, "Laura Fernandez and Rick Jacobson," pp. 24-27.

ONLINE

Canadian Review of Materials Online, http://www.umanitoba.ca/cm/ (April 27, 2001), Val Nielsen, review of *Anne of Green Gables*; (October 29, 2004) Ann Stinner, review of *Picasso*; (May 13, 2005) Ann Stinner, review of *The Mona Lisa Caper.*

Transatlantic Literary Agency Web site, http://www.tla1.com/ (April 27, 2006), "Rick Jacobson."*

K

KEEP, Richard 1949-
(Richard Cleminson Keep)

Personal
Born December 21, 1949, in Fort Atkinson, WI; married Linda Lowery (an author); children: Kris Truelsen. *Education:* University of Wisconsin, Whitewater, B.A. (art education).

Addresses
Home—San Miguel de Allende, Guanajuato, Mexico. *Office*—220 N. Zapata Hwy., No. 11A PMB 69B, Laredo, TX 78043.

Career
Writer and illustrator. Lake Geneva Northwestern Military and Naval Academy, teacher of graphic and studio arts for seventeen years. Graphic designer; workshop presenter, with wife, Linda Lowery.

Awards, Honors
Children's Choice designation, International Reading Association, and Notable Social Studies Trade Book for Young People designation, Children's Book Council/National Council for the Social Studies, both 2005, both for *Clatter Bash!*

Writings
(And illustrator; with wife, Linda Lowery) *Trick or Treat, It's Halloween!*, Random House (New York, NY), 2000.
(And illustrator; with Linda Lowery) *Who Wants a Valentine?*, Random House (New York, NY), 2002.
(And illustrator; with Linda Lowery) *Merry Christmas, Everyone!*, Random House (New York, NY), 2003.
(Self-illustrated) *Clatter Bash!: A Day of the Dead Celebration*, Peachtree Publishers (Atlanta, GA), 2004.
(Self-illustrated) *A Thump from Upstairs: Starring Mr. Boo and Max*, Peachtree Publishers (Atlanta, GA), 2005.

Illustrator and co-creator, with Lowery, of "Jalapeños: Hot Bites for Cool Kids" weekly newspaper feature, *Miami Herald* international edition.

ILLUSTRATOR

Linda Lowery, *One More Valley, One More Hill: The Story of Aunt Clara Brown*, Random House (New York, NY), 2002.
Kathryn O. Galbraith, *Planting the Wild Garden*, Peachtree Publishers (Atlanta, GA), 2006.

Sidelights
An illustrator and author of children's books, Richard Keep recently collaborates with wife and fellow author Linda Lowery. While beginning his career working alongside Lowery on picture books that include *Trick or Treat, It's Halloween!* and *Merry Christmas, Everyone!*, Keep has more frequently branched out on his own, and his first solo effort was *Clatter Bash!: A Day of the Dead Celebration*. Earning Keep both recognition and critical praise, the book delves into Mexico's Día de los muertos, or Day of the Dead, a holiday celebration during which living family members celebrate the lives of their ancestors with offerings and upbeat festivities. Reflecting the holiday's fun-filled traditions, Keep's "staccato text and dynamic cut-paper collage artwork capture the essence of this Mexican holiday," commented a *School Library Journal* critic. Coop Renner, also of *School Library Journal*, wrote that *Clatter Bash!* "will be a popular title in Mexican-American communities and an eye-opener for others."

Together with his wife, Keep resides much of the year in San Miguel de Allende, a colonial town in central Mexico where he continues to pursue his passion for writing and illustrating. In addition to gaining inspira-

Richard Keep brings to life the noisy fun surrounding Mexico's Día de los muertos in his self-illustrated Clatter Bash!: A Day of the Dead Celebration. (Text and illustrations © 2004 by Richard C. Keep. Published by Peachtree. Reproduced by permission.)

tion from his south-of-the-border surroundings, he has also been inspired in his work by the family cat, Max, who is featured in *A Thump from Upstairs: Starring Mr. Boo and Max*. Illustrated with a mix of drawing, photomontage, and digital imaging, this humorous tale finds a nervous cat-owner imagining all sorts of horrible things when he hears a loud noise coming from the second floor of his house. The unperturbable Max has other things on his mind, however, resulting in a low-key picture book that "may help to reassure . . . children who frighten easily," in the opinion of *School Library Journal* contributor Kara Schaff Dean.

Biographical and Critical Sources

PERIODICALS

Kirkus Reviews, September 1, 2004, review of *Clatter Bash!: A Day of the Dead Celebration*, p. 867.
School Library Journal, February, 2005, Coop Renner, review of *Clatter Bash!*, p. 104; September, 2005, Kara Schaff Dean, review of *A Thump from Upstairs: Starring Mr. Boo and Max*, p. 175; October, 2005, review of *Clatter Bash!*, p. 38.

ONLINE

Linda Lowery & Richard Keep Web site, http://www.richardkeep.net (April 11, 2006), "Meet Richard Keep."

* * *

KEEP, Richard Cleminson
See KEEP, Richard

* * *

KIMMEL, Elizabeth Cody

Personal
Born New York, NY; married; children: Emma. *Education:* Attended Kenyon College. *Hobbies and other interests:* Reading, hiking, singing, rock climbing.

Addresses
Home—Cold Spring, NY. *Agent*—c/o Author Mail, HarperCollins, 10 E. 53rd St., 7th Fl., New York, NY 10022. *E-mail*—codykimmel@earthlink.net.

Career
Children's book writer.

Writings

FICTION

In the Stone Circle, Scholastic (New York, NY), 1998.
Balto and the Great Race, illustrated by Nora Koerber, Random House (New York, NY), 1999.
Visiting Miss Caples, Dial (New York, NY), 2000.
To the Frontier ("Adventures of Young Buffalo Bill" series), HarperCollins (New York, NY), 2001.
One Sky above Us ("Adventures of Young Buffalo Bill" series), illustrated by Scott Snow, HarperCollins (New York, NY), 2002.
My Wagon Will Take Me Anywhere, illustrated by Tom Newsom, Dutton (New York, NY), 2002.

In the Eye of the Storm ("Adventures of Young Buffalo Bill" series), HarperCollins (New York, NY), 2003.
West on the Wagon Train ("Adventures of Young Buffalo Bill" series), illustrated by Scott Snow, HarperCollins (New York, NY), 2003.
Lily B. on the Brink of Cool, HarperCollins (New York, NY), 2003.
What Do You Dream?, Candlewick (Cambridge, MA), 2003.
My Penguin Osbert, illustrated by H.B. Lewis, Candlewick (Cambridge, MA), 2004.
Lily B. on the Brink of Love, HarperCollins (New York, NY), 2005.
Lily B. on the Brink of Paris, HarperCollins (New York, NY), 2006.

Kimmel's "Lily B." books have been translated into several languages.

NONFICTION

Ice Story: Shackleton's Lost Expedition, Clarion (New York, NY), 1999.
Before Columbus: The Leif Eriksson Expedition, Random House (New York, NY), 2003.
As Far as the Eye Can Reach: Lewis and Clark's Westward Quest, Random House (New York, NY), 2003.
The Look-It-up Book of Explorers, Random House (New York, NY), 2004.
Ladies First: Forty Daring American Women Who Were Second to None, National Geographic (Washington, DC), 2005.

Work in Progress

Osbert in Love, for Candlewick Press; a book for the "Little House" series published by HarperCollins.

Sidelights

Elizabeth Cody Kimmel grew up in both New York and Brussels, Belgium. As a writer of fiction and nonfiction for children and young adults, she has worked to weave subjects she finds interesting—from Antarctica to ghost stories to medieval history—into her books. Many of her nonfiction titles, such as *Ice Story: Shackleton's Lost Expedition* and *As Far as the Eye Can Reach: Lewis and Clark's Westward Quest,* tell the stories of explorers, while her teen novels deal with such themes as multi-generational friendships and being true to yourself.

The Lewis and Clark Expedition is the subject of *As Far as the Eye Can Reach,* which follows the explorers' efforts to locate a northern route to the Pacific Ocean. The book was considered "a well written, lively account for young readers" by a contributor to *Kirkus Reviews.* As *Booklist* critic Carolyn Phelan commented, "this clearly written summary provides a useful overview for students," while Renee Steinberg commented in *School Library Journal,* commented that "a book

Kimmel presents the story of the eleventh-century Viking who bravely sailed from Greenland to North America in Before Columbus: The Leif Eriksson Expedition. *(Copyright © 2003 by Elizabeth Cody Kimmel. Published by Landmark Books. Reproduced by permission of Random House Children's Books, a division of Random House, Inc.)*

such as this can excite young readers to delve further into U.S. history." Another of Kimmel's nonfiction titles, *Before Columbus: The Leif Eriksson Expedition,* introduces readers to the Viking exploration of the Americas. The book is a "small, readable volume," according to *Booklist* contributor Roger Leslie, while a *Kirkus Reviews* contributor deemed it "more a quick once-over than a systematic study" and "well designed to stimulate an early interest" in its subject. Ginny Gustin, writing in *School Library Journal,* noted that the nonfiction title reads more like an historical novel, and acknowledged that "Kimmel's book will captivate and entertain young readers." The author's reference resource, *The Look-It-up Book of Explorers,* covers the expeditions of explorers through the ages. Carol Wichman, writing in *School Library Journal,* considered the work "a concise and useful guide to virtually all of the explorers usually studied in public schools."

Kimmel's first teen novel, *Visiting Miss Caples,* is the story of thirteen-year-old Jenna, whose father abandons her family. To make things worse, her best friend no longer speaks to her. Jenna assumes that a class project to visit an elderly-shut in will be another bad thing in her year, but she learns that Mrs. Caples, despite her difference in age, understands a lot of what Jenna is going through. "Kimmel ably articulates a young person's experience," wrote Gillian Engberg in *Booklist*.

Kimmel has written three books in the "Lily B." series, all of them featuring the spunky teen heroine and her misadventures. In *Lily B. on the Brink of Cool* Lily is convinced that her family is anything but cool. When she meets distant cousin Karma and Karma's family, Lily is determined to fit in, becoming more sophisticated by proximity. However, it soon appears that Karma's family has more in mind than befriending Lily, and the teen ultimately learns that sometimes first impressions are deceiving. "Lily is a likable teen who wants more than she has, only to discover that what she has is pretty darn good," wrote Linda Binder in *School Library Journal*. A *Kirkus Reviews* contributor found Lily to be "a delightful heroine, sweeter than [other teen heroines] and hilarious," while Louise Bruggemann noted in her *Booklist* review that the book is a

Joe's Christmas wish to Santa goes slightly awry in Kimmel's amusing picture book **My Penguin Osbert,** *featuring whimsical illustrations by H.B. Lewis.* (Text copyright © 2004 by Elizabeth Cody Kimmel. Illustrations copyright © 2004 by H.B. Lewis. Reproduced by permission of the publisher Candlewick Press, Inc., Cambridge, MA.)

"funny, fast-moving, if somewhat self-conscious, novel." A *Publishers Weekly* critic considered Lily "by turns chirpy, sardonic, glib, and melodramatic—and always likable."

Lily's adventures continue in *Lily B. on the Brink of Love,* wherein, as her middle-school paper's advice columnist, she discovers that dealing with love in her own life is more difficult than answering readers' love questions. "Lily's journal entries and advice columns . . . deliver laughs and substance," wrote Wendi Hoffenberg in *School Library Journal*. A *Kirkus Reviews* contributor found the book "heartwarming and funny," and Heidi Hauser Green felt that "Lily's over-the-top narrative voice will likely appeal to many middle school readers."

Cover of Kimmel's **Lily B. on the Brink of Cool,** *featuring artwork by Nathalie Dion.* (Text copyright © 2003 by Elizabeth Cody Kimmel. Jacket art © 2003 by Nathalie Dion. Jacket © 2003 by HarperCollins Publishers, Inc. Published by HarperTrophy. Used by permission of HarperCollins Publishers.)

Along with nonfiction and novels, Kimmel has also crafted picture books, including *My Penguin Osbert*. The book tells the story of a Christmas wish gone wrong; Joe wanted a live penguin, but when Osbert is delivered by Santa, the boy realizes that having a pet penguin is not quite what he imagined. When Joe finally brings Osbert to a new home in the zoo, both boy and penguin end up happy. "Kimmel sneaks some sly humor into the well-told, nicely paced tale," wrote Ilene Cooper in *Booklist*. A *Kirkus Reviews* contributor found the tale to be "salutary reading for all children campaigning for a pet," and *Horn Book* critic Lauren E.

Raece likewise found the story to be a "satisfying tale." Readers should "find much to enjoy in this lighthearted fantasy with realistic holiday roots," according to a *Publishers Weekly* contributor.

On her home page, Kimmel explained where she came up with the idea for *My Penguin Osbert*. "I love the idea of all that ice and snow and wind," she wrote, referring to the weather in Antarctica, "and I can imagine myself bundling up to hike through the winter wonderland. But when reality sets in, I can't stand the cold, and I think that is how Osbert was born." Kimmel expects to write additional books about Osbert, including *Osbert in Love*.

Biographical and Critical Sources

PERIODICALS

Booklist, May 15, 2000, Gillian Engberg, review of *Visiting Miss Caples,* p. 1739; January 1, 2003, Carolyn Phelan, "Lewis & Clark on the Road Again," p. 885; July, 2003, Roger Leslie, review of *Before Columbus: The Leif Eriksson Expedition* p. 1882; October 1, 2003, Lauren Peterson, review of *What Do You Dream?,* p. 328; December 1, 2003, Louise Brueggemann, review of *Lily B. on the Brink of Cool,* p. 666; December 1, 2004, Ilene Cooper, review of *My Penguin Osbert,* p. 659; October 1, 2005, Anne O'Malley, review of *Lily B. on the Brink of Love,* p. 58.

Bulletin of the Center for Children's Books, April, 2000, review of *Visiting Miss Caples,* p. 285; February, 2004, review of *Lily B. on the Brink of Cool,* p. 237.

Horn Book, November-December, 2004, Lauren E. Raece, review of *My Penguin Osbert,* p. 662.

Kirkus Reviews, December 15, 2002, review of *As Far as the Eye Can Reach,* p. 1851; July 15, 2003, review of *Before Columbus,* p. 965; October 15, 2003, review of *Lily B. on the Brink of Cool,* p. 1272; November 1, 2004, review of *My Penguin Osbert,* p. 1051; August 1, 2005, review of *Lily B. on the Brink of Love,* p. 851.

Kliatt, July, 2004, Sherri Ginsberg, review of *Lily B. on the Brink of Cool,* p. 53; September, 2005, Heidi Hauser Green, review of *Lily B. on the Brink of Cool,* p. 20.

Publishers Weekly, December 10, 2001, review of *Visiting Miss Caples,* p. 73; June 9, 2003, review of "Adventures of Young Buffalo Bill" series, p. 54; December 8, 2003, review of *Lily B. on the Brink of Cool,* p. 62; June 14, 2004, audiobook review of *Lily B. on the Brink of Cool,* p. 38; November 22, 2004, review of *My Penguin Osbert,* p. 60.

School Librarian, autumn, 2004, Chris Brown, review of *Lily B. on the Brink of Cool,* p. 156.

School Library Journal, July, 2002, Anne Knickerbocker, review of *My Wagon Will Take Me Anywhere,* p. 94; March, 2003, Renee Steinberg, review of *As Far as the Eye Can Reach,* pp. 172, 253; October, 2003, Ginny Gustin, review of *Before Columbus,* p. 152, and Linda Binder, review of *Lily B. on the Brink of Cool,* p. 169; February 2004, Sanda Kitain, review of *What Do You Dream?,* p. 116; January, 2005, Wendi Hoffengberg, review of *Lily B. on the Brink of Love,* p. 104, and Carol Wichman, review of *The Look-It-up Book of Explorers,* p. 149; October, 2005, review of *The Look-It-up Book of Explorers,* p. S48.

Voice of Youth Advocates, August, 2000, review of *Ice Story,* p. 165; October, 2003, review of *Lily B. on the Brink of Cool,* p. 312.

ONLINE

Elizabeth Cody Kimmel Home Page, http://www.codykimmel.com (April 27, 2006).

Kids Reads Web site, http://www.kidsreads.com/ (April 27, 2006), profile of Kimmel.*

* * *

KULIKOV, Boris 1966-

Personal

Born 1966; immigrated to United States, 1997; married Yelena Romanova (a writer). *Education:* Institute of Theatre, Music, and Cinema (St. Petersburg, Russia), graduated, 1992.

Addresses

Home—Brooklyn, NY. *Agent*—c/o Author Mail, Farrar, Straus & Giroux, 19 Union Square W., New York, NY 10003. *E-mail*—boriskulikov@aol.com.

Career

Illustrator and painter. Formerly worked as a set and costume designer in Russia.

Illustrator

Lore Segal, *Morris the Artist,* Farrar, Straus & Giroux (New York, NY), 2003.

John Lithgow, *Carnival of the Animals,* Simon & Schuster Books for Young Readers (New York, NY), 2004.

Nina Bernstein, *Magic by the Book,* Farrar, Straus & Giroux (New York, NY), 2005.

Kathleen Krull, *Leonardo da Vinci* ("Giants of Science" series), Viking (New York, NY), 2005.

Yelena Romanova, *The Perfect Friend,* Farrar, Straus & Giroux (New York, NY), 2005.

B.G. Hennessy, *The Boy Who Cried Wolf,* Simon & Schuster Books for Young Readers (New York, NY), 2006.

Kathllen Krull, *Isaac Newton,* Viking (New York, NY), 2006.

Kathllen Krull, *Sigmund Freud* ("Giants of Science" series), Viking (New York, NY), 2006.

Kate Banks, *Max's Words,* Farrar, Straus & Giroux (New York, NY), 2006.

Nancy Crocker, *Betty Lou Blue,* Dial Books for Young Readers (New York, NY), 2006.

Linda Heller, *The Castle on Hester Street,* Simon & Schuster (New York, NY), 2007.

Contributor of illustrations to *New York Times Book Review.*

Sidelights

Born and educated in the former Soviet Union, illustrator Boris Kulikov graduated from St. Petersburg, Russia's Institute of Theatre, Music, and Cinema before immigrating to the United States in 1997. He worked at a variety of odd jobs before establishing his artistic career as an illustrator for the *New York Times Book Review.* Expanding his clients to include the *Wall Street Journal* and the *Los Angeles Times,* among others, Kulikov eventually found a way to make a much-hoped-for transition into children's-book illustration. His first illustration project, Lore Segal's *Morris the Artist,* drew critical praise and many other illustration opportunities. Among his more recent illustrated books are *Carnival of the Animals* by actor John Lithgow, *Magic by the Book* by Nina Bernstein, *The Boy Who Cried Wolf,* by B.G. Hennessy, *Max's Words,* by Kate Banks, and *The Perfect Friend,* the last by Kulikov's wife, writer Yelena Romanova. The illustrator's "witty illustrations" for *The Perfect Friend* "are sure to intrigue children and adults alike," noted a *Publishers Weekly* contributor, while in the same periodical another critic wrote that "Kulikov's voluptuous pen-and-ink" drawings for *Magic by the Book* add to the work's "elegant storybook feel."

Kulikov's illustrations for *Morris the Artist* stand out due to their contrast with Segal's modern story line about a creative boy who is unwilling to relinquish the gift of artist's paints he has brought to a friend's birthday party. Drawing from his training in theatrical costuming, Kulikov dresses the story's characters in clothing from a more-distant era, such as sailor suits, fedoras, and even knickers. The illustrator's "creative style . . . is enhanced by his brightly hued palette," commented a *Kirkus Reviews* critic, while a *Publishers Weekly* reviewer stated that "an off kilter, funhouse feeling pervades the full-spread compositions, and the children . . . sport big heads . . . and eyes with the unsettling fixed gaze of marionettes." Gillian Engberg, writing in *Booklist,* called Kulikov's artwork "noteworthy," writing that "an unusual, visually stimulating story about the dynamic of children's play and letting creativity loose."

Biographical and Critical Sources

PERIODICALS

Booklist, August, 2003, Gillian Engberg, review of *Morris the Artist,* p. 1990; November 1, 2004, Diane Foote, review of *Carnival of the Animals,* p. 485; April 15, 2005, Jennifer Mattson, review of *Magic by the Book,* p. 1464.

Kirkus Reviews, May 1, 2003, review of *Morris the Artist,* p. 683; March 1, 2006, review of *Giants of Science: Isaac Newton,* p. 233.

Publishers Weekly, April 7, 2003, review of *Morris the Artist,* p. 66; June 30, 2003, "Flying Starts," p. 18; April 15, 2005, *Magic by the Book,* p. 57.

School Library Journal, March, 2005, Caitlin Augusta, review of *Magic by the Book,* p. 206; March, 2006, John Peters, review of *Isaac Newton,* p. 243.

ONLINE

Boris Kulikov Home Page, http://www.boriskulikov.com (May 10, 2006).

L-M

LEAVITT, Martine 1953-
(Martine Bates)

Personal
Born July 19, 1953, in Taber, Alberta, Canada; daughter of James (in the military) and Mary Webster; married first husband, c. 1975 (divorced); married Greg Leavitt, 1995; children: (first marriage) Sterling, Sarah, Rachel, Russell, Candace, Derek; (second marriage) Dallas. *Education:* University of Calgary, graduated (first-class honors), 1996; Vermont College, M.F.A., 2003.

Addresses
Home—908 Emerson Rd., High River, Alberta T1V 1B1, Canada. *E-mail*—wmleavitt@aol.com.

Career
Copy editor for SMART Technologies, Inc.; freelance writer.

Member
Canadian Society of Children's Authors, Illustrators, and Performers, Writer's Union of Canada.

Awards, Honors
American Association of Mormon Letters Award, for *Dragon's Tapestry, The Prism Moon,* and *The Taker's Key;* Our Choice Award, Canadian Children's Book Centre, for *The Prism Moon* and *The Taker's Key;* finalist, American Association of Mormon Letters Award, and Best Books for Young Adults designation, American Library Association, 2002, both for *The Dollmage;* Mr. Christie Award for Young-Adult Literature, Benjamin Franklin Award, and Top Fifty International Best Books for Young Adults designation, all 2004, all for *Tom Finder;* named laureate, Governor General's award (Canada), 2004, for *Heck Superhero.*

Writings

FANTASY NOVELS

The Dollmage, Red Deer Press (Calgary, Alberta, Canada), 2001.
Tom Finder, Red Deer Press (Calgary, Alberta, Canada), 2003.
Heck Superhero, Front Street Books (Asheville, NC), 2004.
Keturah and Lord Death, Front Street Books (Asheville, NC), 2006.

"MARMAWELL" FANTASY TRILOGY; UNDER NAME MARTINE BATES

The Dragon's Tapestry, Red Deer Press (Red Deer, Alberta, Canada), 1992.
The Prism Moon, Red Deer Press (Calgary, Alberta, Canada), 1993.
The Taker's Key, Red Deer Press (Calgary, Alberta, Canada), 1998.

Author's books have been translated into Danish.

Adaptations
The Prism Moon and *The Dragon's Tapestry* were adapted as audiobooks by Alberta Education, 1994.

Sidelights
Canadian young-adult novelist Martine Leavitt wrote her first three books, which comprise the award-winning "Marmawell" fantasy trilogy featuring Marwen the Oldwife's apprentice, while she was studying writing at the University of Calgary. Published under her then-name Martine Bates, the trilogy follows Marwen's adventures as she progresses to her destiny as a wizard, on the way falling in love with a prince. The third novel in the series, *The Taker's Key,* is written as part of Leavitt's honor's thesis. Reviewing the book, a *Quill & Quire* contributor noted that the author's "magic is in the

Cover of Martine Leavitt's The Taker's Key, *published under Leavitt's pen name, Martine Bates.* (Copyright © 1998 by Martine Bates. Illustrations by Limner Imagery, Ltd. Published by Red Deer Press, a Fitzhenry & Whiteside Company. Reproduced by permission.)

words, both literally in her plot and stylistically in her writing." The quest of Marwen "is one that will absorb readers completely," the critic added.

At the conclusion of Leavitt's "Marmawell" trilogy, the wizard Marwen must come to terms with the wanning of her power. A similar predicament confronts the title character of *The Dollmage,* a wise woman who protects the people of Seekvalley with her magic and her secret ability to make story dolls. When Dollmage realizes that her power is weakening, she sets out to choose a successor. She knows her successor will be born on a certain date, and on the prescribed day a woman in the village gives birth to twin girls. After the sisters come of appropriate age, Dollmage chooses Reenoa as her successor, but sister Annakey also has magical powers. When catastrophe threatens to strike the village, Annakey must convince Dollmage that she can help, despite the fact that few have faith in her power to so. Writing in *Resource Links,* Ingrid Johnston called *The Dollmage* a "compelling fantasy" and went on to comment that Leavitt "creates a world of magic that is easy to believe in with characters that we come to care about." *School Library Journal* contributor Patricia A. Dollisch described the novel as "a tightly plotted story of pride, jealousy, magic, passion, and regret," and deemed *The Dollmage* "extraordinary for its characterizations and plot."

In *Tom Finder* Leavitt tells the story of a fifteen year old who is living on the streets and knows nothing about himself except his first name. As he tries to figure out who he is, a First Nations medicine man tells the teen he is a "Finder." The man agrees to help Tom discover his true identity, but only after the teen helps find the medicine man's missing son, Daniel. During his quest to find Daniel, Tom has the feeling that Mozart's *The Magic Flute* has played a crucial role in his life; ultimately answers to his many questions are answered during a performance of the noted opera.

Praising Leavitt's "depth and insight," Erin Lukens Darr wrote in *Kliatt* that *Tom Finder* "provides an eye-opening view of the hardships of those less fortunate whom we often ignore." In *Resource Links* Donna K. Johnson Alden also commended the book as "rich in character development," with "a compelling plot, a realistic male protagonist who easily engages a reader's sympathies," and a plot that is "valuable for its social message of homelessness in a modern Canadian city."

A change of pace for Leavitt, *Heck Superhero* focuses on a thirteen year old who has artistic talents, especially as a cartoonist. Life has been hard for Heck's mother, a woman suffering from depression, and the family now live day-to-day, surviving on little money. Heck turns to drawing cartoon superheroes as a way to cope with this harsh reality, but after his mom disappears, he finds himself in a situation his art cannot save him from. On the streets, with no home and no money, he searches for his mother and ultimately encounters a tragic situation. A confrontation with drug abuse and the suicide of a new but troubled teen friend lead Heck to realize that he must ask for help in order to locate his mother and get his life together. Betty Carter, writing in *Horn Book,* noted that Leavitt's young protagonist "emerges as a true hero, a complex boy armed with optimism, wit, heart, and commitment." *Booklist* contributor Shelle Rosenfeld felt that while some parts of *Heck Superhero* are "more appropriate for mature readers," "Heck is a well-drawn, sympathetic protagonist who learns that compassion is a superpower, and that asking for help can be the most heroic act of all."

Biographical and Critical Sources

PERIODICALS

Booklist, October 1, 2004, Shelle Rosenfeld, review of *Heck Superhero,* p. 323.

Books in Canada, October, 1993, review of *The Prism Moon,* p. 57.
Canadian Children's Literature, winter, 2002, M. Sean Saunders, "Weaving the Self: The Struggle for Identity in Martine Bates's 'Marmawell Trilogy,'" p. 39.
Canadian Review of Materials, September, 1992, review of *The Dragon's Tapestry,* p. 219; January-February, 1994, review of *The Prism Moon,* pp. 24-25; October 29, 1999, review of *The Taker's Key.*
Horn Book, January-February, 2005, Betty Carter, review of *Heck Superhero,* p. 96.
Kirkus Reviews, September 1, 2004, review of *Heck Superhero,* p. 869.
Kliatt, November, 2003, Erin Lukens Darr, review of *Tom Finder,* p. 16.
Quill & Quire, May, 1992, review of *The Dragon's Tapestry,* p. 32; April, 1993, review of *The Prism Moon,* p. 32; January, 1999, review of *The Taker's Key,* p. 46.
Resource Links, February, 1999, review of *The Taker's Key,* p. 23; June, 2002, Ingrid Johnston, review of *The Dollmage,* p. 26; October, 2003, Donna K. Johnson Alden, review of *Tom Finder,* p. 36.
School Library Journal, August, 2002, Patricia A. Dollisch, review of *The Dollmage,* p. 192; October, 2004, Maria B. Salvadore, review of *Heck Superhero,* p. 171.

ONLINE

Canadian Society of Children's Authors, Illustrators, and Performers Web site, http://www.canscaip.org/ (May 10, 2006), "Martine Leavitt."
Martine Leavitt Home Page, http://www.martineleavitt.com (May 10, 2006).*

* * *

LEHMAN, Barbara 1963-

Personal
Born December 14, 1963, in Chicago, IL; daughter of Donald and Patricia Lehman. *Education:* Pratt Institute, B.F.A. (illustration). *Hobbies and other interests:* Letterpress printing, Aikido, gardening, bookbinding.

Addresses
Home—Claverack, NY. *Agent*—c/o Author Mail, Candlewick Press, 2067 Massachusetts Ave., 5th Fl., Cambridge, MA 02140.

Career
Illustrator, author, and commercial artist. Self-employed freelance artist; clients include *New York Times,* New York City Transit Authority, and McGraw-Hill.

Awards, Honors
Parents' Choice illustration award, 1993, for *Moonfall;* Caldecott Medal Honor Book designation, 2005, for *The Red Book.*

Writings

SELF-ILLUSTRATED

The Red Book, Houghton Mifflin (Boston, MA), 2004.
Museum Trip, Houghton Mifflin (Boston, MA), 2006.

ILLUSTRATOR

Nancy Lecourt, *Abracadabra to Zigzag: An Alphabet Book,* Lothrop, Lee & Shepard (New York, NY), 1991.
Marsha Wilson Chall, *Mattie,* Lothrop, Lee & Shepard (New York, NY), 1992.
Florence Parry Heide and Roxanne Heide Pierce, *Timothy Twinge,* Lothrop, Lee & Shepard (New York, NY), 1993.
Susan Whitcher, *Moonfall,* Farrar, Straus & Giroux (New York, NY), 1993.
Lynda Graham Barber, *A Chartreuse Leotard in a Magenta Limousine, and Other Words Named after People and Places,* Hyperion (New York, NY), 1994.
Susan Whitcher, *Something for Everyone,* Farrar, Straus & Giroux (New York, NY), 1995.
Lynda Graham Barber, *Say Boo!,* Candlewick Press (Cambridge, MA), 1996.
Susan Devins, *Christmas Cookies!: A Cookbook with Cookie Cutters,* Candlewick Press (Cambridge, MA), 2003.

Sidelights
Award-winning commercial artist, illustrator, and children's book author Barbara Lehman has been praised for her imaginative, colorful cartoon art, which has appeared in both her own books and those with texts by other writers. In 2005 she was honored for her talents when *The Red Book,* a wordless picture book that captures the excitement and adventure to be found through reading, earned Lehman a prestigious Caldecott Honor designation.

Lehman was born in Chicago, Illinois, and grew up in New Jersey. As a child, she loved to visit the art museums in nearby New York City. She began to draw at an early age, inspired in part by the prints of John Tenniel's illustrations for Lewis Carroll's *Alice in Wonderland* that her father hand-colored and hung over her crib. To prepare herself for a career as an artist, she attended New York City's Pratt Institute and earned a B.F.A. in illustration. As a professional artist as well as an illustrator, she has worked as an animator, a graphic designer, and a window designer, although she admits that creating book illustrations gives her the most satisfaction.

Inspired by Lehman's view of the landscape from high atop a Manhattan skyscraper, *The Red Book* finds a young girl carried on a magical journey after she discovers a bright red book peeking out of a snow bank on a cold winter day during her walk to her city school.

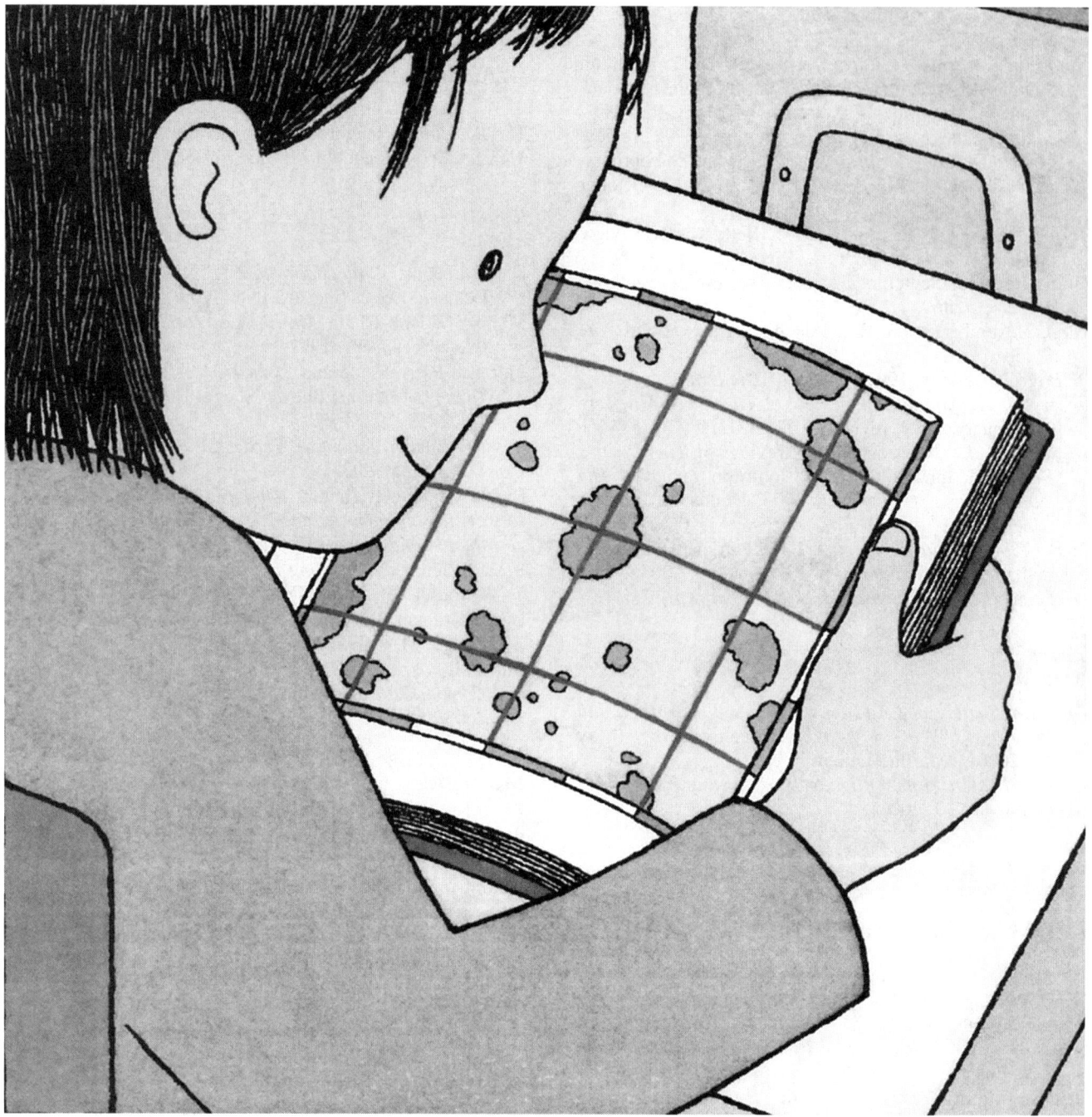

In Barbara Lehman's imaginative picture book **The Red Book** *a young girl takes a journey of the imagination that leads her to a new friend.* (Text and illustrations copyright © 2004 by Barbara Lehman. Reproduced by permission of Houghton Mifflin Company.)

Opening the book at school, she realize that it is magical; its pictures move, revealing a sun-lit island scene and a boy perusing a similar book. With a turn of the page, the boy's view zooms in, revealing the girl sitting at her desk in the city, and suddenly the two children are able to see each other! Inspired by the book, the girl buys a large bunch of balloons and rises into the air, determined to find the boy's island and leave her own world behind.

Telling its story through Lehman's pen-and-ink, watercolor, and gouache illustrations and ending with an interesting twist, *The Red Book* was praised by *Horn Book* contributor Joanna Rudge Long for presenting a "pleasing puzzle that will challenge young imaginations and intellects." "As visually uncluttered as it is conceptually rich, Lehman's red book is a little treasure of its own," wrote a *Publishers Weekly* contributor, while in *School Library Journal* Kathy Krasniewicz deemed the book a "perfectly eloquent" work that "captures the magical possibility that exists every time readers open a book." In *Booklist* Jennifer Mattson recommended *The Red Book* as "ideal for fueling creative-writing exercises."

Museum Trip was inspired by Lehman's childhood visits to New York art museums. A wordless book, it follows a young boy on a class trip to the museum. When the boy bends over to tie his shoe, his class moves on without him, and when he stands up he finds himself alone. At first frightened, the boy soon discovers a tantalizing display of mazes. He negotiates his way through one maze after another, and at the end of the final maze he wins a medal for his skill, then rejoins his classmates who are boarding the bus back home. Gillian Engberg, reviewing *Museum Trip* for *Booklist*, wrote that "Lehman's clever celebration of the fun and power found in art and daydreamed departures will easily draw an audience."

In her work as a picture-book artist, Lehman has produced humorous watercolor illustrations for Florence Parry Heide and Roxanne Heide Pierce's *Timothy Twinge*, in which a young worrier learns to be brave after his fear that aliens might enter his room at night comes true. "Lehman's bright cartoon-style watercolors will have plenty of appeal for children," predicted Janice Del Negro in *Booklist*. Discussing Nancy Lecourt's unusual alphabet book, *Abracadabra to Zigzag: An Alphabet Book*, several reviewers cited Lehman's illustrations for their ability to illuminate Lecourt's text, which introduces children to some of the more colorful expressions in the English language. "The clever and colorful watercolors make the title much more accessible than might be expected given the words involved," asserted Kathy Piehl in *School Library Journal*, adding that Lehman exploits both variety and identity to increase the appeal of the illustrations—varying the layout of the pictures but including a yellow dog somewhere in each in order to help sustain the interest of young audiences.

Lehman's signature watercolor cartoons for Susan Whitcher's *Moonfall* won the Parents' Choice illustration award. In Whitcher's story, one night Sylvie witnesses the moon's fall into a neighbor's lilac bush. After fifteen nights without a moon in the sky, the pragmatic young girl ventures out into the neighbor's garden to rescue the orb, but finds it tarnished and dented. A resourceful girl, she washes it in Magic Bubble solution, whereupon the moon dissolves. When Sylvie blows a huge bubble with the solution, the pearly globe floats up into the sky, a perfect moon replacement. "Whitcher's deceptively simple, effective text is engagingly partnered by Lehman's pleasantly satisfying watercolors," remarked Janice Del Negro in *Booklist*, while Susan Scheps wrote in *School Library Journal* that *Moonfall* "is destined to become a read-aloud favorite in many a household."

Lehman once told *SATA*: "Like many people in publishing I grew up loving books, and reading, and I 'always knew' I wanted to work professionally with books. Illustrating books gives me great pleasure. As a hobby I also do letterpress printing, using metal type and wood and linoleum cuts, as well as hand bookbinding. And I also read a lot—books for all age groups. My most favorite illustrators are: Hergé, Winsor McCay, and George Herriman."

Biographical and Critical Sources

PERIODICALS

Booklist, April 15, 1992, Kay Weisman, review of *Mattie*, p. 1527; July, 1993, Janice Del Negro, review of *Moonfall*, p. 1978; September 15, 1993, Janice Del Negro, review of *Timothy Twinge*, p. 157; October 1, 2004, Jennifer Mattson, review of *The Red Book*, p. 335; April 15, 2006, Gillian Engberg, review of *Museum Trip*, p. 46.

Horn Book, September-October, 2004, Joanna Rudge Long, review of *The Red Book*, p. 570.

Kirkus Reviews, September 1, 2004, review of *The Red Book*, p. 869.

New York Times Book Review, November 14, 2004, Roger Sutton, review of *The Red Book*, p. 22.

Publishers Weekly, April 26, 1991, p. 59; June 14, 1993, p. 69.

School Library Journal, June, 1991, Kathy Piehl, review of *Abracadabra to Zigzag: An Alphabet Book*, p. 84; August, 1992, p. 134; October, 1993, Susan Scheps, review of *Moonfall*, p. 114; November, 2004, Kathy Krasniewicz, review of *The Red Book*, p. 110.

* * *

LEHMANN, Debra Lynn
See VANASSE, Deb

* * *

MANSIR, A. Richard 1932-

Personal

Born March 19, 1932, in New York, NY; son of Allen (a paper-company executive) and Helen Mansir; married Carol Lynch (a commercial artist) June, 1966 (divorced). *Education:* Attended Cleveland Institute of Art, Ohio State University, and Western Reserve University; Cranbrook Academy of Art, graduate.

Addresses

Home—801 Manevar Rd., Cardiff by the Sea, CA 92007.

Career

Writer and art director. Ameron Corp., Pasadena, CA, advertising manager; freelance art director.

Writings

SELF-ILLUSTRATED

A Modeler's Guide to Hull Construction, Moonraker Publications (Dana Point, CA), 1980.
A Modeler's Guide to Rigging, Moonraker Publications (Dana Point, CA), 1981.
Planking Model Ships: A Step-by-Step Procedure for Beginning and Advanced Modelers, 1982.
A Modeler's Guide to Ancient and Medical Ships to 1650, Aero Publishers (Fallbrook, CA), 1982.
The Art of Ship Modeling, 1983, revised as *How to Build Ship Models: A Beginner's Guide,* Aero Publishers (Fallbrook, CA), 1988.
How to Model Small Boats: Moonraker Workbook, 1983.
(With Henry Bridenbeck) *A Scratch Modeler's Log,* Aero Publishers (Fallbrook, CA), 1984.
(Author of annotation) William Bligh, *The Journal of Bounty's Launch,* Kittiwake Publications (Los Angeles, CA), 1989.
Quest for the Northeast Passage, Kittiwake Publications (Los Angeles, CA), 1989.
Build a Wells Fargo Stagecoach, Charlesbridge (Watertown, MA), 1999.
Stagecoach: The Ride of a Century, Charlesbridge (Waterdown, MA), 1999.

Work in Progress

Qoya, a Novel of Colonial Peru; Mary Ann and the Clipper Ship.

Sidelights

A. Richard Mansir told *SATA:* "The advertising industry provided me a living for some years, though my heart wasn't in it. I wanted to write and publish, which I finally began to do full time in 1989 with my "Moonraker" books for ship modelers. Maritime history interest spread into history in general, which inspired illustrations of past events to accompany my books."

Biographical and Critical Sources

PERIODICALS

Social Education, May, 2000, review of *Stagecoach: The Ride of a Century,* p. 11.*

* * *

MARCHETTA, Melina 1965-

Personal

Born 1965, in Sydney, New South Wales, Australia. *Education:* Attended business college; Australian Catholic University, bachelor's degree (education). *Religion:* Roman Catholic.

Addresses

Home—Sydney, New South Wales, Australia. *Office*—c/o St. Mary's Cathedral College, 2 St. Mary's Rd. Sydney, New South Wales 2000, Australia.

Career

Novelist and author of screenplays and short fiction. Has worked for a bank and as a commercial consultant in a large travel company; high school teacher in Sydney, New South Wales, Australia.

Awards, Honors

Book of the Year designation, Children's Book Council of Australia, Multicultural Book of the Year Award for older readers, Kids Own Australian Literature Award, 3M Talking Book of the Year Award, and Fairlight Talking Book Award for outstanding talking book of the past ten years in young people's category, 2000, all for *Looking for Alibrandi;* Australian Film Institute Award, New South Wales Premier's Literary Award, and Film Critics Circle of Australia Award, all for screenplay version of *Looking for Alibrandi.*

Writings

Looking for Alibrandi (young-adult novel), Puffin Books (Ringwood, Victoria, Australia), 1992, Orchard Books (New York, NY), 1999.
Looking for Alibrandi (screenplay; based on the author's novel; produced, 2000), Currency Press (Sydney, New South Wales, Australia), 2000.
Saving Francesca (young-adult novel), Knopf (New York, NY), 2004.

Contributor of short stories to anthologies, including *Family,* edited by Agnes Nieuwenhuizen, Reed Books, 1994, and *Nothing Interesting about Cross Street,* HarperCollins, 1996.

Adaptations

Looking for Alibrandi was adapted for audio cassette, Bolinda Audio, 2000; *Saving Francesca* was adapted for audio cassette, Bolinda Audio, 2004.

Sidelights

Australian writer and educator Melina Marchetta is the author of the highly acclaimed novels *Looking for Alibrandi* and *Saving Francesca.* Though categorized as young-adult fiction, both books span several generations through their focus on Italian-Australian teens completing their final years of Catholic school. Marchetta knows the world of her adolescent characters well: in addition to attending Catholic secondary school herself, she has worked as a teacher in an all-boys school in Sydney, New South Wales, Australia since graduating from college.

Born into a working-class family of Italian descent, Marchetta experienced a school experience that had its ups and downs. Because of an undiscovered learning disability, as a first grader she had trouble learning to read. Fortunately, with the help of her mother, who had wanted to become a teacher, Marchetta overcame her learning difficulties, although the experience left her with a residual shyness and lack of self-confidence.

Because of her lack of confidence with regard to academics, at age fifteen Marchetta left school. A course at a business school taught her useful office skills, including typing, and she found work in banks and then at a travel agency. There she met teenagers who were planning travels abroad after their high-school graduation. "I used to look forward to them coming in," the author noted to an interviewer for *Australian Catholic* online. "It made me realize I really liked being involved with young people." Working allowed her to gain the confidence to return to school and get her teaching credential; it also prompted her to begin writing.

While Marchetta began taking her writing seriously at age twenty-one, she did not find any success until she began mining her own experiences as inspiration for her fiction. "It was only when I started to write about my own world that things really clicked and I was able to produce a novel," the writer recalled in an interview posted on the *Dymocks* Web site.

Like Marchetta, the main character in *Looking for Alibrandi* is a third-generation, Italian-Australian schoolgirl. The young-adult novel tells the story of Josie, who is in her last two years of high school and trying to find herself as she deals with an overbearing grandmother, the social upper crust of her high school, and inner questions about her heritage and her status as lover or friend to the boys in her life. Although popular, Josie is viewed as an outcast both in terms of her Italian heritage and because of the fact that her mother never married her father. The reappearance of her father into her life leads the teen to ask important questions and confront the coming-of-age problems that face many high school students.

In a *Booklist* assessment of *Looking for Alibrandi*, Anne O'Malley commented: "What emerges from this delightful first-person narrative is a strong, fresh, adolescent female voice." The reviewer also commended Marchetta for her "lively, well-drawn characters and realistic teen concerns." A *Publishers Weekly* contributor wrote that "the casting or plot may sound . . . [clichéd] but the characterizations are unusually insightful and persuasive." Writing in *Horn Book,* a reviewer called the novel "a quintessential girl book" and added that "adolescent readers will relish the friendships, rivalries, and romance—as well as the thrilling bits of rebellion." A critical and commercial success in Australia, *Looking for Alibrandi* garnered several of the country's top awards for juvenile literature and went on to sell over 300,000 copies. In addition to being published around the world in numerous translations, the novel has also been made into a film, with Marchetta writing the screenplay.

Cover of Melina Marchetta's Saving Francesca, *featuring artwork by Liz Steketee.* (Copyright © 2003 by Melina Marchetta. Cover photo copyright © 2004 by Liz Steketee. Liz Steketee/Photonica /Getty Images. Published by Thorndike Press.)

Marchetta continues to focus on teen life and angst in her next book, *Saving Francesca*. Transferring to the formerly all-boy's Catholic school St. Sebastian's, sixteen-year-old Francesca faces a crisis of confidence which is compounded by the fact that her mother is currently suffering from severe depression. His wife's condition baffles Francesca's father, and he seems unable to cope with the situation as the family begins to fall apart. With both parents preoccupied, Francesca is forced to find her own way amid her new environment, and she must make decisions with no guidance from the adults in her life. Determined to make a success of her time at St. Sebastian's, she becomes friends with girls and boys she would never have thought to speak to at her previous school, where she held a prized membership in an exclusive clique. Challenged by this new social situation, Francesca gradually discovers a new dimension of her personality, builds some close relationships, and even develops a romantic interest.

Writing in the *Bulletin of the Center for Children's Books,* Deborah Stevenson observed that in *Saving Francesca* Marchetta "takes what could be a predictable problem novel and turns it into a rich exploration of maturation, identity, family, and friendship." *Booklist* writer Ilene Cooper noted that the mother's illness "doesn't work" as a plot device, but added that, "this flaw aside, teens will find the novel is a realistic satisfying reflection of their lives." In a review for *Horn Book,* Lauren Adams concluded of *Saving Francesca* that "Marchetta proves her craft in this fresh, funny, and heartfelt portrait."

In her *Australian Catholics* interview, Marchetta explained her interest in writing for a young-adult audience. "Although I was in the workforce, I was totally confused when I was seventeen," she noted. "My friends were still at school. I had no idea if I was an adult or a child. I think that's why I will always concentrate on that age group in my writing. Because that's when I was most confused about where I belonged and what my identity was."

Biographical and Critical Sources

PERIODICALS

Age (Melbourne, Victoria, Australia), March 28, 2003, "Looking beyond Alibrandi."

Booklist, February 15, 1999, Anne O'Malley, review of *Looking for Alibrandi,* p. 1063; September 15, 1999, Stephanie Zvirin, review of *Looking for Alibrandi,* p. 249; January 1, 2000, review of *Looking for Alibrandi,* p. 820; October 1, 2004, Ilene Cooper, review of *Saving Francesca,* p. 323.

Bookseller, September, 2004, Sarah Amond, review of *Saving Francesca,* p. 212.

Bulletin of the Center for Children's Books, April, 1999, review of *Looking for Alibrandi,* p. 287; October, 2004, Deborah Stevenson, review of *Saving Francesca,* p. 88.

Horn Book, May, 1999, review of *Looking for Alibrandi,* p. 334; September-October, 2004, Lauren Adams, review of *Saving Francesca,* p. 591.

Journal of Adolescent & Adult Literacy, November, 2001, Carol Reinhard, review of *Looking for Alibrandi,* p. 195.

Kirkus Reviews, September 1, 2004, review of *Saving Francesca,* p. 870.

Kliatt, September, 2004, Claire Rosser, review of *Saving Francesca,* p. 14.

Publishers Weekly, March 8, 1999, review of *Looking for Alibrandi,* p. 69; September 6, 2004, review of *Saving Francesca,* p. 64.

SCAN (Sydney, New South Wales, Australia), October, 1993, interview with Marchetta.

School Library Journal, September, 2000, Barbara Wysocki, review of *Looking for Alibrandi,* p. 84; May, 2002, review of *Looking for Alibrandi,* p. 52; July, 2004, Francisca Goldsmith, review of *Saving Francesca,* p. 61.

Voice of Youth Advocates, June, 1999, review of *Looking for Alibrandi,* p. 115; October, 2004, Betsy Fraser, review of *Saving Francesca,* p. 304.

ONLINE

AustLit Web site, http://www.austlit.edu.au/ (February 23, 2005), "Melina Marchetta."

Australian Catholics Web site, http://www.australiancatholics.com.au/ (winter, 2003), Michael McGirr, "The Best Days, The Worst Days"; (October 16, 2005) "A Class of Her Own" (interview).

Dymocks Web site, http://www.dymocks.com.au/ (February 23, 2005), interview with Marchetta.

Lateral Learning Speakers' Agency Web site, http://www.laterallearning.com/ (May 10, 2006), "Melina Marchetta."

Puffin at Penguin Books Australia Web site, http://www.penguin.com.au/puffin/ (February 23, 2005), "Melina Marchetta."*

* * *

MASON, Cherie

Personal
Born in Milwaukee, WI; married, 1962; husband's name Kenneth (a business executive). *Education:* Northwestern University, B.S. (speech and journalism), 1947.

Addresses
Home—P.O. Box 39, Sunset, ME 04683.

Career
Writer, journalist, and wildlife advocate. Worked in advertising in Chicago, IL, 1950-70; Defender of Wildlife, Chicago, lobbyist, 1967-70; freelance voice actress, 1970-80; Marine Environmental Research Institute, public spokesperson and advisor, beginning 2001; host of *Wildlife Journal* (radio program), WERU-FM, for thirteen years. Former trustee, Nature Conservancy's Maine chapter; former board member, Humane Society of the United States; member of board of directors, Marine Environmental Research Institute, 2003—.

Awards, Honors
Lupine Award, Maine Library Association, 1993; honorary doctorate, University College of Maine, 1999.

Writings

Wild Fox: A True Story, illustrated by Jo Ellen McAllister Stammen, Down East Books (Camden, ME), 1993.

Everybody Is Somebody's Lunch, illustrated by Gustav Moore, Tilbury House (Gardiner, ME), 1998.

The dicey side of nature is presented in Cherie Mason's Everybody Is Somebody's Lunch, *featuring detailed illustrations by Rosemary Giebfried.* (Text copyright © 1998 by Cherie Mason and Judy Kellogg Markowsky. Illustrations copyright © 1998 by Rosemary Giebfried. Published by Tilbury House, Publishers. Reproduced by permission.)

Adaptations

Wild Fox was adapted as an audiobook, music by Paul Sullivan, River Music, 1994.

Sidelights

A long-time wildlife advocate who hosted the local radio program *Wildlife Journal* for over a dozen years, Cherie Mason shares her love of nature with young people through the pages of her books *Wild Fox: A True Story* and *Everybody Is Somebody's Lunch*. Avoiding the sugar-coated view of nature present in many children's books, Mason attempts to give young people a realistic portrait of the natural world, where every creature is part of the food chain. Using its young narrator's pragmatic discussion of the fate of the late great family cat Mouser as a starting point, *Everybody Is Somebody's Lunch* discusses the importance of life and death among young and old throughout the natural world, creating a book that, according to *Science Activities* contributor James O'Leary, "will give students and teachers alike a greater appreciation for wildlife."

In *Wild Fox* Mason describes her experience with a red fox who entered her life while she was living on Deer Isle, off the Maine coast. The fox had lost one of its legs, most likely by becoming snared in a hunter's trap. As Mason watched it over the coming months, the creature learned to thrive in spite of its handicap. Impressionistic illustrations accompany the storybook text, in which the author also presents animal facts and discusses the threats poised against North America's diverse wild areas and the need for preserving regions untouched by humans. "Mason's respect and fascination for this wild creature . . . is dearly evident, as is her enthusiasm for her subject," commented a *Publishers Weekly* critic. Another *Publishers Weekly* contributor noted that the author "communicates her innate awe" at tapping into the day-to-day rhythms of a wild creature, "and her riveting book pinpoints that charged, mysterious intersection where humans can meet the wild without taming it."

Biographical and Critical Sources

PERIODICALS

Booklist, June 1, 1993, Carolyn Phelan, review of *Wild Fox: A True Story,* p. 1824; September 15, 1995, Denise Perry Donavin, review of *Wild Fox,* p. 184.

Fifty Plus, October, 1988, Susan Hand Shetterly, "She's Wild about the Wild," p. 92.

Language Arts, October, 1994, review of *Wild Fox,* p. 463.

Newsweek, November 22, 1993, review of *Wild Fox,* p. 55.

New York Times Book Review, November 14, 1993, Sara Stein, review of *Wild Fox,* p. 1993.

Publishers Weekly, June 7, 1993, review of *Wild Fox,* p. 70; October 17, 1994, review of *Wild Fox* (audiobook), p. 38.

School Library Journal, August, 1993, Lynnea McBurney, review of *Wild Fox,* p. 160; May, 1995, Linda W. Braun, review of *Wild Fox* (audiobook), p. 67; April, 1999, review of *Everybody Is Somebody's Lunch,* p. 105.

Science Activities, fall, 1999, James O'Leary, review of *Everybody Is Somebody's Lunch,* p. 45.

Science Books & Films, March, 1999, review of *Wild Fox,* p. 55.

Smithsonian, November, 1993, review of *Wild Fox,* p. 183.

ONLINE

Marine Environmental Research Institute Web site, http://www.meriresearch.org/ (March 27, 2003), "Cherie Mason Joins MERI's Board of Directors."*

* * *

McKENDRY, Joe 1972-

Personal

Born April 20, 1972, in Lowell, MA; son of Donald (a potter) and Judith (a teacher) McKendry; married Susan Hass (a marketing manager), August, 1999; children: Elsie, Owen. *Ethnicity:* "Caucasian." *Education:* Rhode Island School of Design, B.F.A.

Joe McKendry (Pencil drawing courtesy of Joe McKendry)

Addresses

Home—Boston, MA. *Agent*—c/o Author Mail, David R. Godine, Publisher Inc., 9 Hamilton Pl., Boston, MA 02108-4715. *E-mail*—joemckendry@joemckendry.com.

Career

Freelance artist and author. Rhode Island School of Design, Providence, teacher; Massachusetts College of Art, teacher.

Writings

Beneath the Streets of Boston: Building America's First Subway, David R. Godine (Boston, MA), 2005.

Sidelights

An author and illustrator, Joe McKendry graduated from the Rhode Island School of Design and then stayed on there as a teacher of illustration. He made his publishing debut by offering readers a fascinating glimpse into the history of America's first underground transit system in *Beneath the Streets of Boston: Building America's First Subway.* McKendry analyzes the traffic problems that plagued Boston's maze of streets during the late 1800s and prompted the development of an alternative form of public transportation. After a lengthy battle, the famous "T" system was built, sparking a longstanding transportation trend. McKendry follows the ongoing development of the city's subway system, highlighting both problem areas as well as accomplishments. "New England history buffs and those interested in the origins of mass transport will welcome this look at the beginnings of America's first subway," commented Nancy Menaldi-Scanlan in *School Library Journal.* A *Kirkus Reviews* critic referred to McKendry's book as "a stunning examination" of a challenging advance in transportation technology.

McKendry told *SATA:* "During the creation of *Beneath the Streets of Boston* my goal was to present as simply as possible the story of how and why America's first subway came to be built. Research was gathered from turn-of-the-twentieth-century transit commission reports that detailed every facet of the subway's construction. To learn about the public's reaction to the subway, I read newspaper articles or microfilm from important moments in the subway's development (i.e., when particular parts of the tunnel were first opened to the public). Illustrations are watercolor paintings based on photographs primarily from the collection of *Historic New England.*"

Biographical and Critical Sources

PERIODICALS

Booklist, June 1, 2005, Jennifer Mattson, review of *Beneath the Streets of Boston: Building America's First Subway,* p. 1802.
Boston Globe, June 5, 2005, Jennifer Schuessler, "The First Big Dig."
Horn Book, September-October, 2005, Margaret A. Bush, review of *Beneath the Streets of Boston,* p. 605.
Kirkus Reviews, June 1, 2005, review of *Beneath the Streets of Boston,* p. 640.
Publishers Weekly, July 19, 2004, Sally Lodge, "Climbing aboard the Subway," p. 92.
School Library Journal, September, 2005, Nancy Menaldi-Scanlan, review of *Beneath the Streets of Boston,* p. 226.
Trains, September, 2005, Kathi Kube, review of *Beneath the Streets of Boston,* p. 74.

ONLINE

Joe McKendry Home Page, http://joemckendry.com (April 11, 2006).

* * *

MILLIGAN, Bryce 1953-

Personal

Born 1953, in Dallas, TX; son of J.B. (a consulting mechanic) and Maxine Carey (an elementary school teacher) Milligan; married Mary Guerrero (a librarian), May 24, 1975; children: Michael Bryce, Brigid Aileen.

Bryce Milligan (Photo by Brigid A. Milligan.)

Ethnicity: "Irish, Choctaw, Norwegian, Cherokee." *Education:* University of North Texas, B.A., 1977; University of Texas at Austin, M.A. (language and linguistics), 1980. *Politics:* Democrat. *Religion:* "Catholic with pagan leanings." *Hobbies and other interests:* Restoration of antique instruments, limestone sculpture, study of ancient Near-Eastern languages; "I enjoy restoring antique guitars and occasionally making instruments. I have played music my entire life—cello, trumpet, flute, guitar, and other instruments, and I sculpt in both wood and stone. I am interested in astronomy . . . and in the history of science."

Addresses

Home and office—627 E. Guenther, San Antonio, TX 78210. *E-mail*—milligan@wingspress.com.

Career

Guadalupe Cultural Arts Center, San Antonio, TX, director of literature program 1985-86, 1994-2000; North East School of Arts, San Antonio, director of creative writing program, 2000-02; Wings Press (publisher), San Antonio, owner, 1995—. Editor, *Pax: A Journal for Peace through Culture,* 1983-87; book critic for *San Antonio Express News,* 1983-87, and *San Antonio Light,* 1987-90; founding editor, *Vortex: A Critical Review,* 1986-90; coeditor, *Huehuetitlan* (journal), 1989-96.

Member

PEN American Center, National Book Critics Circle, Texas Institute of Letters.

Awards, Honors

Lone Star Award, Texas Library Association, 1991, for *With the Wind, Kevin Dolan;* Library Champion Award, San Antonio Public Library, 1998, for enhancement and involvement in San Antonio Public Library; Most Influential Teacher Award, North East School of the Arts, 2001; Bank Street College Best Book of the Year designation, 2002, for *Brigid's Cloak.*

Writings

FOR YOUNG ADULTS

With the Wind, Kevin Dolan, Corona (San Antonio, TX), 1987.
Battle of the Alamo: You Are There, illustrated by Charles Shaw, Texas Monthly Press (Austin, TX), 1990.
Comanche Captive: You Are There, illustrated by Charles Shaw, Texas Monthly Press (Austin, TX), 1990.
Lawmen: Stories of Men Who Tamed the West, illustrated by Charles Shaw, Disney Press (New York, NY), 1994.
The Mountain Men: Stories of Men Who Tamed the Wilderness, Disney Press (New York, NY), 1995.

FOR CHILDREN

Brigid's Cloak: An Ancient Irish Story, illustrated by Helen Cann, Eerdmans Publishing (Grand Rapids, MI), 2002.
The Prince of Ireland and the Three Magic Stallions, illustrated by Preston McDaniels, Holiday House (New York, NY), 2003.

POETRY; FOR ADULTS

Daysleepers & Other Poems, Corona (San Antonio, TX), 1984.
Litany Sung at Hell's Gate, M & A Editions (San Antonio, TX), 1990.
From Inside the Tree, Calberg Productions (San Antonio, TX), 1990.
Working the Stone, illustrated by Angela de Hoyos, Wings Press (Houston, TX), 1993.
Alms for Oblivion: A Poem in Seven Parts, Aark Arts (London, England), 2002.
Lost and Certain of It, Aark Arts (London, England), 2006.

OTHER

(Editor) Don Everett, *Albert Steves: A Paternal Portrait,* Watercress Press (San Antonio, TX), 1983.

(Editor) Kathleen Silber and Phyllis Speedlin, *Dear Birthmother,* Corona Publishing (San Antonio, TX), 1983.

(Editor) Cecilio Garcia-Camarillo, *And the Ground Spoke: Poems and Stories,* Guadalupe Cultural Arts Center (San Antonio, TX), 1986.

From Inside the Tree (poetry and songs), Calberg Productions (San Antonio, TX), 1990.

(Editor) *Linking Roots: Writing by Six Women of Diverse Ethnic Origins,* M & A Editions (San Antonio, TX), 1993.

(Editor, with others) *American Journeys: The Hispanic American Experience* (CD ROM), Primary Source Media (Farmington Hills, MI), 1995.

(Editor with Angela de Hoyos and wife, Mary Guerrero Milligan) *Daughters of the Fifth Sun: A Collection of Latina Fiction and Poetry,* Riverhead Books (New York, NY), 1995.

(Editor) *This Promiscuous Light: Young Women Poets of San Antonio,* Wings Press (San Antonio, TX), 1996.

(Editor) *Corazón del Norte: Writing by North Texas Latinos,* Wings Press (San Antonio, TX), 1996.

(Editor, with Angela de Hoyos and Mary Guerrero Milligan) *¡Florricanto Sí!: A Collection of Latina Poetry,* Penguin Books (New York, NY), 1998.

Contributing editor to *Stone Drum,* 1988-93. Contributor to books, including *Texas Trees, A Friendly Guide* by Paul W. Cox and Patty Leslie; *Sonnets to Human Beings and Other Selected Works,* edited by Ernesto Padilla; and *Writers at the Lake* edited by Marylyn Croman. Contributor to periodicals, including *Albuquerque Journal, Chicago Tribune, Current, Dallas Morning News, Los Angeles Times, New York Times, Our Kids, Publishers Weekly,* and *San Antonio Kids.*

Work in Progress

Princess, Priestess, Poet: Enheduanna of Ur for Eerdmans Publishing. Researching Sumerian and cuneiform for young-adult novels to be published as a trilogy.

Sidelights

Texas-based writer and publisher Bryce Milligan told *SATA:* "I have been called a 'literary wizard,' a 'jack of all genres,' and 'a contemporary muse poet' (Edward Hirsch), among other things. The fact is, for most of my life I have always functioned in several endeavors (and often several genres) at once. I believe that I am naturally inclined to do so, and that my best writing is done while I am actively engaged in other more physical pursuits. I am interested in astronomy (my son is a professional astronomer) and in the history of science. My interests appear in my writing, which is in itself simply another way to explore them."

In *Daughters of the Fifth Sun: A Collection of Latina Fiction and Poetry* Milligan served as coeditor, together with Angela de Hoyos and Milligan's wife, Mary Guerrero Milligan, of a collection of poems and fiction written by Latinas. The title includes a wealth of contemporary poets and authors, including Sandra Cisneros, Julia Alvarez, Ana Castillo, and Denise Chavez, among others. *Daughters of the Fifth Sun* extends to a far-reaching audience; both adults and young adults are meant to benefit from this collection of literatures. *USA Today* critic Steven G. Kellman noted that the collection includes a "distinctive combination of gender and ethnicity" and is a title that readers will treasure. On a similar note, Donna Seaman commented in *Booklist* that *Daughters of the Fifth Sun* is an "all-out celebration" of Latina writers that presents "a vibrant history of Latina literature."

Bryce Milligan retells the story of the Irish slave girl who eventually became a saint in Brigid's Cloak, *illustrated by Helen Cann.* (Text copyright © 2002 by Bryce Milligan. Illustrations © 2002 by Helen Cann. Eerdmans Books for Young Readers, 2002. Reproduced by permission.)

Brigid's Cloak: An Ancient Irish Story focuses on the legendary tale of a much-loved Irish saint and her celebrated generosity. Critics have applauded Milligan for his narrative abilities in *Brigid's Cloak.* A *Publishers Weekly* critic, for instance, noted that the story is "told with the gripping delivery of a well-seasoned storyteller," adding that Milligan "draws in readers" with his evocative use of words. The story of *Brigid's Cloak* begins when the infant Brigid is presented with a blue cloak by a Druid wizard who also blesses the young girl with magic. The magic bestowed onto Brigid presents itself many years later while she is tending to her flock of sheep. Somehow, Brigid is transported back in time to Jerusalem where she meets Mary and Joseph and witnesses the birth of Jesus. Brigid's renowned act of generosity occurs when she offers Mary her cloak, after which Brigid returns to her own time bearing her blue cloak, now adorned with ethereal stars. *Brigid's Cloak* also includes illustrations by Helen Cann, whose watercolor and mixed-media artwork was described by *Booklist* contributor Diane Foote as contributing "both authenticity and wonder to the tale." *Brigid's Cloak* was named a best-of-the-year book by both *Publishers Weekly* and Bank Street College.

Milligan acquaints young readers with an ancient Irish folktale that tells the story of a young prince who is sent on a quest to find three magic stallions owned by a giant in *The Prince of Ireland and the Three Magic Stallions*. A "geis" (curse) is placed on the prince of Ireland by his calculating stepmother who wants her own sons to rule Ireland. The prince can break the curse only if he succeeds in bringing back the three magic stallions. The story then follows the prince and his two stepbrothers as they seek out and bargain with a giant named Sean O'Donal for the magical steeds. A critic for *Kirkus Reviews* cited Milligan's "lilt of the language," while Jeanne Clancy Watkins noted in *School Library Journal* that the author's "poetic prose demands to be read aloud with a lilt and a brogue, and comely turns of phrase . . . beg readers to join in."

As Milligan continued to *SATA:* "My daughter is a published translator and scholar of comparative literature, which perhaps reflects my own life-long fascination with etymology, ancient languages and literatures from different times and places. In graduate school, it was my honor to study with Dr. Ruth Lehmann, a world-class interpreter of Old Irish and Anglo-Saxon, and with Dr. Winfred Lehmann, an internationally recognized scholar of Indo-European.

"After finishing my M.A., I settled in San Antonio, Texas, and became the weekly book critic for the *San Antonio Express-News* and the *San Antonio Light*. During this period I founded and edited two literary magazines, *Pax: A Journal for Peace through Culture* and *Vortex: A Critical Review*. . . . My interest in contemporary Latina literature led me to edit the first major anthology of all-Latina writing *Daughters of the Fifth Sun*, which spent three years on the New York Public Library's Best Books for the Teen Age list. I also edited the first Penguin anthology of Latina poetry, *¡Floricanto Sí!*

"In 1995, I purchased Wings Press. The press had published my book of poems, *Working the Stone*, and then went bankrupt. As the owner/publisher/editor/book designer, I enjoy having complete control over what and who I publish, and I very much enjoy the designing. Since 1995, Wings has published over one hundred titles, over half by women, mostly Latina, black, and Native American.

"My wife is a librarian, and we have shared many years reading aloud. Sharing a life filled with mutual loves—children, books, the change of seasons—is what keeps

Milligan teams with illustrator Preston McDaniels to retell an traditional tale of magic in **The Prince of Ireland and the Three Magic Stallions.** (Text copyright © 2003 by Bryce Milligan. Illustrations copyright © 2003 by Preston McDaniels. Reproduced by permission of Holiday House, Inc.)

me grounded and stable. Literature and writing are a great part of my life, but they are not everything. Creativity and craft are crucial, especially as they concern the idea of 'making.' Not much that is good in life just happens by accident. One makes a family, makes a song or poem, makes a book, makes a guitar, makes a garden, one even makes an old house continue to keep out the rain. This is why writers do not retire—to stop making is to stop living."

Biographical and Critical Sources

PERIODICALS

Booklist, September 15, 1995, review of *Daughters of the Fifth Sun: A Collection of Latina Fiction and Poetry,* p. 129; October 15, 2002, Diane Foote, *Brigid's Cloak: An Ancient Irish Story,* p. 408.
Kirkus Reviews, March 1, 2003, review of *The Prince of Ireland and the Three Magic Stallions,* p. 392.
Publishers Weekly, September 9, 2002, review of review of *Brigid's Cloak,* p. 64.
School Library Journal, February, 2003, Sally Dow, review of *Brigid's Cloak,* p. 136; June, 2003, Jeanne Clancy Watkins, review of *The Prince of Ireland and the Three Magic Stallions,* p. 131.

USA Today, May, 1996, Steven G. Kellman, review of *Daughters of the Fifth Sun,* p. 80.

ONLINE

Wings Press Web site, http://www.wingspress.com/ (April 8, 2006), "Bryce Milligan."

* * *

MUNGER, Nancy

Personal
Born February 28, in Charlotte, MI; daughter of Robert S. and Phyllis E. Munger; married Douglas Anderson, 1977; children: Jessie, Joshua. *Education:* Art Center of Design, B.F.A. (illustration; with honors).

Addresses
Home and office—P.O. Box 425, Delton, MI 49046. *E-mail*—nancymunger@aol.com.

Career
Illustrator.

Awards, Honors
CBA Gold Medallion Book Award.

Illustrator
Eleanor Doan, compiler, *A Child's Treasury of Verse,* Zondervan (Grand Rapids, MI), 1977.

Bernice Hogan, *My Grandmother Died—but I Won't Forget Her,* Abingdon Press (Nashville, TN), 1983.

Peter S. Seymour, *Baby Animals at Play,* Franklin Watts (New York, NY), 1983.

Janice Kempe, *Growing up Together,* Discovery House (Grand Rapids, MI), 1989.

Kenneth Nathaniel Taylor, *Good New for Little People,* Tyndale (Wheaton, IL), 1991.

Betty Aldridge, *The Toddler's Activity Bible,* Thomas Nelson (Nashville, TN), 1992.

Amy Houts, *An A.B.C. Christmas,* Standard Pub. (Cincinnati, OH), 1993.

Vesta Seek, *Old Ruff and Life on the Farm,* Chariot Books (Elgin, IL), 1993.

Diane M. Stortz, *A 1-2-3 Christmas,* Standard Pub. (Cincinnati, OH), 1993.

Debbie Trafton O'Neal, *Now I Lay Me down to Sleep: Action Prayers, Poems, and Songs for Bedtime,* Augsburg (Minneapolis, MN), 1994.

Debbie Trafton O'Neal, *Thank You for This Food,* Augsburg (Minneapolis, MN), 1994.

L.J. Sattgast, *When Stars Come Out: Bedtime Psalms for Little Ones,* God 'n' Honey Books (Sisters, OR), 1994.

Kenneth Nathaniel Taylor, *Stories about Jesus,* Tyndale House (Wheaton, IL), 1994.

Kenneth Nathaniel Taylor, *Small Talks about God,* Moody Press (Chicago, IL), 1995.

Liz Curtis Higgs, *The Pumpkin Patch Parable,* Thomas Nelson (Nashville, TN), 1995.

Teresa Olive, *My Merry Christmas: Luke 2:1-20 for Children,* Concordia Pub. House (St. Louis, MO), 1995.

Mary Manz Simon, *Little Visits for Toddlers,* revised edition, CPH (St. Louis, MO), 1995.

Teresa Olive, *Mary's Christmas Story: Luke 1:26-56, Luke 2:1-20 for Children,* Concordia Pub. House (St. Louis, MO), 1996.

L.J. Sattgast, *A Light on the Path: Proverbs for Growing Wise,* Gold 'n' Honey Books (Sisters, OR), 1996.

Liz Curtis Higgs, *The Parable of the Lily,* Thomas Nelson (Nashville, TN), 1997.

Liz Curtis Higgs, *The Pine Tree Parable,* Thomas Nelson (Nashville, TN), 1997.

Liz Curtis Higgs, *The Sunflower Parable,* Thomas Nelson (Nashville, TN), 1997.

Michael A. VanderKlipp, *Joy to the World!: A Christmas Counting Book,* Zondervan (Grand Rapids, MI), 1998.

Alice Joyce Davidson, *The "J" Is for Jesus: The Candy Cane Story,* Zondervan (Grand Rapids, MI), 1998.

Jesslyn Deboer, *Follow the Star,* Zondervan (Grand Rapids, MI), 1998.

Jesslyn Deboer, *Getting Ready for Christmas,* Zondervan (Grand Rapids, MI), 1998.

Helen Haidle, *What Would Jesus Do?,* Multnomah Publishers (Sisters, OR), 1998.

Tracy L. Harrast, *My Bible 1-2-3's,* Zondervan (Grand Rapids, MI), 1998.

Tracy L. Harrast, *My Bible ABC's,* Zondervan (Grand Rapids, MI), 1998.

Tracy L. Harrast, *My Bible Animals,* Zondervan (Grand Rapids, MI), 1998.

Tracy L. Harrast, *My Bible Colors,* Zondervan (Grand Rapids, MI), 1998.

Liz Curtis Higgs, *Go Away, Dark Night,* WaterBrook Press (Colorado Springs, CO), 1998.

Patricia A. Hoffman, *In Bethlehem Town: Luke 2:1-19,* Concordia Pub. House (St. Louis, MO), 1999.

Holly Davis, *My Birthday, Jesus' Birthday,* Zondervan (Grand Rapids, MI), 1999.

Helen Haidel, *What Did Jesus Promise?,* Zondervan (Grand Rapids, MI), 2000.

Debbie Trafton O'Neal, *Thank You for This Day: Action Prayers, Songs, and Blessing for Every Day,* Augsburg (Minneapolis, MN), 2000.

Janette Oke, *The Impatient Turtle,* Bethany Backyard (Minneapolis, MN), 2000.

Janette Oke, *The Prodigal Cat,* Bethany Backyard (Minneapolis, MN), 2000.

Janette Oke, *Spunky's Diary,* Bethany Backyard (Minneapolis, MN), 2000.

Janette Oke, *This Little Pig,* Bethany Backyard (Minneapolis, MN), 2001.

Janette Oke, *Maury Had a Little Lamb,* Bethany Backyard (Minneapolis, MN), 2001.

Janette Oke, *New Kid in Town,* Bethany Backyard (Minneapolis, MN), 2001.

Janette Oke, *Pordy's Prickly Problem,* Bethany Backyard (Minneapolis, MN), 2001.

Janette Oke, *Prairie Dog Town*, Bethany Backyard (Minneapolis, MN), 2001.
Janette Oke, *Trouble in a Fur Coat*, Bethany Backyard (Minneapolis, MN), 2001.
Janette Oke, *Who's New at the Zoo?*, Bethany Backyard (Minneapolis, MN), 2001.
Elspeth Campbell Murphy, *The Birthday Present Mystery*, Bethany Backyard (Minneapolis, MN), 2001.
Elspeth Campbell Murphy, *The Sneaky Thief Mystery*, Bethany Backyard (Minneapolis, MN), 2001.
Janette Oke, *A Cote of Many Colors*, Bethany Backyard (Minneapolis, MN), 2001.
Janette Oke, *Ducktails*, Bethany Backyard (Minneapolis, MN), 2001.
Elspeth Campbell Murphy, *The Chalk Drawings Mystery*, Bethany Backyard (Minneapolis, MN), 2002.
Elspeth Campbell Murphy, *The Flying Pigs Mystery*, Bethany Backyard (Minneapolis, MN), 2002.
Elspeth Cambell Murphy, *The Giant Chicken Mystery*, Bethany Backyard (Minneapolis, MN), 2002.
Patricia A. Pingry, *David and Goliath: Based on 1 Samuel 17:1/50*, CandyCane Press (Nashville, TN), 2004.
Patricia A. Pingry, *Jesus in the Temple: Based on Luke 2:40/52*, CandyCane Press (Nashville, TN), 2004.
Patricia A. Pingry, *The Story of The Star-Spangled Banner*, CandyCane Press (Nashville, TN), 2004.
Scott Tunseth, *Tomorrow Begins at Bedtime*, Augsburg (Minneapolis, MN), 2004.

Biographical and Critical Sources

PERIODICALS

Publishers Weekly, March 24, 1997, review of *The Parable of the Lily*, p. 76; October 26, 1998, review of *Go Away, Dark Night*, p. 62.
School Library Journal, December, 1983, review of *My Grandmother Died—but I Won't Forget Her*, p. 56.

ONLINE

Nancy Munger Home Page, http://www.nancymunger.com (April 11, 2006).*

N-O

NÄSLUND, Görel Kristina 1940-
(Görel Kristina Carheden)

Personal
Born 1940, in Röbäck, Sweden; married (divorced, c. 1970); partner's name Gullmar. *Education:* Degree in home economics; University of Minnesota, studied journalism; Karolinska Institutet, Ph.D. (psychology). *Hobbies and other interests:* Skiing, cooking.

Addresses
Home—Near Stockholm, Sweden. *Agent*—c/o Author Mail, Kärnhuset, Drottning Kristinas väg 19, 193 35 Sigtuna, Sweden. *E-mail*—gorel.kristina.naslund@psyk.ks.s.

Career
Psychologist, educator, pomologist, and writer. Established French cooking school. Teacher of Swedish in Denver, CO, c. 1960s; *Expressen* (daily newspaper), Stockholm, Sweden, journalist beginning 1970; freelance writer; apple expert; currently psychologist in private practice.

Writings

- (As Görel Kristina Carheden) *Foods and Festivals, Swedish Style*, illustrated by Dick Sutphen, Dillon Press (Minneapolis, MN), 1968.
- (Translator, as Görel Kristina Carheden) *Swedish Cooking*, Inca Forlaget, 1971.
- *Vår Skona Grona Mat* (for children), illustrated by Kristina Digman, Raben & Sjogren (Stockholm, Sweden), 1977, translated by Lauren Brown as *Our Apple Tree*, Roaring Brook Press (New Milford, CT), 2005.
- *Vår första svampbok*, Raben & Sjogren (Stockholm, Sweden), 1998.
- *100 älskade äpplen*, illustrated by Ingrid af Sandeberg, Kärnhuset (Sigtuna, Sweden), 2002.
- *Lilla äppelboken* (for children), illustrated by Kristina Digman, Raben & Sjogren (Stockholm, Sweden), 2002.
- *Lilla vinterboken* (for children), illustrated by Kristina Digman, Raben & Sjogren (Stockholm, Sweden), 2005.
- *Vem var det där?: en bok om ansiktsblindhet*, Kärnhuset (Sigtuna, Sweden), 2006.

Author of numerous other books published in Swedish, including stories for children and books on cooking, psychology, and apples.

Biographical and Critical Sources

PERIODICALS

Booklist, August, 2005, Gillian Engberg, review of *Our Apple Tree*, p. 2035.
Children's Bookwatch, February, 2006, review of *Our Apple Tree*.
Kirkus Reviews, July 15, 2005, review of *Our Apple Tree*, p. 794.
School Library Journal, November, 2005, Genevieve Gallagher, review of *Our Apple Tree*, p. 118.

ONLINE

Kärnhuset Web site, http://www.karnhuset.com/ (May 29, 2006), "Görel Kristina Näslund."*

* * *

NEUBECKER, Robert

Personal
Born in Rochester, NY; married; wife's name Ruth; children: two daughters. *Education:* Parsons School of Design, B.F.A., 1975. *Hobbies and other interests:* Skiing, surfing, reading.

N-O

NÄSLUND, Görel Kristina 1940-
(Görel Kristina Carheden)

Personal
Born 1940, in Röbäck, Sweden; married (divorced, c. 1970); partner's name Gullmar. *Education:* Degree in home economics; University of Minnesota, studied journalism; Karolinska Institutet, Ph.D. (psychology). *Hobbies and other interests:* Skiing, cooking.

Addresses
Home—Near Stockholm, Sweden. *Agent*—c/o Author Mail, Kärnhuset, Drottning Kristinas väg 19, 193 35 Sigtuna, Sweden. *E-mail*—gorel.kristina.naslund@psyk.ks.s.

Career
Psychologist, educator, pomologist, and writer. Established French cooking school. Teacher of Swedish in Denver, CO, c. 1960s; *Expressen* (daily newspaper), Stockholm, Sweden, journalist beginning 1970; freelance writer; apple expert; currently psychologist in private practice.

Writings

(As Görel Kristina Carheden) *Foods and Festivals, Swedish Style,* illustrated by Dick Sutphen, Dillon Press (Minneapolis, MN), 1968.
(Translator, as Görel Kristina Carheden) *Swedish Cooking,* Inca Forlaget, 1971.
Vår Skona Grona Mat (for children), illustrated by Kristina Digman, Raben & Sjogren (Stockholm, Sweden), 1977, translated by Lauren Brown as *Our Apple Tree,* Roaring Brook Press (New Milford, CT), 2005.
Vår första svampbok, Raben & Sjogren (Stockholm, Sweden), 1998.
100 älskade äpplen, illustrated by Ingrid af Sandeberg, Kärnhuset (Sigtuna, Sweden), 2002.
Lilla äppelboken (for children), illustrated by Kristina Digman, Raben & Sjogren (Stockholm, Sweden), 2002.
Lilla vinterboken (for children), illustrated by Kristina Digman, Raben & Sjogren (Stockholm, Sweden), 2005.
Vem var det där?: en bok om ansiktsblindhet, Kärnhuset (Sigtuna, Sweden), 2006.

Author of numerous other books published in Swedish, including stories for children and books on cooking, psychology, and apples.

Biographical and Critical Sources

PERIODICALS

Booklist, August, 2005, Gillian Engberg, review of *Our Apple Tree,* p. 2035.
Children's Bookwatch, February, 2006, review of *Our Apple Tree.*
Kirkus Reviews, July 15, 2005, review of *Our Apple Tree,* p. 794.
School Library Journal, November, 2005, Genevieve Gallagher, review of *Our Apple Tree,* p. 118.

ONLINE

Kärnhuset Web site, http://www.karnhuset.com/ (May 29, 2006), "Görel Kristina Näslund."*

* * *

NEUBECKER, Robert

Personal
Born in Rochester, NY; married; wife's name Ruth; children: two daughters. *Education:* Parsons School of Design, B.F.A., 1975. *Hobbies and other interests:* Skiing, surfing, reading.

Janette Oke, *Prairie Dog Town,* Bethany Backyard (Minneapolis, MN), 2001.
Janette Oke, *Trouble in a Fur Coat,* Bethany Backyard (Minneapolis, MN), 2001.
Janette Oke, *Who's New at the Zoo?,* Bethany Backyard (Minneapolis, MN), 2001.
Elspeth Campbell Murphy, *The Birthday Present Mystery,* Bethany Backyard (Minneapolis, MN), 2001.
Elspeth Campbell Murphy, *The Sneaky Thief Mystery,* Bethany Backyard (Minneapolis, MN), 2001.
Janette Oke, *A Cote of Many Colors,* Bethany Backyard (Minneapolis, MN), 2001.
Janette Oke, *Ducktails,* Bethany Backyard (Minneapolis, MN), 2001.
Elspeth Campbell Murphy, *The Chalk Drawings Mystery,* Bethany Backyard (Minneapolis, MN), 2002.
Elspeth Campbell Murphy, *The Flying Pigs Mystery,* Bethany Backyard (Minneapolis, MN), 2002.
Elspeth Cambell Murphy, *The Giant Chicken Mystery,* Bethany Backyard (Minneapolis, MN), 2002.
Patricia A. Pingry, *David and Goliath: Based on 1 Samuel 17:1/50,* CandyCane Press (Nashville, TN), 2004.
Patricia A. Pingry, *Jesus in the Temple: Based on Luke 2:40/52,* CandyCane Press (Nashville, TN), 2004.
Patricia A. Pingry, *The Story of The Star-Spangled Banner,* CandyCane Press (Nashville, TN), 2004.
Scott Tunseth, *Tomorrow Begins at Bedtime,* Augsburg (Minneapolis, MN), 2004.

Biographical and Critical Sources

PERIODICALS

Publishers Weekly, March 24, 1997, review of *The Parable of the Lily,* p. 76; October 26, 1998, review of *Go Away, Dark Night,* p. 62.
School Library Journal, December, 1983, review of *My Grandmother Died—but I Won't Forget Her,* p. 56.

ONLINE

Nancy Munger Home Page, http://www.nancymunger.com (April 11, 2006).*

Addresses

Home—Park City, UT. *Agent*—Tammy Shannon, Shannon Associates, 333 W. 57th St., Ste. 801, New York, NY 10019. *E-mail*—Robert@neubecker.com.

Career

Artist and illustrator. Push Pin Press, former researcher; *New York Times*, New York, NY, contributing editorial illustrator, 1974-84; Inxs, Inc. (artists' political illustration collective), co-founder, 1980; freelance illustrator, beginning 1980s. Teacher of illustration and design at Brigham Young University, School of Visual Arts, and University of Utah. *Exhibitions:* Drawings and paintings exhibited in solo and group shows in New York, NY.

Awards, Honors

Awards from American Illustration, *Print, Communication Arts*, Society of Illustrators, *3x3* magazine, and American Institute of Graphic Arts; Key Award for Best Comedy Poster, 2004; American Library Association Notable Book Award, 2005, for *Wow! City!*

Writings

Wow! City!, Hyperion Books for Children (New York, NY), 2004.
Beasty Bath, Orchard Books (New York, NY), 2005.
Wow! America!, Hyperion Books for Children (New York, NY), 2006.
Courage of the Blue Boy, Tricycle Press (Berkeley, CA), 2006.
(Illustrator) Christine Loomis, *Hattie Hippo*, Orchard Books (New York, NY), 2006.

Contributor to periodicals, including *Business Week, Time, Washington Post, Wall Street Journal,* and *Los Angeles Times.*

Work in Progress

Writing and illustrating more books for children.

Sidelights

After graduating from New York City's Parsons School of Design, Robert Neubecker remained in Manhattan, working as a freelance illustrator for twenty years, his work appearing in publications such as the *New York Times, Washington Post, Business Week, Time, Newsweek,* and *Wall Street Journal.* Neubecker moved to Utah in 1994. In 2004 he made his publishing debut with the children's picture book *Wow! City!,* and he has gone on to create the follow-up volume *Wow! America!* as well as the picture book *Beasty Bath.* Dubbed an "ebullient bedtime book . . . full of toddler enthusiasm" by a *Publishers Weekly* contributor, *Beasty Bath*

Cover of Robert Neubecker's self-illustrated Wow! City! (Text and illustrations copyright © 2004 by Robert Neubecker. All rights reserved. Reprinted by permission of Hyperion Books for Children.)

features an imaginative girl making the most of bath time by morphing into a succession of very un-scary creatures, from sea monsters to lion. The *Publishers Weekly* contributor went on to dub Neubecker's book "an inventive bedtime romp," while in *School Library Journal* Angela J. Reynolds compared the book's "colorful, playful, and imaginative watercolor-and-ink cartoon illustrations" to those of noted illustrator Maurice Sendak.

Wow! City!, published in 2004, was inspired by Neubecker's own experience while on a vacation to New York City with his two-year-old daughter, Izzy. Excited by the bustle and energetic atmosphere surrounding her, the young girl in Neubecker's picture book exclaims her excitement at a variety of sights and sounds using her somewhat limited vocabulary. A related book, *Wow! America!,* expands the girl's sightseeing to a panorama that encompasses America's diversity. "Children should adore exploring the numerous details of each scene," commented a *Publishers Weekly* critic of *Wow! City!,* referring to the street scenes in which readers can hunt for yellow-haired Izzy and her father in the crowd. In *School Library Journal* Jane Barrer commented on the "life, action, and detail" present in the colorful art, which Neubecker created by combining inked drawings and computerized coloration. Noting the artist/author's use of thick outlines and saturated colors, Jennifer Mattson praised Neubecker's work in *Booklist,* calling *Wow! City!* "a dazzling picture-book debut that beautifully transmits the wonder of the view from a baby-carrier backpack."

Biographical and Critical Sources

PERIODICALS

Booklist, November 1, 2004, Jennifer Mattson, review of *Wow! City!,* p. 480.

Kirkus Reviews, September 1, 2004, review of *Wow! City!,* p. 871; September 15, 2005, review of *Beasty Bath,* p. 1031.

Publishers Weekly, September 20, 2004, review of *Wow! City!,* p. 61; December 19, 2005, review of *Beasty Bath,* p. 63.

School Library Journal, September, 2004, Jane Barrer, review of *Wow! City!,* p. 176; September, 2005, Barbara Auerbach, review of *Wow! City!,* p. 59; January, 2006, Angela J. Reynolds, review of *Beasty Bath,* p. 110; June 2006, Jodi Kearns, review of *Wow! America!,* p. 139.

ONLINE

Robert Neubecker Home Page, http://www.neubecker.com (April 11, 2006).

BookPage.com, http://www.bookpage.com/ (April 11, 2006), "Meet Robert Neubecker."

Hyperion Web site, http://www.hyperionbooksforchildren.com/ (April 11, 2006), "Robert Neubecker."

* * *

OSTOW, Micol 1976-

Personal
Born April, 29, 1976. *Ethnicity:* "Puerto Rican and Jewish." *Education:* College graduate. *Hobbies and other interests:* Reading, running, watching inappropriate quantities of bad TV.

Addresses
Home—New York, NY. *Agent*—c/o Author Mail, Simon Pulse/Simon & Schuster, 1230 Avenue of the Americas, New York, NY 10020.

Career
Writer and editor. Simon & Schuster, New York, NY, editor in trade nonfiction, then young-adult division. Creator of *Fireplace in a Box* and *Executive Desk Gong,* for Running Press, 2003.

Writings

FOR YOUNG ADULTS

(Compiler with Steven Brizenoff) *The Quotable Slayer* (based on television series *Buffy the Vampire Slayer*), Simon Pulse (New York, NY), 2003.

30 Guys in 30 Days, Simon Pulse (New York, NY), 2005.

Changeling Places (based on television series *Charmed*), Simon Spotlight Entertainment (New York, NY), 2005.

Westminster Abby ("Students across the Seven Seas" series), Speak (New York, NY), 2005.

Ultimate Travel Games, Price, Stern, Sloan, 2006.

Emily Goldberg Learns to Salsa, Razorbill (New York, NY), 2006.

Also author (uncredited) of young-adult novels based on television series, including *American Dreams,* and for novel series, including "Fearless" and "Camp Confidential."

Sidelights
After graduating from college, Micol Ostow hired on with New York City publisher Simon & Schuster, and her job as editor eventually led to her second career as the author of young-adult novels. Describing her move to author as "a very organic" process in an online interview with *NYC24* contributor Catherine Shu, Ostow ex-

Cover of Micol Ostow's Westminster Abby, *featuring artwork by Yuko Sugimoto.* (Text copyright © 2005 by Micol Ostow. Cover illustration copyright © 2005 by Yugo Sugimoto. Published by Speak. Used by permission of Puffin Books, a division of Penguin Young Readers Group, a member of Penguin Group (USA) Inc., 345 Hudson Street, New York, NY 10014. All rights reserved.)

plained that she started as a ghostwriter for novelizations of popular ongoing series such as *Buffy the Vampire Slayer*, *Charmed*, and *Fearless*, some published under house pseudonyms. From there, Ostow has begun to make her own name known to teen readers; her novels *30 Guys in 30 Days* and *Westminster Abby* appeared in 2005. Praising the first book as "tastefully written," *Kliatt* contributor Annette Wells added that older teens "will love this cleverly constructed novel" about a college freshman who decides to overcome her shyness by talking to a different guy each day for a month.

Part of the "Students across the Seven Seas" series, *Westminster Abby* centers around sixteen-year-old Abby, who has been sent to London for the summer by her parents as punishment for lying to them about her boyfriend James. While abroad, Abby meets up with a charming Brit named Ian and strikes up a fun relationship. A quandary arises when James appears in London, hoping to rekindle their relationship despite the fact that he cheated on her: should Abby chose between Ian and James or opt for staying single? "This is as much a travel book as a romance, and for the most part, Ostow does a good job of fitting all the sights, sounds, and smells into the story," commented Ilene Cooper in a *Booklist* review of *Westminster Abby*.

Catherine Ensley, writing in *School Library Journal*, also enjoyed the teen read, commenting that while "light in conflict," Ostow's story "will appeal to teens . . . whose lives are similarly sheltered and somewhat economically privileged."

Biographical and Critical Sources

PERIODICALS

Booklist, August, 2005, Ilene Cooper, review of *Westminster Abby*, p. 2016.

Kliatt, July, 2005, Annette Wells, review of *30 Guys in 30 Days*, p. 24.

School Library Journal, June, 2005, Catherine Ensley, review of *Westminster Abby*, p. 167.

ONLINE

NYC24 Web site, http://www.nyc24.org/ (April 11, 2005), Catherine Shu, "Confessions of an Undercover Author."*

P

PAVER, Michelle

Personal
Born in Malawi; immigrated to England at age three. *Education:* Oxford University, graduated.

Addresses
Home—Wimbledon, England. *Agent*—c/o Author Mail, Katherine Tegen Books, 1350 Avenue of the Americas, New York, NY 10019.

Career
Writer. Formerly worked as an attorney specializing in patent litigation.

Awards, Honors
Gold Award, Parents' Choice List, 2005, for *Wolf Brother*.

Writings

FOR ADULTS

Without Charity (fiction), Corgi (London, England), 2000.
A Place in the Hills (fiction), Corgi (London, England), 2001.

"DAUGHTERS OF EDEN" SERIES; FOR ADULTS

The Shadow Catcher, Corgi (London, England), 2002.
Fever Hill, Bantam (London, England), 2004.
The Serpent's Tooth, 2005

"CHRONICLES OF ANCIENT DARKNESS" SERIES; FOR YOUNG READERS

Wolf Brother, HarperCollins (New York, NY), 2004.
Spirit Walker, Katherine Tegen Books (New York, NY), 2006.
Soul-Eater, Katherine Tegen Books (New York, NY), in press.

Adaptations
Wolf Brother was released as an audio book, HarperCollins, 2005.

Work in Progress
Three more novels in the "Chronicles of Ancient Darkness" series.

Sidelights
Michelle Paver earned a degree in biochemistry from Oxford University and worked for some time as a lawyer specializing in patent litigation, but she gave up that career to focus on her dream of writing full time. She succeeded in that aim, establishing herself as an author of adult fiction before beginning to write children's books. The British author's love of myth, folklore and history has informed all her writing, such as the "Daughters of Eden" series, set in Jamaica, and the novel *A Place in the Hills,* set in the Pyrenees mountains.

Paver's children's book series, "Chronicles of Ancient Darkness," is set in northeastern Europe some six thousand years ago, after the end of the last Ice Age. It was a time before agriculture, when people lived as hunter-gatherers. To research her story, the author traveled to remote areas in Finland, living outdoors in primitive conditions. Her dedicated research makes her work vivid and compelling, according to numerous reviewers. Discussing the genesis of the series with Dirk Vander Ploeg in *PSI Talk,* Paver recalled, "I got the inspiration for the 'Chronicles of Ancient Darkness' [series] one afternoon at home. I was sitting in my garden and the glimmer of an idea suddenly came to me and in a few hours I had mapped out the entire series of six books!"

The first book of the series, *Wolf Brother*, was inspired by the author's encounter with a bear while she was in Southern California. In the book Torak sees his father fatally attacked by a bear that is possessed by a demon spirit. Torak's father commands him to take up a quest to the Mountain of the World Spirit, the only force that can defeat the demon bear. Joined on this journey by an orphaned wolf pup that is also his spirit guide, Torak comes to realize that he is the Listener, destined to hold back the evil Shadow from overrunning the land. *Booklist* reviewer Sally Estes described the book as "fantasy adventure on a grand scale," and also praised Paver's characterizations and well-realized wilderness setting. *Kliatt* reviewer Michele Winship observed that "Paver has done her research and done it well," giving her book a firm archaeological foundation with insights into the lives of hunter-gatherer societies such as the Inuits, many African tribes, and Native Americans.

Wolf Brother won more praise from Karen T. Bilton, a reviewer for *School Library Journal*, who noted that the book immerses readers in spirituality and mysticism in a way that is unusual in a children's book, doing so in a way that is "intriguing and believable." *Wolf Brother* was recommended by a *Publishers Weekly* writer, who described it as "part riveting nature story, part rite of passage saga," and added that the complex plot "remains involving thanks to Paver's unusual setting and eccentric characters,"

Biographical and Critical Sources

PERIODICALS

Booklist, March 1, 2005, Sally Estes, review of *Wolf Brother*, p. 1185.
Kirkus Reviews, January 15, 2005, review of *Wolf Brother*, p. 124.
Kliatt, March, 2005, Michele Winship, review of *Wolf Brother*, p. 15.
MBR Bookwatch, May, 2005, Vicki Arkoff, review of *Wolf Brother*.
Publishers Weekly, January 10, 2005, review of *Wolf Brother*, p. 57.
School Library Journal, February, 2005, Karen T. Bilton, review of *Wolf Brother*, p. 140.

ONLINE

Michelle Paver Home Page, http://www.michellepaver.com (September 1, 2005).
PSI Talk, http://www.psitalk.com/ (September 1, 2005), Dirk Vander Ploeg, interview with Michelle Paver.

* * *

PEREZ, Lana
See PEREZ, Marlene

PEREZ, Marlene
(Lana Perez)

Personal
Female.

Addresses
Home—Southern CA. *Agent*—c/o Author Mail, Roaring Brook Press, 2 Old New Milford Rd., Brookfield, CT 06804. *E-mail*—marlene@marleneperez.com.

Career
Writer.

Awards, Honors
Quick Pick for Reluctant Readers, and Best Book for Young Adults nomination, both 2005, both for *Unexpected Development*.

Writings

Unexpected Development, Roaring Brook Press (Brookfield, CT), 2004.

UNDER PSEUDONYM LANA PEREZ

Bright Lights for Bella ("Star Sisterz" series), Mirrorstone (Renton, WA), 2005.
Figure in the Frost ("Knights of the Silver Dragon" series), Mirrorstone (Renton, WA), 2005.
Bella goes Hollywood ("Star Sisterz" series), Mirrorstone (Renton, WA), 2006.

Sidelights
Marlene Perez made her publishing debut with the young-adult novel *Unexpected Development*. The Southern California-based writer became inspired to write the diary-style book after attending a conference in Los Angeles held by the Society of Children's Book Writers and Illustrators. During the day-long schedule of seminars and round tables, noted YA author Norma Fox Mazer discussed the obstacles presented by a writer's internal critic, Mazer suggested ways of turning off one's internal editor and focusing on writing freely. Returning home, Perez sat down at her desk the very next day and started on the manuscript that would become *Unexpected Development*. In addition to this novel, she has published several books for role-playing-game and book publisher Wizards of the Coast, all under the pen name Lana Perez. Part of the "Star Sisterz" series designed for pre-teens and featuring characters from a related game, *Bright Lights for Bella* and *Bella Goes Hollywood* follow the adventures of a fourteen year old as she struggles through the first year of high school and

successfully resolves an assortment of dilemmas that many teens can relate to. In an online review for *BookLoons,* Ricki Marking-Camuto noted that Perez "has an uncanny ability to capture in her writing the way a young teenager thinks."

Unexpected Development follows seventeen-year-old Megan, a teen plagued with overly large breasts. Made uncomfortable by the constant notice paid her double-D cleavage by ogling men, Megan begins to question the motive behind male attention, particularly after her boss at the pancake house attempts to fondle her. Feeling doomed in romance due to being upstaged by her chest, Megan questions the seeming romantic possibilities that arise when her long-time crush, Jake Darrow, asks her out. Readers follow Megan as she weighs her romantic options in a novel *Booklist* reviewer Hazel Rochman praised as a "wry" story in which Perez conveys a "rare honesty about body image, romance, and sex." "Perez is an author worth watching," commented Susan Riley in *School Library Journal,* while a *Publishers Weekly* critic concluded that "Megan's appealing character will draw readers in, and will likely make the audience hope for more from this promising writer."

Biographical and Critical Sources

PERIODICALS

Booklist, November 15, 2004, Hazel Rochman, review of *Unexpected Development,* p. 598.
Bulletin of the Center for Children's Books, October, 2004, Deborah Stevenson, review of *Unexpected Development,* p. 95.
Journal of Adolescent & Adult Literacy, September, 2005, June Harris, review of *Unexpected Development,* p. 79.
Kirkus Reviews, September 1, 2004, review of *Unexpected Development,* p. 872.
Publishers Weekly, September 6, 2004, review of *Unexpected Development,* p. 64.
School Library Journal, October, 2004, Susan Riley, review of *Unexpected Development,* p. 175; November 25, 2005, Mary R. Hoffmann, review of *Unexpected Development,* p. 60.
Voice of Youth Advocates, December, 2004, review of *Unexpected Development,* p. 392.

ONLINE

BookLoons.com, http://www.bookloons.com/ (April 11, 2006), Ricki Marking-Camuto, review of *Bright Lights for Bella.*
Crescent Blues Online, http://www.crescentblues.com/ (April 11, 2006), Lynne Marie Pisano, review of *Unexpected Developments.*
Kidsreads.com, http://www.kidsreads.com/ (April 11, 2006), Paula Jolin, review of *Bright Lights for Bella.*
Marlene Perez Home Page, http://members.cox.net/mardperez (April 11, 2006).*

* * *

PLUME, Ilse

Personal

Born in Dresden, Germany; immigrated to United States. *Education:* Duke University, B.A., 1968, M.F.A., 1970; studied printmaking at Santa Reparata Studio, Florence, Italy.

Addresses

Home—MA. *Agent*—c/o Author Mail, David R. Godine, Publisher, 9 Hamilton Place, Boston, MA 02108-4715. *E-mail*—ilse@ilseplume.com.

Career

Reteller and illustrator of children's books. School for the Museum of Fine Arts, Boston, MA, art instructor; art teacher at schools, including Iowa State University, Minneapolis College of Art and Design, University of Minnesota, and University of Wisconsin—Eau Claire, c. 1970s. *Exhibitions:* Lincoln Public Library, Lincoln, MA; DeCordova Museum, Lincoln; and Federal Reserve Bank of Boston.

Awards, Honors

Caldecott Honor designation, 1980, for *The Bremen Town Musicians* and 2004, for *The Farmer in the Dell;* Ezra Jack Keats Award, 1985.

Writings

RETELLER; SELF-ILLUSTRATED

The Bremen Town Musicians, Doubleday (Garden City, NY), 1980, reprinted, 1998.
The Story of Befana: An Italian Christmas Tale, David R. Godine (Boston, MA), 1981.
The Shoemaker and the Elves, Harcourt Brace Jovanovich (San Diego, CA), 1991.
The Christmas Witch, Hyperion (New York, NY), 1991.
(And editor) *Lullaby and Goodnight: Songs and Poems for Babies,* HarperCollins (New York, NY), 1994.

ILLUSTRATOR

Margery Williams, *The Velveteen Rabbit; or, How Toys Become Real,* David R. Godine (Boston, MA), 1983.
Jane Langton, *The Hedgehog Boy: A Latvian Folktale,* Harper & Row (New York, NY), 1985.
Nancy Willard, *Night Story,* Harcourt Brace Jovanovich (San Diego, CA), 1986.

Cover of Ilse Plume's self-illustrated The Farmer in the Dell. (Text and illustrations copyright © 2004 by Ilse Plume. Reprinted by permission of David R. Godine, Publisher, Inc.)

Charlotte Zolotow, *Sleepy Book,* Harper & Row (New York, NY), 1988.
Twelve Days of Christmas, Harper & Row (New York, NY), 1990, reprinted, 2005.
Jane Langton, *Salt: From a Russian Folktale,* translated by Alice Plume, Hyperion (New York, NY), 1992.
Jane Langton, *The Queen's Necklace: A Swedish Folktale,* Hyperion (New York, NY), 1994.
The Farmer in the Dell, David R. Godine (Boston, MA), 2004.

Sidelights

Ilse Plume was born in Dresden, Germany, but her family immigrated to the United States when she was a child. Her love for drawing developed early in childhood and continued throughout her adolescent years. After spending time as an art instructor at various universities, Plume published her first self-illustrated book, *The Bremen Town Musicians.* A retelling of the fairy tale by the Brothers Grimm, the work was selected as a Caldecott Honor Book on the strength of Plume's artwork. Other books illustrated by Plume include the traditional stories *The Story of Befana: An Italian Christmas Tale* and *The Farmer in the Dell,* as well as original picture books by well-known writers Nancy Willard, Charlotte Zolotow, and Margery Williams. While not working on her own projects, Plume works as a fine-arts painter and teaches at schools in her native Massachusetts and elsewhere.

Plume's work accompanying *The Farmer in the Dell* was described as "delicate, colored-pencil illustrations" that give the traditional story "an old-fashioned feel," according to *School Library Journal* reviewer Robin L. Gibson. *Booklist* critic Ilene Cooper wrote of the same title that "Plume's colored-pencil artwork has a timeless quality and depth." With *The Twelve Days of Christmas* Plume "adds another outstanding accomplishment to her credit," according to a reviewer for *Publishers Weekly.*

Several titles featuring Plume's illustrations have accompanied Jane Langton's folk-story retellings, among them *The Hedgehog Boy: A Latvian Folktale, Salt: From a Russian Folktale,* and *The Queen's Necklace: A Swedish Folktale.* Of the illustrations in *Salt,* a *Publishers Weekly* contributor wrote that "Plume's richly patterned illustrations are filled with Russian folklore motifs and framed in decorative golden borders." *The Queen's Necklace* "features art that is airy and light in color," wrote *Booklist* reviewer Julie Corsaro.

Continuing to mine the rich vein of traditional children's literature, Plume collects songs and poetry in *Lullaby and Goodnight: Songs and Poems for Babies.* Most of the selections are well-known poems and songs, and include Johannes Brahms's classic "Lullaby" and the folk song "Kentucky Babe." Calling the book "nostalgic," a *Publishers Weekly* critic dubbed Plume's work "an old-fashioned Valentine to the very young."

Biographical and Critical Sources

PERIODICALS

Booklist, October 15, 1992, Carolyn Phelan, review of *Salt: From a Russian Folktale,* p. 434; October 1, 1994, Julie Corsaro, review of *The Queen's Necklace: A Swedish Folktale,* p. 327; September 15, 2004, Ilene Cooper, review of *The Farmer in the Dell,* p. 247.

Five Owls, November, 1991, review of *The Shoemaker and the Elves,* p. 34.

Kirkus Reviews, September 1, 2004, review of *The Farmer in the Dell,* p. 873.

Publishers Weekly, June 26, 1987, review of *The Bremen Town Musicians,* p. 75; June 10, 1988, Kimberly Olson Fakih and Diane Roback, review of *Sleepy Book,* p. 78; September 14, 1990, Diane Roback and Richard Donahue, review of *The Twelve Days of Christmas,* p. 123; September 21, 1992, review of *Salt,* p. 94; September 5, 1994, review of *Lullaby and Goodnight: Songs and Poems for Babies,* p. 111.

School Library Journal, December, 1988, Anna Biagioni Hart, review of *Sleepy Book,* p. 96; October, 1990, Susan Helper, review of *The Twelve Days of Christmas,* p. 40; January, 1992, Martha Rosen, review of *The Shoemaker and the Elves,* p. 102; December, 1992, Denise Anton Wright, review of *Salt,* p. 97; October, 1994, Sally R. Dow, review of *Lullaby and Goodnight,* p. 114; October, 1994, Donna L. Scanlon, review of *The Queen's Necklace,* p. 110; December, 2004, Robin L. Gibson, review of *The Farmer in the Dell,* p. 128.

ONLINE

Ilse Plume Home Page, http://www.ilseplume.com (April 8, 2006).*

R

REEVE, Philip

Personal
Born in Brighton, England; married; children: one son. *Hobbies and other interests:* Walking, drawing, writing, reading.

Addresses
Home—Devon, England. *Agent*—c/o Author Mail, Scholastic, Ltd., Euston House, 24 Eversholt St., London NW1 1DB, England.

Career
Illustrator, author, and bookseller. Children's book illustrator, 1994—. Producer and director of stage plays.

Awards, Honors
Whitbread Children's Book Award shortlist, and Gold Award, Nestlé Smarties Book Prize, both 2002, and Best Book of the Year designation, *Washington Post*, Best Book for Young Adults designation, American Library Association (ALA), and Blue Peter Book Award Book of the Year, all 2003, all for *Mortal Engines*; Best Book for Young Adults designation, ALA, and W.H. Smith People's Choice Award shortlist, 2004, for *Predator's Gold*.

Writings

(Self-illustrated) *Horatio Nelson and His Victory* ("Dead Famous" series), Hippo (London, England), 2003.
Larklight, Bloomsbury (New York, NY), 2006.

Coauthor, with Brian P. Mitchell, of musical *The Ministry of Biscuits*.

"HUNGRY CITY CHRONICLES" SERIES; YOUNG-ADULT SCIENCE FICTION

Mortal Engines, Scholastic (London, England), 2001, HarperCollins (New York, NY), 2003.
Predator's Gold, Eos (New York, NY), 2004.
Infernal Devices, Eos (New York, NY), 2006.
A Darkling Plan, Scholastic (London, England), 2006.

"BUSTER BAYLISS" SERIES; FOR CHILDREN

Night of the Living Veg, illustrated by Graham Philpot, Scholastic Children's Books (London, England), 2002.
The Big Freeze, illustrated by Graham Philpot, Scholastic Children's Books (London, England), 2002.
Day of the Hamster, illustrated by Graham Philpot, Scholastic Children's Books (London, England), 2002.
Custardfinger, illustrated by Graham Philpot, Scholastic Children's Books (London, England), 2003.

ILLUSTRATOR

Terry Deary, *Wicked Words* ("Horrible Histories" series), Andre Deutsch (London, England), 1996.
Terry Deary, *Dark Knights and Dingy Castles* ("Horrible Histories" series), Andre Deutsch (London, England), 1997.
Terry Deary, *The Angry Aztecs* ("Horrible Histories" series), Andre Deutsch (London, England), 1997, published with *The Incredible Incas,* 2001.
Chris D'Lacey, *Henry Spaloosh!,* Hippo (London, England), 1997.
Michael Cox, *Awful Art* ("The Knowledge" series), Hippo (London, England), 1997.
Michael Cox, *Mind-Blowing Music* ("The Knowledge" series), Hippo (London, England), 1997.
Peter Corey, *Coping with Love,* Hippo (London, England), 1997.
Michael Cox, *Smashin' Fashion* ("The Knowledge" series), Hippo (London, England), 1998.

Kjartan Poskitt, *More Murderous Maths,* Hippo (London, England), 1998.

Chris D'Lacey, *Snail Patrol,* Hippo (London, England), 1998.

Terry Deary and Barbara Allen, *Space Race* ("Spark Files" series), Faber (London, England), 1998.

Terry Deary and Barbara Allen, *Shock Tactics* ("Spark Files" series), Faber (London, England), 1998.

Terry Deary and Barbara Allen, *Chop and Change* ("Spark Files" series), Faber (London, England), 1998.

Terry Deary and Barbara Allen, *Bat and Bell* ("Spark Files" series), Faber (London, England), 1998.

Kjartan Poskitt, *Isaac Newton and His Apple* ("Dead Famous" series), Hippo (London, England), 1999.

Hayden Middleton, *Come and Have a Go if You Think You're Cool Enough!,* Hippo (London, England, 1999.

Hayden Middleton, *Come and Have a Go if You Think You're Mad Enough!,* Hippo (London, England), 1999.

Alan MacDonald, *Henry VIII and His Chopping Block,* Scholastic (London, England), 1999.

Alan MacDonald, *Al Capone and His Gang,* Scholastic (London, England), 1999.

Terry Deary, *Rowdy Revolutions* ("Horrible Histories" series), Scholastic (London, England), 1999.

Terry Deary and Barbara Allen, *Magical Magnets* ("Spark Files" series), Faber (London, England), 1999.

Margaret Simpson, *Cleopatra and Her Asp,* Hippo (London, England), 2000.

Alan MacDonald, *Oliver Cromwell and His Warts* ("Dead Famous" series), Hippo (London, England), 2000.

Terry Deary and Barbara Allen, *The Secrets of Science* ("Spark Files" series), Faber (London, England), 2000.

Margaret Simpson, *Elizabeth I and Her Conquests,* Hippo (London, England), 2001.

Margaret Simpson, *Mary, Queen of Scots and Her Hopeless Husbands,* Hippo (London, England), 2001.

Kjartan Poskitt, *Do You Feel Lucky?: The Secrets of Probability* ("Murderous Maths" series), Hippo (London, England), 2001.

Mike Goldsmith, *Albert Einstein and His Inflatable Universe* ("Dead Famous" series), Hippo (London, England), 2001.

Michael Cox, *Elvis and His Pelvis,* Hippo (London, England), 2001.

Phil Robins, *Joan of Arc and Her Marching Orders* ("Dead Famous" series), Scholastic (London, England), 2002.

Kjartan Poskitt, *Vicious Circles and Other Savage Shapes* ("Murderous Maths" series), Hippo (London, England), 2002.

Kjartan Poskitt, *Professor Fiendish's Book of Diabolical Brainbenders* ("Murderous Maths" series), Hippo (London, England), 2002.

Kjartan Poskitt, *Numbers: The Key to the Universe* ("Murderous Maths" series), Hippo (London, England), 2002.

Kjartan Poskitt, *Urgum the Axeman,* Scholastic (London, England), 2006.

Adaptations

The "Buster Bayliss" novels were adapted as audiobooks by Chivers Children's Audio Books, 2003. *Larklight* was scheduled to be adapted for a film, produced by Denise Di Novi, for Warner Brothers.

Sidelights

A former bookseller and a highly successful illustrator of children's books, Philip Reeve has earned fame and critical acclaim for his "Hungry City Chronicles" science-fiction series, which includes the novels *Mortal Engines, Predator's Gold, Infernal Devices,* and *A Darkling Plain.* Imaginative and clever, these novels have been compared to Philip Pullman's "His Dark Materials" trilogy, and have earned positive reviews as well as a large readership. In addition to his novels, as well as his humorous "Buster Bayliss" series for younger readers, Reeve is a popular cartoonist and illustrator who has contributed substantially to artwork for Terry Deary's popular "Horrible Histories" nonfiction series.

Mortal Engines takes place in a bleak time thousands of years in the future, "in which larger, faster cities literally gobble up the resources of smaller towns in order to feed the never-ending need for fuel," as Janice M. Del Negro explained in the *Bulletin of the Center for Children's Books.* In a mobile London, scavenger Thaddeus Valentine has discovered an ancient energy source that will enable his city to overwhelm the stationery but well-defended cities of Asia. When a horribly disfigured girl named Hester attempts to take Valentine's life, loyal young apprentice historian Tom Natsworthy saves his mentor. To Tom's surprise, instead of rewarding him, Valentine shoves both he and Hester down a waste chute and out of London. Learning several unpleasant truths about Valentine—including that the man killed Hester's parents—Tom joins the girl's quest for vengeance as the two set out across a landscape rife with pirates and slave traders in pursuit of east-bound London.

"The grimy yet fantastical post-apocalyptic setting; the narrow escapes, deepening loyalties, and not-infrequent bitter losses—all keep readers' attention riveted," commented Anita L. Burkam in a review of *Mortal Engines* for *Horn Book. Kliatt* reviewer Paula Rohrlick described Reeve's "wildly imaginative British tale" to be "full of marvelous details . . . humor, and grand adventures," and *Chronicle* contributor Don D'Ammassa found the book "well worth the time of readers of any age."

The second book in the "Hungry City Chronicles" series, *Predator's Gold* finds Tom and Hester in Anchorage, Alaska, a city that, like many in Reeve's futuristic world, moves from place to place, searching for comfortable climes and incorporating smaller cities that cross its path. Anchorage is now under the control of a pretty young woman named Freya, and when she recalls the town's history and the lush fields it once controlled in its original stationary site in the old continental United States, she decides to take Anchorage on the perilous journey back across the ice wastes. When Hester sees Tom kissing Freya, a jealous rage causes her to betray Anchorage's location to the predatory city of Arkangel. At the same time, a gang of baddies known as the Lost Boys are spying on the city and trying to kidnap Tom, while the Anti-Traction League seeks to destroy Anchorage with the help of a horrible cyborg. For *Horn Book* contributor Anita L. Burkam, "the technological wizardry" in *Predator's Gold* "will gratify young sci-fi gearheads, while the intense emotions drive the thrilling plot at top speed." In *Kliatt,* Rohrlick commended the author's "marvelous imagination and emotional depth, the sympathetic young protagonists, and the thrilling adventures," while *Booklist* contributor Sally Estes noted that, despite a complex plot and multiple characters, Reeve's story "is still easy to follow [and] gripping enough to leave readers anxious to find out what's to come."

Infernal Devices and *A Darkling Plain* finish up Reeve's "Hungry City Chronicles" saga featuring Tom and Hester. In *Infernal Devices* the two protagonists now have a daughter, and as a teen this girl is threatened by the same Lost Boys who once pursued her father. In the closing volume, the middle-aged Tom watches as Earth's population fractures into the competing Traction League and Green Storm; meanwhile, a powerful weapon created by humans prior to the apocalyptic war that destroyed the first human civilization hangs in the sky, poised to destroy everything. While commenting on the "fabulous streak of frivolity running through absolutely everything that Reeve writes," London *Guardian* contributor Josh Lacey added that the author also has a more serious side: "Municipal Darwinism. A perfect expression of the true nature of the world: that the fittest survive," as one character explains. While noting that the author's prose alternates between complex and "sparkling and witty," Lacey concluded that in the "Hungry City Chronicles" "Reeve has created an extraordinary imaginative achievement" that ends with a "cunning twist."

Biographical and Critical Sources

PERIODICALS

Booklist, November 1, 2003, Sally Estes, review of *Mortal Engines,* p. 491; August, 2004, Sally Estes, review of *Predator's Gold,* p. 1920.

Bookseller, August 10, 2001, Tara Stephenson, review of *Mortal Engines,* p. 33.

Bulletin of the Center for Children's Books, March, 2004, Janice M. Del Negro, review of *Mortal Engines,* p. 294; November, 2004, Timnah Card, review of *Predator's Gold,* p. 141.

Chronicle, January, 2004, Don D'Ammassa, review of *Mortal Engines,* p. 31.

Horn Book, November-December, 2003, Anita L. Burkam, review of *Mortal Engines,* p. 755; September-October, 2004, Anita L. Burkam, review of *Predator's Gold,* p. 596.

Guardian (London, England), April 8, 2006, Josh Lacey, review of *A Darkling Plain.*

Kirkus Reviews, October 15, 2003, review of *Mortal Engines,* p. 1275; August 15, 2004, review of *Predator's Gold,* p. 216.

Kliatt, November, 2003, Paula Rohrlick, review of *Mortal Engines,* p. 10; September, 2004, Paula Rohrlick, review of *Predator's Gold,* p. 16.

Magpies, May, 2002, review of *Mortal Engines,* p. 38; March, 2004, Rayma Turton, review of *Predator's Gold,* p. 43.

Publishers Weekly, October 27, 2003, review of *Mortal Engines,* p. 70; August 16, 2004, review of *Predator's Gold,* p. 64.

School Librarian, winter, 2001, review of *Mortal Engines,* p. 214; winter, 2002, review of *Night of the Living Veg,* p. 202; spring, 2004, Michael Holloway, review of *Predator's Gold,* p. 34.

School Library Journal, December, 2003, Sharon Rawlins, review of *Mortal Engines,* p. 864; September, 2004, Sharon Rawlins, review of *Predator's Gold,* p. 216.

Tribune Books (Chicago, IL), November 23, 2003, review of *Mortal Engines,* p. 4.

Voice of Youth Advocates, October, 2004, Sarah Flowers, review of *Predator's Gold,* p. 318.

ONLINE

British Broadcasting Corporation Web site, http://www.bbc.co.uk/ (September 29, 2004), interview with Reeve.

ContemporaryWriters.com, http://www.contemporarywriters.com/ (September 29, 2004), "Philip Reeve."

Philip Reeve Home Page, http://www.philipreeve.co.uk (April 29, 2006).*

* * *

RICHARDS, Chuck 1957-

Personal

Born 1957; children: one son, one daughter. *Education:* University of Illinois, Urbana-Champaign, B.F.A., 1979; University of Wisconsin, Madison, M.F.A., 1983.

Addresses

Home—Ames, IA. *Office*—Iowa State University, Art and Design Department, 158 College of Design, Ames, IA 50011. *E-mail*—chuckrichards11@mchsi.com.

Career

Educator, illustrator, and author. Teacher of art at colleges and art schools beginning c. 1983; Iowa State University, Ames, associate professor of art and design.

When Dad's creativity goes too far, Jerry's backyard playscape turns terrifying in Chuck Richards' self-illustrated Jungle Gym Jitters. (Text and illustrations copyright © 2004 by Chuck Richards. Published by Walker & Company. Reproduced by permission.)

Writings

(Self-illustrated) *Jungle Gym Jitters*, Walker & Co. (New York, NY), 2004.
(Illustrator) Robin Pulver, *Author Day for Room 3T*, Clarion Books (New York, NY), 2005.

Sidelights

After working as an art teacher for over two decades, illustrator Chuck Richards made his publishing debut with *Jungle Gym Jitters*, a picture book for children about the evolution of a simple backyard playscape into something almost scary. Inspired by cartoon artists such as Basil Wolverton of *Mad* magazine fame, Richards creates what a *Publishers Weekly* contributor described as "extraordinarily crafted drawings" that reveal hidden elements upon close examination. Noting that it took Richards five years to create the artwork for *Jungle Gym Jitters*, *New York Times Book Review* contributor David Small wrote that the illustrator's "fanatic, careful, obsessive art-making" results in a book that is "lively and spontaneous, page after exuberant page." In addition to his original story, the author/illustrator has also created art for Robin Pulver's *Author Day for Room 3T*.

Featuring a rhyming text, *Jungle Gym Jitters* focuses on the plight of Jerry J. Jingle, a boy whose dad, George Jingle, decides to build the best backyard jungle gym ever. As George sets to work to make his son's dreams come true, only the best will do. He follows jungle gym plans to a T and his efforts result in a sturdy but commonplace construction. Determined to create something special, the man begins rebuilding parts of his invention incorporating a mechanical silver loop-de-loop, a seesaw, jungle-creature decorations, and even live animals. Richards' colored-pencil illustrations, done on grey paper, follow the project of the compulsive builder and depict the huge celebration held after George's creation is complete, with children and grown-ups alike amazed by the awe-inspiring contraption. A *Kirkus Reviews* critic commented that "children will pore delightedly over the teeming artwork" and added that Jerry's "playful, painfully competent" dad provides a "refreshing change of pace" from the typical picture-book father. Richards' illustrations were widely praised, Wendy Lukehart commenting in *School Library Journal* that the author/illustrator's "surreal scenes . . . are reminiscent of Chris Van Allsburg's work in *Jumanji*," and another *Publishers Weekly* contributor deemed the volume a "spectacularly illustrated, over-the-top tale." Richards' images in *Jungle Gym Jitters* are "more crowded and frenetic," Lukehart added, "but the extreme perspectives, retro setting, and monochromatic tones" will fascinate young readers. In *Booklist*, Ilene Cooper cited the illustrator's "incredible eye for detail."

Biographical and Critical Sources

PERIODICALS

Booklist, November 1, 2004, Ilene Cooper, review of *Jungle Gym Jitters*, p. 493.
Kirkus Reviews, September 15, 2004, review of *Jungle Gym Jitters*, p. 919.
New York Times Book Review, April 10, 2005, David Small, review of *Jungle Gym Jitters.*
Publishers Weekly, September 20, 2004, review of *Jungle Gym Jitters*, p. 61; December 20, 2004, "Flying Starts," pp. 30-34.
School Library Journal, October, 2004, Wendy Lukehart, review of *Jungle Gym Jitters*, p. 128.

ONLINE

Chuck Richards Home Page, http://www.chuckrichards.us (April 11, 2006).
Iowa State University Web site, http://www.design.iastate.edu/ (April 11, 2006), "Chuck Richards."

* * *

ROCHE, Luane 1937-

Personal

Born February 12, 1937, in Wilkes Barre, PA; daughter of Stanley Louise (a supervisor for Western News Company) and Marguerite Monica (a homemaker; maiden name, Schulte) Hattler; married Francis Joseph Roche (a manager for Alnor Inc.) April 11, 1964 (deceased); children: John, Michael. *Education:* Sacred Heart Junior College, A.A., 1958; Mercy School of Nursing, graduated, 1958. *Politics:* Republican. *Religion:* Roman Catholic. *Hobbies and other interests:* Baking, cooking, canning, puzzling, gardening, crocheting, reading.

Addresses

Home—1080 Lancaster Court, Hoffman Estates, IL 60169. *Agent*—c/o Author Mail, Liguori Publications, One Liguori Dr., Liguori, MO 63057-9999.

Career

St. Anne's Hospital, Chicago, IL, surgical floor nurse, 1958-59; Swedish Covenant Hospital, Chicago, IL, assistant supervisor, 1959-66; St. Thomas Hospital School of Nursing, Akron, OH, operating room and clinical instructor, 1962-63; St. Hubert Elementary School, Hoffman Estates, IL, fifth-grade teacher, 1967; Churchill Elementary School, Schaumburg, IL, fourth through sixth-grade S.T.E.P. teacher's aide, 1981-83; writer.

Awards, Honors

Bishop Walter's Medal for Religion, American Poetry Society, 1955, for poem "The Beloved Master"; Angel Award, 1980, for *The Proud Tree*.

Writings

The Proud Tree, illustrated by Jim Corbett, Liguori Publications (Liguori, MO), 1981.
The Promise, illustrated by Chris Sharp, Liguori Publications (Liguori, MO), 1996.

Sidelights

Luane Roche told *SATA:* "One day, in the 1970s I was busy washing clothes in the laundry room and talking to the Lord about the fact that there were no religious children's books that told the story of the passion of Christ. I thought about the cross especially. It was once a beautiful tree—what a humiliating ending. The story played out in my mind. I wrote it down. The name of the story had to be *The Proud Tree*.

"Eventually, the book, winner of an Angel Award, took off and became an English and Spanish video. I always felt a less-expensive Spanish soft-cover edition would have sold much better. Later a colored edition in a trade book came out also.

"Although *The Proud Tree* is geared for young school children, I learned a good story has no age limits: a four year old refused to go to sleep until the story was read; an 81-year-old woman used it to get into the spirit of Lent, as did a church community of adults in Wisconsin; and a fourth-grade class used the book as a script to put on a Lenten play with costumes, posters, and music.

"My goal was to convey a message, to teach children in a way they could relate to without their being frightened. I hoped they might be open to incorporating into their young lives some of the values and lessons they learned from the story. I believe I did that with *The Proud Tree* and *The Promise,* the sequel that was published in 1995. It has been a fun and rewarding experience."

Biographical and Critical Sources

ONLINE

Ligouri Speakers Bureau Web site, http://mission.liguori.org/ (April 11, 2006).
St. Veronica Catholic Church and School Bulletin Online, http://www.stveronica.net/ (June 15, 2006), review of *The Proud Tree*.

* * *

ROMANO, Ray 1957-
(Raymond Romano)

Personal

Born December 21, 1957, in New York, NY; son of Albert (a civil engineer and real estate broker) and Lucie (a piano teacher) Romano; married Anna Scarpulla, 1986; children: Alexandra, Matthew and Gregory (twins), Joseph. *Education:* Attended Queens College.

Addresses

Office—c/o Talk Productions, Warner Bros. Studios, Warner Blvd., Burbank, CA 91522.

Career

Comedian and actor. During early career, worked variously as a gas station attendant, bank clerk, and truck driver. Stand-up comedian; wrote, produced, and played Ray Barone in television series *Everybody Loves Raymond,* Columbia Broadcasting System (CBS), 1996-2005. Actor in films, including *El anima de sayula,* 1982; (as voice of Manfred the Mammoth) *Ice Age* (animated), Twentieth Century-Fox, 2002; (as himself) *Comedian,* 2002; (as himself) *Bitter Jester,* 2003; *Eulogy,* 2003; and (as Handy Harrison) *Welcome to Mooseport,* 2004. Has appeared in numerous television specials (as himself unless otherwise noted), including *15th Annual*

Young Comedians Show, Home Box Office (HBO), 1992; (as host) Night of about 14 CBS Stars (also known as CBS Fall Preview), Comedy Central, 1996; Catch a Rising Star 50th Anniversary—Give or Take 26 Years, CBS, 1996; HBO Comedy Half-Hour: Ray Romano, HBO, 1996; CBS: The First 50 Years, CBS, 1998; (as Ray Barone) The 51st Annual Primetime Emmy Awards, 1999; America: A Tribute to Heroes, 2001; Diet Coke with Lemon Celebrates 40 Years of Laughter: At the Improv, 2002; The 54th Annual Primetime Emmy Awards, 2002; and A&E Biography: Peter Boyle, 2003. Guest on episodes of television series, including Tonight Show Starring Johnny Carson, National Broadcasting Company (NBC), 1991; Late Show with David Letterman, CBS, 1994; Full Frontal Comedy, Showtime, 1995; Late Late Show with Craig Kilborn, CBS, 1999, 2000; Saturday Night Live, NBC, 1999, 2003; The Martin Short Show, 1999; (as celebrity contestant) Who Wants to Be a Millionaire?, American Broadcasting Companies (ABC), 2000; Rove Live, Ten Network, 2001; SportsCenter, 2002; Sesame Street, Public Broadcasting System (PBS); E! Stand up, Sit down Comedy, E! Entertainment Television; An Evening at the Improv, Arts and Entertainment (A&E); Hollywood Squares, syndicated; Late Night with Conan O'Brien, NBC; MTV Half-Hour Comedy Hour, Music Television (MTV); Showtime Comedy Club Network, Showtime; and The Tonight Show with Jay Leno, NBC.

Guest on television-show episodes as Ray Barone, including "Lucas Raymondicus," Cosby, CBS, 1997; "The Reunion Show," The Nanny, CBS, 1998; and "Road Rayge," The King of Queens, CBS, 1999. Voice in episodes of animated series Dr. Katz: Professional Therapist, 1995-96.

Awards, Honors

First prize, K-Rock Miller Light Comedy Riot, 1989; named best new television actor, Entertainment Weekly, 1996; ranked top-ten television show, Entertainment Weekly, and Time, both 1997; favorite male television performer, People's Choice Awards, 1999; outstanding individual achievement in comedy, Television Critics Association, 1999; named favorite actor in a comedy, TV Guide, 1999; Emmy Award for outstanding lead actor in a comedy, National Academy of Television Arts and Sciences, 2000; voted funniest male lead in a television series, American Comedy Awards, 2000; best comedy and best actor awards, Viewers for Quality Television Awards, 2000; named actor of the year in a comedy series, TV Guide, 2001; voted best male television performer, People's Choice Awards, 2004.

Writings

Everything and a Kite: A Book of Comic Observations, Bantam (New York, NY), 1998.

(With Phil Rosenthal) Everybody Loves Raymond: Our Family Album, photographs by Tom Caltabiano, foreword by Norman Lear, interviews by Heather Havrilesky, Pocket Books (New York, NY), 2004.

(With brothers, Richard and Robert Romano) Raymie, Dickie, and the Bean: Why I Love and Hate My Brothers (for children; includes CD-ROM), Simon & Schuster Books for Young Readers (New York, NY), 2005.

Also author of episodes for television series Everybody Loves Raymond, CBS, 1996-2005, and Dr. Katz: Professional Therapist, Comedy Central.

Adaptations

Everything and a Kite was adapted for audio (unabridged; four CDs), Simon & Schuster, 1998.

Sidelights

In 2003 actor and comedian Ray Romano became the highest-paid star on television when he signed a forty-million-dollar contract with Columbia Broadcasting System (CBS) for the eighth season of his top-rated sitcom, Everybody Loves Raymond, which Romano also wrote and produced. Based on Romano's own family life and his stand-up comedy routines, the show stars Romano as Ray Barone, a sports journalist who lives on Long Island with his wife and children in a house that is across the street from his prying parents and miserable, divorced brother.

Like his character, Romano has a daughter, twin sons, and a brother who is a New York City police officer. Until he was twenty-nine, Romano lived in the basement of his parents' Queens home, sharing space with a water heater that has since been memorialized in his stand-up routines. During those years, Romano worked at a variety of daytime jobs. He quit one as a gas station attendant after the second time he was robbed at gunpoint. He met his wife, Anna, while working as a bank teller (she was also a teller), and he delivered futons. Later in the day, he performed his stand-up comedy routine, sometimes as many as seven times in one night. Romano and Anna lived in Queens until they moved to the Los Angeles area during the last years of the show.

Romano got his big break when he appeared on David Letterman's late-night talk show in 1995. Letterman's production company was impressed with the young comedian and offered him his own show, which first aired in the fall of 1996. At first languishing in its ratings, it later took off when it was moved from its Friday night slot to Monday, where it continued successfully for nine seasons until the final episode aired in 2005.

Romano has also published several books, including Everything and a Kite: A Book of Comic Observations, which is based on his comedy routines. His riffs on the little annoyances of life, especially married life, have been favorably compared to the comedy of such famous stand-up comics as Jerry Seinfeld, Paul Reiser, and Bill Cosby. A *Publishers Weekly* contributor wrote that Romano "can mine the family/kids/guyhood comedy lode with the best of 'em." In 2005, Romano released *Raymie, Dickie, and the Bean: Why I Love and Hate My Brothers*, a picture book for children based on his childhood relationship with his own brothers. A *Publishers Weekly* reviewer called the story, set in an amusement park, "funny and warm."

Biographical and Critical Sources

BOOKS

Contemporary Theatre, Film, and Television, Volume 17, Thomson Gale (Detroit, MI), 1997.
Newsmakers, Issue 4, Thomson Gale (Detroit, MI), 2001.

PERIODICALS

Broadcasting & Cable, December 7, 1998, Joe Schlosser, "Why CBS Loves 'Raymond,'" p. 42.
Daily Variety, May 12, 2003, Josef Adalian, "Pay Day for Ray: CBS Loves 'Raymond' to Tune of $40 mil," p. 1.
Entertainment Weekly, December 13, 1996, Bret Watson, "Ray Romano," p. 34; April 11, 1997, Bruce Fretts, "Everybody Loves Raymond," p. 67; November 28, 1997, Bruce Fretts, "Everything's Relative," p. 44; September 15, 2000, Bruce Fretts, "Amore the Merrier: Living la Dolce Vita, Ray Romano and the Everybody Loves Raymond Gang Invade Italy for a Bellissimo Season Opener," p. 34; November 29, 2002, Dalton Ross, "Pass the Romano Cheese: The 'Everybody Loves Raymond' Star Cools off with Some Mini-Mammoth-size Stupid Questions" (interview), p. 84.
Esquire, May, 2003, Scott Raab, "Sing a Song of Ray Romano" (interview), p. 120.
In Style, December, 1998, "The Host with the Most: What's that Old Joke—Guests and Fish Overstay Their Welcome after Three Days?," p. 321; November 1, 2002, Lisa Arbetter, "Romano Empire," p. 478.
Kirkus Reviews, March 1, 2005, review of *Raymie, Dickie, and the Bean: Why I Love and Hate My Brothers*, p. 294.
Knight Ridder/Tribune News Service, September 12, 1996, Steve Hall, "Standup Comedian Ray Romano Waiting to See If Everybody Loves 'Raymond,'" p. 912K2655; June 10, 2003, Rebecca Louie, "To His Old Pals, TV's Highest-paid Star Is Just Ray from Queens," p. K1647.
People, February 21, 2000, "Pop Quiz with Ray Romano," p. 21.
Publishers Weekly, October 19, 1998, review of *Everything and a Kite: A Book of Comic Observations*, p. 62; February 28, 2005, review of *Raymie, Dickie, and the Bean*, p. 65.

Time, June 14, 1999, "Ray Romano," p. 241.

ONLINE

Hollywood.com, http://www.hollywood.com/ (July 26, 2003), "Ray Romano."
Internet Movie Database, http://us.imdb.com/ (July 8, 2003), "Ray Romano."
Jam! Online, http://jam.canoe.ca/ (April 27, 2005), Samantha Critchell, review of *Raymie, Dickie, and the Bean*.
Official Web Site of Ray Romano, http://www.rayromano.com (June 14, 2005).*

* * *

ROMANO, Raymond
See ROMANO, Ray

* * *

ROSS, Michael Elsohn 1952-

Personal

Born June 30, 1952, in Utica, NY; son of William L. (in business) and Jeanne E. (a homemaker and artist) Ross; married Lisa L. Rhudy (a registered nurse), July 16, 1977; children: Nick F. *Education:* Attended University of California—Irvine, 1970-71; University of California—Berkeley, B.S., 1974; California State University—Fresno, teaching credential, 1981. *Politics:* "Green." *Religion:* "Pantheist." *Hobbies and other interests:* Gardening, bird watching, botany, cross-country skiing/hiking/backpacking, Breema bodywork.

Addresses

Home and office—P.O. Box 295, El Portal, CA 95318. *E-mail*—meross@inreach.com.

Career

Children's author and naturalist. National Park Service, Yosemite National Park, CA, ranger, 1976-77; Yosemite Association, Yosemite National Park, naturalist, 1977—; educational director, Yosemite Guides, 1999—. Mariposa County Schools, Mariposa, CA, teacher, 1981-84; Life Lab Science Program, Santa Cruz, CA, curriculum developer, 1988-92. Merced Canyon Committee, vice president, 1985-86; El Portal Child Development Center, chair, 1990-91. Member, Children's Literature Council of Southern California.

Member

Society of Children's Book Writers and Illustrators, Authors Guild, Sierra Club, Nature Conservancy, California Native Plant Society.

Michael Elsohn Ross (Photograph reproduced by permission.)

Awards, Honors

Outstanding publication citation, U.S. National Park Service, 1988, for *Yosemite Fun Book;* first place, National Park Service Publications Competition, and honorable mention, American Association of Museums Publications, both 1994, both for *The World of Small;* Notable Children's Book selection, *Smithsonian* magazine, 1995, for *Sandbox Scientist;* first place, National Park Service Publications Competition, and honorable mention, American Association of Museums Publications, both 1996, both for *The Happy Camper Handbook;* Young Readers Award, *Scientific American,* 1996, for *Cricketology;* Best of the Best citation, Chicago Public Library, 1996, for *Rolypolyology;* California Arts Council writers fellowship, 1997; honorable mention, National Park Service Publications Competition, 1998, for *A Kid's Golden Gate!;* Outstanding Science Trade Books for Children, National Council of Science Teachers/Children's Book Council, 1998, for *Bird Watching with Margaret Morse Nice,* and 2001, for *Pond Watching with Ann Morgan* and *Exploring the Earth with John Wesley Powell;* Eureka book list, California State Library Association, 2001, for *Nature Art with Chiura Obata;* Best Books for Children citations, *Science Books and Films,* all 1998, for *Bird Watching with Margaret Morse Nice, Wildlife Watching with Charles Eastman, Flower Watching with Alice Eastwood, Bug Watching with Charles Henry Turner, Caterpillarology,* and *Ladybugology,* 2002, for *Cricketology* and *Rolypolyology,* and 2003, for *Kitchen Lab* and *Indoor Zoo;* Honor List citation, *Voice of Youth Advocates,* 2000, for *Children of Northern Ireland;* Young-Adult Top-Forty listee, Pennsylvania School Librarians, 2000, for *Pond Watching with Ann Morgan;* California Reader's List California Collection, 2000, for *Wormology* and 2003-04, for *Wormology* and *Millipedeology;* Best Books of the Year selection, Bank Street College, 2001, for *Pond Watching with Ann Morgan, Millipedeology,* and *Spiderology,* and 2003, for *A Mexican Christmas;* Independent Publisher Award finalist for best multicultural nonfiction title, 2003, for *A Mexican Christmas;* Arizona Young Reader's Award in Nonfiction nomination, 2007, for *What's the Matter in Mr. Whisker's Room?*

Writings

Cycles, Cycles, Cycles, Yosemite Association (El Portal, CA), 1979.

What Makes Everything Go?, Yosemite Association (El Portal, CA), 1979.

(With David Gaines and Becky Shearin) *Mono Lake Color and Learn Book,* Mono Lake Comm., 1981.

(Illustrator) Deborah Durkes, *Easy Day Hikes in Yosemite,* Yosemite Association (El Portal, CA), 1985.

Faces in All Kinds of Places, Yosemite Association (El Portal, CA), 1986.

The Yosemite Fun Book, Yosemite Association (El Portal, CA), 1987.

Become a Bird and Fly!, illustrated by Peter Parnall, Millbrook Press (Brookfield, CT), 1992.

The World of Small: Exploration with a Hand Lens, illustrated by Cary Michael Trout, Yosemite Association (El Portal, CA), 1993.

The Happy Camper Handbook (activity guide with flashlight and whistle), Yosemite Association (El Portal, CA), 1994.

Sandbox Scientist: Real Science Activities for Little Kids, illustrated by Mary Anne Lloyd, Chicago Review (Chicago, IL), 1996.

Cricketology ("Backyard Buddies" series), illustrations by Darren Erickson, Carolrhoda Books (Minneapolis, MN), 1996.

Rolypolyology ("Backyard Buddies" series), illustrated by Darren Erickson, Carolrhoda Books (Minneapolis, MN), 1996.

Snailology ("Backyard Buddies" series), illustrated by Darren Erickson, Carolrhoda Books (Minneapolis, MN), 1996.

Wormology ("Backyard Buddies" series), illustrated by Darren Erickson, Carolrhoda Books (Minneapolis, MN), 1996.

Caterpillarology ("Backyard Buddies" series), illustrations by Darren Erickson, Carolrhoda Books (Minneapolis, MN), 1997.

Ladybugology ("Backyard Buddies" series), illustrations by Darren Erickson, Carolrhoda Books (Minneapolis, MN), 1997.

Bird Watching with Margaret Morse Nice ("Naturalist's Apprentice" series), illustrations by Laurie A. Caple, Carolrhoda Books (Minneapolis, MN), 1997.
Bug Watching with Charles Henry Turner ("Naturalist's Apprentice" series), illustrations by Laurie A. Caple, Carolrhoda Books (Minneapolis, MN), 1997.
Wildlife Watching with Charles Eastman ("Naturalist's Apprentice" series), illustrations by Laurie A. Caple, Carolrhoda Books (Minneapolis, MN), 1997.
Flower Watching with Alice Eastwood ("Naturalist's Apprentice" series), illustrations by Laurie A. Caple, Carolrhoda Books (Minneapolis, MN), 1997.
A Kid's Golden Gate!: Guide to Family Adventures in the National Parks at the Golden Gate, illustrated by Scott Ramsey, Golden Gate National Parks Association (San Francisco, CA), 1997.
Fish Watching with Eugenie Clark ("Naturalist's Apprentice" series), illustrations by Wendy Smith, Carolrhoda Books (Minneapolis, MN), 2000.
Millipedeology ("Backyard Buddies" series), illustrated by Darren Erickson, Carolrhoda Books (Minneapolis, MN), 2000.
Spiderology ("Backyard Buddies" series), illustrated by Darren Erickson, Carolrhoda Books (Minneapolis, MN), 2000.
Nature Art with Chiura Obata ("Naturalist's Apprentice" series), illustrated by Wendy Smith, Carolrhoda Books (Minneapolis, MN), 2000.
Pond Watching with Ann Morgan ("Naturalist's Apprentice" series), illustrated by Wendy Smith, Carolrhoda Books (Minneapolis, MN), 2000.
Exploring the Earth with John Wesley Powell ("Naturalist's Apprentice" series), illustrated by Wendy Smith, Carolrhoda Books (Minneapolis, MN), 2000.
Children of Northern Ireland ("World's Children" series), photographs by Felix Rigau, Carolrhoda Books (Minneapolis, MN), 2001.
Earth Cycles, illustrated by Gustav Moore, Millbrook Press (Brookfield, CT), 2001.
Life Cycles, illustrated by Gustav Moore, Millbrook Press (Brookfield, CT), 2001.
Children of Ireland ("World's Children" series), photographs by Felix Rigau, Carolrhoda Books (Minneapolis, MN), 2002.
Children of Puerto Rico ("World's Children" series), photographs by Felix Rigau, Carolrhoda Books (Minneapolis, MN), 2002.
Body Cycles, illustrated by Gustav Moore, Millbrook Press (Brookfield, CT), 2002.
Re-cycles, illustrated by Gustav Moore, Millbrook Press (Brookfield, CT), 2002.
Mexican Christmas, photographs by Felix Rigau, Carolrhoda Books (Minneapolis, MN), 2002.
Toy Lab ("You're the Scientist" series), illustrated by Tim Seeley, Carolrhoda Books (Minneapolis, MN), 2002.
Junk Lab ("You're the Scientist" series), illustrated by Tim Seeley, Carolrhoda Books (Minneapolis, MN), 2002.
Kitchen Lab ("You're the Scientist" series), illustrated by Tim Seeley, Carolrhoda Books (Minneapolis, MN), 2002.
Indoor Zoo ("You're the Scientist" series), illustrated by Tim Seeley, Carolrhoda Books (Minneapolis, MN), 2003.
Salvador Dali and the Surrealists for Kids, Chicago Review Press (Chicago, IL), 2003.
Snug as a Bug, illustrated by Sylvia Long, Chronicle (San Francisco, CA), 2004.
What's the Matter in Mr. Whisker's Room?, illustrated by Paul Meisel, Candlewick Press (Cambridge, MA), 2004.
Baby Bear Isn't Hungry, illustrated by Connie Powell, Yosemite Association (El Portal, CA), 2006.
Mama's Milk, illustrated by Ashley Wolff, Tricycle Press (Berkeley, CA), 2007.

Also principal author and developer of science-teacher activity guides *Great Explorations, Earth Is Home,* and *Changes around Us,* published by Videodiscovery, 1992.

Sidelights

Michael Elsohn Ross is the author of dozens of books for young readers, most with an emphasis on nature and science. Ross is known for his engaging style and obvious enthusiasm for all aspects of the natural world. In addition to stand-alone titles such as *Snug as a Bug, Baby Bear Isn't Hungry,* and *What's the Matter in Mr. Whisker's Room?,* he has contributed to several book series, including the "World's Children" books, which help inform young readers about their contemporaries elsewhere in the world, from Northern Ireland to Puerto Rico. In a series of books dealing with natural cycles, Ross introduces readers to the many rhythms to be found in nature, while the "You're the Scientist" books provide a creative outlet for budding experimenters.

Born in Utica, New York, in 1952, Ross grew up dreaming of becoming a cartoonist or artist. "During my youth in Huntington, New York," the author once commented, "the countless hours I spent browsing *New Yorker* cartoons seriously molded my impressionable mind. By the time I was ten I was drawing my own cartoons. I thought for sure that I was headed for a career in art, but I was sidetracked when I attended University of California—Berkeley, and became intrigued by, of all things, bugs! I got a degree in conservation of natural resources with an emphasis in entomology and environmental education." Graduating with honors and going on to earn his teaching credential, Ross pursued his love of nature, which led him to work as a ranger in Yosemite National Park for a time. Then he went into the classroom and worked developing curricula for a number of years before leaving to write full time; he was inspired to do so by seeing the voids in many science subject areas.

"Nobody had ever written a kid's book about cycles," Ross once commented. "Each day, each year, each breath is a cycle. Without these circular patterns life would cease. I had been teaching five-to eighteen year olds about cycles for several years. They enjoyed learning about life cycles, water cycles, and nutrient cycles, but they only knew about cycles because I was their teacher. What would happen if I wasn't there? There wasn't a book to take my place, so when a friend encouraged me to write one, I got out my pen and started writing and illustrating *Cycles, Cycles, Cycles.* My employer, the Yosemite Association, a nonprofit publisher and educational organization, was anxious to publish it. It took only a month and a half to complete the book, and after [many] years it is still selling and doing its job of teaching kids about cycles."

Ross's writing soon led him into nature studies in general. His fanciful picture book *Become a Bird and Fly!* follows the adventures of young Nicky, who loves to watch birds and wants to try flying for himself. Nicky, with the help of a neighbor, slowly turns into a pelican, soaring in the wind. When he awakes from this pleasant dream he is simply a boy again, but in his hand he holds a feather. Jim Jeske, writing in *Booklist,* felt that author Ross and illustrator Peter Parnall have created "an enchanting story." The author meets his goal of creating a book to help youngsters prepare for a productive outdoor experience in *The Happy Camper Handbook.* A contributor to the *Los Angeles Times Book Review* felt that this work serves as a "nice guide for campers of all ages," and is "sturdy and small enough to carry in a backpack." Covering topics from equipment to clothing, and from setting up camp to map reading, Ross's book also includes a flashlight and rescue whistle.

Other picture books by Ross that contain science facts couched in an entertaining story include *Snug as a Bug* and *What's the Matter in Mr. Whiskers' Room?* Curling up for the night is the focus of the first title, in which Ross shows how everything from bugs to slugs to bumblebees take their daily rest. In *Kirkus Reviews* a critic praised the author's "whimsical rhyming couplets" as well as the "lush watercolor illustrations" by Sylvia Long, and predicted that young children will "connect with the [book's] homey, comforting theme." An inspiring teacher who encourages his eight students in hands-on study is the focus of *What's the Matter in Mr. Whiskers' Room?* Reflecting current educational standards in science, Mr. Whiskers arranges his lessons around seven science centers, each of which present an interesting experiment that reveals an important scientific concept. Praising the author for including information on how adults can set up similar learning experiences, the book was cited by *School Library Journal* critic Sandra Welzenbach for "encouraging students to learn through interacting with one another as well as with adults" as part of the learning process.

In *Sandbox Scientist: Real Science Activities for Little Kids* Ross provides a wealth of hands-on activities for budding scientists. *Booklist* reviewer Carolyn Phelan concluded that "preschool and primary-grade teachers and parents will find this an upbeat, practical guide to science activities for young children." Another hands-on title, *Toy Lab* uses Silly Putty, Slinkies, and building blocks to illustrate basic physics concepts, such as gravity and waves, in a manner that will "pique youngsters' interest," in the opinion of *School Library Journal* reviewer Peg Glisson. In *The World of Small: Exploration with a Hand Lens* Ross presents an introduction to the world of the miniscule by the use of a hand-held lens, one of which is included with the book. Reviewing the title for *Publishers Weekly,* a contributor called the book an "ingenious package" and praised Ross for his use of "humorous language and oddball perspectives." The same reviewer concluded that *The World of Small* is a "source of entertainment and reference that could keep some enthusiasts busy for years." J. Baldwin, writing in the *Whole Earth Review,* dubbed the book "irresistible" and the "perfect gift for a kid you like."

In the eight titles in the "Backyard Buddies" series, Ross introduces readers to insects and invertebrates from snails to ladybugs, and from caterpillars to millipedes, all in a user-friendly and light manner. Reviewing *Cricketology* and *Snailology* in *School Library Journal,* Karey Wehner found the series installments to emphasize "hands-on learning," with each title describing how to collect, house, and care for the animal in question. These simple guides also explain observation techniques for the backyard naturalist, as well as the behavior and life cycle of each creature. *Caterpillarology* and *Ladybugology* "encourage kids to observe and inquire into the lives of our most commonly found creatures," remarked Arwen Marshall in a *School Library Journal* review of the two titles. Marshall also noted that what sets these books apart is the author's "aim to foster children's natural curiosity and get them to think about the world around them." *Booklist* reviewer Susan Dove Lempke noted that in *Caterpillarology* and *Ladybugology,* "Ross conveys the pleasure and fascination of studying one creature carefully," and that he also includes "semihumorous tips for convincing parents to accept critters in the house." A *Kirkus Reviews* contributor commented that in *Ladybugology* Ross "includes some good facts about ladybugs and their care, defining their scientific names and covering some ladybug lore." In a review of *Millipedeology* and *Spiderology,* Patricia Manning noted in *School Library Journal* that these books "will be enthusiastically received by students and teachers alike."

Ross has contributed many titles to the ongoing series "Naturalist's Apprentice," which feature books about naturalists and their fields of study. Part biography and part field guide, the titles in this series deal with birds, beasts, bugs, and plants. Many of the naturalists featured are members of minority groups, allowing Ross to

Part of the "Backyard Buddies" series, Ross's Caterpillarology *is an enticing guide for budding etymologists that suggests basic experiments and presents a wealth of facts.* (Text copyright © 1997 by Michael Elshohn Ross. Photograph copyright © 1997 by Brian Grogan. Published by Carolrhoda Books. Reproduced by permission.)

address social themes as well as scientific ones in his text. "Ross takes an innovative approach to biography, using the lives of these pioneering naturalists as a framework on which to hang an introduction to nature study," wrote Ruth S. Vose in a *School Library Journal* review of both *Bird Watching with Margaret Morse Nice* and *Wildlife Watching with Charles Eastman*. While Nice grew up at the turn of the twentieth century, a time when women generally stayed in the home rather than pursuing careers, she nonetheless managed to combine child rearing with her passion for bird watching and making a detailed study of bird behavior. Likewise, Charles Eastman, born into the Dakota Nation, became a physician and ardent nature lover. Writing in *School Library Journal*, Frances E. Millhouser called Ross's *Pond Watching with Ann Morgan* a "unique combination for biography and natural history," while Patricia Manning, also writing in *School Library Journal*, deemed *Fish Watching with Eugenie Clark* a "sparkling addition to a lively series."

African-American zoologist Charles Henry Turner and self-trained female botanist Alice Eastwood are featured in two other "Naturalist's Apprentice" installments, *Bug Watching with Charles Henry Turner* and *Flower Watching with Alice Eastwood*. Reviewing both titles in *Booklist*, Phelan concluded that "effective writing and attractive presentation should encourage readers' enthusiasm for studying nature." A *Kirkus Reviews* contributor found *Flower Watching with Alice Eastwood* to be a biography that "lovingly presents the life" of the renowned botanist. Though self-taught, Eastwood ultimately became the curator of botany at the California Academy of Sciences and at age of ninety-one was honorary president of the Seventh International Botanical Congress in Sweden. Another contributor for *Kirkus Reviews* called *Bug Watching with Charles Henry Turner* a "well-researched biography of a lesser-known scientist, complete with project ideas that extend the book's usefulness." Turner had to overcome many obstacles in his career, being the first African American in his college class, the first to serve on the faculty of his university, and the first to become a member of the St. Louis Academy of Science.

Moving from science to art, Ross profiles another person who overcame prejudice in *Nature Art with Chiura Obata*. The life of Japanese-American artist Chiura

Obata is covered, from his early days in Japan to his move to California. Covering Obata's use of Asian techniques to depict the nature of his adopted country and the irony of the artist's internment during World War II, Ross creates a "well-written, historically illuminating biography [that] will inspire appreciation of the beauty and wonder in nature," according to *Booklist* contributor Shelle Rosenfeld. A related title, *Salvador Dali and the Surrealists: Their Lives and Ideals* focuses on the early-twentieth-century Spanish painter whose dreamlike images have intrigued art fans as much as has his colorful and eccentric life story. Calling the book "respectful and thorough," *Horn Book* reviewer Nell Beram noted that Ross follows Dali's creative evolution from impressionist to cubist and surrealist, and cites the man's wide-ranging influence on fashion, literature, and film. Beram praised Ross for presenting "admirably succinct and lucid interpretations" of Dali's "often flummoxing work," and in *School Library Journal* Cris Riedel dubbed the text "eminently readable" and "crisply written."

Ross revisits the theme of nature's cycles that he addressed in earlier books in a series which includes *Earth Cycles, Life Cycles, Body Cycles,* and *Re-Cycles*. Reviewing *Earth Cycles* in *Booklist*, Gillian Engberg noted that Ross uses "clear language suitable for beginning readers" to explain the "Earth's cycles of rotation" and deemed the book "direct, simple, and ideal for classroom support." Appraising the same title in *School Library Journal*, Eunice Weech commented that Ross deals with his subject in "easy-to-read but expressive language." The functions of the human body with regard to growth, respiration, and circulation are just a few of the things covered in *Body Cycles,* while in *Life Cycles* Ross maps the live cycles of a mushroom, grasshopper, and sunflower using what *Booklist* reviewer Lauren Peterson praised as "clear, direct language." *Re-Cycles* covers the cycle of regeneration as it plays out in the soil and water, and covers composting and the other recycling practices that allow people to participate in the cycle. The book's inclusion of fact boxes combine with "a generous assortment of color illustrations" to "clearly illustrate" the regeneration cycle, according to *Booklist* contributor Shelle Townsend-Hudson.

Somewhat of a change of direction for Ross are his titles for the "World's Children" series. Reviewing *Children of Northern Ireland, School Library Journal* contributor Tammy K. Baggett noted that Ross's book allows readers "to learn about another country through an exploration of the daily lives of children living there." Accompanied by full-color photographs, each text examines the lives of children both in and out of school and provides some historical background to the country in question.

"What impresses me years later is that I wrote a kids' book without knowing much about children's literature," Ross once remarked. "Ignorance was bliss, because I wrote and illustrated free of the constraints of trying to fit a mold. I created with kids in mind, and because I was a teacher I had ample opportunity to listen to kids. This process started me off on the path of creating unconventional science books. Ideas for new books are not a problem. They simply grow out of my life and work."

Biographical and Critical Sources

PERIODICALS

Booklist, January 15, 1993, Jim Jeske, review of *Become a Bird and Fly!,* p. 924; February 1, 1996, Carolyn Phelan, review of *Sandbox Scientist: Real Science Activities for Little Kids,* p. 936; March 15, 1996, p. 1260; March 1, 1998, Carolyn Phelan, review of *Bug Watching with Charles Henry Turner* and *Flower Watching with Alice Eastwood,* p. 1132; July, 1998, Susan Dove Lempke, review of *Caterpillarology* and *Ladybugology,* p. 1880; December 1, 1998, p. 680; February 1, 2000, Shelle Rosenfeld, review of *Nature Art with Chiura Obata,* p. 1021; January 1, 2001, Gillian Engberg, review of *Earth Cycles,* p. 964; August, 2001, Lauren Peterson, review of *Life Cycles,* p. 2112.

Children's Playmate, July-August, 1996, p. 14; November 1, 2002, Shelley Townsend-Hudson, review of *Re-Cycles,* p. 502; November 1, 2003, Stephanie Zvirin, review of *Salvador Dali and the Surrealists: Their Lives and Ideas,* p. 510.

The cycles of day to night, as well as seasonal shifts and the changing face of Moon are the focus of Ross's Earth Cycles, *illustrated by Gustav Moore.* (Text copyright © 2001 by Michael Elsohn Ross. Illustration copyright © 2001 by Gustav Moore. Reproduced in the U.S. by permission of Gustav Moore, in the rest of the world by permission of Millbrook Press.)

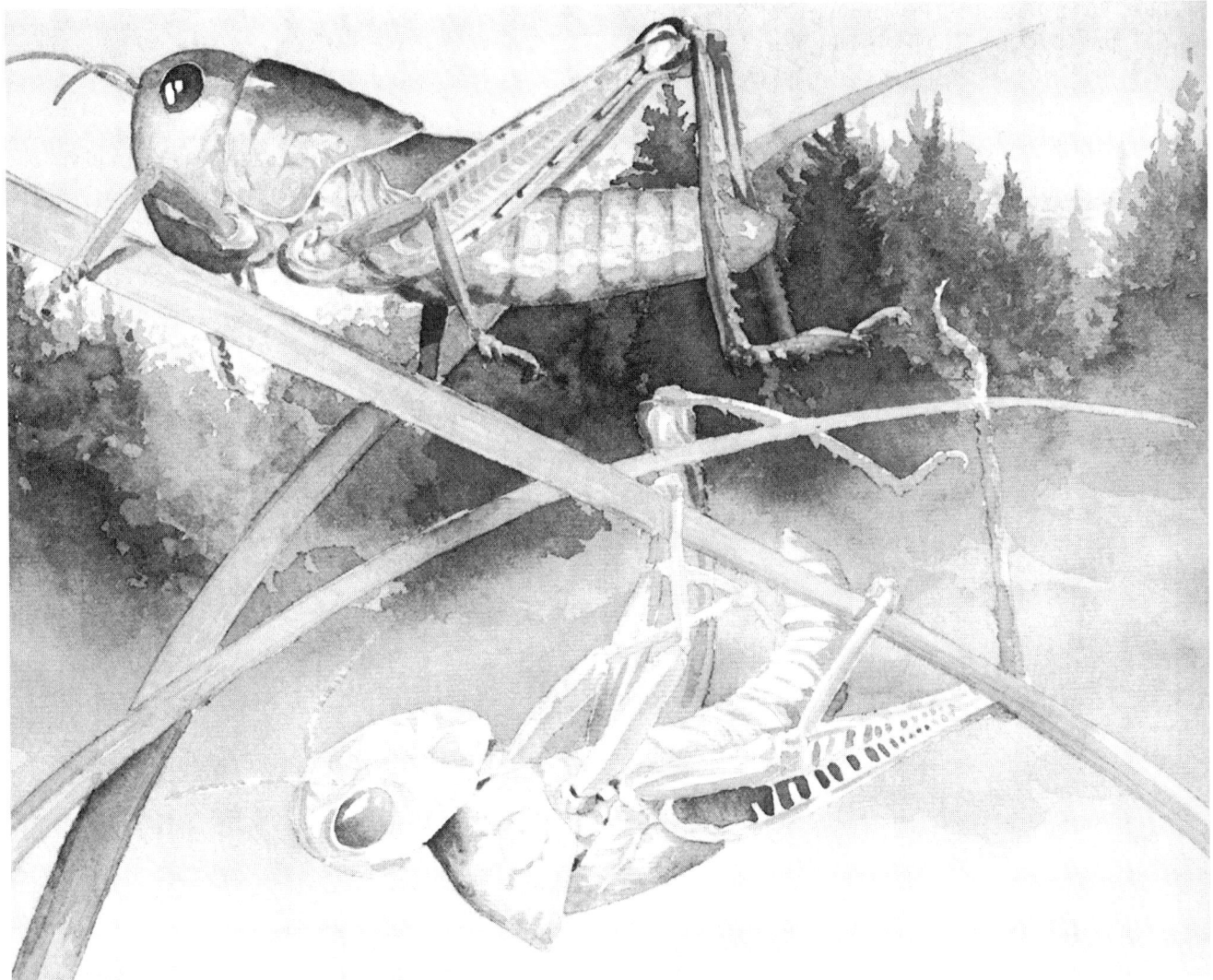

Ross uses the transformations of a mushroom, sunflower, and grasshopper to help young readers understand the process of growth in Life Cycles, *illustrated by Gustav Moore.* (Text copyright © 2001 by Michael Elsohn Ross. Illustration copyright © 2001 Gustav Moore. Reproduced in the U.S. by permission of Gustav Moore, in the rest of the world by permission of Millbrook Press.)

Horn Book, January-February, 2004, Nell Beram, review of *Salvador Dali and the Surrealists,* p. 106.

Kirkus Reviews, November 15, 1997, review of *Flower Watching with Alice Eastwood,* p. 1712; December 1, 1997, review of *Bug Watching with Charles Henry Turner,* pp. 1778-1779; January 15, 1998, review of *Ladybugology,* p. 117; April 1, 2004, review of *Snug as a Bug,* p. 337; August 15, 2004, review of *What's the Matter in Mr. Whiskers' Room?,* p. 812.

Kliatt, March, 2004, Jennifer Baldwin, review of *Salvador Dali and the Surrealists,* p. 35.

Los Angeles Times Book Review, September 17, 1995, review of *The Happy Camper Handbook,* p. 9.

Publishers Weekly, May 17, 1993, review of *The World of Small: Exploration with a Hand Lens,* p. 82.

School Library Journal, February, 1993, p. 78; March, 1996, p. 132; July, 1996, Karey Wehner, review of *Rolypolyology* and *Wormology,* pp. 80-81; August, 1996, Karey Wehner, review of *Cricketology* and *Snailology,* p. 160; March, 1998, Arwen Marshall, review of *Caterpillarology* and *Ladybugology,* pp. 202-203; March, 1998, Ruth S. Vose, review of *Bird Watching with Margaret Morse Nice* and *Wildlife Watching with Charles Eastman,* p. 241; February, 1999, p. 39; July, 2000, Frances E. Millhouser, review of *Pond Watching with Ann Morgan,* p. 121; July, 2000, Patricia Manning, review of *Fish Watching with Eugenie Clark, Millipedeology,* and *Spiderology,* p. 121; August, 2000, Andrew Medlar, review of *Exploring the Earth with John Wesley Powell,* p. 206; June, 2001, Tammy K. Baggett, review of *Children of Northern Ireland,* p. 136; July, 2001, Eunice Weech, review of *Earth Cycles,* p. 98; January, 2002, Michele Capozzella, review of *Life Cycles,* p. 124; February, 2002, Linda Greengrass, review of *Children of Puerto Rico,* p. 126; August, 2002, Martha Gordon, review of *Body Cycles,* p. 179; February, 2003, Peg Glisson, review of *Toy Lab,* p. 168; December, 2003, Cris Riedel, review of *Salvador Dali and the Surrealists,* p. 173;

June, 2004, Rachel G. Payne, review of *Snug as a Bug,* p. 118; October, 2004, Sandra Welzenbach, review of *What's the Matter in Mr. Whiskers' Room?,* p. 148.

Scientific American, December, 1996, pp. 121-122.

Skipping Stones, March, 2000, p. 34.

Whole Earth Review, summer, 1993, J. Baldwin, review of *The World of Small,* p. 124.

ONLINE

Michael Elsohn Ross Web site, http://www.bugauthor.com (May 18, 2006).

S-T

SABUDA, Robert 1965-
(Robert James Sabuda)

Personal
Born March 8, 1965, in Pinckney, MI; son of Bruce Edward (a tool-and-die maker) and Judith Elaine (a singer; maiden name, Barnes) Sabuda; partner of Matthew Reinhart (an author and illustrator). *Education:* Pratt Institute, B.F.A. (communication design; summa cum laude), 1987. *Hobbies and other interests:* Yoga.

Addresses
Home—New York, NY. *Agent*—c/o Dunham Literary, Inc., 156 5th Ave., Ste. 625, New York, NY 10010-7002. *E-mail*—robert.sabuda@robertsabuda.com.

Career
Children's book author and illustrator, 1988—.

Member
Society of Children's Book Writers and Illustrators, Movable Book Society, New York Genealogical and Biographical Society.

Awards, Honors
Notable Children's Trade Book in the Field of Social Studies designation, Children's Book Council, and New York Public Library Best Children's Book of the Year designation, both 1990, both for *Walden;* Magic Reading Award, *Parenting* magazine, and *Hungry Mind Review* Children's Book of Distinction designation, both 1992, both for *Saint Valentine;* Boston Globe/Horn Book Honor Award, 1994, for *A Tree Place;* Gold Medal, Dimension Illustration Awards, 1994, for *A Christmas Alphabet.*

Writings

SELF-ILLUSTRATED

Saint Valentine, Atheneum (New York, NY), 1992.
Tutankhamen's Gift, Atheneum (New York, NY), 1994.
The Christmas Alphabet (pop-up book), Orchard (New York, NY), 1994.
The Knight's Castle (pop-up book), Golden Books (New York, NY), 1994.
The Mummy's Tomb (pop-up book), Golden Books (New York, NY), 1994.
Help the Animals (pop-up books), 4 volumes, Reader's Digest, 1995.
Arthur and the Sword, Atheneum (New York, NY), 1995.
The Twelve Days of Christmas (pop-up book), Simon & Schuster (New York, NY), 1996.
ABC Disney (pop-up book), Disney Press (New York, NY), 1998.
Cookie Count: A Tasty Pop-Up, Simon & Schuster (New York, NY), 1998.
The Blizzard's Robe, Atheneum (New York, NY), 1999.
The Movable Mother Goose (pop-up book), Simon & Schuster (New York, NY), 1999.
(Reteller) L. Frank Baum, *The Wonderful Wizard of Oz* (pop-up book), Little Simon (New York, NY), 2000.
(With partner, Matthew Reinhart) *Young Naturalist's Pop-up Handbook: Butterflies,* Hyperion (New York, NY), 2001.
(With Matthew Reinhart) *Young Naturalist's Pop-up Handbook: Beetles,* Hyperion (New York, NY), 2001.
The Adventures of Providence Traveler, 1503: Uh-oh, Leonardo!, Atheneum (New York, NY), 2002.
(Reteller) Lewis Carroll, *Alice's Adventures in Wonderland* (pop-up book), Little Simon (New York, NY), 2003.
(With Matthew Reinhart) *Encyclopedia Prehistorica: Dinosaurs,* Candlewick (Cambridge, MA), 2005.
Winter's Tale (pop-up book), Little Simon (New York, NY), 2005.
(With Matthew Reinhart) *Encyclopedia Prehistorica: Sharks and Other Sea Monsters,* Candlewick (Cambridge, MA), 2006.

ILLUSTRATOR

Eugene Coco, *The Fiddler's Son,* Green Tiger Press, 1988.
Eugene Coco, *The Wishing Well,* Green Tiger Press, 1988.

Artwork from Sabuda's self-illustrated The Movable Mother Goose, *featuring pop-up artwork.* (Copyright © 1999 Robert Sabuda. Reproduced by permission of Little Simon, an imprint of Simon & Schuster Children's Publishing Division.)

Henry David Thoreau, *Walden*, text selections by Steve Lowe, Putnam (New York, NY), 1990.

Walt Whitman, *I Hear America Singing*, Putnam (New York, NY), 1991.

J. Patrick Lewis, *Earth Verses and Water Rhymes*, Atheneum (New York, NY), 1991.

Christopher Columbus, *The Log of Christopher Columbus*, text selections by Steve Lowe, Putnam (New York, NY), 1992.

Roy Owen, *The Ibis and the Egret*, Putnam (New York, NY), 1993.

Constance Levy, *A Tree Place and Other Poems*, Margaret K. McElderry Books (New York, NY), 1994.

Nancy Williams, *A Kwanzaa Celebration* (pop-up book), Simon & Schuster (New York, NY), 1995.

Marguerite W. Davol, *The Paper Dragon*, Atheneum (New York, NY), 1997.

Clement C. Moore, *The Night before Christmas*, Little Simon (New York, NY), 2002.

Katharine Lee Bates, *America the Beautiful*, Little Simon (New York, NY), 2004.

Kyle Olmon, *Sabuda and Reinhart Present Castle*, Orchard (New York, NY), 2006.

Sidelights

Robert Sabuda is an author and illustrator who has received wide-ranging acclaim as one of the foremost designers of interactive "pop-up" books. His delightful creations for the preschool set incorporate bright colors, stand-out graphics, and what a *School Library Journal* contributor termed "striking" examples of paper engineering in a review of *A Kwanzaa Celebration*. Sabuda has designed graphic illustrations for such classic works as the tales of Mother Goose, Henry David Thoreau's *Walden,* and a 1991 edition of nineteenth-century American poet Walt Whitman's *I Hear America Singing.* The busy Sabuda has also built a solid reputation as a traditional illustrator by bringing to life such picture books as *The Tree Place and Other Poems*, by Constance Levy, and *The Ibis and the Egret,* by Roy Owen.

In addition to his work as an illustrator, and as a way to allow himself greater creative latitude, Sabuda has also penned several original stories, including *Saint Valentine, Tutankhamen's Gift,* and *The Blizzard's Robe,* all of which feature his unique artwork. *The Blizzard's Robe,* a story about the origin of the Northern Lights, was praised for both its text and illustrations. *School Li-*

brary *Journal* contributor Tina Hudak called it a "tale of survival and compassion . . . [that] will warm the hearts of children and adults alike."

Born in 1965 and raised in a small, rural Michigan town, Sabuda always knew he would be an artist when he grew up; among his favorite illustrators were Tomi Ungerer, Arnold Lobel, and Norman Bridwell. Sabuda first discovered pop-up picture books after a horrible trip to the dentist. Waiting in the lobby the next time he visited the dentist, he found a thick and heavy book. "When I opened it, I was shocked and delighted when something leapt right off the page," he told Patricia J. Murphy for *Highlights for Children.* "I forgot all about the dentist."

"I should have known I was going to be a children's book illustrator when I presented my mom with *The Wizard of Oz* ('a pop-up book complete with cyclone!') made with my own dirty little hands," Sabuda once recalled to *SATA*. "My bedroom was a mess from all my projects. Now I get paid to make messes! My mother can't believe it (but of course she's thrilled; she was sure I'd starve to death)!" Sabuda credits his knack for engineering to his father, who was a mason and carpenter in addition to working as a tool-and-die maker. He explained to Murphy that he experimented over and over as a child. "With each failure . . . I learned a better solution, one that I wouldn't have even imagined," Sabuda said.

Attending New York's Pratt Institute after high school, Sabuda graduated summa cum laude in 1987. With his B.F.A. in communications design in hand, he began his first illustration project for Green Tiger Press: a pair of books he designed with writer Eugene B. Coco titled *The Fiddler's Son* and *The Wishing Well.* In the late 1990s Sabuda returned to Pratt to teach a course in the craft of pop-up design. As he explained in a *Publishers Weekly* interview, "There isn't a place you can go to learn how to make pop-ups. I learned by experimenting, and looking at my favorites to see how things were done."

Sabuda's *Cookie Count: A Tasty Pop-Up* reflects the author/illustrator's whimsical approach to his art. In the story, an ever-growing number of spatula-wielding mice stir up batch after batch of delicious cookies: everything from Linzer cookies to a gingerbread house. A reviewer for *Publishers Weekly* was impressed by Sabuda's "elaborate" two-page spreads, "each more inventive than the last." In a review of *The Movable Mother Goose* for *School Library Journal,* contributor John Peters noted that Sabuda "is as much an artist as a paper engineer, capable not only of designing cutting-edge special effects, but of using them in ingeniously creative ways."

Sabuda designs pop-up history in his *The Knight's Castle* and *The Mummy's Tomb,* helping relics from the past pop into the present, accompanied by simple rhyming texts and a small mouse hidden in the illustrations

An Arctic folk tale about the creation of the Northern Lights is brought to life by Robert Sabuda's brilliantly colored batik-inspired illustrations in **The Blizzard's Robe.** (Text and illustrations copyright © 1999 Robert Sabuda. Reproduced by permission of Atheneum Books for Young Readers, an imprint of Simon & Schuster Children's Publishing Division.)

on each page. By opening and closing the pages, "the figures can be made to move in amusing ways," commented *Horn Book* contributor Lolly Robinson. Sabuda has also illustrated nonfiction texts for other authors, including *A Kwanzaa Celebration,* in which his pop-up designs "extend" the text, according to Henrietta M. Smith in *Booklist.*

Sabuda retells L. Frank Baum's classic *The Wonderful Wizard of Oz,* abridging the tale and providing extensive pop-up art to accompany Baum's story. In the center of the book, the Emerald City stretches out on a full two-page spread; other prominent features of the story are the silver shoes of the Wicked Witch of the East sticking out from beneath Dorothy's house, and, like Sabuda's childhood inspiration, the cyclone that lifts Dorothy's house to Oz. "Baum himself would have been enchanted with this inventive interpretation of his famous fairy tale," wrote *Horn Book* reviewer Michael Patrick Hearn.

Using the traditional Christmas poem by Clement C. Moore, Sabuda created *The Night before Christmas,* incorporating white paper for all the pop-ups, movable parts, and flaps. Sabuda explained to Shannon Maughan of *Publishers Weekly* why he chose to use all-white paper. "I think it goes back to when I was a boy in rural Michigan. The winters were so big there," he wrote. "Everything was so white. We would build all kinds of snow forts and snowmen. I always go back to the pure simplicity of exploring shapes in white. I have not lost my love for that yet." Susan Patron commented in *School Library Journal* on the "clever techniques, original design, and a unique graphic style" that make Sabuda's work stand out.

Providence Traveler, daring mouse explorer, is the heroine of *The Adventures of Providence Traveler, 1503: Uh-oh, Leonardo!* Accidentally transported back in time with her friends, Providence encounters Leonardo da Vinci, her hero. "The bright pencil-and-watercolor cartoons are packed with loads of cultural information about old Florence," wrote Christine E. Carr in *School Library Journal,* who noted the book's educational value. *Booklist* reviewer Karin Snelson commented on the book's "colorful, mouse-eye's view of Renaissance culture."

Sabuda adapts another classic novel as a pop-up book in *Alice's Adventures in Wonderland*. Abridging Lewis Carroll's classic children's book, Sabuda was inspired by the originally published illustrations of Sir John Tenniel. He told Joy Bean for *Publishers Weekly* that he "sort of leaned to Tenniel's original illustrations. If you're paying homage to something, I agree with the adage, 'if it ain't broke, don't fix it.'" Sabuda chose to adapt *Alice's Adventures in Wonderland,* he told Bean, because it had been a favorite in his childhood. "When reading the book as a child, the artist said he was struck by the wordplay throughout the story," explained Bean, who then quoted Sabuda as saying, 'It was so silly and it was the adults who were so silly, which wasn't common at the time.'"

Carroll, who himself worked paper-engineering projects, "would be pleased" with this adaptation, according to a *Kirkus Reviews* contributor, while a *Publishers Weekly* reviewer felt that "readers will be astonished by every tableau in this pop-up extravaganza." Anita L. Burkam, in *Horn Book,* noted of Sabuda's abridgement that "the story moves at an over-fast pace but still manages to cohere," and concluded that the pop-up makes "a cunning addition to any Alice collection." The book "establish[es] Sabuda as the foremost visionary of the genre," according to Jennifer Mattson in *Booklist.*

America the Beautiful takes the words of the song by Katharine Lee Bates and uses them to create a pop-up trip across the United States. Covering such locations as Mount Rushmore, the National Capitol, the Statue of Liberty, and the Golden Gate Bridge, all done in white paper and occasional foil trim, *America the Beautiful* introduces readers to many of the nation's landmarks. "Each opening will elicit gasps, and the poem's soaring imagery has never been better served," wrote John Peters in *Booklist.* A *Kirkus Reviews* contributor considered the book "a masterpiece in design, in execution, in boldness of vision, and in artistic and historical integrity."

Cover of Sabuda's self-illustrated **Winter's Tale.** (Copyright © 2005 Robert Sabuda. Reproduced by permission of Little Simon, an imprint of Simon & Schuster Children's Publishing Division.)

With his partner Matthew Reinhart, Sabuda has worked on two books exploring prehistoric animals: *Encyclopedai Prehistorica: Dinosaurs* and *Encyclopedia Prehistorica: Sharks and Other Sea Monsters.* The first title features creatures from the Mesozoic era, all standing up from the page in multi-colored hides. "The coauthors balance the lively 3D material with sidebars on extinction, palentologists' discoveries, . . . and practical details," wrote a *Publishers Weekly* critic. The book will be "gobbled up as voraciously as one spread's allosaurus tucks into a lump of dinoflesh," assured Mattson in *Booklist.* Joy Fleishhacker, writing in *School Library Journal,* noted that "the book is so enticing that children will find it impossible to keep their hands off it."

Sabuda's solo title, *Winter's Tale,* celebrates a snow-covered winter environment, and like *The Night before Christmas* and *America the Beautiful,* all of the moving pieces and pop-up art are done in white paper. Sabuda explained to an interviewer for the *Powells Books Web site* where he came up with the idea for *Winter's Tale*: "During winter when I was a boy, my father would walk with me through the snow-covered terrain of rural Michigan and point out all the different animal tracks. He knew exactly which track belonged to which animal. *Winter's Tale* is a celebration of all those winter animals." A critic for *Kirkus Reviews* commented that "one is hard-pressed to find appropriate superlatives for this wonderful new offering," and Claire E. Gross, in *Horn Book,* considered the book a "paper-engineered miracle of bright white ingenuity."

Sabuda normally designs a book over the course of eight months. "We sketch with scissors, not pencils," the artist told Martha Pickerill of *Time for Kids.* Once designed, the books are hand-assembled by teams of over 1,000 workers, who produce about 15,000 copies in a week, according to the *Entertainment Weekly* reporter. On his home page, Sabuda described how he looks at his work: "It's hard work but the best part is not having to worry about making a mess. When being an artist is your job, you can make as many messes as you want to!"

Biographical and Critical Sources

PERIODICALS

Advocate, December 25, 2001, Michael Glitz, "Not Just Kid Stuff," p. 66.

Book, September-October, 2003, review of *Alice's Adventures in Wonderland,* p. 41.

Booklist, November 15, 1992, p. 603; April 15, 1994, Ilene Cooper, review of *Tutankhamen's Gift,* p. 1537; November 1, 1995, Kathy Broderick, review of *Arthur and the Sword,* p. 478; September 1, 1996, review of *The Twelve Days of Christmas,* p. 138; October 15, 1997, Susan Dove Lempke, review of *The Paper Dragon,* p. 402; December 15, 1997, review of *Cookie Count: A Tasty Pop-Up,* p. 700; November 15, 1999, Linda Perkins, review of *The Blizzard's Robe,* p. 637; December, 1999, Ilene Cooper, review of *The Movable Mother Goose,* p. 786; February 15, 2001, Henrietta M. Smith, review of *A Kwanzaa Celebration,* p. 1161; June 1, 2003, Karin Snelson, review of *The Adventures of Providence Traveler, 1503: Uh-oh, Leonardo!,* p. 1779; November 1, 2003, Jennifer Mattson, "Alice Pops Up," p. 513; January 1, 2004, review of *Alice's Adventures in Wonderland,* p. 782; November 15, 2004, Jennifer Mattson, review of *America the Beautiful,* p. 578; July, 2005, Jennifer Mattson, review of *Encyclopedia Prehistorica: Dinosaurs,* p. 1929; September 1, 2005, Jennifer Mattson, review of *Winter's Tale,* p. 146.

Bulletin of the Center for Children's Books, March, 1998, Deborah Stevens, review of *Cookie Count,* p. 359; December, 1998, Deborah Stevenson, review of *ABC Disney,* p. 145.

Child, October, 2003, Julie Yates Walton, review of *Alice's Adventures in Wonderland,* p. 48.

Entertainment Weekly, June 10, 2005, Tina Jordan, review of *Encyclopedia Prehistorica: Dinosaurs,* p. 118; December 16, 2005, "The King of Pop-ups," p. 89.

Five Owls, January, 1993, p. 63.

Highlights for Children, March, 2006, Patricia J. Murphy, "Popping in with Robert Sabuda," p. 34.

Horn Book, spring, 1993, p. 87; spring, 1995, Lolly Robinson, review of *The Knight's Castle,* p. 53; spring, 1999, Peter D. Sieruta, review of *ABC Disney,* p. 42; September, 2000, Michael Patrick Hearn, review of *The Wonderful Wizard of Oz,* p. 547; November-December, 2003, Anita L. Burkam, review of *Alice's Adventures in Wonderland,* p. 735; September-October, 2005, Danielle J. Ford, review of *Encyclopedia Prehistorica: Dinosaurs,* p. 607.

Kirkus Reviews, November 15, 1992, p. 1447; October 15, 1995, review of *Arthur and the Sword,* p. 1500; April 1, 2003, review of *The Adventures of Providence Traveler, 1503,* p. 539; September 15, 2003, review of *Alice's Adventures in Wonderland,* p. 1181; December 1, 2003, review of *Alice's Adventures in Wonderland,* p. 1405; October 1, 2004, review of *America the Beautiful,* p. 968; September 1, 2005, review of *Winter's Tale,* p. 982; November-December, 2005, Claire E. Gross, review of *Winter's Tale,* p. 697.

Library Journal, January, 1993, p. 17; May, 1993, p. 26.

New Advocate, spring, 1993, p. 140.

Newsweek, September 26, 2005, Bao Ong, "Pop Culture Phenomenon," p. 9.

Publishers Weekly, August 16, 1991, review of *I Hear America Singing,* p. 59; December 20, 1991, review of *The Log of Christopher Columbus,* p. 83; October 26, 1992, p. 72; October 23, 1993, review of *The Ibis and the Egret,* p. 61; October 17, 1994, review of *The Knight's Castle,* p. 80; September 18, 1995, review of *A Kwanzaa Celebration,* p. 94; September 30, 1996, review of *The Twelve Days of Christmas,* p. 88; November 25, 1996, Cindi Di Marzo, "In the Studio with Robert Sabuda," p. 30; December 1, 1997, review of *Cookie Count,* p. 55; October 25, 1999, review of *The Movable Mother Goose,* p. 79; November 29, 1999, review of *The Blizzard's Robe,* p. 70; December 8, 2002, Shannon Maughan, "Pop! Go the Sales," p. 19; February 10, 2003, review of *The Adventures of a Providence Traveler, 1503,* p. 187; September 22, 2003, review of *Alice's Adventures in Wonderland,* p. 101; September 29, 2003, Joy Bean, "A Double Take on Alice," p. 25; November 10, 2003, review of *Alice's Adventures in Wonderland,* p. 36; September 13, 2004, review of *America the Beautiful,* p. 77; June 20, 2005, review of *Winter's Tale,* p. 75, and review of *Encyclopedia Prehistorica: Dinosaurs,* p. 77.

Reading Teacher, April, 1993, p. 592.

School Library Journal, November, 1992, p. 86; April, 1994, Meg Stackpole, review of *A Tree Place,* p. 140; October, 1995, review of *A Kwanzaa Celebration,* p. 43; November, 1997, Margaret A. Chang, review of *The Paper Dragon,* p. 79; October, 1999, Tina Hudak, review of *The Blizzard's Robe,* p. 125; February, 2000, John Peters, review of *The Movable Mother Goose,* p. 97; October, 2002, Susan Patron, review of *The Night before Christmas,* p. 61; June, 2003, Christine E. Carr, review of *The Adventures of Providence Traveler, 1503,* p. 116; November, 2004, John Peters, review of *America the Beautiful,* p. 130; September, 2005, Joy Fleishhacker, review of *Winter's Tale,* p. 186, and review of *Encyclopedia Prehistorica: Dinosaurs,* p. 195.

Time for Kids, September 23, 2005, Martha Pickerill, "The Kings of Pop," p. 7.

ONLINE

Powells Books Web site, http://www.powells.com/ (April 25, 2006), interview with Sabuda.

Robert Sabuda Home Page, http://www.robertsabuda.com (April 25, 2006).

SABUDA, Robert James
   See SABUDA, Robert

* * *

SKYE, Obert

Personal
Male. *Hobbies and other interests:* Collecting old maps, water polo, roller coasters.

Addresses
Agent—c/o Author Mail, Deseret Book Company, P.O. Box 30178, Salt Lake City, UT 84130-0178.

Career
Writer.

Writings
Leven Thumps and the Gateway to Foo (children's fiction), illustrated by Ben Sowards, Shadow Mountain (Salt Lake City, UT), 2005.

Work in Progress
Four more books in the "Foo" series, including book two, *Leven Thumps and the Whispered Secret.*

Sidelights
Obert Skye's first book, *Leven Thumps and the Gateway to Foo,* is the initial offering in a series of books about an Oklahoma teenager who finds himself enmeshed in a world where reality and dreams meet. In an interview with Doug Wright, posted on *DeseretBook.com,* the author explained that "the entire idea started to come to me because of a certain part of the earth that I was at, I was in a forest, . . . and how the ground was connecting with the trees and [all,] just started in my mind thinking about the existence of where dreams and hopes might be and where they might be hidden. And so that was really the first strings and strands of a beginning of the discovery of Foo."

The book's hero, Leven—"Lev"—is introduced to the world of Foo—a type of metaphysical dreamland inhabited by an assortment of strange beings—by three Foovians who have come to recruit Lev to save both their world and his own. Sabine, an inhabitant of this world is so evil that his own shadow tries to run away from him. Sabine is on a mission to find and cross the gate between reality and Foo, thus merging the two together into a world of evil. Lev is chosen to help thwart Sabine's plan because, as the only descendent of the gate's creator, he alone has the ability to destroy the portal. Lev also has a personal stake in thwarting the villain; Sabine is intent on killing him. In addition to his newfound Foo allies, one of whom has taken on the form of a toothpick, Lev is assisted in his quest by a young girl named Winter who appears to be average until circumstances prove otherwise. In a review of *Leven Thumps and the Gateway to Foo* in *School Library Journal,* Steven Engelfried called the book a "lighthearted fantasy" and noted that the "complicated plot unwinds through a playful narrative." A *Kirkus Reviews* contributor commented that the book has "splendidly unpredictable plot twists" and an "intriguing vision of a reality that is wider than most of us suspect."

Biographical and Critical Sources

PERIODICALS

Kirkus Reviews, March 1, 2005, review of *Leven Thumps and the Gateway to Foo,* p. 296.
School Library Journal, April, 2005, review of *Leven Thumps and the Gateway to Foo,* p. 142.
Voice of Youth Advocates, April, 2005, review of *Leven Thumps and the Gateway to Foo,* p. 62.

ONLINE

Deseret Book Web site, http://deseretbook.com/ (April 24, 2005), Doug Wright, interview transcript from KSL Radio.
Leven Thumps and the Gateway to Foo Web site, http://www.leventhumps.com/ (August 21, 2005).*

* * *

SMITII, Z.Z.
   See WESTHEIMER, David

* * *

STILLE, Darlene R. 1942-
   (Darlene Ruth Stille)

Personal
Born April 17, 1942, in Chicago, IL; daughter of Theodore E. (a house painter) and Edna Pue (a telephone operator; maiden name, Cook) Stille. *Education:* University of Illinois—Urbana, B.A., 1965. *Politics:* Democrat. *Religion:* Protestant. *Hobbies and other interests:* Travel, SCUBA diving.

Addresses
Home—200 N. Eagle St., New Buffalo, MI 49117.

Career
Encyclopedia Britannica, Chicago, IL, production editor, 1968-69; *Compton's Encyclopedia,* Chicago, IL, staff writer, 1969-71; World Book, Chicago, IL, senior

editor, *The Year Book, Science Year,* 1971-78, managing editor, *Science Year,* 1978-91, executive editor, *Annuals,* 1991-2000, editor-in-chief, annual and online supplements, 2000-03; full-time writer, 2003—. Worked as a travel writer and Web design consultant for Envoy Travel, Inc.

Member

American Association for the Advancement of Science, Women Employed (chair, 1973-76).

Writings

Extraordinary Women Scientists ("Extraordinary People" series), Children's Press (Chicago, IL), 1995.
Extraordinary Women of Medicine ("Extraordinary People" series), Children's Press (Chicago, IL), 1997.
Jaguars ("First Report" series), Compass Point Books (Minneapolis, MN), 2001.
Snakes ("First Report" series), Compass Point Books (Minneapolis, MN), 2001.
(With Susan Heinrichs Gray) *The White House* ("Let's See Library—Our Nation" series), Compass Point Books (Minneapolis, MN), 2001.
(With Dana Meachen Rau) *The Statue of Liberty* ("Let's See Library—Our Nation" series), Compass Point Books (Minneapolis, MN), 2001.
Octopuses ("Sea Creatures" series), Heinemann Library (Chicago, IL), 2003.
Cheetahs ("First Report" series), Compass Point Books (Minneapolis, MN), 2004.

"TRUE BOOKS" SERIES

Air Pollution, Children's Press (Chicago, IL), 1990.
Water Pollution, Children's Press (Chicago, IL), 1990.
Soil Erosion and Pollution, Children's Press (Chicago, IL), 1990.
The Greenhouse Effect, Children's Press (Chicago, IL), 1990.
The Ice Age, Children's Press (Chicago, IL), 1990.
Oil Spills, Children's Press (Chicago, IL), 1991.
Ozone Hole, Children's Press (Chicago, IL), 1991.
Space Craft, Children's Press (Chicago, IL), 1991.
The Circulatory System, Children's Press (Chicago, IL), 1997.
The Nervous System, Children's Press (Chicago, IL), 1997.
The Respiratory System, Children's Press (Chicago, IL), 1997.
Trains, Compass Point Books (Minneapolis, MN), 1997.
Trucks, Compass Point Books (Minneapolis, MN), 1997.
The Digestive System, Children's Press (Chicago, IL), 1997.
Deserts, Children's Press (Chicago, IL), 1999.
Tropical Rain Forest, Children's Press (Chicago, IL), 1999.
Wetlands, Children's Press (Chicago, IL), 1999.
Grasslands, Children's Press (Chicago, IL), 1999.
Oceans, Children's Press (Chicago, IL), 1999.

"LET'S SEE LIBRARY—COMMUNICATION" SERIES

Radio, Compass Point Books (Minneapolis, MN), 2001.
Satellite, Compass Point Books (Minneapolis, MN), 2001.
Telephones, Compass Point Books (Minneapolis, MN), 2001.
Television, Compass Point Books (Minneapolis, MN), 2001.

"SIMPLY SCIENCE" SERIES

Electricity, Compass Point Books (Minneapolis, MN), 2001.
Fall, Compass Point Books (Minneapolis, MN), 2001.
Winter, Compass Point Books (Minneapolis, MN), 2001.
Hot and Cold, Compass Point Books (Minneapolis, MN), 2001.
Magnets, Compass Point Books (Minneapolis, MN), 2001.
Sound, Compass Point Books (Minneapolis, MN), 2001.
Spring, Compass Point Books (Minneapolis, MN), 2001.
Summer, Compass Point Books (Minneapolis, MN), 2001.
Satellites, Compass Point Books (Minneapolis, MN), 2002.
Radio, Compass Point Books (Minneapolis, MN), 2002.

"TRANSPORTATION" SERIES

Airplanes, Compass Point Books (Minneapolis, MN), 1997.
Helicopters, Children's Press (Chicago, IL), 1997.
Blimps, Children's Press (Chicago, IL), 1997.
Big Rigs, Compass Point Books (Minneapolis, MN), 2001.
Freight Trains, Compass Point Books (Minneapolis, MN), 2001.
Race Cars, Compass Point Books (Minneapolis, MN), 2002.
Tractors, Compass Point Books (Minneapolis, MN), 2002.
Police Cars, Compass Point Books (Minneapolis, MN), 2003.
Fire Trucks, Compass Point Books (Minneapolis, MN), 2003.
Boats, Compass Point Books (Minneapolis, MN), 2003.
Helicopters, Compass Point Books (Minneapolis, MN), 2004.
Bulldozers, Compass Point Books (Minneapolis, MN), 2004.
Submarines, Compass Point Books (Minneapolis, MN), 2004.
Space Shuttle, Compass Point Books (Minneapolis, MN), 2004.
Ships, Compass Point Books (Minneapolis, MN), 2004.
Motorcycles, Compass Point Books (Minneapolis, MN), 2004.

"AMAZING SCIENCE" SERIES

Matter: See It, Touch It, Taste It, Smell It, Picture Window Books (Minneapolis, MN), 2004.
Energy: Heat, Light, and Fuel, Picture Window Books (Minneapolis, MN), 2004.

Electricity: Bulbs, Batteries, and Sparks, Picture Window Books (Minneapolis, MN), 2004.
Temperature: Heating Up and Cooling Down, Picture Window Books (Minneapolis, MN), 2004.
Air: Outside, Inside, and All Around, Picture Window Books (Minneapolis, MN), 2004.
Motion: Push and Pull, Fast and Slow, Picture Window Books (Minneapolis, MN), 2004.

"OUR GALAXY AND BEYOND" SERIES

Mars, Child's World (Chanhassen, MN), 2004.
Earth, Child's World (Chanhassen, MN), 2004.
The Sun, Child's World (Chanhassen, MN), 2004.
Pluto, Child's World (Chanhassen, MN), 2004.
Neptune, Child's World (Chanhassen, MN), 2004.
Mercury, Child's World (Chanhassen, MN), 2004.
Uranus, Child's World (Chanhassen, MN), 2004.

"I LIVE IN THE OCEAN" SERIES

I Am a Whale: The Life of a Humpback Whale, illustrated by Todd Ouren, Picture Window Books (Minneapolis, MN), 2005.
I Am a Shark: The Life of a Hammerhead Shark, illustrated by Todd Ouren, Picture Window Books (Minneapolis, MN), 2005.
I Am a Seal: The Life of an Elephant Seal, illustrated by Todd Ouren, Picture Window Books (Minneapolis, MN), 2005.
I Am a Sea Turtle: The Life of a Green Sea Turtle, illustrated by Todd Ouren, Picture Window Books (Minneapolis, MN), 2005.
I Am a Fish: The Life of a Clown Fish, illustrated by Todd Ouren, Picture Window Books (Minneapolis, MN), 2005.
I Am a Dolphin: The Life of a Bottlenose Dolphin, illustrated by Todd Ouren, Picture Window Books (Minneapolis, MN), 2005.

"SCIENCE AROUND US" SERIES

Magnetism, Child's World (Chanhassen, MN), 2005.
Light, Child's World (Chanhassen, MN), 2005.
Energy, Child's World (Chanhassen, MN), 2005.
Electricity, Child's World (Chanhassen, MN), 2005.
Solids, Liquids, and Gases, Child's World (Chanhassen, MN), 2005.
Motion, Child's World (Chanhassen, MN), 2005.
Matter and Material, Child's World (Chanhassen, MN), 2005.

"EXPLORING SCIENCE" SERIES

Erosion: How Land Forms, How It Changes, Compass Point Books (Minneapolis, MN), 2005.
Soil: Digging into Earth's Vital Resource, Compass Point Books (Minneapolis, MN), 2005.
Plant Cells: The Building Blocks of Plants, Compass Point Books (Minneapolis, MN), 2005.
Natural Resources: Using and Protecting Earth's Supplies, Compass Point Books (Minneapolis, MN), 2005.
Minerals: From Apatite to Zinc, Compass Point Books (Minneapolis, MN), 2005.
Waves: Energy on the Move, Compass Point Books (Minneapolis, MN), 2005.
Physical Change: Reshaping Matter, Compass Point Books (Minneapolis, MN), 2006.
Manipulating Light: Reflection, Refraction, and Absorption, Compass Point Books (Minneapolis, MN), 2006.
Genetics: A Living Blueprint, Compass Point Books (Minneapolis, MN), 2006.
DNA: The Master of Molecule of Life, Compass Point Books (Minneapolis, MN), 2006.
Chemical Change: From Fireworks to Rust, Compass Point Books (Minneapolis, MN), 2006.
Animal Cells: The Smallest Units of Life, Compass Point Books (Minneapolis, MN), 2006.

"SIGNATURE LIVES" SERIES

Eva Peron, First Lady of Argentina, Compass Point Books (Minneapolis, MN), 2006.
Anne Hutchinson: Puritan Protester, Compass Point Books (Minneapolis, MN), 2006.

Sidelights

Darlene R. Stille's interest in science is reflected in most, if not all, of her nonfiction books for younger readers. As she once commented to *SATA:* "I became a science writer and editor largely because I could not become a doctor. I started out in pre-med in 1960. Medicine, at that time, was not very open to women—to say the least. One needed strong family support to go forth in that direction. My family was dead set against the idea." "Fortunately," the author and editor added, "I had another love in addition to science: writing. I pursued a degree in English, went into the reference publishing field, and was soon able to put together my love of science and of words in science editing and writing." Among Stille's books for younger readers are titles such as *Extraordinary Women Scientists* as well as books in a number of nonfiction series.

In *Extraordinary Women Scientists* Stille focuses on women's role in science throughout history. The book features biographies of fifty important female scientist from various scientific disciplines, and includes information on women scientists from numerous countries. Margaret M. Hagel, writing in the *School Library Journal,* noted that while this work can be "used as a reference book, . . . it [also] introduces readers to the diversity of science." Her next book for the "Extraordinary People" series, titled *Extraordinary Women of Medicine,* Stille narrows her focus to present an overview of the history of medicine as well as highlighting women's achievements in that field. Like its companion volume, *Extraordinary Women of Medicine* also includes biographies and covers various ethnic groups, such as Americans, African Americans, and Europeans. Reviewing the work for *Booklist,* Lauren Peterson noted that it contains a "wealth of information" presented in an "accessible format."

In *Erosion: How Land Forms, How It Changes,* a title from the "Exploring Science" series, Stille explores how elements of the environment contribute to natural erosion. The book features full-color illustrations that provide a quick source for pertinent data, while the text is directed toward older students. *Booklist* reviewer Carolyn Phelan remarked that Stille writes with a "straightforward approach" that addresses "the pros and cons of attempting to control erosion." The book also features a table of contents, graphs, an index, and a glossary. Other titles in the "Exploring Science" series include *Waves: Energy on the Move, Manipulating Light: Reflection, Refraction, and Absorption,* and *Genetics: A Living Blueprint.*

Stille surveys the realm of physical science in the "Science around Us," series which includes such titles as *Magnetism, Energy,* and *Solids, Liquids, and Gases.* John Peters reviewed the companion titles *Energy* and *Solids, Liquids, and Gases* for *Booklist.* The critic noted that the titles "ably introduce topics in the physical sciences," by describing how energy is made and by detailing the difference between solids, liquids, and gases. Both titles include full-color photographs, a list of suggested books, and links to the publisher's Web site, resources for further information on the topics.

Stille's scientific background is also evident in the books she has written for the "True Book" series published by Children's Press. Included among these is *The Circulatory System,* a book that presents basic information about the heart, flow of blood, and the function of lungs. As with her other books, Stille includes a glossary as well as a list of resources for more information. Another book is titled *The Nervous System.* Once again using simple language and diagrams, she explains the interaction between brain, nerves, and muscles. Reviewing this work for *Booklist,* Lauren Peterson noted that Stille does an "admirable" job of explaining a complex subject. Other titles by Stille for the "True Book" series include *The Wetlands* and *Tropical Rain Forests.* Both follow the familiar, simple format of her earlier books, focusing on basic facts about the topics under discussion accompanied by photographs and a list of resources for further study.

In addition to books on natural science, Stille has also written numerous titles for her "Transportation" series, including *Airplanes* and *Trains.* In both of these works, she includes information that will be relevant to school-age children who are just beginning to write reports on various technological subjects. In addition to descriptions of planes and trains, both books also include photographs and a list of sources for further study. In *Freight Trains* and *Race Cars* Stille offers descriptions of an assortment of railway carriers and racing vehicles. *Booklist* reviewer Carolyn Phelan remarked that both titles "provide simple, solid information on the topics at hand." Other books in this series include *Helicopters, Blimps,* and *Trucks.*

Earth's solar system is explored in the "Our Galaxy and Beyond" series published by Child's World. Focusing on a single planet, each volume in the series introduces budding scientists to the solar system by describing the distinguishing features of that particular celestial body. The titles also provide historical backgrounds of the first astronomers as well as current NASA missions. John Peters, in *School Library Journal,* noted that the series contains fundamental information that is not "couched in generalities." Each title is further enhanced by full-color and archival photographs.

Stille delves into the oceanic world with such titles as *I Am a Seal: The Life of the Elephant Sea, I Am a Shark: The Life of a Hammerhead Shark,* and *I Am a Whale: The Life of a Humpback Whale.* All the titles are part of the "I Live in the Ocean" series published by Picture Window Books. Each title is narrated by an ocean animal who explains their diets, anatomy, and their daily activities. Cynde Suite, in *School Library Journal,* wrote that the "I Live in the Ocean" books are "perfect for young animal lovers."

Biographical and Critical Sources

PERIODICALS

Booklist, October 1, 1997, Lauren Peterson, review of *Extraordinary Women of Medicine,* p. 316; September 15, 1997, Ilene Cooper, review of *Airplanes* and *Trains,* p. 233; December 1, 1997, Hazel Rochman, review of *The Circulatory System,* p. 632; February 15, 1998, Lauren Peterson, review of *The Nervous System,* p. 1006; October 15, 1999, Hazel Rochman, review of *Tropical Rain Forests,* p. 440; December 15, 2001, Carolyn Phelan, review of *Freight Trains* and *Race Cars,* p. 737; November 1, 2004, John Peters, review of *Energy: Heat, Light, and Fuel* and *Solids, Liquids, and Gases,* p. 478; April 1, 2005, Carolyn Phelan, review of *Erosion: How Land Forms, How It Changes,* p. 1384.

School Library Journal, December, 1995, Margaret M. Hagel, review of *Extraordinary Women Scientists,* pp. 125-126; February, 1998, Martha Gordon, reviews of *The Circulatory System, The Respiratory System,* and *The Digestive System,* p. 105; January, 2004, John Peters, review of "Our Galaxy and Beyond" series, p. 122; January, 2005, Cynde Suite, review of "I Live in the Ocean" series, p. 116.

* * *

STILLE, Darlene Ruth
See STILLE, Darlene R.

TABACK, Simms 1932-

Personal
Born February 13, 1932, in New York, NY; son of Leon (a house painter and contractor) and Thelma (a seamstress) Taback; married Gail Baugher Kuenstler (a writer), March 1, 1980; children: Lisa, Jason, Emily. *Education:* Cooper Union, B.F.A., 1953.

Addresses
Agent—c/o Author Mail, Viking, Penguin Putnam, 375 Hudson St., New York, NY 10014.

Career
Illustrator. CBS Records, New York, NY, graphic designer, 1956-57; *New York Times*, New York, NY, designer, 1957-58; William Douglas McAdams, New York, NY, art director, 1958-60; freelance illustrator, 1960-63, 1970—; Ruffins/Taback Design Studio, New York, NY, partner, 1963-70. Teacher of illustration and design at Syracuse University and School of Visual Arts. Member of board, Graphic Artists Guild, for twenty years. *Military service:* U.S. Army, private first class, 1953-55.

Member
Illustrators Guild (president, 1975-77), New York Graphics Artists Guild (president, 1978-83), Society of Illustrators, Art Directors Club.

Awards, Honors
Best Illustrated Books designation, *New York Times*, 1965, for *Please Share That Peanut! A Preposterous Pageant in Fourteen Acts;* Children's Book of the Year selection, American Institute of Graphic Arts, 1970, for *There's Motion Everywhere,* 1979, for *Joseph Had a Little Overcoat,* and 1980, for *Laughing Together;* Notable Book designation, American Library Association (ALA), 1998, and Caldecott Honor Book, ALA, 1998, both for *There Was an Old Lady Who Swallowed a Fly;* Caldecott Medal, 2000, for newly illustrated edition of *Joseph Had a Little Overcoat.*

Writings

SELF-ILLUSTRATED

Joseph Had a Little Overcoat, Random House (New York, NY), 1978, published with new illustrations, Viking (New York, NY), 1999.
(Adaptor) *There Was an Old Lady Who Swallowed a Fly,* Viking (New York, NY), 1997.
This Is the House That Jack Built, Putnam (New York, NY), 2002.
Simms Taback's Big Book of Words, Chronicle Books (New York, NY), 2004.
Kibitzers and Fools: Tales My Zayda Told Me, Viking (New York, NY), 2005.

ILLUSTRATOR

Lewis Carroll, *Jabberwocky and Other Frabjous Nonsense,* Harlan Quist, 1964.
Sesyle Joslin, *Please Share That Peanut! A Preposterous Pageant in Fourteen Acts,* Harcourt (Boston, MA), 1965.
Ann McGovern, *Too Much Noise,* Houghton (Boston, MA), 1967.
John Travers Moore, *There's Motion Everywhere,* Houghton (Boston, MA), 1970.
(With Reynold Ruffins) Harry Hartwick, *The Amazing Maze,* Dutton (New York, NY), 1970.
Janet Barkas, *Meatless Cooking, Celebrity Style,* Grove Press (New York, NY), 1975.
Barbara K. Walker, compiler, *Laughing Together: Giggles and Grins from around the World,* Four Winds Press (New York, NY), 1977, published as *Laughing Together: Giggles and Grins from around the Globe,* Free Spirit, 1982.
Harriet Ziefert, *Where Is My House?,* Grosset, 1982.
Katy Hall and Lisa Eisenberg, *Fishy Riddles,* Dial (New York, NY), 1983.
Harriet Ziefert, *Where Is My Dinner?,* Grosset, 1984.
Harriet Ziefert, *Where Is My Friend?,* Grosset, 1984.
Harriet Ziefert, *On Our Way,* four volumes (includes *On Our Way To the Forest, On Our Way to the Water, On Our Way to the Zoo,* and *On Our Way to the Barn*), Harper (New York, NY), 1985.
Katy Hall and Lisa Eisenberg, *Buggy Riddles,* Dial (New York, NY), 1985.
Harriet Ziefert, *Jason's Bus Ride,* Viking (New York, NY), 1987.
Science Activity Book, Galison, 1987.
Harriet Ziefert, *Zoo Parade,* Harper (New York, NY), 1990.
Harriet Ziefert, *Noisy Barn!,* Harper (New York, NY), 1990.
Katy Hall and Lisa Eisenberg, *Snakey Riddles,* Dial (New York, NY), 1990.
Michele Urvater, *The Monday to Friday Cookbook,* Workman (New York, NY), 1991.
Gail MacColl, *The Book of Cards for Kids,* Workman (New York, NY), 1992.
Katy Hall and Lisa Eisenberg, *Spacey Riddles,* Dial (New York, NY), 1992.
B.G. Hennessy, *Road Builders,* Viking (New York, NY), 1994.
Harriet Ziefert, *Where Is My Baby?,* Harper (New York, NY), 1994.
Nancy Antle, *Sam's Wild West Show,* Dial (New York, NY), 1995.
Michele Urvater, *Monday to Friday Pasta,* Workman (New York, NY), 1995.
Mary Calhoun, *Euphonia and the Flood,* Parents Magazine Press, 1996.

Harriet Ziefert, *Who Said Moo?*, Harper (New York, NY), 1996.
Harriet Ziefert, *Two Little Witches: A Halloween Counting Story*, Candlewick Press (New York, NY), 1996.
Harriet Ziefert, reteller, *When I First Came to This Land*, Putnam (New York, NY), 1998.
Harriet Ziefert, *Noisy Forest!*, Chronicle Books (New York, NY), 2004.
Harriet Ziefert, *Beach Party!*, Chronicle Books (New York, NY), 2005.

Taback's works are included in the Kerlan Collection at the University of Minnesota.

Adaptations

Taback's books adapted for video include *There Was an Old Lady Who Swallowed a Fly*, Weston Woods, 2002; *Joseph Had a Little Overcoat* was adapted for audiocassette, with musical accompaniment, Live Oak Media, 2001.

Sidelights

A prolific and highly lauded illustrator of books for young children, Simms Taback is best known for his Caldecott Medal-winning picture book *Joseph Had a Little Overcoat*, as well as for his many collaborations with popular children's author Harriet Ziefert. Experienced in many media, Taback uses pen and ink and watercolor for most of his illustrations. In addition to works by Ziefert, he has created artwork for authors such as Barbara Walker, Mary Calhoun, Katy Hall, Lisa Eisenberg, and B.G. Hennessy, and has also illustrated his original adaptations of traditional rhymes and stories. Praising Taback's contribution to Hennessy's picture book *Road Builders*, *Booklist* contributor Hazel Rochman maintained that "kids will pore over the detailed, brightly colored pen-and-ink drawings . . . [that] show the precision and the power of these marvelous machines." Reviewing the same work, a *Publishers Weekly* reviewer commended Taback's use of "bold, attention-grabbing colors" in his "oversized, up-close-and-personal illustrations."

Born in a working-class neighborhood in the Bronx, New York, in 1932, Taback originally planned to follow in the footsteps of his father, a painting contractor who had immigrated from Eastern Europe in the wake of anti-Jewish sentiment. However, his creative instincts won out, and he attended the Cooper Union, where he studied under Ray Baxter Dowden and Sid Delevanty before receiving his bachelor of fine arts degree in 1953. Beginning his career as a graphic artist with CBS Records, Taback worked as a designer for the *New York Times* as well as for other Manhattan-based businesses before opening his own design studio in 1963. His first illustration project, an adaptation of the nonsense verses of Lewis Carroll titled *Jabberwocky and Other Frabjous Nonsense*, was published in 1964.

Taback's second illustration project, Sesyle Joslin's *Please Share That Peanut! A Preposterous Pageant in Fourteen Acts*, was named one of the *New York Times*' best illustrated books of 1965. Paired with several other authors to produce a variety of picture books—and, in one instance, a cookbook—Taback linked up with author Ziefert on the beginning reader *Where Is My House?*, the first of many Ziefert texts featuring illustrations by Taback. In *On Our Way to the Forest*, part of a series of four beginning readers, Taback includes stickers of his animal characters and encourages readers to make their own pictures. *Two Little Witches: A Halloween Counting Story* finds a growing group of trick-or-treaters winding up at a house so scary that most turn and run for home . . . while one runs to fetch her broomstick. Praising Taback's introduction of humorous illustrated embellishments to Zeifert's story, *Booklist* contributor Susan Dove Lempke noted that "he keeps the design simple and clear to make the counting easy." In *School Library Journal*, Claudia Cooper commented that the illustrator's "large, primitive, watercolor-and-ink cartoons are especially delightful, both spooky . . . and reassuringly familiar."

Riddle books are popular with children new to reading on their own, and Taback has illustrated several such works for authors Katy Hall and Lisa Eisenberg. *Snakey Riddles* offers scads of jokes and other wordplay featuring the slithery, scaly creatures, as well as Taback's "cleverly drawn, lively cartoon illustrations," which *School Library Journal* contributor Sharon McElmeel considered "the best thing about the book." *Fishy Riddles*, *Buggy Riddles*, and *Spacey Riddles* continue the fun, bringing "groans of enjoyment to primary-grade children and even bigger groans from adults who share them," according to the critic.

In addition to illustrating the works of others, Taback has adapted traditional tales as picture-book texts, gracing each with his whimsical drawings. First published in 1978 and cited as a notable children's book by the American Institute of Graphic Arts, *Joseph Had a Little Overcoat* earned its creator the prestigious Caldecott Medal when it was reissued with new illustrations in 1999. In its simple text based on a Yiddish folk song, the book tells the story of a Polish tailor who salvages the increasingly worn fabric left from a cherished plaid overcoat into, a jacket, and then as each garment wears out in succession, a vest, scarf, tie, handkerchief, and ultimately a button. Designed as an interactive, die-cut book in which readers can watch the amount of plaid fabric gradually whittle away in size, Taback's tale ends with the tailor's decision to weave the remaining threads of his fabric into a story: the story the reader is now reading. "With its effective repetition and an abundance of visual humor, this is tailor-made for reading aloud," noted a *Publishers Weekly* contributor, while in *Horn Book* Martha V. Parravano deemed the tale "clever, visually engrossing, [and] poignant."

As Parravano noted, to create *Joseph Had a Little Overcoat* Taback draws on his Eastern European cultural heritage to "create a veritable pageant of pre-[World War II] . . . Jewish-Polish life," adding "broad com-

In his characteristic quirky style, Simms Taback presents an upbeat rendition of a traditional rhyme in his self-illustrated This Is the House That Jack Built. (Text and illustrations copyright © 2002 by Simms Taback. All rights reserved. Used by permission of G.P. Putnam's Sons, a division of Penguin Young Readers Group, a member of Penguin Group (USA) Inc.)

edy" as well as a wealth of historical references; Indeed, the book "is a story set in a world I heard so much about as a child, filled with memories of my family and of a thriving culture that no longer exists," the author/illustrator recalled in an essay for the *Children's Book Council Web site*. "It embodies the values and struggles of life in the *shtetl*, the small villages where Jews lived in Eastern Europe. These were not big-city Jews, but families of farmers and tradesmen of mixed economic class." In creating his illustrations, Taback explained, "I decided to take some artistic license and mix it up with more traditional Polish and Ukrainian designs, This made it more like the shtetl of my imagination." Noting that the book depicts a way of life that has now disappeared, the author added: "What I find special about making picture books is that this old world can be reimagined and presented to children in an appealing way" so that they can "learn . . . something special about the world as it once was."

Taback opens other windows onto the past with the books *There Was an Old Lady Who Swallowed a Fly* and *This Is the House That Jack Built,* both based on folk tales. Teaching the valuable moral "never swallow a horse," the award-winning *There Was an Old Lady Who Swallowed a Fly* entertains with a wealth of "details and humorous asides, from the names of different types of birds, to a recipe for spider soup," according to *School Library Journal* contributor Martha Topol. Taback's illustrations prove equally entertaining; Topol maintained that the old lady of the title, whose incredible appetite gets her into all sorts of trouble, "looks wacky enough to go so far as to swallow a horse" in this "eye-catching, energy-filled" work. Praising the book's collage-like format—Taback patchworks everything from the pages of nature guides to clips from the *Wall Street Journal* in his humorous drawings—a *Publishers Weekly* contributor maintained that "children of all ages will joyfully swallow this book whole." Gahan Wilson enthusiastic praise for the book in his *New York Times Book Review* assessment, lauding the "widely varied gallery of flies" that appears on the book's back cover and applauding the concept for punching a hole through the page that allows the reader to see inside the gluttonous old lady, "a neat little gross-out in itself. . . . [that] converts the book into a marvelous toy and gives [readers] many wonderful chances to get inventive."

This Is the House That Jack Built follows a similar plan, featuring what a *Kirkus Reviews* writer called "deeply colorful, intricately detailed and witty mixed-media illustrations" of each of the creatures that call Jack's house "home." Dubbing Taback's adaptation "downright hilarious," Barbara Buckley added in *School Library Journal* that the illustrator's use of strong, saturated colors, imaginative endpapers, and a humorous text make the work "a natural for storyhour." "Taback puts a new house on the market and hits the nail on the head with this boisterous, rollicking version," concluded Julie Cummins in *Booklist*.

With *Kibitzers and Fools: Tales My Zayda Told Me* Taback immerses young readers in Yiddish wit and wisdom, using Yiddish expressions—a glossary is included—and cadence in this collection of stories told by his zayda (grandfather) to a boy named Yankel. Praising the stories as "short but very wise," a *Kirkus Reviews* writer added that the tales are drawn from "a world of poverty imbued with spiritual richness and a strong dose of practicality." The "warmhearted silliness" of these thirteen tales, "combined with Taback's characteristically irrepressible drawing style easily transcends the boundaries of time and ethnicities," noted a *Publishers Weekly* contributor, while in *Booklist* Hazel Rochman called *Kibitzers and Fools* an "uproarious book [that] celebrates the shtetl scene" in "bright, folk-art style."

Biographical and Critical Sources

PERIODICALS

Booklist, February 1, 1992, p. 1042; May 1, 1994, Hazel Rochman, review of *Road Builders,* p. 1603; July, 1995, p. 1885; September 1, 1996, Susan Dove Lempke, review of *Two Little Witches: A Halloween Counting Story,* p. 138; January 1, 2000, Tim Arnold, review of *Joseph Had a Little Overcoat,* p. 936; March 1, 2002, Nancy McCray, review of *Joseph Had a Little*

Kibitzers and Fools: Tales My Zayda Told Me *collects stories once told by author/illustrator Taback's Polish grandfather.* (Text and illustrations copyright © 2005 by Simms Taback. Viking, 2005. All rights reserved. Used by permission of Viking Children's Books, a division of Penguin Young Readers Group, a member of Penguin Group (USA) Inc.)

Overcoat, p. 1151; October 1, 2002, Julie Cummins, review of *This Is the House That Jack Built*, p. 323; October 15, 2005, Hazel Rochman, review of *Kibitzers and Fools: Tales My Zayda Told Me*, p. 60.

Bulletin of the Center for Children's Books, March, 2000, review of *Joseph Had a Little Overcoat*, p. 257.

Horn Book, January, 2000, Martha V. Parravano, review of *Joseph Had a Little Overcoat*, p. 68; July, 2000, Reynold Ruffins, "Across the Drawing Board from Simms Taback," p. 409; November-December, 2002, Martha V. Parravano, review of *This Is the House That Jack Built*, p. 769; September-October, 2005, Susan P. Bloom, review of *Kibitzers and Fools*, p. 595.

Kirkus Reviews, July 15, 2002, review of *This Is the House That Jack Built*, p. 1045; August 15, 2005, review of *Kibitzers and Fools*, p. 923.

New York Times Book Review, November 16, 1997, Gahan Wilson, review of *There Was an Old Lady Who Swallowed a Fly*, p. 56.

Publishers Weekly, June 21, 1993, p. 103; June 20, 1994, review of *Road Builders*, p. 104; September 30, 1996, p. 85; August 18, 1997, review of *There Was an Old Lady Who Swallowed a Fly*, p. 91; May 4, 1998, p. 212; November 1, 1999, review of *Joseph Had a Little Overcoat*, p. 82; July 22, 2002, review of *This Is the House That Jack Built*, p. 176; August 8, 2005, review of *Kibitzers and Fools*, p. 233.

School Library Journal, December, 1987, p. 96; May, 1988, p. 90; April, 1990, Sharon McElmeel, review of *Snakey Riddles*, p. 108; June, 1992, Sharon McElmeel, review of *Spacey Riddles*, p. 108; September, 1994, p. 208; August, 1995, p. 114; December, 1996, Claudia Cooper, review of *Two Little Witches*, p. 110; December, 1997, Martha Topol, review of *There Was an Old Lady Who Swallowed a Fly*, p. 101; January, 2000, Linda Ludke, review of *Joseph Had a Little Overcoat*, p. 112; September, 2002, Barbara Buckley, review of *This Is the House That Jack Built*, p. 218; December, 2004, Wanda Meyers-Hines, review of *Simms Taback's Big Book of Words*, p. 122; October, 2005, Susan Scheps, review of *Kibitzers and Fools*, p. 130.

ONLINE

Children's Book Council Web site, http://www.cbcbooks.org/cbcmagazine/ (May 18, 2006), "Simms Taback."

* * *

TEAGUE, Mark 1963-
(Mark Christopher Teague)

Personal
Born February 10, 1963, in La Mesa, CA; son of John Wesley (an insurance agent) and Joan (Clay) Teague; married Laura Quinlan (an insurance claims examiner), June 18, 1988; children: Lily, Ava. *Education:* University of California, Santa Cruz, B.A., 1985. *Politics:* Democrat. *Religion:* Christian. *Hobbies and other interests:* Soccer, running.

Addresses
Home—Coxsackie, NY. *Agent*—c/o Author Mail, Scholastic, 555 Broadway, New York, NY 10012.

Career
Freelance illustrator and writer, 1989—.

Member
Authors Guild, Authors League of America.

Awards, Honors
Christopher Award, 2003, for *Dear Mrs. LaRue: Letters from Obedience School*.

Writings

SELF-ILLUSTRATED

The Trouble with the Johnsons, Scholastic (New York, NY), 1989.

Mark Teague (Photograph by Laura Teague. Reproduced by permission of Mark Teague.)

Moog-Moog, Space Barber, Scholastic (New York, NY), 1990.
Frog Medicine, Scholastic (New York, NY), 1991.
The Field beyond the Outfield, Scholastic (New York, NY), 1991.
Pigsty, Scholastic (New York, NY), 1994.
How I Spent My Summer Vacation, Crown (New York, NY), 1995.
The Secret Shortcut, Scholastic (New York, NY), 1996.
Baby Tamer, Scholastic (New York, NY), 1997.
The Lost and Found, Scholastic (New York, NY), 1998.
One Halloween Night, Scholastic (New York, NY), 1999.
Dear Mrs. LaRue: Letters from Obedience School, Scholastic (New York, NY), 2002.
Detective LaRue: Letters from the Investigation, Scholastic (New York, NY), 2004.

ILLUSTRATOR

What Are Scientists, What Do They Do?, Scholastic (New York, NY), 1991.
Adventures in Lego Land, Scholastic (New York, NY), 1991.
Chris Babcock, *No Moon, No Milk!*, Crown (New York, NY), 1993.
Dick King-Smith, *Three Terrible Trins*, Crown (New York, NY), 1994.
Tony Johnston, *The Iguana Brothers, A Perfect Day*, Blue Sky Press (New York, NY), 1995.
Audrey Wood, *The Flying Dragon Room*, Blue Sky Press (New York, NY), 1996.
Dick King-Smith, *Mr. Potter's Pet*, Hyperion (New York, NY), 1996.
Cynthia Rylant, *Poppleton*, Blue Sky Press (New York, NY), 1997.
Cynthia Rylant, *Poppleton and Friends: Book Two*, Blue Sky Press (New York, NY), 1997.
Cynthia Rylant, *Poppleton Forever*, Blue Sky Press (New York, NY), 1998.
Audrey Wood, *Sweet Dream Pie*, Blue Sky Press (New York, NY), 1998.
Cynthia Rylant, *Poppleton Everyday*, Blue Sky Press (New York, NY), 1998.
Cynthia Rylant, *Poppleton in Fall*, Blue Sky Press (New York, NY), 1999.
Cynthia Rylant, *Poppleton in Spring*, Blue Sky Press (New York, NY), 1999.
Cynthia Rylant, *Poppleton Has Fun*, Blue Sky Press (New York, NY), 2000.
Cynthia Rylant, *Poppleton in Winter*, Blue Sky Press (New York, NY), 2001.
Cynthia Rylant, *The Great Gracie Chace*, Blue Sky Press (New York, NY), 2001.
Shana Corey, *First Graders from Mars: Episode One, Horus's Horrible Day*, Scholastic (New York, NY), 2001.
Shana Corey, *First Graders from Mars: Episode Two, The Problem with Pelly*, Scholastic (New York, NY), 2002.
Shana Corey, *First Graders from Mars: Episode Three, Nergal and the Great Space Race*, Scholastic (New York, NY), 2002.
Shana Corey, *First Graders from Mars: Episode Four, Tera, Star Student*, Scholastic (New York, NY), 2003.
Anne Isaacs, *Pancakes for Supper!*, Scholastic (New York, NY), 2006.

ILLUSTRATOR; "HOW DO DINOSAURS" SERIES

Jane Yolen, *How Do Dinosaurs Say Goodnight?*, Blue Sky Press (New York, NY), 2000.
Jane Yolen, *How Do Dinosaurs Get Well Soon?*, Blue Sky Press (New York, NY), 2003.
Jane Yolen, *How Do Dinosaurs Clean Their Rooms?*, Blue Sky Press (New York, NY), 2004.
Jane Yolen, *How Do Dinosaurs Count to Ten?*, Blue Sky Press (New York, NY), 2004.
Jane Yolen, *How Do Dinosaurs Eat Their Food?*, Blue Sky Press (New York, NY), 2005.
Jane Yolen, *How Do Dinosaurs Learn Their Colors?*, Blue Sky Press (New York, NY), 2006.
Jane Yolen, *How Do Dinosaurs Play with Their Friends?*, Blue Sky Press (New York, NY), 2006.

Sidelights

Mark Teague has a quirky sense of humor, and just how quirky can easily be discovered by reading any of his books for children. Peopled with characters with names like Elmo Freem and Wallace Bleff, Teague's books poke fun at things that kids dread—homework, cleaning one's room, ritual first-day-of-school haircuts, and the like—while his illustrations bring to life his quasi-realistic settings. Comparing Teague to author and illustrator William Joyce due to the nostalgic quality of his acrylic paintings, a *Publishers Weekly* contributor remarked that Teague's "combination of deadpan text and unbridled art is a sure-fire recipe for a crowd-pleaser."

"I managed to graduate from college without having any idea what I was going to do with my life," Teague once admitted to *SATA*. "My degree was in U.S. history but I wasn't interested in teaching. I enjoyed art but had no formal training. I liked to write but was unsure how to make it pay." The solution? Pack up the auto and head East to New York City. By the spring of 1986 Teague had arrived and was living with his brother, who helped the author-to-be get a job in the display department at the giant Barnes and Noble bookstore at Rockefeller Center in Manhattan. "The job provided a sort of crash course in design and graphic arts techniques," Teague explained, "and exposed me to a lot of new books. Looking at children's books in the store reminded me of how much I had enjoyed picture books as a child and how much fun it had been to write and illustrate my own stories at that age."

Remembering the fun of being an author sparked *The Trouble with the Johnsons,* Teague's first picture book for children. Published in 1989, the book tells the story of Elmo Freem, who longs to return to the country after his family moves to the big city. Together with his equally homesick cat, Elmo returns to the old house for a visit, where he meets the new owners, the Johnsons. While they seem nice enough, the Johnsons are a bit odd (for one thing, they're a family of dinosaurs). Ultimately, Elmo goes back to the city with the knowledge that home is really where your family is. "The book came out of my experience living in Brooklyn," Teague recalled to *SATA*. "The theme was somewhat melancholy, but I tried to offset this with humor and a plot which was energetic and bizarre." A *Publishers Weekly* commentator stated that "Teague's unique perspective is utilized magnificently both in words and pictures to produce a noteworthy first book." The same year as *The Trouble with the Johnsons* was accepted by its eventual publisher, Scholastic, Teague was able to escape the city, moving with his wife to upstate New York where he continues to make his home.

Elmo reemerges in Teague's next book, *Moog-Moog, Space Barber.* Taking as its premise "the apparently universal horror inspired by a bad haircut," according to Teague, *Moog-Moog, Space Barber* is much more a fantasy than *The Trouble with the Johnsons,* incorporating elements of science fiction as well. The amazingly calm Elmo awakes one morning to find several rotund space aliens, suitably green in color, hanging around the refrigerator in his kitchen. What has Elmo more concerned than close encounters of the alien kind is the razzing he expects to take from fellow schoolmates as a result of his perfectly horrid back-to-school haircut. Fortunately, the aliens are the ones to turn to when looking for a competent stylist; they fly Elmo off to Moog-Moog, barber to the extraterrestrials, and the boy's problems are solved. Stephanie Zvirin praised the book as "sure-footed silliness, sometimes amusingly sly, with just the right touch of irony," in her *Booklist* review.

Fans of Elmo get another glimpse of the boy's off-kilter world in *Frog Medicine,* which involves "that dreaded subject: homework," as well as giant frogs, and "things of that sort," according to its author. Unfortunately for Elmo, fear of an impending book report causes him to sprout frog feet, and only a consultation with noted frog medicine practitioner Dr. Frank Galoof gives him hope of de-amphibianizing anytime soon. Once more, Teague reveals his "knack for dealing with the kinds of predicaments that loom large on children's horizons in a fresh and funny way," according to a *Publishers Weekly* contributor. The book was also praised for containing acrylic illustrations with an attention to detail that reflects the hero's gradual transformation. "Every scene is bathed in curiously pure light," noted a *Kirkus Reviews* critic, "with plenty of clever, funny details to discover."

Equally bizarre is the world casually inhabited by one Wendell Fultz, who, in the book *Pigsty,* is not surprised to find a large hog dozing on his bed. In fact, the abominable condition of Wendell's room makes the pig the cleanest thing in it, but instead of cleaning up the mess like his mother requested, the sly Wendell just pushes a few things out of sight and settles in to play with his new porcine companion. Problems arise, however, after the rest of the curly tailed gang shows up, and their antics cause a commotion. Finally, Wendell himself is forced to lay down the law; the pigs grudgingly help clean up the room and then leave for messier parts. "Especially evident in [Teague's] artwork, there's enough fun to carry the story," maintained *Booklist* reviewer Ilene Cooper, while a *Publishers Weekly* critic lauded the author/illustrator's "gleefully inventive imagination" and stated that "much of the tale's fun resides in [his] quirky acrylic art."

Books by Teague continue to defy traditional classification. In *The Field beyond the Outfield,* a story about summer baseball camp becomes a full-scale fantasy involving a major-league playoff between teams of giant insects. Commented *School Library Journal* critic Dorothy Houlihan, "Teague's window to childhood is wide open, allowing him to address the realities of youthful fantasies without trivializing them." Readers opening the innocent-sounding *How I Spent My Summer Vacation* are drawn into the classroom of one Wallace Bleff and then immediately carried away to the Wild West, amid cowpokes, lariats, and stampeding cattle. "One rootin' tootin' tall tale," applauded a *Publishers Weekly* reviewer, pointing out "some laugh-out-loud funny expressions on animal faces." *Baby Tamer,* Teague's 1997 contribution to the annals of quirky children's literature, depicts a face-off between incredibly

Friends Floyd, Mona, and Wendell find their Halloween brimming with supernatural magic in Teague's self-illustrated beginning reader One Halloween Night. (Text and illustrations copyright © 1999 by Mark Teague. Reprinted by permission of Scholastic Inc.)

competent, fully certified baby-sitter Amanda Smeedy and the Egmont children. When making a lot of noise does not cause even a raised eyebrow from the stoic Amanda, the twins grow desperate, finally resorting to producing a full-blown circus complete with fireworks before admitting defeat. Teague's "bright, sassy acrylics careen across the pages at near-warp speed," according to a *Publishers Weekly* critic.

The mixture of reality and fantasy on the Halloween holiday provide the setting for *One Halloween Night*. Featuring Wendell (from *Pigsty*) and his friends, *One Halloween Night* is the story of a perfectly awful Halloween: Wendell's "mad scientist" costume has turned pink in the wash, good candy is replaced by vegetable flavored candy, and school bully Leona Fleebish is determined to make the night even worse. Luckily for Wendell and company, their costumes give them special powers to deal with the night's problems. "Teague's illustrations are, as always, imaginative, quirky, and exuberant," wrote *Booklist* critic Susan Dove Lempke. Wendell and his friend Floyd star in *The Lost and Found*, in which the two dive into the lost-and-found box at school only to get sucked into a realm of lost hats and missing items. "Teague's latest sly take on the wild flights of childhood fancy is as entertaining as always, and he doles out his deadpan artistic style with a wink," according to a reviewer for *Publishers Weekly*.

As *Booklist* critic Stephanie Zvirin noted, "children will . . . love the crazy notion at the heart of the story."

In 2002, Teague introduced his readers to Ike, a dog at obedience school who is incredibly homesick for his owner, Mrs. LaRue, in *Dear Mrs. LaRue: Letters from Obedience School.* To hear Ike tell the tale, the obedience school is worse than prison; Teague's clever illustrations show Ike's version of the tale in black and white, while in full color, the true story is revealed. Obedience school actually is not all that bad: the lucky dog is essentially being treated to a spa-style environment. Ike is not one to stay put, however, and he escapes obedience school just in time to save Mrs. LaRue from danger, so all his transgressions are forgiven. A *Publishers Weekly* critic considered the title "a tail-wagger of a book that will have readers howling with amusement." Roxanne Burg, in *School Library Journal,* considered the "humorous acrylic illustrations" to be "a howl," while *Booklist* contributor Ilene Cooper wrote that "the wonderfully arch text is matched with Teague's sly pictures." Sue Grossman, writing in *Childhood Education,* noted that "children will have fun comparing Ike's story to what is really going on."

Ike's return in *Detective LaRue: Letters from the Investigation* features him once again writing from prison—this time literally. Accused of kidnaping the neighbor's cats, Ike decides to take the case himself and clear his good name. Again, his descriptions of what is actually going on do not exactly match the true events. "Lively acrylics paired with comical correspondence result in a picture book that will have fans howling," wrote a reviewer for *Publishers Weekly.* A *Kirkus Reviews* contributor acknowledged that "Teague's innovative approach to storytelling is fun, but educational as well." As *School Library Journal* contributor Steven Engelfried wrote, "Teague's visual characterizations of animals and people are also a treat," while Jennifer Mattson, in *Booklist,* noted that "children will get a thrill out of piecing together the mystery alongside the wily, self-serving, yet eminently lovable Ike."

Teague has also illustrated the work of other authors such as Dick King-Smith, Audrey Wood, and Cynthia Rylant. A *Publishers Weekly* contributor, appraising Wood's *The Flying Dragon Room,* asserted that the plot "gets a vital boost from Teague's buoyant whimsical art," while Cooper, reviewing *No Moon, No Milk!* in *Booklist,* noted that "Teague's ebullient artwork captures a very determined cow in . . . uncowlike settings . . . with humor and panache." Audrey Wood's *Sweet Dream* "is a funny and clever story, taken a notch further by Teague's illustrations," according to Elizabeth Drennan in *Booklist.* Teague illustrates the story of a lost dog in *The Great Gracie Chase,* about which Beth Tegart wrote in *School Library Journal:* "In the hands of Rylant and Teague, this basic event has charm, hu-

A puppy accused of cat-chasing links up with the law to clear his reputation in Teague's humorous Detective LaRue: Letters from the Investigation. (Text and illustrations copyright © 2004 by Mark Teague. Reprinted by permission of Scholastic Inc.)

mor, and joy." Sue Grossman, writing in *Childhood Education,* commented that "The simple pictures and story will delight young children."

Working with author Shana Corey on the "First Graders from Mars" series, Teague has created a Martian vision of elementary school. The children are brilliantly colored and have long tentacles; a *Publishers Weekly* critic called the setting a "Seussian landscape" in a review of the first title in the series, *First Graders from Mars: Episode One, Horus's Horrible Day.* Carol Schene, reviewing the same title, commented: "The nonhuman students are done in assorted colors from green to purple, and the teacher, Ms. Vortex, is really a standout with eyes . . . in the back of her head." Shelle Rosenfeld, writing about *First Graders from Mars: Episode Two, The Problem with Pelly* in *Booklist,* noted that Teague's "Martian setting clearly and humorously shows that normality is relative."

Teague has also teamed up with award-winning author Jane Yolen on the "How Do Dinosaurs" picture-book series intended to encourage good manners to readers through the humorous behaviors of dinosaur children. While the dinosaurs are depicted as having human parents, they are "specifically identified with cunningly placed labels within each double-paged spread," as well as at the end of the book, according to a critic for *Kirkus Reviews* in a review of *How Do Dinosaurs Get Well Soon?* Ilene Cooper, in *Booklist,* noted of the same book that "Teague, always tops when it comes to mining humor in art, does a great job here."

As a father, Teague often gets inspiration from his two children. "My daughters keep it fresh for me. They provide all kinds of inspiration. They're very funny and we have a good time. I read to my daughters all the time," he told an interviewer for the *Reading Is Fundamental Web site.* In the same interview, Teague gave his advice for young writers and illustrators: "Practice is everything. You should read a lot. I think that both writing and illustrating come from a love of books. That was the first thing for me. For as long as I remember, I just loved books."

Biographical and Critical Sources

PERIODICALS

Booklist, November 1, 1990, Stephanie Zvirin, review of *Moog-Moog, Space Barber,* p. 531; September 1, 1991, p. 64; September 1, 1993, Ilene Cooper, review of *No Moon, No Milk!,* pp. 66-67; September 15, 1994, Ilene Cooper, review of *Pigsty,* p. 145; September 15, 1996, p. 251; February 15, 1998, Elizabeth Drennan, review of *Sweet Dream,* p. 1021; July, 1998, Stephanie Zvirin, review of *The Lost and Found,* p. 1890; September 1, 1999, Susan Dove Lempke, review of *One Halloween Night,* p. 151; February 15, 2002, Shelle Rosenfeld, review of *First Graders from Mars: Episode Two, The Problem with Pelly,* p. 1019; November 1, 2002, Ilene Cooper, review of *Dear Mrs. LaRue: Letters from Obedience School,* p. 494; January 1, 2003, Ilene Cooper, review of *How Do Dinosaurs Get Well Soon?,* p. 881; January 1, 2003, review of *Dear Mrs. LaRue,* p. 799; October 15, 2004, Jennifer Mattson, review of *Detective LaRue: Letters from the Investigation,* p. 411.

Childhood Education, winter, 2001, Sue Grossman, review of *The Great Gracie Chase,* p. 112; spring, 2003, Sue Grossman, review of *Dear Mrs. LaRue,* p. 180.

Five Owls, March-April, 1998, pp. 80-81.

Horn Book, March-April, 2003, Christine M. Hepperman, review of *How Do Dinosaurs Get Well Soon?,* p. 208.

Instructor, August, 2001, Judy Freeman, review of *First Graders from Mars: Episode One, Horus's Horrible Day,* p. 22.

Kirkus Reviews, August 15, 1991, review of *Frog Medicine,* pp. 1094-1095; March 15, 1992, p. 399; August 1, 1995, p. 1117; July 1, 1996, p. 975; August 15, 1997, p. 1313; December 1, 2001, review of *First Graders from Mars: Episode Two,* p. 1683; August 1, 2002, review of *Dear Mrs. LaRue,* p. 1145; December 1, 2002, review of *How Do Dinosaurs Get Well Soon?,* p. 1776; August 15, 2004, review of *Detective LaRue: Letters from the Investigation,* p. 814.

Library Journal, June, 1992, Dorothy Houlihan, review of *The Field beyond the Outfield, School* pp. 103-104.

New York Times Book Review, July 12, 1992, p. 23.

Publishers Weekly, September 8, 1989, review of *The Trouble with the Johnsons,* p. 69; October 4, 1991, review of *Frog Medicine,* p. 88; July 11, 1994, review of *Pigsty,* p. 78; July 10, 1995, review of *How I Spent My Summer Vacation,* p. 56; January 22, 1996, review of *The Flying Dragon Room,* p. 73; August 26, 1996, review of *The Secret Shortcut,* p. 98; August 11, 1997, review of *Baby Tamer,* p. 401; July, 1998, Stephanie Zvirin, review of *The Lost and Found,* p. 1890; September 27, 1999, review of *One Halloween Night,* p. 47, and review of *The Secret Shortcut,* p. 107; July 16, 2001, review of *First Graders from Mars: Episode 1, Horus's Horrible Day,* p. 180; July 22, 2002, review of *Dear Mrs. LaRue,* p. 177; September 15, 2002, Jason Britton, "In the Studio with Mark Teague," pp. 23-24; March 10, 2003, "Christopher Awards Presented," p. 18; July 19, 2004, review of *Detective LaRue,* p. 160.

School Library Journal, April, 1995, p. 103; March, 1996, p. 184; April, 2001, Beth Tegart, review of *The Great Gracie Chase,* p. 121; September, 2001, Carol Schene, review of *First Graders from Mars: Episode One,* p. 185; October, 2001, Patricia Manning, review of *Poppleton in Winter,* p. 130; April, 2002, Dona Ratterree, review of *First Graders from Mars: Episode Two,* p. 102; September, 2002, Roxanne Burg, review of *Dear Mrs. LaRue,* p. 207; February, 2003, Jody McCoy, review of *How Do Dinosaurs Get Well Soon?,* p. 126; October, 2004, Steven Engelfried, review of *Detective LaRue,* p. 135.

Time, December 11, 1995, p. 77.

Tribune Books (Chicago, IL), December 15, 2002, review of *Dear Mrs. LaRue,* p. 5.

ONLINE

Children's Book Council Magazine Web site, http://cbcbooks.org/cbcmagazine/ (April 25, 2006), profile of Teague.

Houghton Mifflin Education Place Web site, http://www.eduplace.com/kids/ (April 25, 2006), profile of Teague.

Reading Is Fundamental Web site, http://www.rif.org/ (April 25, 2006), interview with Teague.

Scholastic Web site, http://www.scholastic.com/ (April 25, 2006), profile of Teague.*

* * *

TEAGUE, Mark Christopher See TEAGUE, Mark

* * *

TOFT, Kim Michelle 1960-

Personal

Born February 29, 1960, in Dalby, Queensland, Australia; daughter of Beryl Newly Anders (a retailer); partner of Allan Sheather; children: Casey Elle. *Education:* Diploma of Teaching; Certificate of Design. *Politics:* "Green." *Hobbies and other interests:* Collecting glasses and crockery, cooking and dining out, swimming, astrology, live music, walking on the beach.

Addresses

Home—12/4-10 Grandview St., Shelly Beach, East Ballina, New South Wales 2478, Australia. *Office*—P.O. Box 693, Ballina, New South Wales 2478, Australia. *Agent*—Rod Hare, Unit 4/21 Mary St., Surrey Hills, New South Wales 2010, Australia. *E-mail*—silkimbooks@dodo.com.au.

Kim Michelle Toft (Photo courtesy of Kim Michelle Toft.)

Career

Primary school teacher in North Queensland, Australia, 1979-84; graphic designer in South Australia, Australia, 1984-88; silk artist, Shelly Beach, New South Wales, Australia, 1991—; illustrator and author, 1995—; Silkim Books (publishing company), founder and owner, 2005—. Artist-in-residence at Underwater World Mooloolaba; Barrier Reef Aquarium; Out of the Box '98 Brisbane; Ipswich Children's Literature Festival; Somerset Children's Literature Festival, Gold Coast, Queensland, Australia; and Freemantle Children's Centre, Perth, Western Australia, Australia. Motivational speaker; leads silk workshops for adults and children. *Exhibitions:* Work exhibited at Sheraton Mirage, Port Douglas, Queensland, Australia; Sheraton Mirage, Gold Coast, Queensland; Marriott, Surfers Paradise, Queensland; 12th Annual Maui Marine Art Expo, Maui, Hawaii; and elsewhere in Hawaii.

Member

World Wildlife Foundation (member, local dune care group).

Awards, Honors

Honour Book Award, Australia Book Council, and Whitley Award for Best Children's Book, both 1998, Best Children's Book designation, Benjamin Franklin Awards for Independent Publishing, and Teacher's Choice Award, both 1999, and Best Primary Book designation, Royal Zoological Awards, all for *One Less Fish;* notable book citation, Children's Book Council of Australia (CBCA), 2000, and Whitley Award Certificate of Merit, both for *Neptune's Nursery;* notable book designation in the children's information book category, CBCA, Best Picture Book designation, Australian Wilderness Society, and Green Earth Book Award, and Whitely Award Australia, all for *The World That We Want.*

Writings

SELF-ILLUSTRATED PICTURE BOOKS

(With Allan Sheather) *One Less Fish,* University of Queensland Press (St. Lucia, Queensland, Australia), 1997, Charlesbridge (Watertown, MA), 1998.
(With Allan Sheather) *Neptune's Nursery,* University of Queensland Press (St. Lucia, Queensland, Australia), 1999, Charlesbridge (Watertown, MA), 2000.
The World That We Want, University of Queensland Press (St. Lucia, Queensland, Australia), 2004, Charlesbridge (Watertown, MA), 2005.
A Sea of Words: An ABC of the Deep Blue Sea, Charlesbridge (Watertown, MA), 2006.

ILLUSTRATOR

Alan Brown, *Turtle's Song* (picture book), University of Queensland Press (St. Lucia, Queensland, Australia), 2001.

Work in Progress

12 Underwater Days of Christmas; The Forgotten Ocean, about the evolution of central Australia.

Sidelights

Kim Michelle Toft is the author and illustrator of several books that introduce children to the wonders of the fragile ocean ecosystem. In her first book, *One Less Fish,* Toft counts down from twelve fish to zero as the creatures are killed by fishermen, discarded trash, and other marine hazards. Another book, *Neptune's Nursery,* shows how various sea creatures, including humpback whales, manta rays, and seahorses, are born and raised by their parents. This title was described as "a radiant peek into an oceanic nursery" by *School Library Journal* contributor Patricia Manning. In a more recent title, *The World That We Want,* Toft's cumulative rhyme shows how all of the ecosystems of the earth depend on each other, including the "This is the beach that meets the mangrove that follows the river that weaves through the forest that filters the air that circles the world that we want." However, her books are most notable for their illustrations. As Kathy Piehl described in a review of *The World That We Want* for *School Library Journal,* "The arresting, brilliantly hued illustrations were drawn and painted on silk." A *Publishers Weekly* also praised Toft's artwork for that title, calling it "luminous."

Toft told *SATA*: "As I sat in my room at the age of four, spending hours upon hours drawing my favorite Walt Disney characters like Mickey Mouse and Donald Duck, I had no idea that one day I would be creating my own characters and writing stories about them.

"Growing up in suburbia in Brisbane in the 1960s and 1970s, I always had a feeling that there was more to the world than my backyard. I was an only child and I often felt very lonely, as my mum and stepfather worked full time. I would amuse myself drawing and watching far too much television! I believe both things helped fuel my imagination and would take me to different worlds. Drawing was the one thing I did well and therefore it was something I always got great satisfaction out of.

"School was hard for me because I always felt like an outsider. Instead of playing sport, I would prefer to draw. Then in high school I ran the school magazine and once again, I felt like I didn't fit in with the 'norm.' Art was my elective subject all through school and I loved it. I also love learning about the history of art and the artists' lives.

"Even though I wanted to be an art teacher I opted for the primary-school teaching course and once completed I taught for four and a half years in far north Queensland, where I discovered the immense beauty of tropical Australia. The strong feelings I developed there toward the environment would stay with me all through my life. Although I loved teaching I felt I was moving further and further away from my art. I decided to go back to college to study art and design. I moved to Adelaide, moved into a share house on the beach, and completed a two-year course in graphic design. I then worked as a graphic designer for another two years, designing wine bottle labels, cat food labels, and logos for businesses. I enjoyed the designing, but the commercial aspect of the advertising industry did little to enrich my soul. However, I learnt a lot about layout and design, typesetting and photography—little did I know then that I would use these skills to produce the children's books I create today.

"I decided to make another change and moved from Adelaide, back closer to my mum who was living on the Gold Coast. I set up house in northern New South Wales, a place I had always loved, and I still live here today. Still on the water and still being 'blown away' by the timeless beauty of the ocean.

"I have made many changes in my life. It was not easy at times making such major decisions, like giving up a good career to move to a totally different place and do a totally different thing. Each time it was like starting from scratch, but I knew there was more to discover about myself and my career path.

"My goal when I moved to northern New South Wales was to become a full-time artist and make a living out of it! However, you need money to pay the rent and buy food, so I worked in bars, restaurants and galleries part-time so I could draw and paint at home. It was in these early days that I worked with a lady who was painting on silk to produce unique clothing. I learnt a lot about the medium and marveled at the incredible range of colours you could achieve on silk. It was like no other medium I had ever used. I started experimenting more and more with the silk, until finally I went out on my own and started creating large underwater paintings.

"I was fortunate enough in the beginning of my silk painting career to meet the right people who helped me set up exhibitions of my work at the big hotels like the Sheraton Hotels in Port Douglas, Gold Coast and Hawaii. I was also lucky enough to find my market, people who loved the coastal habitats I painted and had the money to buy them. I have met some amazing people over the past fourteen years of exhibiting. People from all around the world, and one of my biggest highlights was selling a painting to Mick Jagger (from the Rolling Stones) and his wife then, Jerry Hall. But once again I felt there was something missing. Painting to sell has limited rewards and I wanted to do something more meaningful.

"In 1992 I did do something more meaningful: I gave birth to my beautiful daughter Casey Elle. Perhaps it was the emergence of picture books again in my life that got me thinking about writing and illustrating my own books. I had always collected children's books and I had also kept all my treasured Golden Books from when I was a child. So I decided that books were where I wanted to head.

"With the help of Casey's dad, Allan Sheather, we wrote *One Less Fish* together. Then armed with my silk portfolio and the manuscript, I begged to see noted publishers University of Queensland Press, who signed me up two weeks after our first meeting. *Neptune's Nursery* was my next book. It was also co-written by Allan Sheather. Both books are still being published and can be found in countries all around the world. *Turtle's Song* was next, which was written by an English author, Alan Brown. I painted the illustrations, once again on silk and once again all with strong environmental emphasis. My first totally solo effort is *The World That We Want*. It is my favorite to date and looks at the fragile balance in nature and in particular the coastal habitats of far north Queensland. It took three years to complete and some of the illustrations took three months to paint. One illustration is 4.5 meters long and 1.2 meters wide! *All* the illustrations from this book are on a national tour. The total wall space needed to exhibit all the illustrations is 30 meters! I was very proud when I saw them altogether for the first time.

"It has also been an honor to win many national and international awards for my books. Knowing that they are being read and appreciated by children from all around the world is also a wonderful buzz.

"When I am not touring or teaching, I try to paint and draw for twenty hours per week and spend ten hours writing or researching per week. I also do between 5-10 hours of bookwork, promotional work and work-related activities, i.e. going to the framers, galleries, delivering work, and packing and signing books.

"I love my life now; living on the beach with my daughter Casey, writing and illustrating books about things I feel passionate about like the coastal environment, and touring to teach children about my books and my art.

"I have done a complete cycle, drawing, painting, designing and teaching. It is all an ongoing journey. Each decision I make, each painting I complete and each book which is created brings me closer to my dream of becoming a successful children's book author and illustrator and buying my own house on the beach.

"So my advice to anyone who wants to become a success through artistic pursuits is to keep true to your dreams. DO IT, don't just say it; don't worry about what other people think or do, and just enjoy the journey toward the world that you want."

Biographical and Critical Sources

BOOKS

Toft, Kim Michelle, *The World That We Want,* University of Queensland Press (St. Lucia, Queensland, Australia), 2004, Charlesbridge (Watertown, MA), 2005.

PERIODICALS

Booklist, July, 1998, Carolyn Phelan, review of *One Less Fish,* p. 1883; December 15, 2000, John Peters, review of *Neptune's Nursery,* p. 823.

Publishers Weekly, October 10, 2005, review of *The World That We Want,* p. 60.

School Library Journal, October, 2000, Patricia Manning, review of *Neptune's Nursery,* p. 140; September, 2005, Kathy Piehl, review of *The World That We Want,* p. 197.

ONLINE

Booked Out Speakers Agency Web site, http://www.bookedout.com.au/ (April 8, 2006), "Kim Michelle Toft."

V-W

VANASSE, Deb 1957-
(Debra Lynn Lehmann)

Personal
Born September 12, 1957, in St. Paul, MN; married; husband's name Tim; children: Lynx (son), Jessica. *Education:* Bemidji State University, B.A.; California State University at Dominguez Hills, master's degree. *Hobbies and other interests:* Reading, writing, traveling, music, dance.

Addresses
Home—AK; winters in Baja, Mexico. *Agent*—c/o Author Mail, Sasquatch Books, 119 S. Main, Ste. 400, Seattle, WA 98104. *E-mail*—debv@gci.net.

Career
High school teacher in Nunapitchuk, AK, and other Alaskan villages; university instructor in Bethel and Fairbanks, AK, 1987-88; North Pole High School, educator, 1988-99; real-estate broker.

Writings

YOUNG-ADULT NOVELS

A Distant Enemy, Lodestar Books (New York, NY), 1997.
Out of the Wilderness, Clarion Books (New York, NY), 1999.

PICTURE BOOKS

Alaska Animal Babies, photographs by Gavriel Jecan, Sasquatch Books (Seattle, WA), 2005.
Under Alaska's Midnight Sun, illustrated by Jeremiah Trammell, Sasquatch Books (Seattle, WA), 2005.
A Totem Tale, illustrated by Eric Brooks, Sasquatch Books (Seattle, WA), 2006.

Sidelights
Author Deb Vanasse has spent most of her adult life living in Alaska, much of it teaching high school and college in remote areas. As a result, the unique culture and environment of rural Alaska are key features of her work. Her first two books, *A Distant Enemy* and *Out of the Wilderness,* are young-adult novels, but since then she has also published several picture books. "I could spend many years and many books attempting to capture the essence of Southwestern Alaska, an area so remote that few people get to experience it firsthand," Vanasse wrote on her home page.

Joseph, the protagonist of *A Distant Enemy,* is a half-Eskimo, half-white (*kass'aq* in the Yup'ik Eskimo language), fourteen-year-old boy who lives in a small, remote Alaskan village. After Joseph's kass'aq father abandons the family to return to "civilization," Joseph takes out his anger over this abandonment on every other kass'aq whom he encounters. These include the wildlife rangers, who enforce rules that restrict the Yup'ik from fishing, and Joseph's English teacher. That teacher, Mr. Townsend, and Joseph's grandfather try to help the boy, but Joseph seems to be bent on allowing his rage to destroy him. *Booklist* reviewer Hazel Rochman commented that Vanasse "tries to do too much" in this book, but still praised "the strong sense of place and the drama of Joseph's personal conflict." A *Publishers Weekly* contributor also praised this aspect of the book, calling *A Distant Enemy* "a vivid portrait of modern Eskimo lifestyles, conflicts and fears . . . [and] a sensitive account of one teenager's coming of age."

Josh, the protagonist of *Out of the Wilderness,* has the opposite problem from Joseph: his father loves the Alaskan wilderness far too much. The man takes fifteen-year-old Josh and Josh's older half-brother, Nathan, out to a remote area, where they build a ten-foot-by-twenty-foot cabin and survive by hunting, gathering, and building the things they need. Josh wants nothing more than to return to his friends and school, but Nathan and their father love this life. However, Nathan's passion for the wilderness causes him to take dangerous risks as he tries to get closer to nature, and it falls to Josh to save him. "Pragmatic Josh, intense Nathan, and the boys' guilt-ridden father are intriguingly drawn," Debbie Carton wrote in *Booklist,* and a *Publishers Weekly* reviewer deemed the book a "chilling winter's tale."

Under Alaska's Midnight Sun, one of Vanasse's first picture books, examines a unique aspect of life in Alaska: on the solstice (the longest day of the year) the sun never sets. A young girl struggles to stay awake to see the midnight sun, as she, her mother, and her baby brother walk out into the country to observe the animals frolicking in the late-night sunshine. "The text is fresh and vivid," Carol L. MacKay wrote in *School Library Journal,* while according to *Booklist* reviewer Carolyn Phelan, Vanese "conveys [the girl's] excitement as well as her determination not to fall asleep before midnight."

Biographical and Critical Sources

PERIODICALS

ALAN Review, winter, 2000, Deb Vanasse, "On Taking Ourselves Too Seriously, and Other Tragic Mistakes."
Booklist, January 1, 1997, Hazel Rochman, review of *A Distant Enemy,* p. 846; March 15, 1999, Debbie Carton, review of *Out of the Wilderness,* p. 1330; May 1, 2005, Carolyn Phelan, review of *Under Alaska's Midnight Sun,* p. 1594.
Children's Bookwatch, September, 2005, review of *Under Alaska's Midnight Sun.*
Publishers Weekly, January 13, 1997, review of *A Distant Enemy,* p. 76; February 15, 1999, review of *Out of the Wilderness,* p. 108.
School Library Journal, August, 2005, Carol L. MacKay, review of *Under Alaska's Midnight Sun,* p. 107.

ONLINE

Deb Vanasse Home Page, http://www.debvanasse.com/ (April 8, 2006).

* * *

VanOOSTING, James 1951-

Personal

Born 1951; son of Jean Reed; stepson of Robert Reed; married twice (divorced); married Dawn LaJuana Williams (a university dean), September 15, 2001. *Education:* Taylor University, graduated; Northwestern University, Ph.D. (performance studies).

Addresses

Office—Fordham University, Rose Hill Campus, Bronx, NY 10458. *E-mail*—vanoosja@shu.edu.

Career

Educator and author. Southern Illinois University, Carbondale, professor of English for 16 years, and department chair for 8 years; Seton Hall University, NJ, dean of arts and sciences, beginning c. 1998;. Visiting professor and St. Edmund Campion fellow, Fordham University, beginning 2005; visiting professor at University of California, San Diego, and Louisiana State University.

Writings

FICTION

Maxie's Ghost, Farrar, Straus (New York, NY), 1987.
Electing J.J., Farrar, Straus (New York, NY), 1990.
The Last Payback, HarperCollins (New York, NY), 1997.
Walking Mary, HarperCollins (New York, NY), 2005.

OTHER

Business Correspondence: Writer, Reader, and Text, Prentice-Hall (Englewood Cliffs, NJ), 1983.
The Business Report: Writer, Reader, and Text, Prentice-Hall (Englewood Cliffs, NJ), 1983.
The Business Speech: Writer, Reader, and Text, Prentice-Hall (Englewood Cliffs, NJ), 1985.
Practicing Business: Communication in the Workplace, Houghton Mifflin (Boston, MA), 1992.
(With Paul H. Gray) *Performance in Life and Literature,* Allyn & Bacon (Boston, MA), 1996.
And the Flesh Became Word: Reflections Theological and Aesthetic, Crossroad (New York, NY), 2005.

Sidelights

In addition to working as a college English professor, James VanOosting has written several novels for young-adult readers, among them *The Last Payback, Electing J.J.,* and *Walking Mary.* Narrated by twelve-year-old Dorothea "Dimple" Dorfman, *The Last Paycheck* focuses on a grief-stricken girl's desire for revenge immediately following the accidental death of her twin brother. Praising VanOosting for creating realistic characters, *Horn Book* reviewer Elizabeth S. Watson added that the novel's "intriguing plot and fast-paced dialogue" keep readers turning pages. In *Booklist* GraceAnne A. DeCandido also praised the work, calling *The Last Payback* "startling in its unsentimental, first-person approach." In praise of *Electing J.J.,* a humorous story about a middle-school newcomer who decides to run for town mayor of Framburg, Illinois and shake up stodgy town politics, a *Publishers Weekly* contributor deemed the novel "cleverly written and highly entertaining."

VanOosting tells what *School Library Journal* contributor Nancy P. Reader called a "dark, disturbing tale of mental instability and sexual abuse" in his young-adult

Cover of James VanOosting's *Walking Mary,* featuring artwork by Gary Isaacs. (Text copyright © 2005 by James VanOosting. Jacket art copyright © 2005 by Gary Isaacs. Used by permission of HarperCollins Publishers.)

novel *Walking Mary. Walking Mary* draws readers back once again to Framburg, Illinois. This time they arrive during the 1940s and 1950s, as Pearl and Franklin Keenan are attempting to survive a harsh childhood under the sway of an abusive home and an authoritarian father. Almost drowning at age six, Pearl is pulled to safety by an elderly black woman known as Walking Mary; a poignant town fixture, the woman haunts the train station, awaiting the arrival of a beloved son who was actually killed during World War II. As a way of avoiding her own problems, Pearl becomes increasingly fascinated with Mary and takes up the habit of shadowing the woman, dressing in similar mourning black, and spending time at the train station. Although the two never speak, their lives ultimately reconnect during another tragic set of circumstances. In *Booklist* Frances Bradburn called VanOoosting's story "quietly disturbing with undercurrents of foreboding" that will captivate readers, while a *Kirkus Reviews* critic praised the novel as "wonderfully expressive" work that "captures the magic and intensity of childhood" while also dealing with more serious themes.

Biographical and Critical Sources

PERIODICALS

Booklist, June 1, 1997, GraceAnne A. DeCandido, review of *The Last Payback,* p. 1706; August, 2005, Frances Bradburn, review of *Walking Mary,* p. 2017.

Bulletin of the Center for Children's Books, January, 1988, review of *Maxie's Ghost,* p. 104; June, 1997, review of *The Last Payback,* p. 377.

Horn Book, July-August, 1997, Elizabeth S. Watson, review of *The Last Payback,* p. 465.

Kirkus Reviews, April 15, 2005, review of *Walking Mary,* p. 484.

Kliatt, May, 2005, Janis Flint-Ferguson, review of *Walking Mary,* p. 19.

Publishers Weekly, October 30, 1987, review of *Maxie's Ghost,* p. 72; June 29, 1990, review of *Electing J.J.,* p. 102.

School Library Journal, January, 1988, Martha Rosen, review of *Maxie's Ghost,* p. 78; August, 1990, Joel Shoemaker, review of *Electing J.J.,* p. 150; July, 1997, Jana R. Fine, review of *The Last Payback,* p. 98; July, 2005, Nancy P. Reeder, review of *Walking Mary,* p. 110.

Voice of Youth Advocates, August, 2005, Susan Allen, review of *Walking Mary,* p. 227.*

* * *

WALSH, Lawrence 1942-

Personal

Born 1942; married; wife's name Suella (a teacher and writer).

Addresses

Home—1803 Wornall Rd., Excelsior Springs, MO 64024. *E-mail*—landswalsh@prodigy.net.

Career

Bayer Corporation Quality Assurance Water Analysis Laboratory, former chemist; freelance writer. *Red Herring Mystery Magazine,* founding editor. Whispering Prairie Press, member of board of directors and president; Potpourri Publications, member of board, 1989-95, treasurer, 1993-95. Teacher at writing workshops and at libraries and schools, including Johnson County Community College, and Maplewoods College. Judge for writing contests, including Longview College Scriptwriting Contest, 1991, and Kansas Coffin Awards, 1992.

Member

Society of Children's Book Writers and Illustrators, Missouri Writers' Guild, Oklahoma Writers' Federation.

Awards, Honors

Kansas Governor's Arts Award (with Suella Walsh), 1994.

Writings

WITH WIFE, SUELLA WALSH

The Unicorn and Other Children's Stories, Potpourri Publications, 1993.
They Would Never Be Friends, Royal Fireworks Press (Unionville, NY), 1996.
Through a Dark Tunnel, Royal Fireworks Press (Unionville, NY), 2001.

Also author, with Suella Walsh, of books, including *Viewpoint in Fiction* for Potpourri Publications; *Running Scared, The Case of Erica's Weird Behavior* (uncredited), *Through a Dark Tunnel,* and *In the Middle of the Night,* for Royal Fireworks Press; and *Creating Fiction That Sells,* for Shannon River Press. Contributor to books, including *Chocolate for a Teen's Soul,* Simon & Schuster; and to periodicals, including *Highlights for Children, Writers' Journal, Buffalo Spree, Good Old Days, Byline, Mystery Forum, Friend, Potpourri, Missouri,* and *Missouri Life.**

* * *

WALSH, Suella

Personal
Married Lawrence Walsh (a chemist and writer).

Addresses
Home—1803 Wornall Rd., Excelsior Springs, MO 64024. *E-mail*—landswalsh@prodigy.net.

Career
Editor and author. Former elementary school teacher; freelance writer. Whispering Prairie Press, member of board of directors; Potpourri Publications, member of board, 1989-95, secretary, 1991-95. Teacher at writing workshops and at libraries and schools, including Johnson County Community College, and Maplewoods College. Judge for writing contests, including Longview College Scriptwriting Contest, 1991, and Kansas Coffin Awards, 1992.

Member
Society of Children's Book Writers and Illustrators, Missouri Writers' Guild, Oklahoma Writers' Federation.

Awards, Honors
Kansas Governor's Arts Award (with Lawrence Walsh), 1994.

Writings

WITH HUSBAND, LAWRENCE WALSH

The Unicorn and Other Children's Stories, Potpourri Publications, 1993.
They Would Never Be Friends, Royal Fireworks Press (Unionville, NY), 1996.
Through a Dark Tunnel, Royal Fireworks Press (Unionville, NY), 2001.

Also author, with Lawrence Walsh, of books, including *Viewpoint in Fiction* for Potpourri Publications; *Running Scared, The Case of Erica's Weird Behavior, Through a Dark Tunnel,* and *In the Middle of the Night,* for Royal Fireworks Press; and *Creating Fiction That Sells,* for Shannon River Press. Contributor to books, including *Chocolate for a Teen's Soul,* Simon & Schuster; and to periodicals, including *Highlights for Children, Writers' Journal, Buffalo Spree, Good Old Days, Byline, Mystery Forum, Friend, Potpourri, Missouri,* and *Missouri Life.* Former columnist.*

* * *

WATKINS, Gloria Jean
See hooks, bell

* * *

WATTS, Jeri Hanel 1957-

Personal
Born June 6, 1957, in Lynchburg, VA; daughter of Robert C. (an insurance salesman) and Dorothy B. (a secretary) Hanel; married Charles L. Watts, Jr. (a juvenile probation director), April 16, 1982; children: Mary, Ellen. *Ethnicity:* "Caucasian." *Education:* College of William & Mary, B.A., 1979; University of Virginia, M.Ed. (reading), 1991. *Religion:* Protestant.

Addresses
Home—409 Harvest Court, Lynchburg, VA 24502.

Career
Educator and writer. Harrington Waddell School, Lexington, VA, teacher, 1979-2006; Lynchburg College, Lynchburg, VA, assistant professor, 2006—.

Member
Shenandoah Reading Council Board, Central Virginia Writers Project Board.

Writings

Keepers, illustrated by Felicia Marshall, Lee & Low Books (New York, NY), 1997.

Work in Progress
Wonder.

After spending the money saved for a special gift, Kendall finds another way to honor his grandmother in Jeri Hanel Watts's Keepers, *featuring illustrations by Felicia Marshall.* (Text copyright © 1997 by Jeri Hanel Watts. Illustrations copyright © 1997 by Felicia Marshall. Reproduced by permission of Lee & Low Books, Inc.)

Sidelights

Longtime teacher Jeri Hanel Watts is the author of *Keepers,* a story about a young boy's strong emotional bond with his grandmother. Kenyon loves to hear his grandmother, Little Dolly, tell stories, and when the woman's birthday approaches, the boy decides he will use his savings to buy her a wonderful gift. However, Kenyon's love of playing baseball overcomes him; instead of using his hard-earned money on a gift for Little Dolly, he buys a baseball glove for himself. Afterward, Kenyon feels remorse, but his understanding grandmother shows that neither her love nor her respect for him have diminished: She now gives him a responsibility: to be the keeper of the family stories. Watts's "acrylic oil paintings in muted colors supply warm, loving portraits of a close-knit African American family" stated Denia Hester in *Booklist.* A *Publishers Weekly* critic commented that Watt's storytelling "comes alive with language, particularly the playful dialogue; the lessons she delivers are sturdy and multilayered."

Watts told *SATA:* "I began writing because I felt compelled to tell stories. A junior high school teacher let me know I was 'a real writer' and I took her word to heart.

"Real life has, however, interfered with being a full-time writer. Being a full-time teacher and a wife and mother means I don't write every day or for the amount of time I'd like. But I write often and continue to produce stories. I try to always be aware of the myriad of ideas that surround me.

"I often combine my work as a writer and my work as a teacher. I work on writing with the fifth-grade students at my school and I find my own experiences as a writer inform my instruction. This 'collaboration' makes both of these aspects of my life richer and more meaningful."

Biographical and Critical Sources

PERIODICALS

Childhood Education, April 11, 2006.
Booklist, January 1, 1998, Denia Hester, review *Keepers,* p. 825.
Publishers Weekly, November 24, 1997, review of *Keepers,* p. 73.
School Library Journal, January, 1998, Marie Wright, review of *Keepers,* p. 94.

ONLINE

Lee & Low Books Web site, http://www.leeandlow.com/ (April 11, 2006).

* * *

WEBBER, Desiree Morrison 1956-

Personal

Born May 22, 1956, in La Mesa, CA; daughter of William (a metallurgist) and Juanita (a homemaker and secretary) Morrison; married Stephen Webber (a television producer), June 28, 1980; children: Clayton. *Ethnicity:* "Caucasian." *Education:* University of California, San Diego, B.A., 1982; University of Oklahoma, M.L.I.S., 1990.

Addresses

Home—322 Country Club Terrace, Mustang, OK 73064.

Career

Librarian and writer. Moore Public Library, Moore, OK, head of children's services, 1990-97; Oklahoma Department of Libraries, Oklahoma City, public library consultant, 1997-2002; Mustang Public Library, Mustang, OK, director, 2002—.

Member

Society of Children's Book Writers and Illustrators, American Library Association, Rotary International.

Awards, Honors

Storytelling World award, International Reading Association, 1999, for *Travel the Globe: Multicultural Story Times;* Oklahoma Book Award finalist, 2000, and Delta

Kappa Gamma State Author Award, 2001, both for *The Buffalo Train Ride;* Oklahoma Book Award finalist, 2004, for *Bone Head.*

Writings

CHILDREN'S NONFICTION

The Buffalo Train Ride, illustrated by Sandy Shropshire, Eakin Press (Austin, TX), 1999.
Bone Head: Story of the Longhorn, illustrated by Sandy Shropshire, Eakin Press (Austin, TX), 2003.

OTHER

(With others) *Travel the Globe: Multicultural Story Times,* illustrated by Sandy Shropshire, Libraries Unlimited (Englewood, CO), 1998.
The Kids' Book Club: Lively Reading and Activities for Grades 1-3, illustrated by Sandy Shropshire, Libraries Unlimited (Englewood, CO), 2001.

Sidelights

In addition to her work as a library administrator, Desiree Morrison Webber is the author of several storytelling guides for teachers and librarians, as well as of *Bone Head: Story of the Longhorn* and *The Buffalo Train Ride,* two titles that reflect her research skills and her knowledge of the history of the American plains. In *Bone Head* Webber recounts the history of the often-overlooked Texas longhorn, and the reasons why this hardy breed was eclipsed by short-horned, more-easily domesticated cattle breeds by the end of the nineteenth century. John Sigwald, writing in *School Library Journal,* called the volume "thoroughly engaging," and added that "*Bone Head* evokes empathy for the cowhands and drovers who endured the elements, outlaws, and dangerous horns of stampede-prone cattle." Focusing on the same era, *The Buffalo Train Ride* follows the path of American bison toward extinction when their grazing lands were fenced in by increasing human settlement. The book focuses on the efforts of zoologist William Hornaday to preserve the species by creating the Wichita National Forest and Game Preserve as a home for the remaining buffalo at the turn of the twentieth century. In *School Library Journal* Coop Renner wrote that Webber's "unusual story is sure to interest animal lovers" as well as young ecology-minded readers.

Webber told *SATA:* "As a librarian and a writer, I have written books for fellow educators and also for children in middle elementary. My professional books are written to help teachers and librarians to encourage young people to enjoy books and to use the library. Books that I write for children are nonfiction and, hopefully, are something interesting from which to read and learn.

Cover of Desiree Morrison Webber's Bone Head, *featuring cover art by Chad Payne.* (Text copyright © 2003 by Desiree Morrison Webber. Illustrations by Sandy Shropshire. Published by Eakin Press. Reproduced by permission.)

"With co-workers, I jointly wrote *Travel the Globe: Multicultural Story Times,* which gives a series of story-hour programs for children aged four to eight. Each chapter covers a different country and includes stories, action rhymes, finger plays, activities, and crafts. Some of the stories are retellings of folk stories and some are original tales based on a country's traditions. For example, on visiting China, I wrote an original story about a young dragon that wants to eat the sun. This is based on an ancient belief that a solar eclipse was caused by a dragon swallowing the sun. People would rush into the streets banging on pots and kettles to scare the dragon away. Apparently it was an effective method of scaring dragons because the sun always returned.

"After *Travel the Globe,* I wrote a children's nonfiction title about fifteen buffalo that rode a train from the Bronx Zoo to Oklahoma Territory, in 1907, to start the first federal bison preserve in the United States. The research for *The Buffalo Train Ride* took two years, plus one year of writing. I read diaries, letters, articles, and books plus a first-hand account of the train ride by a Bronx Zoo employee.

"While working on *The Buffalo Train Ride*, colleague Sandy Shropshire and I began a new program in the children's department of the Moore Public Library. We developed a young readers' book discussion group for children ages five to eight. We had conducted book discussion programs for children aged nine and older, but then considered a discussion group for emerging readers. It turned out to be a great success and we learned that young children enjoyed sharing their opinions.

"After several years, Sandy and I wrote *The Kids' Book Club: Lively Reading and Activities for Grades 1-3*. It was our hope that other librarians would pick up the book and start a young readers' club at their libraries. Sandy and I found that the book club inspired children to read and drew them and their families to the library on a weekly basis. In addition, the reading club attracted both boys and girls, accomplished and unaccomplished readers.

"*Bone Head* is a children's nonfiction book about the near demise of the long horn cattle breed. In my opinion, this animal carved out the Wild West. If not for the longhorns, there may never have been the American cowboys, chuck wagons, or trail drives. *Bone Head* focuses on their colorful history to the near extinction of the breed before they, too, were also located to a federal preserve.

"I became interested in writing while attending college. I wrote articles for my college paper and sought out internships with weekly newspapers and, for a year, worked for a wire service that covered the San Diego City Council and the San Diego County Commissioners' meetings. I thought I wanted to be a journalist but discovered that I enjoyed writing longer pieces. It gave me an opportunity to delve into the topic more and conduct further research.

"I finished my undergraduate degree in communications at the University of California, San Diego, and I later completed a master's degree in library and information sciences at the University of Oklahoma. Following graduation I became a children's librarian. This position inspired me not only to write for children but also to share ideas on getting children interested in books and in using the library. It is a pleasure to write something that you are interested in or inspired by.

"As someone with a full-time career, I had to write before and after hours. Each morning I awoke at four o'clock in the morning and worked for an hour and half to two hours before getting ready for work. In the evenings I tried to write for another hour. At first I thought I would never get anything accomplished writing only two or three hours each day, but I was like Aesop's turtle—slow and steady met the goal."

Biographical and Critical Sources

PERIODICALS

Booklist, August, 1998, Julie Corsaro, review of *Travel the Globe: Multicultural Story Times*, p. 2021.

School Library Journal, February, 1999, Robin L. Gibson, *It's a Small, Small World*, p. 41; May, 2002, Mary Lankford, review of "The Kids' Book Club: Lively Reading and Activities for Grades 1-3," p. 183; March, 2000, Coop Renner, review of *The Buffalo Train Ride*, p. 262; February, 2004, John Sigwald, review of *Bone Head: Story of the Longhorn*, p. 171.*

* * *

WEIGEL, Jeff 1958-

Personal
Born September 9, 1958, in Freeport, IL; son of Lawrence (a butcher) and Phyllis Weigel; married Kim Kent (a copywriter), June 25, 1983; children: Peter, Allison. *Ethnicity:* "Caucasian." *Education:* University of Illinois, B.F.A., 1980.

Addresses
Home—113 Villa Drive, Belleville, IL 62223. *E-mail*—jeffweigel@charter.net.

Career
Comic-book and children's picture book illustrator and author, and graphic artist. Obata Design, St. Louis, MO, creative director, 1989—. Creator of character The Sphinx, for comic-book series *Big Bang*. Creator of character Atomic Ace for children's picture-book series.

Member
Society of Children's Book Writers and Illustrators.

Awards, Honors
Russ Manning Award for Most Promising Newcomer in Comics nomination, 1998, for "The Riddle of the Sphinx"; Don Freeman Award honorable mention, Society of Children's Book Writers and Illustrator, 2004; Parents' Choice Honor Book designation, 2004, for *Atomic Ace*.

Writings

Atomic Ace (He's Just My Dad), Albert Whitman (Morton Grove, IL), 2004.

Atomic Ace and the Robot Rampage, Albert Whitman (Morton Grove, IL), 2006.

While some boys just read about super heroes, the young narrator of Jeff Weigel's Atomic Ace (He's Just My Dad) *actually gets to live with one!* (Text and illustrations copyright © 2004 by Jeff Weigel. Published by Albert Whitman & Company. Reproduced by permission.)

Writer and illustrator for comic-book series *Big Bang*, published by Image Comics.

Sidelights

Writer and illustrator Jeff Weigel entered the world of children's picture books as a refugee from comics. Creator of the comic-book character The Sphinx for the *Big Bang* comic-book series he both writes and illustrates, Weigel is also the creative force behind the books *Atomic Ace (He's Just My Dad)* and *Atomic Ace and the Robot Rampage*. Working as a graphic designer and comic-book artist, Weigel has seen comics skew toward an ever-older audience, and he realized that the kids he hoped to reach through his work could be more easily reached through picture books. He is noted for bringing a comics-style approach to his storytelling, and lets the pictures tell at least as much of the tale as the words. In his imaginative stories, Weigel taps into the same spirit of fun, humor, and adventure as the comics he loved in his youth.

Picture-book super hero Atomic Ace leads a double life, as his young son reveals in his humorous narration to *Atomic Ace (He's Just My Dad)*. As readers watch, Ace spends his days flying around town to fight off bad guys and save the world. At night he morphs into a father and husband, spending time with his family and doing typical dad-type things, like reading the newspaper in his favorite chair. Ace's son wishes that his dad spent more time at home, but admires his father's heroic and noble work. Noting that the book's simple text mimics a child's speech, a *Publishers Weekly* writer wrote that Weigel's "hard-boiled headlines and graphics capture the comedy of Ace's double life." Jennifer Matt-son, writing in *Booklist,* commented that "the juxtapositions between superheroics and regular-guy domesticity are clever, and Weigel's confident artwork, with a slickness that clearly announces his background as a comic book writer and illustrator, is guaranteed to satisfy children obsessed with caped crusaders."

Biographical and Critical Sources

PERIODICALS

Booklinks, May, 2005, Toni Buzzeo, review of *Atomic Ace (He's Just My Dad),* p. 31.
Booklist, March 1, 2004, Jennifer Mattson, review of *Atomic Ace (He's Just My Dad),* p. 1999.
Publishers Weekly, March 15, 2004, review of *Atomic Ace (He's Just My Dad),* p. 74.
School Library Journal, May, 2004, John Sigwald, review of *Atomic Ace (He's Just My Dad),* p. 126.

ONLINE

International Hero.co.uk, http://www.internationalhero.co.uk/ (April 11, 2006), "Big Bang's Sphinx."

*   *   *

WESTHEIMER, David 1917-2005
(Z.Z. Smith, David Kaplan Westheimer)

OBITUARY NOTICE— See index for *SATA* sketch: Born April 11, 1917, in Houston, TX; died of heart failure November 8, 2005, in Los Angeles, CA. Journalist and author. Westheimer was a novelist best known for his books *Von Ryan's Express* and *My Sweet Charlie.* A 1937 graduate of Rice University, his early career was devoted to journalism. He was working for the *Houston Post* when America entered World War II, and he enlisted in the U.S. Army Air Forces. Aboard a B-24 bomber near Italy when it was shot down, Westheimer was captured and became a prisoner of war (P.O.W.). While a prisoner, he spent as much time as he could reading, and this inspired him to become a writer. After the war, he returned to the *Houston Post,* working as an editor for the paper's Sunday magazine and as a television and radio editor until 1960. By that time, he had gained enough success with his first novels, including *Summer on the Water* (1948) and *Watching out for Dulie* (1960), that he decided to write full time. *Von Ryan's Express* (1964) was a bestseller and was adapted as a film starring Frank Sinatra and Trevor Howard. *My Sweet Charlie* (1965) was likewise produced as a film, as well a 1966 Broadway play. Other works by Westheimer include *Lighter than a Feather* (1971; published as *Death Is Lighter than a Feather,* 1995), *Von Ryan's Return* (1980), and *Delay en Route* (2002). In addition, he wrote the television screenplays *Trouble Comes to Town* (1972) and *A Killer among Us* (1990), and the autobiography *Sitting It Out: A World War II POW Memoir* (1992). During the 1980s, Westheimer returned to journalism for a time as a columnist for the *Houston Post*.

OBITUARIES AND OTHER SOURCES:

BOOKS

Westheimer, David, *Sitting It Out: A World War II POW Memoir*, Rice University Press (Houston, TX), 1992.

PERIODICALS

Los Angeles Times, November 12, 2005, p. B17.
New York Times, November 20, 2005, p. A28.
Washington Post, November 19, 2005, p. B7.

* * *

WESTHEIMER, David Kaplan
See WESTHEIMER, David

* * *

WILSON-MAX, Ken 1965-

Personal
Born August 15, 1965, in Harare, Zimbabwe; son of Ken Wilson-Max (a local businessman) and Sophie Elizabeth Pike. *Education:* Attended London College of Printing. *Hobbies and other interests:* Basketball, squash, football, films, looking at magazines, watching television.

Addresses
Home—137 Westbury Ave., London N22 6RY, England. *Agent*—Peters, Fraser & Dunlop, Drury House, 34-43 Russell St., London WC2B 5HA, England. *E-mail*—kenwilsonmax@mac.com.

Career
Graphic designer and illustrator. Barkers Advertising and Marketing, Harare, Zimbabwe, designer, 1985-86; Orchard Books, London, England, book designer, 1986-88; BBC Books, London, book designer, 1988-90; David Bennett Books, St. Albans, England, assistant art director, 1992; freelance designer, 1992—. Worked as an illustrator for *Moto* magazine, designer/typographer for Next Wave design, and designer/finisher for Artist Prontaprint UK; designer of furniture and other objects for retail outlet in Harare, Zimbabwe.

Member
Graphic Designers Association of Zimbabwe.

Ken Wilson-Max (Photograph reproduced by permission.)

Awards, Honors
Illustration of the Year designation (Harare, Zimbabwe), 1985; bronze medal, Brno Biennale, 1986, for illustration for *Moto* magazine; Best Advertisement designation, Annual Advertising Awards (Harare, Zimbabwe), for animation; Children's Choice selection, International Reading Association/Children's Book Council, 1996, for *Little Red Plane*.

Writings

SELF-ILLUSTRATED

The Sun Is a Bright Star, Bloomsbury (London, England), 1995.
Big Yellow Taxi, David Bennett (St. Albans, England), 1995.
Big Blue Engine, Scholastic (New York, NY), 1996.
(With Audra Wilson-Max) *Great Day Out: African Life, African Words*, Chronicle (San Francisco, CA), 1996.
Little Red Plane, Scholastic (New York, NY), 1996.
(With Audra Wilson-Max) *Let's Play: African Life, African Words*, Chronicle (San Francisco, CA), 1996.
Little Green Tow Truck, Scholastic (New York, NY), 1997.

Big Silver Spaceship, David Bennett (St. Albans, England), 1997.
Big Red Fire Engine, David Bennett (St. Albans, England), 1997.
Wake up, Go to Sleep, Bloomsbury (London, England), 1997.
Big Silver Space Shuttle, Scholastic (New York, NY), 1998.
Dexter Gets Dressed!, Kingfisher (New York, NY), 1998.
Halala Means Welcome: A Book of Zulu Words, Hyperion (New York, NY), 1998.
Max, Hyperion (New York, NY), 1998.
Max Loves Sunflowers, Hyperion (New York, NY), 1998.
Max's Letter, Hyperion (New York, NY), 1999.
L Is for Loving: An ABC for the Way You Feel, Hyperion (New York, NY), 1999.
Max's Money, Hyperion (New York, NY), 1999.
Furaha Means Happy: A Book of Swahili Words, Hyperion (New York, NY), 2000.
Ken Wilson-Max Presents Zelda in the City, Phyllis Fogelman Books (New York, NY), 2000.
Max Paints the House, Hyperion (New York, NY), 2000.
Long Train: 101 Cars on the Track, Scholastic (New York, NY), 2001.
Max's Starry Night, Hyperion (New York, NY), 2001.
A Book of Letters, illustrated by Manya Stojic, Scholastic (New York, NY), 2002.
Firefighter: Thirty Years from the Home of Underground Rock, Harry N. Abrams (New York, NY), 2005.
Motorcycle Police: Thirty Years from the Home of Underground Rock, Harry N. Abrams (New York, NY), 2005.

ILLUSTRATOR

Juwanda G. Ford, *K Is for Kwanza: A Kwanza Alphabet Book,* Scholastic (New York, NY), 1997.
Judith Bauer Stamper, *Tic-Tac-Toe: Three in a Row,* Scholastic (New York, NY), 1998.
Angela Shelf Medearis, *Best Friends in the Snow,* Scholastic (New York, NY), 1999.
Liza Baker, *Flush the Potty!,* Scholastic, (New York, NY) 2000.
Ian Whybrow, *Good Night, Monster!,* Alfred A. Knopf (New York, NY), 2001.
Susanna Leonard Hill, *The House That Mack Built,* Little Simon (New York, NY), 2002.
Joan Holub, *Kwanzaa Kids,* Puffin Books (New York, NY), 2002.
Alison Inches, *Snuggle up, Buttercup,* Harcourt (San Diego, CA), 2002.
Dakari Hru, *Tickle, Tickle,* Roaring Brook Press (Brookfield, CT), 2002.
Alison Inches, *Wake up, Buttercup,* Harcourt (San Diego, CA), 2002.
Rebecca O'Connell, *The Baby Goes Beep,* Roaring Brook Press (Brookfield, CT), 2003.
Karen Baicker, *I Can Do It Too!,* Handprint Books (Brooklyn, NY), 2003.
Aamir Lee Bermiss, *I Hate to Be Sick,* Scholastic (New York, NY), 2004.
W. Nikola-Lisa, *Setting the Turkeys Free,* Hyperion (New York, NY), 2004.
Malachy Doyle, *Splash, Joshua, Splash!,* Bloomsbury (London, England), 2004.
Marjorie Newman, *Just like Me,* Walker & Company (New York, NY), 2005.
Suen Anastasia, *Red Light, Green Light,* Harcourt (Orlando, FL), 2005.
Karen Baicker, *You Can Do It Too!,* Handprint Books (Brooklyn, NY), 2005.
Judy Cumberbatch, *Can You Hear the Sea?,* Bloomsbury (London, England), 2006.

Sidelights

Ken Wilson-Max originally joined the world of children's literature as a book designer for the London-based publishers Orchard and BBC Books, then worked as an assistant art director for David Bennett Books. It was not until 1992 that Wilson-Max capitalized on his talents, which extended beyond designing to writing and illustrating. In 1995 he published his first self-illustrated picture books: *The Sun Is a Bright Star* and *Big Yellow Taxi.* Among his other works is 1996's *Little Red Plane,* which was selected a Children's Choice title by the International Reading Association/Children's Book Council.

Critics often describe Wilson-Max's illustrations as vibrant, colorful, and bold, and make note of the artist's signature style: a use of simple shapes embroidered with heavy black outlines. Wilson-Max is also known for his ability to pull children into stories through the interactive elements he employs in many of his books. For instance, in *Little Red Plane* a *Publishers Weekly* reviewer noted that Wilson-Max engages readers by allowing them to "shift a steering wheel from side to side, [while] the view of through the windshield shifts too."

In addition to being entertaining, Wilson-Max's books also educate youngsters in the variety of cultures existing in the world. In *Halala Means Welcome: A Book of Zulu Words* he introduces young readers to a young boy named Chidi, who lives in post-apartheid South Africa. In this bilingual picture book readers follow Chidi and his friend Michael as they spend the day together, while the English and Zulu words for objects that the characters interact with are incorporated into the text. The book also includes a pronunciation guide that allows readers to fully experience the Zulu language. *Booklist* reviewer Hazel Rochman noted that *Halala Means Welcome* allows readers to "recognize the universal friendship story even as they have fun learning the simple vocabulary [and] practicing how to make the 'click' sound."

With the publication of *Furaha Means Happy: A Book of Swahili Words* Wilson-Max introduces young readers to the Swahili language by mixing a simple dictionary within the text of the story. In his tale, Wambui and her

Ken Wilson-Max's bold illustrations for the interactive board book Flush the Potty! *encourage young toddlers to master an important skill.* (Text and illustrations copyright © 2000 by Ken Wilson-Max. Reprinted by permission of Scholastic Inc.)

brother Moses take a trip to the Kenyan zoo with their parents. In the tradition of *Halala Means Welcome, Furaha Means Happy* provides a section that teaches children how to pronounce the Swahili words featured within the book and also includes a map of Africa. In addition, *Furaha Means Happy* engages readers beyond its story and instruction; it also charms youngsters through its illustrations. *School Library Journal* reviewer Alicia Eames notes that "Wilson-Max's choice of rich, full bodied color and the use of bold black outlines give his illustrations instant appeal."

Tickle Tickle, written by Dakari Hru, focuses on the loving bond between father and son when a father playful tickles his infant son. In his role as illustrator, Wilson-Max employs rounded, colorful images to help depict the lively interaction between the two. Anna DeWind Walls, writing in *School Library Journal*, noted that the artist's illustrations "burst off the pages" and "capture the rambunctious activity perfectly."Wilson-Max also illustrates Ian Whybrow's *Good Night, Monster!*, using his signature bold colors and thick black lines to portray the farm animals and monsters inhabiting Whybrow's tale. In *Booklist* Ilene Cooper commented that the book's artwork "invites children to turn the page."

Wilson-Max once told *SATA*: "I learned about art and design in a very unique way and will always be grateful to those who took the time to persuade me to open my mind and look for that spark of hope and possibility that starts the creative juices flowing, particularly Chaz Maviyane Davies, who in my view started me going.

"I've lived in London all my adult life and it is as much a part of me as Zimbabwe was a part of my childhood. The decision to make either of these places my permanent home is therefore never easy to make and is as yet unresolved.

"I've always observed and drawn, made notes and sketches, had ideas and tried to bring them to life, especially those of a three-dimensional variety. I would ideally like to make books and objects for children simultaneously. As a consequence most of the work travels across several different formats, from books to merchandise.

"During the early stages of a new project I tend to do quite a few colour sketches to get into character. The illustrations are intended to be honest, contemporary, and as real in tone and feeling as possible, not to mention fun! It is important to maintain this set of values in my mind while working.

"I enjoy playing most sports, especially basketball, football, and squash. Films and laughing are my favourite pastimes, as well as looking at magazines (not buying them), reading, and watching television. I get my ideas from these places."

Biographical and Critical Sources

PERIODICALS

Booklist, August, 1998, Hazel Rochman, review of *Halala Means Welcome: A Book of Zulu Words,* p. 201; August, 2002, Ilene Cooper, review of *Good Night, Monster!,* p. 1977.

Publishers Weekly, August 21, 1995, review of *Little Red Plane,* p. 64.

School Library Journal, October, 2000, Alicia Eames, review of *Furaha Means Happy: A Book of Swahili Words,* p. 142; August, 2002, Anna DeWind Walls, review of *Tickle Tickle,* p. 158.

ONLINE

Bloomsbury Web site, http://www.bloomsbury.com/ (April 8, 2006), "Ken Wilson-Max."

IdeasforChildren.com, http://www.ideasforchildren.com/ (April 8, 2006), "Ken Wilson-Max."*

Y-Z

YANG, Belle 1960-

Personal
Born 1960, in Taiwan; daughter of Joseph and Yaning Yang; immigrated to United States, 1967. *Education:* Attended Stirling University (Scotland); University of California, Santa Cruz, B.S. (biology; with honors); attended Pasadena Art Center College of Design; attended Beijing Institute of Traditional Chinese Painting, 1986-89.

Addresses
Home—Carmel, CA. *Agent*—Sandra Dijkstra Literary Agency, 1155 Camino Del Mar, PMB 515, Del Mar, CA 92014. *E-mail*—belle@belleyang.com.

Career
Children's author and artist. *Exhibitions:* Works exhibited at Monterey Museum of Art, 1996; Santa Cruz Museum of Art and History, 1997; and Orange County Museum of Art, 1997.

Writings

SELF-ILLUSTRATED

Baba: A Return to China upon My Father's Shoulders, preface by Amy Tan, Harcourt (New York, NY), 1994.
The Odyssey of a Manchurian, Harcourt Brace (New York, NY), 1996.
Chili-Chili-Chin-Chin, Harcourt Brace (San Diego, CA), 1999.
Hannah Is My Name, Candlewick Press (Cambridge, MA), 2004.

Sidelights
Taiwanese-American author and painter Belle Yang is the author of a number of self-illustrated books, several of which relate stories about Yang and her family. In her first book, *Baba: A Return to China upon My Father's Shoulders,* she retells the tales her father, Baba, told to her about his life in Manchuria, China in the early twentieth century. The narrative opens with simple, fairy-tale-like stories about life in rural China that reveal the region's religious beliefs, holidays, and Confucian philosophy. "Beguiled by the musical cadence and bold strokes," Pam Lambert wrote in a review for *People,* readers "only slowly become aware of the underlying seriousness of Yang's dual story," which also encompasses the Japanese invasion of Manchuria in the early days of World War II and the atrocities that followed.

Yang continues her father's story in *The Odyssey of a Manchurian.* The formerly prosperous Yang family loses nearly everything in the civil war that follows World War II in China, and Baba, then seventeen years old, heads from northern China to the south, and eventually to Taiwan, seeking safety. "The story has the appeal of a fairytale hero's travails—as do the illustrations by the author," concluded a *Publishers Weekly* contributor.

Yang tells her family's story from her own perspective, in a somewhat fictionalized manner, in *Hannah Is My Name.* In this book Na-Lin's family moves from Taiwan to San Francisco in 1967, whereupon the girl—also the story's narrator—is renamed Hannah. Although Hannah enjoys her new life in San Francisco, her parents's days are far more stressful: they wait to receive their permanent residency and hope the U.S. immigration authorities will not catch them working illegally before their green cards arrive. "The tension is palpable," noted a *Kirkus Reviews* contributor, and, as Jennifer M. Brabander wrote in *Horn Book,* Yang's "deeply colored paintings match the strong emotions." *School Library Journal* reviewer Marian Creamer also praised *Hannah Is My Name,* noting that "the setting . . . as well as elements of Chinese culture are nicely evoked in both the text and artwork."

Yang is also the author and illustrator of *Chili-Chili-Chin-Chin,* a picture book for younger children about a

In her self-illustrated Hannah Is My Name, *Belle Yang depicts a Chinese family as they learn to adapt to a new life, with new friends and a new language, in San Francisco.* (Text and illustrations copyright © 2004 by Belle Yang. Reproduced by permission of the publisher Candlewick Press, Inc., Cambridge, MA.)

determined little purple donkey and the boy who named it. The little boy is the only one whom Chili-Chili-Chin-Chin will allow to ride him, and together they go off on adventures, such as watching turtles and picking persimmons. *Booklist* reviewer Stephanie Zvirin declared Yang's "slick, striking artwork in high-intensity colors" to be the main attraction in this title. Zvirin's sentiment was echoed by a *Publishers Weekly* contributor who praised Yang's "witty folk-art stylings and . . . exuberant sense of color."

Biographical and Critical Sources

PERIODICALS

Booklist, July, 1999, Stephanie Zvirin, review of *Chili-Chili-Chin-Chin*, p. 1956; September 15, 2004, Hazel Rochman, review of *Hannah Is My Name*, p. 255.

Horn Book, November-December, 2004, Jennifer M. Brabander, review of *Hannah Is My Name*, p. 704.

Kirkus Reviews, September 1, 2004, review of *Hannah Is My Name*, p. 875.

People, December 19, 1994, Pam Lambert, review of *Baba: A Return to China upon My Father's Shoulders*, p. 66.

Publishers Weekly, August 22, 1994, review of *Baba*, p. 45; August 5, 1996, review of *The Odyssey of a Manchurian*, p. 419; April 26, 1999, review of *Chili-Chili-Chin-Chin*, p. 81.

School Library Journal, November, 2004, Marian Creamer, review of *Hannah Is My Name*, p. 120; April, 2005, review of *Hannah Is My Name*, p. S28.

ONLINE

Belle Yang Home Page, http://www.belleyang.com (April 8, 2006).

* * *

ZALBEN, Jane Breskin 1950-

Personal

Born April 21, 1950, in New York, NY; daughter of Murry (a certified public accountant) and Mae (a librarian; maiden name, Kirshbloom) Breskin; married Steven Zalben (an architect), December 25, 1969; children: Jonathan, Alexander. *Education:* Queens College of the City University of New York, B.A., 1971; Pratt Institute Graphic Center, graduate study in lithography, 1971-72. *Religion:* Jewish. *Hobbies and other interests:* Travel, gardening, gourmet cooking, pets.

Addresses

Home—Port Washington, Long Island, NY. *Agent*—Elizabeth Harding, Curtis Brown Ltd., 10 Astor Pl., New York, NY 10003. *E-mail*—janezalben@hotmail.com.

Career

Dial Press, New York, NY, assistant to art director of children's book department, 1971-72; Holt, Rinehart & Winston, Inc., New York, NY, freelance book designer, 1973-74; Thomas Y. Crowell Co., New York, NY, senior designer of children's books, 1974-75; Scribner's, New York, NY, art director of children's books, 1975-76; writer and illustrator of children's books and novels, 1973—. School of Visual Arts, New York, NY, instructor of illustration, design, and writing of children's books, 1976-93; Vassar Publishing Institute, Poughkeepsie, NY, writer and artist-in-residence, 1988; Hofstra University, Long Island, NY, writer-in-residence, 1992. *Exhibitions:* Works exhibited at individual and group shows at various institutions, including Metropolitan Museum of Art, Justin Schiller Gallery, Pierpont Morgan Library, and American Institute of Graphics Art Show, all New York, NY; Port Washington Library; Jericho Library, Bryant Library, Hecksher Museum, Long Island; Every Picture Tells a Story, Storyopolis, and Museum of Tolerance/Simon Wiesenthal Center, Los Angeles, CA; San Francisco Public Library Gallery, San Francisco, CA; Bush Gallery, VT; Books of Wonder, Beverly Hills, CA; Elizabeth Stone Gallery, Birmingham, MI, and Alexandria, VA; Vassar College; Greenfield College; and Findlay College.

Jane Breskin Zalben (Photograph reproduced by permission.)

Member

Authors Guild, Author's League of America, PEN, Society of Children's Book Writers and Illustrators (judge of Golden Kite award).

Awards, Honors

AIGA award, 1978, 1979; *Beni's First Chanukah* named an *American Bookseller* Pick of the Lists, 1988, and a Sidney Taylor Honor Book in younger readers category, Association of Jewish Libraries; Association of Jewish Libraries Notable Book designation, 1989, for *Earth to Andrew O. Blechman; Parents* magazine award, 1993; International Reading Association Teachers' Choice award, 1993; American Library Association (ALA) Notable Book designation, and Children's Book Council award, both 1996, both for *Benji's Family Cookbook;* William Allen White Award finalist, 1997, for *Unfinished Dreams;* Sydney Taylor Children's Book Award Honor Book in younger readers category, 2002, for *Pearl's Passover;* ALA Top-Ten Religion Book of the Year listee, 2003, for *Let There Be Light;* Koret Foundation Award finalist, 2005, for *Baby Babka.*

Writings

SELF-ILLUSTRATED

Cecilia's Older Brother, Macmillan (New York, NY), 1973.
Lyle and Humus, Macmillan (New York, NY), 1974.
Basil and Hillary, Macmillan (New York, NY), 1975.
Penny and the Captain, Collins (New York, NY), 1977.
Norton's Nighttime, Collins (New York, NY), 1979.
Will You Count the Stars without Me?, Farrar, Straus (New York, NY), 1979.
"Oh, Simple!", Farrar, Straus (New York, NY), 1981.
Porcupine's Christmas Blues, Philomel/Putnam (New York, NY), 1982.
Beni's First Chanukah, Holt (New York, NY), 1988.
Happy Passover, Rosie, Holt (New York, NY), 1990.
Leo and Blossom's Sukkah, Holt (New York, NY), 1990.
Goldie's Purim, Holt (New York, NY), 1991.
Beni's Little Library (boxed set), Holt (New York, NY), 1991.
Buster Gets Braces, Holt (New York, NY), 1992.
Happy New Year, Beni, Holt (New York, NY), 1993.
Papa's Latkes, Holt (New York, NY), 1994.
Miss Violet's Shining Day, Boyds Mills Press (Honesdale, PA), 1995.
Pearl Plants a Tree, Simon & Schuster (New York, NY), 1995.
Beni's Family Cookbook for the Jewish Holidays, Holt (New York, NY), 1996.
Pearl's Marigolds for Grandpa, Simon & Schuster (New York, NY), 1997.
Beni's Family Treasury: Stories for the Jewish Holidays, Holt (New York, NY), 1998.
Beni's First Wedding, Holt (New York, NY), 1998.
Pearl's Eight Days of Chanukah, Simon & Schuster (New York, NY), 1998.
To Every Season: A Family Holiday Cookbook, Simon & Schuster (New York, NY), 1999.
Don't Go!, Clarion Books (New York, NY), 2001.
Let There Be Light: Poems and Prayers for Repairing the World, Dutton Children's Books (New York, NY), 2002.
Pearl's Passover: A Family Celebration through Stories, Recipes, Crafts, and Songs, Simon & Schuster (New York, NY), 2002.
(With husband, Steven Zalben) *Saturday Night at the Beastro,* HarperCollins (New York, NY), 2004.
Paths to Peace: People Who Changed the World, Dutton Children's Books (New York, NY), 2006.
Light, Dutton (New York, NY), 2007.

PICTURE BOOKS

Oliver and Alison's Week, illustrated by Emily Arnold McCully, Farrar, Straus (New York, NY), 1980.
A Perfect Nose for Ralph, illustrated by John Wallner, Philomel (New York, NY), 1980.
The Magic Menorah: A Modern Chanukah Tale, illustrated by Donna Diamond, Simon & Schuster (New York, NY), 2001.
Baby Babka: The Gorgeous Genius, illustrated by Victoria Chess, Clarion (New York, NY), 2004.
Hey, Mama Goose, illustrated by Emilie Chollat, Dutton Children's Books (New York, NY), 2005.

YOUNG-ADULT NOVELS

Maybe It Will Rain Tomorrow, Farrar, Straus (New York, NY), 1982.
Here's Looking at You, Kid, Farrar, Straus (New York, NY), 1984.
Water from the Moon, Farrar, Straus (New York, NY), 1987.
Earth to Andrew O. Blechman, Farrar, Straus (New York, NY), 1989.
The Fortuneteller in 5B, Holt (New York, NY), 1991.
Unfinished Dreams, Simon & Schuster (New York, NY), 1996.
Leap, Alfred A. Knopf (New York, NY), 2007.

ILLUSTRATOR

Jan Wahl, *Jeremiah Knucklebones,* Holt (New York, NY), 1974.
Jane Yolen, *An Invitation to the Butterfly Ball: A Counting Rhyme,* Parents Magazine Press (New York, NY), 1976, reprinted, Caroline House (Honesdale, PA), 1991.
Lewis Carroll, *Jabberwocky,* F. Warne (New York, NY), 1977.
Jane Yolen, *All in the Woodland Early: An ABC Book,* Collins (New York, NY), 1979.
Lewis Carroll, *The Walrus and the Carpenter,* Holt (New York, NY), 1986.
William Shakespeare, *Starlight & Moonshine: Poetry of the Supernatural,* foreword by Werner Gundersheimer, Orchard Books (New York, NY), 1987.
Inner Chimes: Poems on Poetry, selected by Bobbye S. Goldstein, Wordsong/Boyds Mills Press (Honesdale, PA), 1992.

Adaptations

"Oh, Simple!" was adapted as a film broadcast on British Broadcasting Corporation television.

Sidelights

Jane Breskin Zalben is an author and illustrator with numerous books to her credit, from simple counting and A-B-C picture books for preschoolers to young-adult novels dealing with topics ranging from the death of a parent and Holocaust survivors to AIDS to coping with first loves and a physical disabilities. Since the 1983 publication of *Beni's First Chanukah,* Zalben has become best known as the creator of several series of picture books about the Jewish holidays that feature lovable animal characters. As an illustrator, she is lauded for her warm, finely detailed watercolor renderings of anthropomorphic animals: including squirrels, monkeys, penguins, lambs, and bears. Alice Digilio noted in a *Washington Post Book World* review of *"Oh, Simple!"* that some stories "can seem too precious when small animal characters are substituted for small human ones" and praised Zalben for avoiding this problem in her "excellent tale" about two chipmunk characters.

Marcia Posner, in a *School Library Journal* appraisal of *Goldie's Purim,* found the pictures "totally charming and accomplished," lauding the author-illustrator's "tiny, intricate patterns and . . . attention to detail."

Born in 1950 in New York City, Zalben enjoyed drawing from the time she could hold a crayon. Formal art study began at age five when her mother took Zalben for weekly arts lessons at the Metropolitan Museum of Art. "I just loved it," Zalben once recalled of her time at the museum school, saying in an interview that "it became like a comfortable second home." In sixth grade she decided that when she reached the ninth grade she would apply to New York City's High School of Music and Art; soon after she began building her portfolio.

After graduating from the specialized High School of Music and Art in Manhattan, Zalben went on to major in art at Queens College, where she was fortunate to study under several inspiring teachers. One was Marvin Bileck, a Caldecott Honor runner-up for his book *Rain Makes Applesauce.* Bileck talked about "the importance of the brushes and papers you use. It changed my life. I started thinking, gee, this would be interesting to do for a living." Another fond memory from Zalben's college years is working in a barn that had been converted into studios for art students' use. "I had my own big space," she once recalled, "so it was the first time in my life I could paint until three in the morning."

Her first job after college was as a part-time assistant in the art department at New York City's Dial Press. One advantage of the job was being in the office only "three days a week, so I could do my own work the other two." It was during this time that Zalben began to really learn about book design, and her passion for the entire process of creating children's books developed. "I was getting advice and knowledge from people who were really the best in the field," she once explained.

Nine months after finishing college, Zalben met Susan Hirschman, then editor-in-chief of children's publishing at Macmillan. Zalben credits Hirschman with having a great effect on her career. "She said certain things to me," Zalben once recalled, "about writing—the clarity, the simplicity, the whole architectural concept of less is more."

A month after meeting Hirschman, Zalben published her first book, *Cecilia's Older Brother,* a tale of sibling rivalry with a twist. In this story about a family of mice, Cecilia is constantly being teased and bullied by her older brother Timothy—that is, until "something better" comes along. That something better is a baby brother, and now both Timothy and Cecilia have someone new to fight with. Zalben drew on personal memories of growing up with an older brother to create the book, which, according to a *Times Literary Supplement* critic, "has its funny moments" and is "neatly and wittily illustrated." Ethel L. Heins in *Horn Book* praised *Cecilia's Older Brother* for its "crisply detailed pictures."

With her first three books published, Zalben found herself drawn toward a different style; what she once called "the elf-and-details direction of *Butterfly Ball.*" Zalben has been developing and refining this warm, sometimes offbeat and whimsical, and, above all, richly detailed style of watercolor and pencil drawing in the more than thirty picture books she has illustrated since.

Reviewers are frequently charmed by Zalben's drawings. For example, Kristi L. Thomas's review of *"Oh, Simple!"* in *School Library Journal* praised Zalben's "exquisite tableaux of anthropomorphic animals." Carolyn K. Jenks, in her *School Library Journal* critique of *Norton's Nighttime,* commented favorably on the way "the soft, dark watercolor illustrations reflect the nighttime atmosphere of the text." The book was ultimately adapted as a short film broadcast by England's British Broadcasting Corporation.

After contributing to some thirteen picture books over ten years' time, Zalben also began writing young-adult novels. She recalled that Sandra Jordan, then editor-in-chief at Farrar, Straus & Giroux, helped encourage this change by suggesting: "I think there's more you need to say than you're able to say in a thirty-two-page picture book." Zalben was then raising a baby and a toddler, and although she had little extra energy, she decided that nap times would provide her the opportunity to start working on a longer story.

Her first novel, *Maybe It Will Rain Tomorrow,* was published in 1982. It is the story of Beth, a sixteen year old who must go to live with her father and his second wife after her mother's suicide. The story focuses on growing up, loss, first love, and, most of all, on about the difficult relationship between Beth and her stepmother, Linda. Symme J. Benoff, writing in *School Library Journal,* called the book "touching" and the relationship between Beth and Linda "real [and] understandable."

Zalben went on to write three novels in a row, inspired by her experiences as a parent of budding teenagers as well as by her own emotional memories. In *Water from the Moon,* teen Nicole Bernstein seems to have it all, except a love interest, and this causes her to misinterpret the friendly overtures of a young man working in her father's office. The young woman's efforts to establish a secure friendship with a fellow art student are also frustrated when her friend announces plans to leave the area when her mother changes jobs. *The Fortuneteller in 5B,* which Zalben published in 1991, focuses on Alexandria Pilaf, a teen whose anguish over the death of her father is transferred into paranoia about an elderly woman living in her apartment building. Alexandria begins to spread rumors that the woman is a vampire, because she is rarely seen during the day. Finally the truth is learned—the woman is a survivor of the Nazi concentration camps where she lost much of her family—and Alexandria finds a way to deal with her own loss. "Readers will be moved by the author's note about the concentration camp at Terezin," noted Kathy Peihl in the *St. James Guide to Young-Adult Writers,* "where thousands of children were sent during World War II."

The 1980s were a time of transition for Zalben. She had left the city in which she had been born and raised, and moved to the Long Island suburbs, where she felt lonely. "I hated it for the first three years," she once explained, "and my first novel starts out like that about suburbia and all the houses looking the same." Although it was a difficult adjustment, her new life in the suburbs inspired her work on the "Beni" books, an illustrated series about the Jewish holidays. Zalben once recalled in an interview the story of driving down the main street of her town with her family. The streets were decorated for Christmas and her younger son Alexander wanted to know where the Chanukah decorations were. "He wanted to have a Christmas tree and the holly trailing down the banister," Zalben explained. "I said, 'Alexander, we're not going to do that, we're Jewish.' And he said, 'Well, if you don't do that then I'm going to marry a girl who's not Jewish when I grow up.'" Zalben was amused at the strong reaction she had to this situation, and it encouraged her to do a Chanukah book.

"The more I thought about it, the more I wanted to give my children, and Jewish children, a gift—something they could cuddle up with during their holiday that wasn't moralistic, pedantic and preachy," Zalben wrote in an essay in the *Miami Jewish Tribune.* She presented the idea of a picture book featuring a cuddly family of bears to her publisher, and the next six months were filled with meetings and discussions trying to answer the question, "How would Jewish people take to animals?" As Zalben wrote in her essay, the response to her idea was generally that "cute little mice were okay for Christmas books, but Jewish children shouldn't have animals."

Ultimately Zalben prevailed. She wrote the book as she had envisioned it, and the first printing of *Beni's First Chanukah*—12,500 copies—sold out in three weeks. A *Publishers Weekly* reviewer called the volume "" "a gentle reminder that children take pleasure in simple things and that holidays need not be elaborate to be memorable." A *School Library Journal* critic termed the book "a pleasant celebration" and "a quiet story of family holiday togetherness."

The critical and popular success of *Beni's First Chanukah* led to books celebrating Passover, Sukkot, Purim, and the Jewish New Year, all featuring Beni's bear family. Zalben once commented that it was not until the fifth book, *Happy New Year, Beni,* that she really started to feel like she "knew" the characters. *Happy New Year, Beni* was inspired by her own experience of Tashlikh, the ritual of throwing bits of bread into a river that symbolizes the casting away of past wrongdoing to start the new year afresh. "It was so spiritual and wonderful," she remembered, "that after the holidays were over, I went home and wrote the book." A review of

Happy New Year, Beni in *Publishers Weekly* pointed to "Zalben's sweet-natured watercolor-and-pencil illustrations" that "portray the festivities in inviting detail, from the table set with lace cloth and candles to the Torah scrolls and prayer shawls in the synagogue." Hazel Rochman, writing in *Booklist,* noted how the "sweetness is nicely undercut by pesky cousin Max, whose practical jokes and wet plastic spiders spoil Beni's fun."

Other "Beni" books include *Beni's Family Cookbook,* which collects recipes organized around each of the Jewish holidays. While the recipes are designed for cooks who know their way around the kitchen, the layout of the book, and its engaging illustrations, will be sure to captivate younger helpers. The young bear experiences yet another first when he hears Uncle Izzy announce his wedding plans. In *Beni's First Wedding* readers share Beni's excitement at being a part of the wedding party, and learn about Jewish customs. Writing in *School Library Journal,* Elizabeth Palmer Abarbanel called *Beni's First Wedding* "a wonderful selection for children anticipating a family wedding, and a must for libraries serving Jewish communities."

In addition to her Beni character, Zalben has introduced a young sheep named Pearl who, with little brother Avi in tow, explores the Jewish tradition from a female perspective. In *Pearl's Eight Days of Chanukah,* published in 1998, Pearl's twin cousins Sophie and Harry come to spend the holidays, allowing readers to share in the crafts, ceremonies, and festivities that comprise Chanukah. Noting that the book's strength "lies in the depiction of Chanukah as a time to celebrate and enjoy the company of friends and family," a *School Library Journal* contributor praised the colored pencil-and-watercolor illustrations as "warm and appealing," while a *Publishers Weekly* reviewer noted that Zalben's "cosy, finely detailed" illustrations are the strength of this book.

Another Jewish holiday is covered in *Pearl's Passover: A Family Celebration through Stories, Recipes, Crafts, and Songs.* Pearl, Avi, Sophie, Harry, and the rest of the family gather together to cook special Passover foods, make holiday crafts, and hear their grandparents tell the story of the first Passover. (The important role played by lamb's blood in the first Passover is, mercifully for the little sheep, not mentioned, and the traditional leg of lamb is not featured on the Seder menu.) Interspersed with the tale are activities for young readers, recipes to make, and songs to sing. The book also includes a glossary, outlines the fifteen steps of the Seder, and provides the words and music for the parts of the Seder that are traditionally sung. Overall, noted a *Kirkus Reviews* contributor, this book is a "quite comprehensive look at the Passover holiday." Zalben's illustrations for *Pearl's Passover* also received favorable comments from reviewers. "The cozy watercolor depictions of the family as pink-cheeked sheep . . . are well suited to this affectionate gathering," Lauren Adams wrote in *Horn Book. School Library Journal* reviewer Linda R.

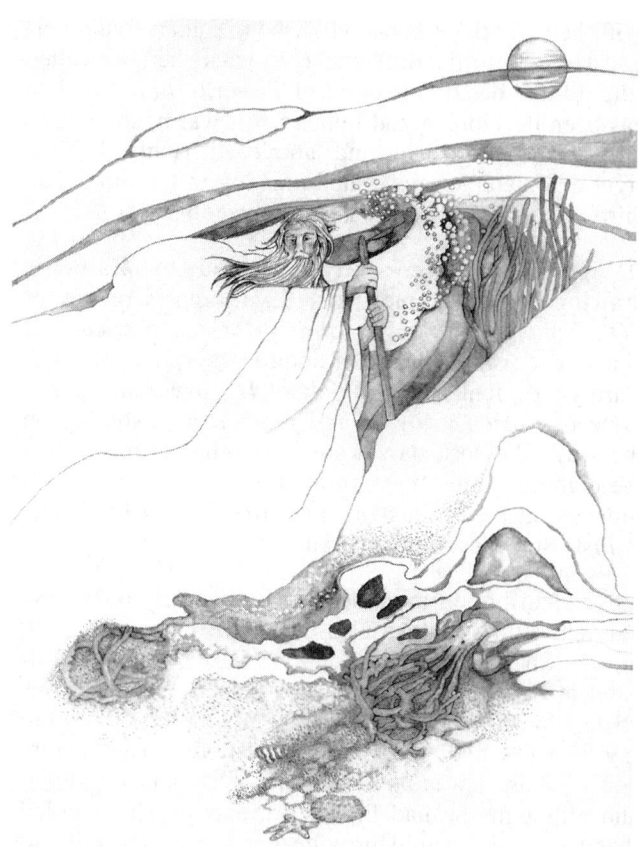

Featuring Zalben's highly detailed illustrations, **Pearl's Passover** *finds siblings Pearl and Avi exited about the holiday but nervous about meeting new cousins.* (Text and illustrations copyright © 2002 by Jane Breskin Zalben. Reproduced by permission of Simon & Schuster Books for Young Readers, an imprint of Simon & Schuster Children's Publishing Division.)

Silver called the artwork "charming," while noting the "humorous touches that make the rather large cast easy to distinguish."

Pearl Plants a Tree describes the "environmental" holiday of Tu B'shvat, as Pearl and her grandfather discuss his first home in America and the tree he once planted there. Pearl decides to follow the tradition by raising an apple tree seedling; the following spring she and her grandfather celebrate the tree-planting holiday together. In the poignant *Pearl's Marigolds for Grandpa,* the young sheep must cope with the loss of her beloved grandfather in a story that *School Library Journal* contributor Susan Scheps noted "will be comfortably reassuring to children who have lost a beloved grandparent." The book also contains information on the mourning customs for six major religious traditions.

Zalben examines religious traditions from another perspective in *Let There Be Light: Poems and Prayers for Repairing the World.* This book is an anthology of inspirational pieces gathered from many different religious writings and traditions, including verses from the Bible and the Qur'an, words from Lao-Tzu, Buddha, the Dalai Lama, and Mahatma Gandhi, and pieces from Native American tribes and the Shona of Zimbabwe. The collages Zalben created to illustrate these pieces are also varied, incorporating materials and color schemes appropriate to the culture of each selection. *Booklist* reviewer Carolyn Phelan commented favorably on the book's "positive message," as well as on its "thoughtful selections and creative illustrations." *Let There Be Light* was selected an American Library Association Top-Ten Religion Book of the Year.

Although Zalben's primary fame rests on her "Beni" and "Pearl" books, she continues exploring many different projects to express herself. A young-adult novel, 1996's *Unfinished Dreams,* focuses on sixth grade student Jason Glass and his relationship with his middle school principal, Mr. Carr, who ultimately dies of AIDS. It is also about music—Mr. Carr had inspired Jason to learn to play the violin—and Zalben's story explores the healing power of art. "Zalben has written an introspective novel, with real people who have real conversations," commented *Voice of Youth Advocates* contributor Ann Bouricius. The critic added that the book "will be savored by those who enjoy a subtly rich and quiet read."

Zalben's other books for older readers include *Paths to Peace: People Who Changed the World.* Sixteen individuals are given one-page profiles in this book, each with a facing illustration. The individuals are from around the world, including the United States (John F. Kennedy, Eleanor Roosevelt, and Martin Luther King Jr.), Kenya (Wangari Maathai), India (Mahatma Gandhi), Britain (Princess Diana), Germany (Anne Frank), and Burma (Aung San Suu Kyi). Despite the hardships and tragic early deaths that befell many of these people, "the focus is very upbeat," Hazel Rochman commented in *Booklist.* Zalben's collages again received much critical attention. As Hope Marie Cook explained in *School Library Journal,* rather than being typical portraits, the somewhat abstract illustrations instead "reflect Zalben's interpretation of these individuals, and the appended notes explain the various symbols and materials in the pictures."

Zalben has also written several non-series books for young readers, including *Saturday Night at the Beastro* (written with her husband, Steven Zalben), *Baby Babka: The Gorgeous Genius,* and *Hey, Mama Goose.* The first title features Halloween monsters heading to a New Orleans-style French "beastro" for a dinner of bugs, slugs, skunks, and other gross fare. The text is "less an actual story than a catalog of gross food," Kathleen Kelly MacMillan commented in *School Library Journal,* but the illustrations are "unique." For these collages, Steven Zalben (his real job is as an architect) took new photographs of a New Orleans restaurant, another in Manhattan, and street scenes all over Eastern Europe, then digitally manipulated them in the computer, pixel by pixel. Then the Zalbens overlaid them with original drawings, paintings, feathers, googly eyes, other found materials, and fabric and paper scraps from around the world.

Baby Babka and *Hey, Mama Goose* are notable for being among the small number of books Zalben has written but not illustrated herself. In the latter title, characters from an assortment of fairy tales become unhappy with their current homes and decide that they want to move into better digs. Hansel and Gretel have eaten their cottage made from candy and now need a new home; Snow White moves in with Rapunzel; the old woman who lived in the shoe and her large family relocate to Snow White and the Seven Dwarves' previous house; and the Three Bears turn the old woman's shoe into a porridge stand. "Lighthearted and inventive, the jaunty text bounces along," Ilene Cooper wrote in *Booklist,* and *School Library Journal* contributor Linda M. Keaton concluded: "This book will provide grand entertainment to children who know the original stories and rhymes."

In addition to writing books about friendship, feelings, warmth, and family, Zalben travels around the world (although you can usually find her at her desk, working), and speaks to young fans about her writing and her art. Her experiences with her readers, her family, and others in her life, continue to fuel her passion for her work. "Sometimes you need to rewrite things that you haven't had in life and wished or hoped for, and other times you also need to duplicate things you have had, revisiting them in different ways in order to remember to appreciate those small gifts and moments. If I've had bad times in my life, I try not to stop my work.

In **Hey, Mama Goose** *Zalben spins a fanciful rhyming tale about a housing shortage in Fairy Tale Land, with illustrations by Emilie Chollat.* (Text copyright © 2005 by Jane Breskin Zalben. Illustrations copyright © 2005 by Emilie Chollat. All rights reserved. Used by permission of Dutton Children's Books, a division of Penguin Young Readers Group, a member of Penguin Group (USA) Inc.)

I get closer to it and go into it more. The art and the writing are like good friends who are there for me. They nourish my journey. They keep me sane."

Biographical and Critical Sources

BOOKS

St. James Guide to Young-Adult Writers, St. James Press (Detroit, MI), 1997.

PERIODICALS

Booklist, December 15, 1975, p. 583; December 15, 1988; March 15, 1990, p. 1464; September 15, 1990; January 1, 1992; July, 1993, Hazel Rochman, review of *Happy New Year, Beni;* August, 1995, Kathy Broderick, review of *Miss Violet's Shining Day,* p. 1958; November 15, 1995, Stephanie Zvirin, review of *Pearl Plants a Tree,* p. 566; June 1, 1996, Susan Dove Lempke, review of *Unfinished Dreams,* p. 1704; September 15, 1996, Stephanie Zvirin, review of *Beni's Family Cookbook,* p. 236; November 1, 1997, Ilene Cooper, review of *Pearl's Marigolds for Grandpa,* p. 485; February 15, 2002, Ilene Cooper, review of *Pearl's Passover: A Family Celebration through Stories, Recipes, Crafts, and Songs,* p. 1023; October 1, 2002, Carolyn Phelan, review of *Let There Be Light: Poems and Prayers for Repairing the World,* p. 342; September 15, 2004, Karin Snelson, review of *Saturday Night at the Beastro,* p. 255; February 15, 2005, Ilene Cooper, review of *Hey, Mama Goose,* p. 1085; January 1, 2006, Hazel Rochman, review of *Paths to Peace: People Who Changed the World,* p. 96.
Bulletin of the Center for Children's Books, November, 1973; February, 1979; November, 1982, October, 1984; December, 1991, p. 111.
Hadassah, August-September, 1993, Rahel Musleah, "Love Pictures," pp. 38-39.
Horn Book, June, 1973, Ethel L. Heins, review of *Cecilia's Older Brother,* pp. 263-264; October, 1978, p. 511; March-April, 1990, p. 197; January-February, 1992, p. 77; September-October, 1996, Elizabeth Watson, review of *Unfinished Dreams,* p. 603; March-April, 2002, Lauren Adams, review of *Pearl's Passover,* p. 207.
Kirkus Reviews, October 1, 2001, review of *The Magic Menorah: A Modern Chanukah Tale,* p. 1436; November 15, 2001, review of *Pearl's Passover,* p. 1616; September 15, 2002, review of *Let There Be Light,* p. 1404; July 1, 2004, review of *Saturday Night at the Beastro,* p. 639; September 1, 2004, review of *Baby Babka, the Gorgeous Genius,* p. 875; February 1, 2005, review of *Hey, Mama Goose,* p. 183; January 1, 2006, review of *Paths to Peace,* p. 47.
Miami Jewish Tribune, December 22, 1989, Jane Breskin Zalben, "Chanukah Story."
Publishers Weekly, November 3, 1975, p. 72; June 26, 1978, p. 117; October 15, 1979, p. 67; December 12, 1980, p. 47; July 3, 1981, p. 146; April 30, 1982; October 15, 1982; April 10, 1987, p. 95; November 11, 1988, review of *Beni's First Chanukah,* p. 55; October 27, 1989, p. 70; January 19, 1990; October 26, 1990, p. 69; January 18, 1991, p. 57; September 20, 1991, p. 135; May 18, 1992, p. 68; August 16, 1993, p. 49; September 20, 1993, review of *Happy New Year, Beni;* October 14, 1996, review of *Beni's Family Cookbook,* p. 85; September 28, 1998, review of *Pearl's Eight Days of Chanukah,* p. 52; September 24, 2001, review of *The Magic Menorah,* p. 48; February 18, 2002, review of *Pearl's Passover,* p. 65; August 9, 2004, review of *Saturday Night at the Beastro,* p. 250; February 14, 2005, review of *Hey, Mama Goose,* p. 75.
School Library Journal, September, 1979, Carolyn K. Jenks, review of *Norton's Nighttime,* p. 125; November, 1981, Kristi L. Thomas, review of *"Oh, Simple!,"* p. 84; May, 1982, Symme J. Bennoff, review of *Maybe It Will Rain Tomorrow,* p. 76; October, 1988, review of *Beni's First Chanukah;* November, 1989, p. 116; April, 1990, p. 101; February, 1991, p. 77; May, 1991, Marcia Posner, review of *Goldie's Purim,* p. 86; December, 1991, p. 120; April, 1992, p. 102; December, 1993, p. 97; January 1, 1996, Marcia W. Posner, review of *Pearl Plants a Tree,* p. 99; February, 1997, Susan Scheps, review of *Beni's Family Cookbook,* p. 126; September, 1997, Susan Scheps, review of *Pearl's Marigolds for Grandpa,* p. 198; May, 1998, Elizabeth Palmer Abarbanel, review of *Beni's First Wedding,* pp. 128-129; October, 1998, review of *Pearl's Eight Days of Chanukah,* p. 39; February, 2000, Augusta R. Malvagno, review of *To Every Season,* p. 116; October, 2001, review of *The Magic Menorah,* p. 71; February, 2002, Linda R. Silver, review of *Pearl's Passover,* p. 116; August, 2004, Kathleen Kelly MacMillan, review of *Saturday Night at the Beastro,* p. 104; November, 2004, Julie Roach, review of *Baby Babka, the Gorgeous Genius,* p. 120; February, 2005, Linda M. Kenton, review of *Hey, Mama Goose,* p. 112; February, 2006, Hope Marie Cook, review of *Paths to Peace,* p. 156.
Times Literary Supplement, November 23, 1973, review of *Cecilia's Older Brother,* p. 1436.
Voice of Youth Advocates, August, 1996, Ann Bouricius, review of *Unfinished Dreams,* p. 164.
Washington Post Book World, August 9, 1981, Alice Digilio, "Young Bookshelf."

ONLINE

Jane Breskin Zalben Home Page, http://www.janebreskinzalben.com (April 8, 2006).

* * *

ZHANG, Song Nan 1942-

Personal

Surname is pronounced "Jung"; born June 22, 1942, in Shanghai, China; immigrated to Canada, 1989; naturalized Canadian citizen, 1995; son of Can Zhang (a textile engineer) and Gengmai Zhu (a homemaker); married Shengli Wang (an accountant); children: Hao Yu, Hao Yong (sons). *Education:* Central Institute of Fine Arts (Beijing, China), undergraduate degree, 1964, graduate degree, 1980; attended École Superieure National des Beaux-Arts (Paris, France), 1984-85. *Hobbies and other interests:* Cooking, reading, traveling.

Addresses

Home—2800 Ch. des Prairies, Brossard, Quebec J4Y 2X4, Canada.

Career

Artist, illustrator, and author. Central Institute of Fine Arts, Beijing, China, art professor, 1980-88, deputy director, 1985-87, dean of mural department, 1985-88; Dominion Gallerie/Westmont Gallerie, Montreal, Quebec, Canada, artist, 1988—. *Exhibitions:* Paintings exhibited throughout the world, including at Montreal Museum of Fine Arts, Montreal, Quebec, Canada; throughout China; Hong Kong; Tokyo, Japan; Paris, France; and Seoul, South Korea.

Member

Chinese Artist Association, Writers' Union of Canada.

Awards, Honors

Mr. Christie's Book Award, 1993, and Children's Literature Roundtables of Canada honor book, 1994, both for *A Little Tiger in the Chinese Night: An Autobiography in Art;* Red Cedar Book Award, 1997, for *The Children of China: An Artist's Journey.*

Writings

SELF-ILLUSTRATED

A Little Tiger in the Chinese Night: An Autobiography in Art, Tundra Books (Plattsburgh, NY), 1993.
Five Heavenly Emperors: Chinese Myths of Creation, Tundra Books (Plattsburgh, NY), 1994.
The Children of China: An Artist's Journey, Tundra Books (Plattsburgh, NY), 1995.
Cowboy on the Steppes, Tundra Books (Plattsburgh, NY), 1997.
(Reteller) *The Ballad of Mulan,* Pan Asian Publications (Union City, CA), 1998.
(With son, Hao Yu Zhang) *A Time of Golden Dragons,* Tundra Books (Plattsburgh, NY), 2000.
(With Hou Yu Zhang) *The Great Voyages of Zheng He,* Pan Asian Publications (Union City, CA), 2005.

Works by Zhang have been translated into Spanish, Vietnamese, and Chinese.

ILLUSTRATOR

Linda Granfield, reteller, *The Legend of the Panda,* Tundra Books (Plattsburgh, NY), 1998.

The Man Who Made Parks: The Story of Parkbuilder Frederick Law Olmsted, Tundra Books (Plattsburgh, NY), 1999.
Jo Bannatyne-Cugnet, *From Far and Wide: A Canadian Citizenship Scrapbook,* Tundra Books (Plattsburgh, NY), 2000.
Aaron Shepard, reteller, *Lady White Snake: A Tale from Chinese Opera,* Pan Asian Publications (Union City, CA), 2001.
Deborah Hodge, *Emma's Story,* Tundra Books (Plattsburgh, NY), 2003.
Arlene Chan, *Awakening the Dragon,* Tundra Books (Plattsburgh, NY), 2004.

Sidelights

Born in China, Song Nan Zhang has since made eastern Canada his home, and has shared his unique cultural heritage with North American readers through his art and his many books for children. While Zhang considers himself to be primarily an oil painter, he has also earned respect as a writer since publishing of his first book for children, the award-winning *A Little Tiger in the Chinese Night: An Autobiography in Art.* Zhang's straightforward text about growing up in communist China is accompanied by realistic paintings in what a *Kirkus Reviews* critic called a "classic Communist style."

Having lived through the Japanese occupation of China during World War II as well as the oppression of the Chinese people by communist leader Mao Zedong during the Chinese Cultural Revolution, Zhang recalls his experiences during this tumultuous time in a way that has captivated young readers. He and his parents hid in the mountains when the Japanese overran the city of Shanghai. After the end of the war, the family's troubles did not end, Zhang explained, because living under China's new Communist government was also difficult. His father was a patriot, and Zhang tried to remain loyal to the government as well, though it often meant putting his natural artistic gifts aside to work as a laborer. Zhang was fortunate to receive an education in art, and it was his talent for painting portraits of Mao that won him a favored status as a college professor and allowed him to marry and raise his two sons in relative comfort.

Things changed for Zhang in the late 1980s. "When I was still in Beijing as a fine arts professor at the Central Institute of Fine Arts, I was commissioned by the government of China to work on a huge mural in the then-new national library," Zhang recalled to *SATA,* revealing how esteemed he was by government officials. However, the actions of the repressive Communist regime was becoming intolerable, and the Tianamen Square incident, wherein the Chinese military massacred a number of demonstrating college students, served as a catalyst. While his father remained in China, the artist managed to escape to Montreal, and his wife and two sons followed him two years later.

The colorful tradition of China's Dragon Boat Festival is the focus of Zhang's Awakening the Dragon, *featuring detailed artwork by Arlene Chan.* (Copyright © 2004 by Arlene Chan. Illustrations copyright © 2004 by Song Nan Zhang. Reproduced by permission of Tundra Books of Northern New York.)

Establishing himself as a full-time artist, Zhang had no plans to become a children's writer. Then May Cuttler, president of Tundra Books, encouraged him to complete *A Little Tiger in the Chinese Night*. "I was not sure how many people, especially young ones, would like the book. But I did my utmost to make sure all the historic details are accurate," Zhang recalled to *SATA* of that first work.

Reviewing *A Little Tiger in the Chinese Night,* critics were enthusiastic about Zhang's unique autobiography. "Radically innovative, it is remarkably successful," stated Janet McNaughton of the book in her review for *Quill & Quire*. Noting the book's educational value and the inclusion of a map of China and a timeline of historical events, McNaughton added that Zhang's "wonderful book will make a complex period of Chinese history comprehensible" to younger readers, while Carla Kozak praised Zhang's artwork in *School Library Journal* by noting that the "vivid, personal, yet oddly detached" writing is complemented by the "emotion" of the illustrations.

Zhang has continued to share his Chinese heritage with young readers. In his book *Five Heavenly Emperors: Chinese Myths of Creation* he uses paintings—"a form of universal language," as he told *SATA*—to relate twelve stories comprising ancient Chinese creation myths. In one story Pangu separates sky from Earth, while other gods create man from clay, shoot down suns to preserve life on earth, and repair the sky following the downpour that caused the Great Flood. The story of a Chinese explorer who made several voyages into the unknown in the 1400s, almost a century before Columbus set sail, is recounted in *The Great Voyages of Zheng He,* a picture book coauthored by Zhang's son, Hao Yu Zhang. In *Booklist* Carolyn Phelan cited the book for combining "an interesting story and unusually good illustrations" to present young readers with a little-known aspect of history. The highly detailed illustrations, which make the early years of the Ming dynasty come to life, are "by turns dramatic, monumental, and intimate," according to Margaret A. Chang in *School Library Journal*.

A similar collaboration between father and son, *A Time of Golden Dragons* explains the importance of the dragon image in Chinese art over five thousand years. In *School Library Journal,* Chang praised the Zhangs' text for presenting "solid, accessible, authentic background on the mythical creatures that symbolize China," while in *Resource Links* a reviewer cited Song Nan Zhang's "arresting illustrations" and the coauthors "fascinating" text as an appropriate celebration of 2000, the only time the Chinese Year of the Dragon and the Western millennium have intersected in 3,000 years.

Several of Zhang's books relate a more personal history. In *Cowboy on the Steppes* the author/illustrator uses the cowboy myth to draw young readers in to the story of his older brother, Yi Nan Zhang. At age eighteen, Yi

In both art and text, Canadian writer Song Nan Zhang tells the story of his older brother's experiences herding cattle in Mongolia in Cowboy on the Steppes. (Text and illustrations copyright © 1997 by Song Nan Zhang. Reproduced by permission of Tundra Books of Northern New York.)

Nan was taken from the comfortable family home in Beijing and, on orders of the Chinese government, sent to a Mongolian commune and trained in his assigned livelihood: to raise and herd cattle. In this harsh terrain, keeping away hungry wolves was the ultimate challenge for the novice cowboy during his first months at his new task. The text—inspired by Yi Nan's diary of the experience—"depict[s] a young man who . . . grows to admire and respect the land and people of his new home," according to *Canadian Review of Materials* contributor Valerie Nielsen. Praising the book as a work "of rare eloquence," *Resource Links* contributor Theo Heras added that "Zhang's superb illustrations recreate life on the Mongolian steppes vividly." In *Booklist* Carolyn Phelan wrote that Zhang's work "reveals an episodic tale of births and deaths, respect and generosity, horsemanship and pride."

Zhang's artwork has been praised for its detail, and several critics had compared his work to that of American artist Norman Rockwell. This is an apt description; as Zhang told *SATA*, "Andrew Wyeth and Norman Rockwell are undoubtedly two of my favorite American artists. They and their works possess something typically [American], as well as universal."

Biographical and Critical Sources

BOOKS

Zhang, Son Nan, *A Little Tiger in the Chinese Night: An Autobiography in Art,* Tundra Books (Plattsburgh, NY), 1993.

PERIODICALS

Booklist, January 1, 1994, p. 821; February 1, 1996, Carolyn Phelan, review of *The Children of China: An Artist's Journey,* p. 931; February 15, 1998, Carolyn Phelan, review of *Cowboy on the Steppes,* p. 1006; December 15, 1998, Karen Morgan, review of *The Legend of the Panda,* p. 753; August, 1999, Carolyn Phelan, review of *The Man Who Made Parks: The Story of Parkbuilder Frederick Law Olmsted,* p. 2061; November 1, 2000, Linda Perkins, review of *A Time of Golden Dragons,* p. 536; October 15, 2005, Carolyn Phelan, review of *The Great Voyages of Zheng He,* p. 48.

Bulletin of the Center for Children's Books, March, 1994, p. 240.

Junior Bookshelf, June, 1994, p. 111.

Kirkus Reviews, December 1, 1993, review of *A Little Tiger in the Chinese Night,* p. 1532.

Maclean's, December 11, 2000, review of *A Time of Golden Dragons,* p. 59.

Publishers Weekly, November 15, 1993, p. 79.

Quill & Quire, January, 1994, Janet McNaughton, review of *A Little Tiger in the Chinese Night,* p. 36; September, 2000, review of *A Time of Golden Dragons,* p. 61.

Resource Links, February, 1998, Theo Heras, review of *Cowboy on the Steppes,* p. 106; October, 2000, review of *A Time of Golden Dragons,* pp. 12-13.

School Librarian, May, 1995, p. 68.

School Library Journal, May, 1994, Carla Kozak, review of *A Little Tiger in the Chinese Night,* p. 127; February, 1998, Margaret A. Chang, review of *Cowboy on the Steppes,* p. 128; October 1999, Lucinda Snyder Whitehurst, review of *The Man Who Made Parks,* p. 143; October, 2000, Margaret A. Chang, review of *A Time of Golden Dragons,* p. 154; November, 2005, Margaret A. Chang, review of *The Great Voyages of Zheng He,* p. 173.

ONLINE

Canadian Review of Materials Online, http://www.umanitoba.ca/cm/ (February 27, 1998), Valerie Nielsen, review of *Cowboy on the Steppes;* (March 30, 2001) review of *A Time of Golden Dragons.*

Writers Union of Canada Web site, http://www.writersunion.ca/ (May 18, 2006), "Song Nan Zhang."